Innovation / Renovation

NEW PERSPECTIVES ON

THE HUMANITIES

A volume in the series

Theories of Contemporary Culture

Center for Twentieth Century Studies

University of Wisconsin-Milwaukee

General Editor, Kathleen Woodward

Innovation/Renovation

NEW PERSPECTIVES ON THE HUMANITIES

EDITED BY

Ihab Hassan & *Sally Hassan*

The University of Wisconsin Press

Published 1983

The University of Wisconsin Press
114 North Murray Street
Madison, Wisconsin 53715

The University of Wisconsin Press, Ltd.
1 Gower Street
London WC1E 6HA, England

First printing

Printed in the United States of America

For LC CIP information see the colophon

ISBN 0-299-09390-5

Chapter 8, "The Remission of Play," first appeared in
Blooded Thought: Occasions of Theatre, *New York,*
Performing Arts Journal Publications, 1982
© 1982 by Herbert Blau.

CONTENTS

ACKNOWLEDGMENTS   vii

INTRODUCTION   3

I   PERSPECTIVES ON *Change*   13

   1   **Ihab Hassan,** *Ideas of Cultural Change*   15
   2   **Claus Uhlig,** *Toward a Chronography of Change*   39
   3   **Dominick LaCapra,** *Intellectual History and*   47
     Defining the Present as "Postmodern"
   4   **Paul Noack,** *Crisis Instead of Revolution: On the*   65
     Instrumental Change of Social Innovation

II   PERSPECTIVES ON *Innovation*   85

    LITERARY THEORY

   5   **Geoffrey H. Hartman,** *The New Wilderness:*   87
     Critics as Connoisseurs of Chaos
   6   **Ralph Cohen,** *The Joys and Sorrows of Literary*   111
     Theory
   7   **Wayne C. Booth,** *Renewing the Medium of*   131
     Renewal: Some Notes on the Anxieties of
     Innovation

    PERFORMANCE THEORY

   8   **Herbert Blau,** *The Remission of Play*   161

9 **Richard Schechner**, *News, Sex, and Performance Theory*   189

10 **Régis Durand**, *Theatre/SIGNS/Performance: On Some Transformations of the Theatrical and the Theoretical*   211

CULTURE

11 **Leslie A. Fiedler**, *The Death and Rebirths of the Novel: The View from '82*   225

12 **Didier Coste**, *Rehearsal: An Alternative to Production/Reproduction in French Feminist Discourse*   243

13 **Matei Calinescu**, *From the One to the Many: Pluralism in Today's Thought*   263

III PERSPECTIVES ON *Postmodernism*   289

14 **Norman N. Holland**, *Postmodern Psychoanalysis*   291

15 **Malcolm Bradbury**, *Modernisms/Postmodernisms*   311

16 **Jean-François Lyotard**, *Answering the Question: What is Postmodernism?*   329

CONTRIBUTORS   345

INDEX   349

ACKNOWLEDGMENTS

The occasion requires some acknowledgments, not bland or formulaic. For though the enterprise which has led to this book was not so complex and arduous as sending a man to the moon, it sufficed. Many made it possible—and some, impossible. The latter will remain unacknowledged.

Two international conferences on "Innovation/Renovation" yielded the essays published here for the first time. The first took place in June 1980, in Würzburg and Munich. Professor Dr. Gerhard Hoffman (Würzburg), the driving force of the project, together with Professor Dr. Klaus Poenicke (Munich) organized the event with intellectual and convivial grace. The second conference took place in September 1981, in Racine and Milwaukee, Wisconsin. The editors coordinated it with much assistance from the staff of the Johnson Foundation's superb Wingspread Conference Center—notably Mr. Henry Halsted and Mrs. Kay Mauer—and from the staff of the Center for Twentieth Century Studies of the University of Wisconsin in Milwaukee—particularly Mrs. Carol Tennessen and Mrs. Jean Lile.

The organizers, quite miraculously, found funds for both conferences in these stringent times: from the University of Würzburg, the University of Munich, and the United States International Communication Agency; from the Johnson Foundation and the Pabst Brewing Company; and from the College of Letters and Science, the School of Fine Arts, the Center for Twentieth Century Studies, the Graduate School, and the Student Union, all at the University of Wisconsin in Milwaukee. The British Council, the French Cultural Services, the Goethe House in Milwaukee, and especially the Goethe Institute in Chicago, under the directorship of Dr. Wolfgang Ule, assisted with travel expenses — the latter also with prompt action, affluent goodwill, and translator fees.

Special thanks are due to two friends in power: Dean William Halloran of the College of Letters and Science, and Dean Robert Corrigan of the School of Fine Arts, whose unwavering confidence in the project proved decisive. Associate Dean Micheal Riley, with effective tact, obliterated all obstacles. Mrs. Judy Friedman kindly guided us through the labyrinthine facilities and procedures of the Union. And Associate Professor Kathleen Woodward, director of the Center for Twentieth Century Studies, generously enabled the metamorphosis of two conferences into this book, which Peter Givler, acquisitions editor of the University of Wisconsin Press, had the foresight to acquire.

Geraldine Simonich and Monica Verona efficiently typed this manuscript of happy Babel, and Mark Luprecht proofread it with an eagle's eye.

Remain the contributors. They would have included two distinguished women scholars, invited to the conference, who were unable to complete their papers on feminist theory. Their lack is felt.

To all, our unexasperated thanks.

February 1982
Milwaukee, Wisconsin

Innovation / *Renovation*

Introduction

"... we need to re-imagine change itself, else we labor to confirm all our errors. How many of us, radical in politics, morality, or art, seem only repetitious there where life cries to remake itself."[1]

I

The authors of this volume engage critical developments in several domains of Western culture. In doing so, their essays become themselves signals of change, both testing and testifying to its evasive forms. Some evasion, or rather intellectual suspicion, constitutes the theme, the very title, of this work. Could it have been otherwise? Who amongst us can still cry, as Zamyatin did in 1923: "Revolution is everywhere, in everything. It is infinite"?[2] That infinity now promises too many horrors and deceptions, all very old.

Yet the reality of change has remained central to our awareness for more than a century, and in the last few decades that awareness has become ever more acute. This does not mean that ideas, values, or institutions of the past cease to inform the present; rather, traditions alter, influences shift, and history moves in measures both continuous and discontinuous. Certainly the complex cultural assumptions of the last century—evoked, say, by Darwin, Marx, Baudelaire, Nietzsche, Cézanne, Debussy, Freud, and Einstein—still pervade the Western mind. Certainly, those assumptions have been reconceived, not once, but many times.

Can we identify such reconceptions in our midst? Do these point to a distinct moment in our culture, perhaps in the very idea of culture itself? Should specific trends in different disciplines—say literary theory, dramaturgy, psychoanalysis, political philos-

3

ophy, cultural criticism, all represented here—join to define a provisional scheme, an emergent pattern in the West? What relations obtain between trends and countertrends, interpretations and reinterpretations, in our arts, our knowledge, our societies? And how assess the implications, moral and political, of all these transformations? On such crucial, on such obdurate, questions our authors reflect.

II

The authors bring to the quandaries of change their several disciplines, theories, experiences, wishes, lacks; of the subject, they each have ideas deeply textured by their lives. But their ideas also fall within three narrowing perspectives which suggest the organization of this work. The first perspective concerns change generically, the second innovation/renovation particularly, the third postmodernism more specifically still. Focused on cultural novation all, each of the three perspectives assumes a different concept of *metanoia,* transformation, a different mental tilt and temporal scale. Most certainly, these perspectives overlap. Yet they provide us also with a variable angle on the problems at hand.

Change itself, in its essential forms, may finally elude our discursive modes. Robert Heilbroner rightly remarks: "It is difficult to 'think' about change, even if it is natural to imagine it. Heraclitus's river is much more easily discussed in its infinite instants of motionlessness than in its single trajectory of movement."[3] Yet from that unspeakable moment, trivialized as the Big Bang, to the present instant of speech (written or read), the universe has done nothing but change, change and repeat itself. This change offers itself to us as a "story." Why is the universe nearly fifteen billion years old? Because it took us that long to ask. Thus "the story" relates the adventure of evolution into human language, a language that some take to have been there always and ready. Will we keep chattering one or two million years hence? "The answer is certainly No," Richard Leakey avers in his book entitled—pace Derrida—*Origins.*[4] Ninety-eight percent of all the earth's species, it seems, have either vanished or reverted into parasitism. But the incalculable future concerns no one here, except in the mind, and should the human race (pun intended) come to some sudden end, another creature may learn in time to make of the earth a brighter place. For in higher evolution, as Konrad Lorenz notes, "each step forward has consisted of a *fulguratio,* a historically unique event in phylogeny which has always had a chance quality about it — the quality, one might say, of something *invented* [italics added]."[5]

"Invention," then, informs even biological change. But doesn't the *fulguratio* flare in culture even more than in nature? Our times are "interesting" enough, as the Chinese say when they curse, to indicate that this may be true. Consider a few items of recent human "interest": nuclear fission and fusion; molecular biology and recombinant DNA (we can now create rabbit/mice, or rabice); jet travel, space shuttle; automation, home computers, cybernetic processes of every kind; radio, television, radar, laser, and satellite communication; hybrid grains which revolutionize even the earlier "green revolution"; massive pollution of the environment; an energy debacle; widespread contraception in the West and a global population explosion withal; torture, terrorism, secession, repression, perpetual crisis; the delegitimation of values, authorities, procedures, and institutions around the world — in short, both planetization and tribalization in thought as in deed. It is enough to drive futurists muttering about "superexponential curves," "third-wave civilizations," and "post-civilizations," and predicting utopia, oblivion, or both.

As for the second perspective, entitled "innovation/renovation," it rests upon a hesitation, not to say tergiversation. Questions here beg one another and end by beggaring our doubt. Is anything wholly original? How recognize, let alone define, that originality? And how relate innovation to renovation, and either to plain novation? Could we agree on some indisputable example of cultural creation? The Gothic flying buttress? Brunelleschi's perspective in the Renaissance? The theory of natural selection — Darwin's or Wallace's? The hypothesis of the unconscious — Freud's or von Hartmann's? The Special Theory of Relativity? The dodecaphonic scale — Schönberg's or Joseph Mathias Hauer's? Or in literature: Dante's *Commedia,* Luther's *Bible,* Montaigne's

Essays, Hamlet, Tristram Shandy, Lyrical Ballads, Leaves of Grass, Un Coup de dés, Finnegans Wake, and *Don Quixote* — of Cervantes or Pierre Menard? Or do we confuse masterpieces with novelties, and the latter with freakish art? Is all discovery anamnesis as Plato thought, all production reproduction, vision misprision, creation recombination — and what of the Imagination, primary, secondary, or otherwise? Harry Levin noted: "When Pound advised disciples to 'make it new,' he was repeating a maxim as old as Confucius, and well aware of the irony, for his studies in the Renaissance had won him insights into the processes of cultural renewal, and shown him how renovation could be innovation."[6] Yet Pound's friend Eliot famously remarked: "It is exactly as wasteful for a poet to do what has been done already, as for a biologist to rediscover Mendel's discoveries."[7] Once "discovered," though, how do innovations make their way in culture? What values and reactions do they release? And have we learned to assess their retentive and protentive character, their long-delayed effects, in these postmodern times?

Postmodernism, third in our perspectives on change, appears anxiously in several of these essays. But we need not vex the term in this introduction, a term that has changed in a few decades from awkward neologism to derelict cliché without ever attaining to the dignity of a concept. We need only recognize that postmodernism has become a current and tenacious trope of tendencies in theatre, dance, music, art, and architecture; in literature and criticism; in philosophy, psychoanalysis, historiography; in mass communications, cybernetic technologies, and sometimes even in the sciences, which are forming "new alliances" with humanistic thought.[8] Does it not deserve, then, to be theorized? The effort to understand our historical presence, to perceive the interactions of language and power in our midst, to valorize the living categories of our existence — surely that reflective effort, that complex cultural nisus, is what an adequate theory of postmodernism requires. Such a theory might clarify current indeterminacies in our modes of thought, action, belief, *and* current immanences of our signs, media, procedures; it might explain, in the West at least, a vast, ironic will to unmaking moving through a seemingly endless technological field. Yet the words

6

"clarify" and "explain" are perhaps not wholly apt; for irony turns also against postmodern theory itself. Contested as both a term and a phenomenon, signifier and signified, postmodernism proves true to itself: true, that is, to its plural, dialogical, problematic, yet pervasive character. This, too, our authors show.

III

The authors of this volume are happily diverse; this does not preclude some passion or anxiety on their part. It seems supererogatory to summarize here what they themselves best convey. Yet a brief outline of their thought may afford the reader some sense of the shape and scope of this work, in which themes cross, concerns overlap.

Part One relates to generic questions of Change, though the essays of Ihab Hassan and Dominick LaCapra allude to postmodernism as well. Hassan considers some theories of change — in myth, history, nature, and the paradigms of science — before suggesting a cultural schema for postmodernism which he terms "Indetermanence." Briefly but appositely, Claus Uhlig discusses certain difficulties inherent in the conception of historical times (always plural) and urges for a "chronography of change" which would recognize the "multidimensionality of historical phenomena as they appear to us in time." More consciously dialogical, LaCapra explores how historians discourse about the present; for him, the constitutive problem of intellectual history, which apprehends change under various deceptive guises, subsumes the *aporias* of both "innovation" and "postmodernism." Writing as a political scientist, Paul Noack propounds still another concept of change, that of "crisis," even permanent crisis, which supplants "revolution" as a description of social change both in its innovative and catastrophic forms.

Part Two, by far the longest, concerns Innovation, or rather innovations. It comprises three sections, which center on Literary Theory, Theory of Performance, the Cultural Criticism, regions in which the Western mind now plays out its agonisms with peculiar vividness and force.

Geoffrey Hartman shows that literary theory casts a long

shadow across culture; his call for an innovative, philosophical criticism challenges traditional demarcations of genres, and subtly probes the social uses of language in a world dominated by the illusions of mass media, the illiteracies of mass education. Similarly, Ralph Cohen examines the strategies of innovation, which he identifies with continual shifts of values, assumptions, and boundaries of literary theory; such shifts, he argues, make the recovery of traditional meanings both pressing and precarious. Unlike Hartman and Cohen, however, Wayne Booth questions the current rage for decreation and re-creation: instead of innovation, he offers a concept of human freedom, textual but also social, ultimately moral, which he believes more relevant to our belated historical condition.

The section on performance opens with the sweeping essay of Herbert Blau; calling on his rich experience as director, he simultaneously reviews the history, theory, and politics of innovative drama in the last few decades, with side glances at music and dance. Richard Schechner, another experienced director, attributes the innovative element in theatre to its restless liminality, to the essential "not-not notness" of all symbolic human actions; thus art and life, absence and presence, slip and slide into one another in that "play-mood" which constitutes performance, whether of drama, ritual, or television news. Similarly, Régis Durand perceives performance as a pervasive metaphor of postmodern society; siding with Barthes and Artaud against Michael Fried, Durand argues for a situational art, which can displace narrative and still serve as a "cybernetic machine." Semiotic in their outlook — since signs are the radical and deceptive means of all our representations — these three writers also address cultural questions that transgress Western bounds.

Cultural criticism, which permeates this volume, becomes perhaps most overt in the third section. Mooting the novel in an explicitly cultural perspective, Leslie Fiedler reviews his own views of a genre that reflects the changing needs, tastes, canons, and alignments of pop and elitist art: what, he asks, happened to the modernist conception of "innovation," of "literature" itself? And as our concepts of literature change, so do our ideas of woman in language, whom Didier Coste finds to have been spoken by men rather than herself; proposing the notion of "rehearsal" — "behavior which is never its own model" — instead of the *bougé* effect of "innovation/renovation," he reads in some current feminist texts a call to otherness. This is not far from the "dialogical pluralism" which Matei Calinescu explores by adverting especially to M. M. Bakhtin; beyond the negations of modernism, Calinescu suggests, a positive diversity of postmodern styles abets cultural innovation and expresses a new historicism that recognizes the claims of the Many and the One.

Part Three focuses wholly on Postmodernism, which already insinuated itself in several earlier texts. In assaying to define a postmodern phase of psychoanalysis, Norman Holland limns as well some general features of postmodernism in the arts; but his interest, like that of D. W. Winnicott, Heinz Kohut, and Heinz Lichtenstein, remains mainly in the new relational, reflexive, and transactive self. More wary of the postmodern phenomenon, which he sees partly as an ambitious critical intervention, Malcolm Bradbury recalls the history of literary modernism and of the artistic avant-gardes from which postmodernism emerged, and cautions against the reification of the latter in our current critical accounts. In the final essay, however, Jean-François Lyotard offers a statement, both partisan and theoretical, in favor of the ideolectic, the marginal, and the ludic impulses of postmodernism, which he forcefully defends against Jürgen Habermas;[9] working through Kant's concept of the sublime, Lyotard redefines both modernism and postmodernism by appealing to the criterion of "unpresentability."

IV

Clearly, the authors of these essays speak in many voices, in many styles and antistyles. Yet their polylogue also sounds some distinct variations on the theme of change. Here are seven of their varied themes:

1. Change has no disciplinary bounds. Thus the innovative concerns of literary theory engage society at large, and those of dramatic performance affect knowledge, action, and art.

9

2. Consequently, change reveals itself best in mutations of genres, shifts of epistemic forms, realignments of need and power, disjunctions or dispersals of discourse, all evident in Western societies during the last two decades.

3. Similarly, change manifests itself in reconceptions of certain ideas, institutions, norms; for instance, "man," "woman," "sexuality," "authority," "high culture," "literature," even "nature" itself.

4. As a result of these shifts and reconceptions, Western societies have experienced tense negotiations between parts and wholes, differences and identities, margins and centers, the Many and the One.

5. As a result, too, those societies have endured anxious mediations between past and future, old and new, flow and rupture —between different kinds of time, linear or cyclical, diachronic or synchronic. (What is postmodernism but another mediation of time and mind?)

6. Nor is change—modern or postmodern, innovative or renovative—ever intellectually naive. Elusive, equivocal, thoroughly problematic, it defies all our schemes, evincing itself as surprise or surmise, perhaps finally a rumor of mortality.

7. And since change always invokes both freedom and constraint, it is neither morally innocent nor politically neutral. Inescapably, we all pay, in private or in public, the price of change.

This last theme, exacerbated in some essays here more than in others, pervades them all. For change summons us finally to judgment. Is the New really a value upon which all criticism is founded, as Roland Barthes thought? Or is it, instead, an expense of the Western spirit in a waste of fashion? Are we not all recidivists—yes, even amateurs of change—and want to throttle mutability till it rattles of eternity? And can mutability yield any *human* meaning without some common nexus of worth, assent, and power: that is, of Authority? What Authority—or rather, which authorities? And how make such authorities congruent with inconstant time and desire? Though such renitent queries may yield us no facile answer, to ask them wakefully, and ask again, may also tease us a little into thought.

10

For what now deserves more our proleptic thought? Change, rapid and irreversible, and some may say irremediable, no longer seems the *hybris* of the West alone: its challenges run with one shock of recognition the whole world round. On a transhumanized earth, where dependence and independence — here the One and the Many appear again — clash into interdependence every day, none escapes the existential jolts of change. Thus the qualifier "Western" cannot finally exclude the pressure of global events on the essays in this volume. If American embassies are burned in distant lands, if religious atavists exorcise the nuclear Great Satan and young Europeans march for unilateral disarmament and chant, is it not perhaps because America has come to embody the radical threat of modernization itself? For though some may believe that America paradoxically serves as "The Archives of Eden" — its energy mainly "custodian" and "exhibitionist," George Steiner says[10] — yet it has become for all the world the scapegoat of change.

But politics is partial. In the end, no adequate view of all our transformations can shun a vaster vision of human being and becoming in this universe. The earth, Rilke thought, rises in us invisibly: "Was, wenn Verwandlung nicht, ist dein drängender Auftrag?" he asked.[11] And so, too, may we ask: does not human destiny lie in some strange region, locked in dreams, where the imagination meets change?

NOTES

1 Ihab Hassan, ed., *Liberations: New Essays on the Humanities in Revolution* (Middletown, Conn.: Wesleyan University Press, 1971), pp. xvf.
2 Yevgeny Zamyatin, *A Soviet Heretic* (Chicago: University of Chicago Press, 1970), p. 107.
3 Robert Heilbroner, *Marxism: For and Against* (New York: W. W. Norton, 1980), p. 32.
4 Richard Leakey, *Origins* (New York: E. P. Dutton, 1977), p. 15.
5 Konrad Lorenz, *Behind the Mirror* (New York: Harcourt Brace Jovanovich, 1977), p. 35.
6 Harry Levin, "What Was Modernism?" in *Refractions* (New York: Oxford University Press, 1966), p. 287.
7 Quoted by William K. Wimsatt, Jr. and Cleanth Brooks, *Literary*

Criticism: A Short History (New York: Alfred A. Knopf, 1957), p. 354.

8 See pp. 24–27 below. See also Ihab Hassan, *The Right Promethean Fire* (Urbana: University of Illinois Press, 1980), pp. 89–173; *The Dismemberment of Orpheus,* 2d ed. rev. (Madison: University of Wisconsin Press, 1982), pp. 259–71; and Ilya Prigogine and Isabelle Stengers, *La Nouvelle alliance* (Paris: Editions Gallimard, 1979).

9 See Jürgen Habermas, "Modernity versus Postmodernity," *New German Critique* 22 (Winter 1981): 3–14. Originally a lecture which Habermas delivered in Frankfurt on the occasion of his acceptance of the Theodor W. Adorno Prize, the German text first appeared in *Die Zeit,* 19 September 1980. Habermas concludes his essay with the bizarre distinction between "the antimodernism of the young conservatives" (Bataille, Foucault, Derrida) from "the premodernism of old conservatives" (Leo Strauss, Hans Jonas, Robert Spaemann) and "the postmodernism of the neoconservatives" (early Wittgenstein, late Gottfried Benn), p. 13.

10 George Steiner, "The Archives of Eden," *Salmagundi* 50–51 (Fall 1980–Winter 1981).

11 Rainer Maria Rilke, *Duino Elegies* (Berkeley and Los Angeles: University of California Press, 1968), p. 72.

I / PERSPECTIVES ON

Change

1 /

Ideas of Cultural Change

Ihab Hassan

We speak much of change and have no theory of it. This may be wiser than we suspect; for change must continually surprise itself. Nothing in the Cambrian age presages dinosaurs in the Jurassic or *homo sapiens* in the Pleistocene—except in retrospect. And nothing in our childhood predicts our end—except in biography. Thus the future, in spite of dull futurists and inspired prophets, remains in large part mercifully concealed.

Yet human beings in culture continue to innovate or renovate and do this now more than in any period of history. How, then, can we understand the strange rush of mutability? How, that is, comprehend the nature of our contemporaneity? We can begin, perhaps, with an act of self-reflexion, not in the Cartesian mode of the *cogito,* but rather in the Nietzschean spirit of a *Wille zur Macht,* a will seeking hopelessly to clarify itself. This is to say that we remain creatures of power, language, and desire; and that all our articulations shadow forth our mortality.

Death indeed takes the measure of every change and inspires its metaphors. For no alteration of seasons or reversal of states impresses us more than this "event of events": suddenly, the body refuses its long intimacy with the will, giving itself to emptiness. The event is visible, irrevocable, mysterious. Men lived, it seems, millennia without conscious knowledge of their deaths; nor do infants today possess such knowledge till they enter late childhood. Yet we all surrender nightly to dreamless sleep; and our civilization rests on burial mounds and cairns. As individuals of

a secular society, we now refuse mythic time and religious conso-
lation, and so feel death all the more acutely as rupture, cessa-
tion. No rebirth for us; no immortality or metempsychosis; no
Heraclitean fire or Brunist transmutation; nor Hölderlin's "aus
dem Bunde der Wesen schwindet der Tod."

Ernest Becker believed that the human body represents the
"curse of fate," and that culture stands on repression, not only of
sexuality as Freud thought, but also of mortality, "because man
[is] . . . primarily an avoider of death."[1] We need not concur
with this sombre view to perceive that every creative act is also a
small exercise in dying. For the new is an aspect of the unknown,
"the undiscovered country from whose bourn / No traveler returns. . . ." Innovation/renovation, creation/re-creation: such
terms conspire deeply against our quotidian being.

Consider two familiar views of change, equally partial, perhaps equally true: one, surpassing even Heraclitus, asserts that
"you can't step into the same stream once" (Cratylus), the other
claims that "nothing is ever new under the sun" (Ecclesiastes).
One favors change and difference, the other repetition and sameness. The first, disjunctive, preserves the gap between concrete
phenomena; the second, conjunctive, fills gaps by its abstract
narratives or metalanguages. We may need both: the first to *perceive* the New, the second to *comprehend* it. Yet each whispers to
us of human mortality. For the discontinuous vision invokes perpetual rebirth, the phoenix rising from its ashes; while the vision
of continuity yearns for retrospective immortality, the sphinx's
anamnesis. Thus mortality may make cowards of us all, making
politics the art of self-avoidance, making history a rehearsal of
desires. Is there no way out of these deadly gyres?

Roland Barthes believed that "the New is not a fashion but a
value" upon which we found our existence. "To escape from the
alienation of present society, there is only one way: *escape forward* . . . ," he said.[2] Which way, in our day, is "forward"?
Which "forward" evades mortality? The questions, though communal, return us to the languages of the self. From Lacan we
know that the symbolic subject, the self in language, constitutes
itself in a *béance* or abysm; and so "no being is ever evoked by
him [the subject] except among the shadows of death."[3] And

from Foucault we learn that death serves as a cognitive principle in "the anonymous flow of speech," displacing continually the present; "to die" is an infinitive we can never complete.[4] In short, more than an existential metaphor, more than an ontology of the new or a politics of innovation, death enters the very language by which we try to understand change; and it acts, as Heidegger saw, as the basis of "authentic history," which finds its weight not in the past, not in the "today," but in the *Geschehen,* the very process of existence, originating from the future, the "Being-toward-death."

Yet change also takes more public forms in culture, assumes historical as well as epistemological shapes. Consider four established models of change.

I commence with the oldest, the mythic-religious model. Though we often believe myth to be ahistorical or static, it offers crucial images of transformation.[5] For despite the nostalgia of archaic societies for some unvarying Golden Age, some ideal Great Time, these societies practice diverse rituals of passage, signal alterations in the inward and outward life of their members, such as initiation and marriage, the shaman's deep trance, the heroic journey down into Hades or beyond the Pillars of Hercules. This journey represents, above all, a labor of self-creation through self-mastery and self-achieved submission to the universe; it thus represents conquest of death, or rather, enactment of rebirth. "Within the soul, within the body social," Joseph Campbell remarks, "there must be—if we are to experience long survival—a continuous 'recurrence of birth' (*palingenesia*) to nullify the unremitting recurrences of death."[6] This is the "monomyth," in which the monster-slaying hero initiates new orders. "For the mythological hero," Campbell continues," is the champion not of things become but of things becoming; the dragon to be slain by him is precisely the monster of the status quo: Holdfast, the keeper of the past."[7] This past, which includes his parents, not only impedes his progress; it further inhibits his individuation, his realization of a self capable of giving itself to the universe. Thus, as Erich Neumann argues, the evolution of consciousness itself, from an undifferentiated pleromatic condition, through the slaying of the Great Mother and the World Parents,

17

toward a "centroverted," autonomous state, represents the supreme creative effort of the race.[8] In this mythic model, then, change is double: the hero creates himself even as he re-creates society, founds a new city. But creation and re-creation combine the highest degree of individuation with the widest cosmic awareness; unlike the zealot, who serves only his totem or tribe, the hero uniquely serves the whole of life.[9]

I come now to the second or historical model. Historiographers agree that history is young. Some would say that a genuine historical awareness emerged not with Old Testament prophets or Greek historians — Herodotus, Thucydides — but with early Renaissance man. "This was nothing less than man's discovery of the new," Daniel Boorstin thinks. "Not of a particular sort of novelty, but of the very possibility of novelty."[10] (Significantly, voyagers of that epoch discovered also the New World.) But history as a *pattern* of change, as historiography, came still later; it awaited Giambattista Vico in the eighteenth century. His *Scienza Nuova* discerns the ontogenetic principles of institutions in "gentile nations," and discriminates between history and nature, poetic wisdom and natural evidence, in ways that still inform our humanities. Vico's threefold scheme of historical evolution, followed by a *recorso,* may seem rather mythic in its cyclical bias. Yet his "new science" remains both a demonstration "of what providence has wrought in history" and a "history of human ideas, on which it seems the metaphysics of the human mind must proceed."[11] Conscious of the constitutive element in history, which is "certain" precisely because "he who creates the things also narrates them," Vico's model of change rests on the self-reflexive capacity of human beings to interpret what they do.[12] But the model derives also from the mythopoetic origins of language and culture, and so testifies to the transformative powers of the imagination no less than to the hermeneutic character of change.[13] "That which did all this was mind, for men did it with intelligence; it was not fate, for they did it by choice; not chance, for the results of their always so acting are perpetually the same," Vico concludes.[14]

The last phrase seems suddenly to undercut the more linear thrust, which Hegel and Marx powerfully introduced in the next century. For Hegel, history is "free," dialectical, irreversible, the work of a Universal Spirit that takes the whole world as its stage. The future, acting upon the past, creates the present, which becomes the future again, till the end of History, the end of Man — not as a sentient being but as an active negation, a crack or error in Being. At that happy terminus, subject and object, time and space, concrete and universal, achieve their reconciliation; the dialectic of change attains to changelessness.[15] Marx, we know, inverted Hegel, refusing all "idealistic humbug." For him, "history does not end by being resolved into 'self-consciousness' as 'spirit of the spirit'"; history rather shows that "at each stage there is found a material result: a sum of productive forces, a historically created relation of individuals to nature and to one another, which is handed down to each generation from its predecessors. . . ."[16] Believing firmly that the consciousness of men does not determine their being, "but, on the contrary their social being . . . determines their consciousness," Marx still sought to reform consciousness by "criticism," sought to expose class conflicts and "unmask human self-alienation"; for though force could be overthrown only by material force, "theory itself becomes a material force when it has seized the masses."[17] In the Marxist model of change, then, "the *entire so-called history of the world* is nothing but the creation of man through human labor, nothing but the emergence of nature for man, so he has the visible, irrefutable proof of his *birth* through himself, of the *process of his creation.*"[18] Materialist as he claimed to be, Marx, we see, believes that man changes his nature by acting upon nature.[19]

We may be inclined to contrast mythic and historical change, the one seemingly cyclical, the other linear. Yet such a contrast would be feckless. For as Lévi-Strauss shows, history now fulfills certain mythical functions in "advanced" societies; and myth or religion, even among "primitive" people, permits metamorphosis, conversion.[20] Furthermore, mythopoesis defines an essential aspect of human creativity, imaginative change.[21] Nor do all historical views shun cycles or epicycles, as the works of Vico, Nietzsche, Spengler, and Toynbee show. Even Marx thought that revolutions repeat some aspect of themselves, that all great events occur, as it were, twice, "the first time as tragedy, the second as farce."[22] Thus both myth and history confirm us in certain features of change that I mean shortly to summarize.

But I must turn now to a third model derived from evolution: the evolution of our earth and the cosmos, the evolution of species. In the seventeenth century, we recall, Archbishop Ussher precisely dated the creation of the earth from the year 4004 B.C. It remained for James Hutton and Charles Lyell, centuries after, to propound the "uniformitarianism theory" of change, in a far older earth, according to uniform physical laws operating then as now in the universe. The world, it seems, was not spontaneously given in its present shape; irreversible time acted as much in nature as in history. That same action of time in living organisms provided Charles Darwin and Alfred Russel Wallace—both influenced by Malthus as by Lyell—with the key to a vast conundrum: how can so much variety in life, so much detail in nature, proceed from a general, invariable design? The answer, of course, lies in the theory of biological evolution, with its twin principles of natural selection and random mutation. Darwin concludes *The Origin of Species* thus: "It is interesting to contemplate a tangled bank, clothed with many plants of many kinds, with birds singing on the bushes, with various insects flitting about, and with worms crawling through the damp earth, and to reflect that these elaborately constructed forms, so different from each other and dependent upon each other in so complex a manner, have all been produced by laws acting around us. . . . There is grandeur in this view of life. . . ."[23] These laws of an immanent grandeur, however, allow greater change in organic than inorganic systems; for the former possess a capacity for self-modification that the latter lack. This is especially true of human beings, as Wallace recognizes: "With our advent, there had come into existence a being in whom that subtle force we term 'mind' became of far more importance than mere bodily structure."[24] Still, we may well ask: is time teleological (Teilhard) or simply teleonomic (Monod)?[25] Are we the product of some strange necessity in the universe or merely of chance?

The question becomes acute wherever science encounters "singularities" like black holes in space or the origins of the universe, where mind seems to encounter itself. As Sir Bernard Lov-

ell asks: "Does man face this difficulty because he has external-
ized the object of his investigation? A remarkable and intimate
relationship between man, the fundamental constants of nature,
and the initial moments of space and time seems to be an inescapable condition of existence."[26] Here is the hermeneutic point
again, hermeneutic and decidedly epistemological, which leads
us to consider still another model of change.

The fourth model concerns the paradigms of science itself,
changes in scientific knowledge. Philosophers of sciences, of
course, no more agree than scientists or historians about how
such changes take place; their paradigms range from the "objec-
tivist" model of Karl Popper to the tacit or "subjectivist" view of
Michael Polanyi.[27] I shall discuss here two younger and more
flamboyant thinkers, Thomas Kuhn and Paul Feyerabend,
whose works may prove more pertinent to our cultural theme.
Kuhn's celebrated theory of paradigms or "disciplinary matrices"
— mildly modified in its later versions — recognizes that science is
not exclusively empirical: "An apparently arbitrary element,
compounded of personal and historical accident, is always a for-
mative ingredient of the beliefs espoused by a given scientific
community at a given time."[28] This consensus of belief defines
"normal science," until anomalies challenge the ruling paradigm,
and scientists begin once again the "extraordinarily arduous"
search for a new one. "Produced inadvertently by a game played
under one set of rules," the assimilation of these anomalies now
". . . requires the elaboration of another set."[29] Thus crises im-
pel scientists to choose between alternate models of reality; and
such choices affect "the scientific imagination in ways that we
shall ultimately need to describe as a transformation of the world
within which scientific work was done."[30] Yet these paradigmatic
changes or choices, these "revolutions" as Kuhn also calls them,
will not necessarily yield a closer approximation of reality itself,
which remains unknowable.[31] Thus, though science makes instrumental progress, it can make no similar ontological claim. "Is
it not possible, or perhaps even likely," Kuhn shockingly asks,
"that contemporary scientists know less of what there is to know
about their world than the scientists of the eighteenth century
knew of theirs?"[32] But how finally do paradigms shift, revolu-

tions in science occur? Kuhn scrupulously declines to answer, though he does show that logic and experiment—in naive attempts of "falsification"—will not explain historic choices between competing theories; social, psychological, even axiological imperatives of the scientific community as a whole prove more decisive. "We shall not . . . ," he concludes, "understand the success of science without understanding the full force of rhetorically induced and professionally shared imperatives like these."[33]

Feyerabend goes farther. This *enfant terrible* of the profession considers himself a "flippant Dadaist and *not* . . . a serious anarchist."[34] Therefore, I do well to let him speak for himself through excerpts from the "Analytical Index" of *Against Method:*

Science is an essentially anarchistic enterprise: theoretical anarchism is more humanitarian and more likely to encourage progress than its law-and-order alternatives.

No theory ever agrees with all the *facts* in its domain, yet it is not always the theory that is to blame. Facts are constituted by older ideologies, and a clash between facts and theories may be proof of progress.

Given science, reason cannot be universal and unreason cannot be excluded. . . . The realization that science is not sacrosanct, and that the debate between science and myth has ceased without having been won by either side, further strengthens the case for anarchism.

Thus science is much closer to myth than a scientific philosophy is prepared to admit. It is one of the many forms of thought that have been developed by man, and not necessarily the best. It is conspicuous, noisy, and impudent, but it is inherently superior only for those who have already decided in favour of a certain ideology. . . .[35]

Himself noisy, impudent, often tendentious—as well as zanily erudite—Feyerabend counterposes to the crypto-ideology of science an ideology of his own, wavering between anarchic libertarianism and Maoist control. Thus, for instance, he demands the separation of science and state, and would overrule "truth" or "expert opinion," subjecting science to "community action" and "democratic judgment," though the latter can turn tyrannical as any state.[36] Calling his philosophy of change "interactionism," Feyerabend drills home his thesis that every scientific argument depends upon an *"attitude,"* "involves *cosmological assumptions* which must be believed or else the argument will not seem plausible."[37] Thus from both Kuhn and Feyerabend we learn that scientific change depends on ideology, belief, even accident, as much as on logic or evidence.

From such varied models of change, what then can we surmise? Perhaps the following seven inconclusive points:

1. There is change. It affects not only the physical universe — exploding supernovae, geological shifts, photosynthesis, random mutations — but also the human world. Indeed, our awareness of change expands with our knowledge of ourselves and the universe.

2. All change depends upon a sense and scale of time. Human nature may not have altered much since Socrates, but it has since the hominids of the Olduvai Gorge. Goethe could quip that humanity progresses though man does not because the span of the one is incommensurate with the other's.

3. In the human world, change appears as a function of imagination and desire, metaphor and value, noetic construct and affective interest — as well as pure chance.

4. In the human world, again, the perception of change depends upon language, and so possesses a distinct hermeneutic dimension; or as Nietzsche might say, every change is already an interpretation.

5. The most powerful agent of change is mind acting upon itself even as it acts upon material reality, a self-transforming system, cybernetic and seemingly exponential in its capacity for altering nature — for better or worse — through knowledge and culture.[38]

6. No universal pattern of transformation applies to all human endeavors; some change seems cyclical, some linear, here dialectical, there dramatic, one kind filiative, another affiliative.

7. Finally, all models of change assume some idea of order or metaphysical principle, which may be variously termed Isis, Providence, History, Omega Point, or God Does Not Play Dice With The Universe.

I come to these inferences without having considered other

models of change: for instance, psychological and cognitive developments of the individual since infancy (Freud, Piaget); the creative process itself, or *Einbildungskraft,* in science and art; shifts in natural languages on the one hand, in informational or algorithmic systems on the other; and perhaps the most proximate to my theme, that evasive form of change we call literary history.

But it is time that I engaged more closely my central theme: innovation and renovation in contemporary culture. Admittedly, innovation/renovation betrays a certain equivocation. This hesitancy is especially pronounced in the humanities: nobly epimethean, they accrue with many backward glances. Yet critical developments in the arts and humanities of twentieth-century culture did take place. Can we begin to distinguish between some of these? Quite provisionally, I would suggest three modes of cultural change in our century. I call these Avant-Garde, Modern, and Postmodern, or—given the notorious instability of such terms—simply A, B, and C. Together, in any case, these modes perpetuate that Western "tradition of the new" which, since Baudelaire, has brought "into being an art whose history, regardless of the credos of its practitioners, has consisted of leaps from vanguard to vanguard, and political mass movements whose aim has been the total renovation not only of social institutions but of man himself."[39]

By Avant-Garde (A) I mean those movements that agitated the earlier part of our century, including "Pataphysics, Cubism, Futurism, Dadaism, Surrealism, Suprematism, Constructivism, Merzism, and so on. Anarchic and disjunctive, these assaulted the bourgeoisie with their art, their manifestos, their antics. But their activism could also turn inward, becoming suicidal—as became later some Postmodernists like Rudolf Schwartzkogler. Once full of brio and bravura, these movements have all but vanished now, leaving only their story, at once fugacious and exemplary.[40] Modernism (B), however, proved more stable, aloof, hieratic, like the French Symbolism from which it derived; even its experiments now seem olympian. Enacted by such "individual talents" as Valéry, Proust, and Gide, Yeats, the earlier Joyce, and Lawrence, Rilke, Mann, and Musil, Pound, Eliot, and Faulkner,

24

it commanded high authority, leading Delmore Schwartz to chant: "Let us consider where the great men are / Who will obsess the child when he can read. . . ."[41] But if much of Modernism appears hieratic, hypotactical, and formalist, Postmodernism (C) strikes us by contrast as playful, paratactical, and deconstructionist.[42] In this, it recalls the irreverent spirit of the Avant-Garde, and so carries sometimes the label Neo-Avant-Garde. Yet Postmodernism remains "cooler," in McLuhan's sense, than older vanguards — cooler, less cliquish, and far less aversive to the pop, electronic society of which it is a part.[43]

No doubt, the question of Postmodernism remains complex and moot.[44] Yet we need no lexical definition of the term to sense the larger questions implied. They are: Can we, or even should we at this time, construct some probative scheme, both historical and theoretical, that may account for current mutations of culture and consciousness? What kind of change — innovative, renovative, simply novative — would such a scheme assume?[45] What values, private or public, physical or metaphysical? And would such a scheme admit various trends and countertrends, admit the diverse strains of Postmodernism: its experimental and kitsch sides, its tendency now to contract reflexively into concept art or verbal games, now to explode riotously into happenings or public gestures? In the end, whatever scheme we devise remains but a scheme or construct, at best heuristic, perhaps proleptic.

Certainly our epoch invites intuitions of things to come. It may not help us much to know that we stand at the threshold of "post-civilization," as Kenneth Boulding insists, making a transition as momentous as the "agricultural revolution proved ten millennia ago."[46] Yet the sense of supervention crowds our moment and affects even prudent and conservative minds.[47] Thus, for instance, Daniel Bell declares: "I believe we are coming to a watershed in Western society: we are witnessing the end of the bourgeois idea — that view of human action and social relations, particularly of economic exchange — which has molded the modern era for the last 200 years. And I believe that we have reached the end of the creative impulse and ideological sway of modernism, which, as a cultural movement, has dominated all the arts, and shaped our symbolic expressions, for the past 125 years."[48]

Disjunctions between the realms of economy, polity, and cultures; the crisis of the Protestant ethic, of middle-class values in general; the advent, beyond rising expectations, of a politics of entitlement or envy; syncretism and the jumbling of styles in culture; the increasing permeability of all society to novelty, without discrimination or resistance; the confusions of fact and fantasy in public as in private life; the enervation of the postmodern self, nourished on hedonism, consumption, febrile affluence—all these, Bell argues, have undermined the Western "order of things." But Bell goes still farther to identify not only technology but also culture (by which he means the entire symbolic universe, managed more and more by postmodern vanguards) as the culprit. For the "post-modernist temper demands that what was previously played out in fantasy and imagination must be acted out in life as well. . . . Anything permitted in art is permitted in life. . . ."[49] Thus cultural vanguards come to assume primacy "in the fields of manners, morals, and, ultimately, politics."[50] Bell, of course, exaggerates the triumph of these movements; and though he writes with acumen, he writes as a conservative sociologist, who finds lamentable that the contemporary imagination should serve to disconfirm our polity. (I wonder if he has read much in classic American literature or sensed its powers of darkness.)

Jean-François Lyotard, however, rejoices in the very same evidence of disconfirmation. His trenchant, brilliant work, *La Condition postmoderne,* both corroborates *The Cultural Contradictions of Capitalism* and profoundly challenges its values. Lyotard's central theme is the desuetude of the "great narratives" and "metanarratives," which organized bourgeois society. The radical crisis, then, is one of "*légitimation*"—compare with Habermas's "legitimation crisis" in *Legitimationsprobleme im Spätkapitalismus*—in every cognitive and social endeavor where a multitude of languages now reign. I paraphrase freely Lyotard's theme:

The postmodern condition is a stranger to disenchantment as to the blind positivity of delegitimation. Where can legitimacy reside after the dissolution of metanarratives? The criterion of functionality is merely technological; it cannot apply to judgments of truth and justice. The consensus obtained by discussion, as Habermas thinks? That criterion violates the heterogeneity of language games. And inventions are always made in dissent. Postmodern knowledge is not only the instrument of power. It refines our sensibilities, awakens them to differences, and strengthens our capacities to bear the incommensurable. It does not find its reason in the agreements or homologies of experts but in the paralogies of inventors.

The open question, then, is this: can a legitimation of social relations, can a just society, be made practicable in accordance with a paradox analogous to that of current scientific activity? And of what would such a paradox consist?[51]

Lyotard thus ushers us, somewhat utopically, into the postmodern era of "*les petites histoires*": paratactical, paradoxical, paralogical narratives meant to open the structures of knowledge as of politics to language games, to imaginative reconstitutions that permit us either a new breakthrough or a change in the rules of the game itself.[52] He concludes: "A politics is taking shape in which the desire for both justice and the unknown are equally respected."[53] Yet "human justice," alas, can sanction bloody terror, and "the unknown" can provoke intolerant reactions, new needs for certainty and authority.

Still, it is of some interest that two thinkers, one conservative and the other radical, respond so differently to a phenomenon that both call by the same name. (Bell, however, protests against postmodernism by hyphenating the word, which neither Lyotard nor I find necessary to do.) But the initial question remains: what useful scheme of postmodern transformations can we devise? The scheme I would propose proves to be less a scheme than a complex double tendency. The two tendencies are not dialectical; for they are not exactly antithetical; nor do they lead to any synthesis. Furthermore, each tendency generates its own contradictions, and contains as well elements of the other tendency. The two tendencies, then, interplay; their actions, ludic and deadly serious, may suggest the pattern of an ambilectic. I believe that this ambilectic now modulates changes in nearly every domain of Western culture in the last half century, changes we cannot ignore.

The first of these tendencies I have elsewhere called Indeterminacy.[54] But the tendency is really compounded of sub-tendencies which the following words evoke: openness, heterodoxy, pluralism, eclecticism, randomness, revolt, deformation. The latter alone subsumes a dozen current terms of unmaking: decreation, disintegration, deconstruction, decenterment, displacement, difference, discontinuity, disjunction, disappearance, decomposition, de-definition, demystification, detotalization, delegitimation — let alone more technical and rhetorical terms, such as chiasmus, lapsus, schism, hiatus, diremption, suture, transumption, idiolect, heteromorph, etc. Through all these signs moves a vast will to unmaking, affecting the body politic, the body cognitive, the erotic body, the psyche of each individual — affecting, in short, the entire realm of human discourse in the West. We may then call that tendency *Indeterminacies,* thus recognizing its plural character, which nonetheless reopens or revokes our familiar modes of thought and being.

I scarcely know where I might begin to document so pervasive, so perverse, a trend. In literature alone, our ideas of author, audience, reading, writing, book, genre, critical theory, and of literature itself have all suddenly become questionable.[55] We now speak of intertextuality and semioclasty (Julia Kristeva), of a hermeneutics of suspicion (Paul Ricoeur), of a criticism of bliss and pedagogy of unlearning (Roland Barthes). We propose schizoanalysis (Gilles Deleuze and Félix Guattari), a humanism of disappearance (Michel Foucault), a grammatology of differences (Jacques Derrida), a politics of delegitimation (Jean-François Lyotard). These *philosophies blanches* truly abound: ideologies of fracture, metaphysics of absence, theologies of the supplement, mystiques of the trace.[56] But Gaul is not the only home of epistemological Gaullism, Gallic *ratures,* and borrowed *Unheimlichkeit.* Others near at hand speak of paracriticism and parabiography (Ihab Hassan), freaks and mutants (Leslie Fiedler), dialogy and the imagination of doubt (Matei Calinescu), surfiction and playgiarism (Raymond Federman), a third-phase psychoanalysis of intimacy and incompleteness (Norman N. Holland), a theatre of impossibility, brought to the vanishing point (Herbert Blau).[57] In so speaking, they testify variously to the indeterminate, or decreative, or antinomian impulse of our moment, a moment that reaches back, half a century ago, to Heisenberg's Principle of Uncertainty in physics and Gödel's Proof of Incompleteness (or Undecidability) in all logical systems. (The two theories, though logically unrelated, express the same spirit of limitation or ambiguity, which leads Douglas Hofstadter to remark: "provability is a weaker notion than truth, no matter what axiomatic system is involved."[58]) Yet in the end, the epistemic factor proves to be only one of many. The force of the antinomian and indeterminate tendency derives from larger dispositions in society: a rising standard of living in the West, the disruption of institutional values, freed desires, liberation movements of every kind, schism and secession around the globe, terrorism rampant—in short, the Many asserting their primacy over the One.

We may now challenge the totalizing will, from Pharaoh or Moses through Louis XIV ("L'état, c'est moi!") and Charlie Wilson ("What's good for General Motors is good for the country") to Stalin, Hitler, Mao, and Castro. But we may not overlook a second major tendency in the postmodern world, dispersing the will of the One. I call that tendency *Immanences,* a term I employ without religious echo, and by which I mean the capacity of mind to generalize itself in the world, to act upon both self and world, and so become more and more, im-mediately, its own environment. Various thinkers have reflected variously upon this tendency, speaking of etherialization (Arnold Toynbee), ephemeralization (Buckminster Fuller), conceptualization (Erwin Laszlo), dematerialization (Paolo Soleri), of nature historicized (Karl Marx) and the earth hominized (Teilhard de Chardin), and of a new technological and scientific gnosis (Ihab Hassan).[59] The tendency—evoked also by such sundry words as dispersal, diffusion, dissemination, diffraction, pulsion, integration, ecumenism, communication, interplay, interdependence, interpenetration, etc. — depends, above all, on the emergence of man as a language animal, *homo pictor* or *homo significans,* a creature constituting himself, and increasingly his universe, by symbols of his own making. Is ". . . this not the sign that the whole of this [classic] configuration is about to topple, and that man is in the process of perishing as the being of language continues to shine ever brighter upon our horizon?" Foucault famously asks.[60]

More than Foucault, however, Lyotard considers the role of media (*l'informatique*) in shaping the languages of self and society in advanced capitalist states; tomorrow's encyclopedias, he suggests, may be data banks which could become "nature" itself for postmodern man.[61] Media, of course, may derealize history even as they disseminate it around the world, often as kitsch or entertainment. But media also project mind to the edge of the universe or into the ghostly interstices of matter, and so abet another type of immanence, which scientists since Heisenberg have recognized as human participation or intervention in nature. Daniel Bell perceives this as the emergent stage of cultural development, implicating human beings in the recreation of reality, and confronting post-Kantian epistemologies with the enigma of artificial intelligence.[62] "Beyond this is a larger dream . . . ," Bell writes. "Just as Pascal sought to throw dice with God . . . so the decision theorists, and the new intellectual technology, seek their own *tableau entier*—the compass of rationality itself."[63] Yet both Lyotard's *"informatique"* and Bell's *"tableau entier"* have already created disquieting constraints in postmodern societies, constraints which demand from us stringent moral and political critiques.

Still other factors further the immanences of which I speak. The explosion of human populations increases the intellectual density of the earth, the possibilities of mental no less than physical interactions. (As everyone knows, a room holding one or two people differs radically from the same space containing seven, or again seventy, more.) Such intense interaction, Bell believes, augments both differences in the social structure (indeterminacies?) and syncretism in the culture (immanences?).[64] "In principle, much of this is not new," Bell adds. "What is distinctive is the change of scale. . . . All what we once knew played out on the scale of the Greek polis is now played out in the dimensions of the entire world. Scale creates two effects: one, it extends the range of control from a center of power. (What is Stalin, an unknown wit remarked, if not Genghis Khan with a telephone?) And two, when linear extension reaches certain thresholds, unsettling changes ensue."[65]

Such immanences we may learn to rue. Still, though one immanence may become totalitarian, complex immanences of languages and indeterminacies of theories or praxis diffract power, and so force us to reconceive the relation between wholes and parts. No doubt, the process will prove violent, perhaps catastrophic. Yet both planetization, on a global scale, and cosmopolitanism, in the city's smaller measure, already reveal the erratic course of that process. The city began, as Lewis Mumford shows, where the gods inhabited a certain space, and people came to mingle in rich human interactions.[66] "We must now conceive the city . . . ," he concludes, "not primarily as a place of business or government, but as an essential organ for expressing and actualizing the new human personality—that of 'One World Man.'"[67] One World Man or Woman, if ever given a chance to appear, will prove anything but homogeneous; heterodox, heteromorph, heteroclite, living in one human universe yet many heterocosms, that creature may still astonish all our expectations.[68] Yet I believe that very same creature is the true protagonist of present and future change: One and Many in ambiguous Hope.

NOTES

1 Ernest Becker, *The Denial of Death* (New York: Free Press, 1975), p. 96.
2 Roland Barthes, *The Pleasure of the Text,* trans. Richard Howard (New York: Hill & Wang, 1975), p. 40.
3 Jacques Lacan, *The Language of the Self,* trans. Anthony Wilden (Baltimore: Johns Hopkins University Press, 1968), p. 85.
4 "'To' die is never localized in the density of a given moment, but from its flux it infinitely divides the shortest moment. To die is even smaller than the moment it takes to think it and yet dying is infinitely repeated on either side of this widthless crack." Michel Foucault, *Language, Counter-Memory, Practice,* trans. Donald F. Bouchard and Sherry Simon (Ithaca: Cornell University Press, 1977), pp. 174f.
5 See Mircea Eliade, *Cosmos and History* (New York: Harper & Brothers, 1959).
6 Joseph Campbell, *The Hero With a Thousand Faces* (New York: Meridian Books, 1956), p. 16.
7 Ibid, p. 337.
8 Erich Neumann, *The Origins and History of Consciousness* (Princeton: Princeton University Press, 1954). For a succinct statement on the evolution of language and deities, hence of mythic consciousness, see Ernst Cassirer, *Language and Myth,* trans. Suzanne K. Langer (New York: Harper & Brothers, 1946). Crucial in this respect

also is the voluminous work of C. G. Jung, especially *The Spirit in Man, Art, and Literature* (Princeton: Princeton University Press, 1966); *Symbols of Transformation* (Princeton: Princeton University Press, 1967); and *Psychology and Alchemy* (Princeton: Princeton University Press, 1968).

9 See Campbell, *The Hero With a Thousand Faces,* pp. 45, 147, 156.
10 Daniel J. Boorstin, *The Republic of Technology* (New York: Harper & Row Pubs., 1978), p. 14.
11 *The New Science of Giambattista Vico,* trans. and abridged from 3d ed. by Thomas Goddard Bergin and Max Harold Fisch (Ithaca: Cornell University Press, 1970), pp. 60, 62.
12 Ibid., p. 63.
13 Ibid., pp. 87f., 90, 117, 123, 241, 260, 285, among many others.
14 Ibid., p. 383.
15 See G. W. F. Hegel, *The Philosophy of History,* trans. J. Sibree (New York: John Wiley & Sons, 1944), pp. 1–79.
16 Karl Marx and Friedrich Engels, *The German Ideology,* ed. C. J. Arthur (New York: International Publishers, 1970), p. 59.
17 *The Marx-Engels Reader,* ed. Robert C. Tucker (New York: W. W. Norton, 1978), pp. 4, 15, 54, 60.
18 Karl Marx, *The Economic and Philosophic Manuscripts of 1844,* ed. Dirk J. Struik (New York: International Publishers, 1964), p. 145.
19 See also *The Marx-Engels Reader,* p. 344, for a relevant excerpt from *Capital.*
20 See Claude Lévi-Strauss, *Myth and Meaning* (New York: Schocken Books, 1979), pp. 38–43, where the author briefly argues that myth and history can be more continuous than we suspect.
21 In addition to the works of Vico, Jung, and Cassirer noted earlier, see Suzanne K. Langer, *Philosophy in a New Key* (Cambridge: Harvard University Press, 1942); Philip Wheelwright, *The Burning Fountain* (Bloomington: Indiana University Press, 1954); Erich Neumann, *Art and the Creative Unconscious* (Princeton: Princeton University Press, 1959); and Harry Slowchower, *Mythopoesis* (Detroit: Wayne State University Press, 1970).
22 Karl Marx, *The Eighteenth Brumaire of Louis Bonaparte,* ed. C. P. Duff (New York: International Publishers, 1964), p. 15. See also, for a brilliant analysis of Marx's essay, Harold Rosenberg, "Politics of Illusion," in *Liberations,* ed. Ihab Hassan (Middletown, Conn.: Wesleyan University Press, 1971); Edward W. Said, "On Repetition," in *The Literature of Fact,* ed. Angus Fletcher (New York: Columbia University Press, 1976); and Jeffrey Mehlman, *Revolution and Repetition* (Berkeley and Los Angeles: University of California Press, 1977).
23 Charles Darwin, *The Origin of Species* (New York: New American Library of World Literature, 1958), p. 450. See also Stanley Edgar

32

Hyman, *The Tangled Bank* (New York: Atheneum Pubs., 1962), for chapters on Darwin and Marx as "imaginative writers."

24 Quoted by Jacob Bronowski, *The Ascent of Man* (Boston: Little, Brown, 1973), p. 302.

25 Cf. Pierre Teilhard de Chardin, *The Phenomenon of Man,* trans. Bernard Wall, intro. Sir Julian Huxley (New York: Harper & Row Pubs., 1959) with Jacques Monod, *Chance and Necessity,* trans. Austryn Wainhouse (New York: Alfred A. Knopf, 1971).

26 *The New York Times Magazine,* 16 November 1975, p. 95.

27 Cf. Karl R. Popper, *The Logic of Scientific Discovery* (New York: Harper & Row Pubs., 1968) and *Conjectures and Refutations* (New York: Harper & Row Pubs., 1965), with Michael Polanyi, *Personal Knowledge* (New York: Harper & Row Pubs., 1964) and *Knowing and Being* (London: Routledge & Kegan Paul, 1969).

28 Thomas S. Kuhn, *The Structure of Scientific Revolutions,* 2d ed. enlgd. (Chicago: University of Chicago Press, 1970), p. 4. The postscript of this work qualifies some statements in the earlier edition. But see also Thomas S. Kuhn, "Second Thoughts on Paradigms," in *The Essential Tension* (Chicago: Chicago University Press, 1977); Imre Lakatos and Alan Musgrave, eds., *Criticism and the Growth of Knowledge* (Cambridge: Cambridge University Press, 1970); Stephen Toulmin, *Human Understanding (Princeton: Princeton University Press,* 1972); and Frederick Suppe, ed., *The Structure of Scientific Theories* (Urbana: University of Illinois Press, 1974) for further discussions of scientific change. For a persuasive application of Kuhn's ideas to literary criticism, see David Bleich, *Subjective Criticism* (Baltimore: Johns Hopkins University Press, 1978).

29 Kuhn, *The Structure of Scientific Revolutions,* p. 52.

30 Ibid., p. 6.

31 As Kuhn elsewhere observes: "The view toward which I grope would also be Kantian but without 'things in themselves' and with categories of the mind which could change with time as the accommodation of language and experience proceed. A view of that sort need not, I think, make the world less real." See Thomas S. Kuhn, "Metaphor in Science," in *Metaphor and Thought,* ed. Andrew Ortony (Cambridge: Cambridge University Press, 1979), pp. 418f.

32 Kuhn, *The Essential Tension,* p. 290.

33 Ibid., p. 292.

34 Paul Feyerabend, *Against Method* (London: NLB, 1975), p. 21.

35 Ibid., pp. 10–15. Drawing on thinkers from Greek Sophists to Feyerabend, Matei Calinescu presents an interesting humanist argument for an "imagination of doubt," relying on dialogy rather than any traditional *logos. Cadmos* 2, no. 7 (Fall 1979).

36 See Paul Feyerabend, *Science in a Free Society* (London: NLB, 1978), pp. 73–122.

37 Ibid., p. 8. But see also pp. 16–31.
38 As Erich Jantsch says: ". . . the human world, analogous to physical and biological evolution, incorporates a basic principle of *self-transcendence,* of venturing out by changing its own physical, social, and cultural structures—above all, by changing its own consciousness." Erich Jantsch and C. H. Waddington, eds., *Evolution and Consciousness* (Reading, Mass.: Addison-Wesley Publishing Co., 1976), p. 2. Speaking as a geneticist, Sir Peter Medawar confirms the point: "In human beings, exogenetic heredity—the transfer of information through non-genetic channels—has become more important for our biological success than anything programmed in DNA." "Technology and Evolution," in *Technology and the Frontiers of Knowledge,* ed. Saul Bellow et al. (Garden City, N.Y.: Doubleday, 1975), p. 103.
39 Harold Rosenberg, *The Tradition of the New* (New York: Grove Press, 1961), p. 9. See also Ihab Hassan, *The Dismemberment of Orpheus,* 2 ed. rev. (Madison: University of Wisconsin Press, 1982) for further elaboration of these modes.
40 See especially Roger Shattuck, *The Banquet Years* (New York: Vintage Books, 1968); Renato Poggioli, *Theory of the* Avant-Garde, trans. Gerald Fitzgerald (Cambridge: Harvard University Press, 1968); Peter Bürger, *Theorie der Avantgarde* (Frankfurt/Main: Suhrkamp Verlag, 1974); Matei Calinescu, *Faces of Modernity* (Bloomington: Indiana University Press, 1977); and Jean Weisgerber, ed., *Les Avant-gardes littéraires au XXe siècle,* 2 vols. (Paris: Éditions John Didier, 1980). The last two works contain useful bibliographies of the Avant-Gardes.
41 Delmore Schwartz, *Shenandoah* (Norfolk, Conn.: New Directions, 1941), p. 20. Works that address Modernism include Edmund Wilson, *Axel's Castle* (New York: Charles Scribner's Sons, 1931): José Ortega y Gasset, *The Modern Theme,* trans. James Cleugh (New York: W. W. Norton, 1933) and *The Dehumanization of Art,* trans. Helene Weyl (Princeton: Princeton University Press, 1948); Lionel Trilling, *Beyond Culture* (New York: Viking Press, 1965); Hassan, *The Dismemberment of Orpheus;* Hugh Kenner, *The Pound Era* (Berkeley and Los Angeles: University of California Press, 1971); Malcolm Bradbury and James McFarlane, eds., *Modernism* (London: Penguin Books, 1976); and Calinescu, *Faces of Modernity.* The last two works contain extensive bibliographies of Modernism as well as Postmodernism.
42 For a discussion of Postmodernism, in addition to the works of Bradbury, Calinescu, and Hassan cited above, see John Barth, "The Literature of Exhaustion," *Atlantic Monthly,* August 1967, and, less persuasive, "The Literature of Replenishment," *Atlantic Monthly,* January 1980; Ihab Hassan, "Joyce, Beckett, and the Postmodern

Imagination," *TriQuarterly* 34 (Fall 1975) and *Paracriticisms* (Urbana: University of Illinois Press, 1975) especially pp. 45f. (which refer to relevant works by Leslie Fiedler, Richard Poirier, Susan Sontag, and George Steiner); Raymond Federman, ed., *Surfiction* (Chicago: Swallow Press, 1975); Charles Russell, ed., *The Avant-Garde Today* (Urbana: University of Illinois Press, 1981); Mas'ud Zavarzadeh, *The Mythopoetic Reality* (Urbana: University of Illinois Press, 1976); and *Amerikastudien* 22, no. 1 (1977). Again, the last two works offer lengthy bibliographies.

43 This is a point that Hans Magnus Enzensberger mistakes in his otherwise witty and perceptive essay, "The Aporias of the Avant-Garde," *The Consciousness Industry* (New York: Seabury Press, 1974). I believe Daniel Bell comes here nearer the mark: "What is most striking about post-modernism is that what was once maintained as esoteric is now proclaimed as ideology, and what was once the property of an aristocracy of the spirit is now turned into the democratic property of the mass." *The Cultural Contradictions of Capitalism* (New York: Basic Books, 1976), p. 52.

44 See Ihab Hassan, "The Question of Postmodernism," in *Romanticism, Modernism, Postmodernism,* ed. Harry R. Garvin, (Lewisburg, Pa.: Bucknell University Press, 1980), as well as other essays in this issue devoted to Postmodernism.

45 Calinescu rightly perceives modernity, in all its various forms, as "the history of the battle to give value to the present." *Faces of Modernity,* p. 267.

46 Kenneth Boulding, *The Meaning of the Twentieth Century* (New York: Harper & Row Pubs., 1964), pp. 1f. Sir Peter Medawar, among other distinguished scientists, makes a similar point: "The coming of technology and the new style of human evolution it made possible was an epoch in biological history as important as the evolution of man himself." "Technology and Evolution" in *Technology and the Frontiers of Knowledge,* p. 108. See also the futurist speculations of Arthur C. Clarke, *Profiles of the Future* (New York: Harper & Row Pubs., 1963); Gerald Feinberg, *The Prometheus Project* (Garden City, N.Y.: Doubleday, 1969); and Herman Kahn and Anthony Wiener, *The Year 2000* (New York: Macmillan, 1967).

47 Saul Bellow, for instance, writes: "So, at the height of technological achievement there blazes the menace of obsolescence. The museum, worse than the grave because it humiliates us by making us dodos, waits in judgment on our ambitions and vanities." "Literature in the Age of Technology," in *Technology and the Frontiers of Knowledge,* pp. 10f. Similarly, Daniel Bell complains: "It used to be that the great literary modifier was the word *beyond.* . . . But we seem to have exhausted the beyond, and today the sociological modifier is post. . . ." *The Coming of Post-Industrial Society* (New York: Basic Books,

1973), p. 53. As in post-industrial, post-civilization, post-culture, post-historic, post-humanist, and post-modern?

48 Bell, *The Cultural Contradictions of Capitalism*, p. 7.

49 Ibid., pp. 53f. Carl Friedrich von Weizsäcker makes the more serious point about the predominance of pleasure in any society: "Und dann sage ich schon in diesem ganz einfachen Sinne von Glück — Erreichen von Angenehmem oder Erwünschtem, Vermeiden von Unangenehmem oder Unerwünschtem, Schmerzhaften: die Orientierung an diesem Kriterium als Fundamentalorientierung einer Gesellschaft ist die Garantie des Untergangs dieser Gesellschaft." *Wachstum und Lebenssinn — Alternative Rationalitäten?* Bergedorfer Gesprächskreis, Protokoll-Nr. 61 (1978), p. 8.

50 Bell, *The Cultural Contradictions of Capitalism*, p. 34.

51 Jean-François Lyotard, *La Condition postmoderne* (Paris: Éditions de Minuit, 1979), pp. 8f.

52 Ibid., pp. 85f., 97f., 107.

53 Ibid., p. 108. Unlike Jürgen Habermas, Lyotard doubts the final value of *Diskurs*, consensus. For a critique of Habermas based on a confrontation between the latter and French thought, especially Derrida, see Dominick LaCapra, "Habermas and the Grounding of Critical Theory," *History and Theory* 16, no. 3 (October 1977).

54 Ihab Hassan, "Culture, Indeterminacy, and Immanence," *The Right Promethean Fire* (Urbana: University of Illinois Press, 1980). This chapter, as well as another entitled "The Re-Vision of Literature," contains material relevant to this discussion.

55 Ibid., pp. 49–52. But see also pp. 109–14.

56 For good introductions to current French literary thought, see Jonathan Culler, *Structuralist Poetics* (Ithaca: Cornell University Press, 1975) and *The Pursuit of Signs* (Ithaca: Cornell University Press, 1981); Edward Said, *Beginnings* (New York: Basic Books, 1975); and Josué V. Harrari, ed., *Textual Strategies* (Ithaca: Cornell University Press, 1979); and for a thoughtful assessment of their impact, see Geoffrey H. Hartman, *Criticism in the Wilderness* (New Haven: Yale University Press, 1980).

57 Many of these authors are represented in this volume. In addition, see such recent attempts to reconceive various disciplines as Norman O. Brown, *Closing Time* (New York: Random House, 1973); David L. Miller, *The New Polytheism* (New York: Harper & Row Pubs., 1974; James Hillman, *Re-Visioning Psychology* (New York: Harper & Row Pubs., 1975); Paul Feyerabend, *Against Method;* Charles Jencks, *The Language of Post-Modern Architecture* (New York: Rizzoli Intl. Pubs., 1977); Hayden White, *Tropics of Discourse* (Baltimore: Johns Hopkins University Press, 1978); and the "Yale Critics'" *Deconstruction and Criticism* (New York: Seabury Press, 1979).

36

58 See Jeremy Bernstein, *Experiencing Science* (New York: Basic Books, 1978), p. 263; and Douglas R. Hofstadter, *Gödel, Escher, Bach: an Eternal Golden Braid* (New York: Basic Books, 1979), p. 19. Both authors explain abstruse problems in such lucid and joyful prose as might put some literary critics to shame.

59 See Hassan, "The New Gnosticism," *Paracriticisms;* and "The Gnosis of Science," *The Right Promethean Fire,* for discussions of this trend.

60 Michel Foucault, *The Order of Things* (New York: Pantheon Books, 1970), p. 386.

61 Lyotard, *La Condition postmoderne,* pp. 84f. See also pp. 16, 30f., and 63.

62 Daniel Bell, "Technology, Nature, and Society," in *Technology and the Frontiers of Knowledge,* pp. 34–42.

63 Ibid., pp. 52f. But see also Hubert L. Dreyfus, *What Computers Can't Do* (New York: Harper & Row Pubs., 1979), for a skeptical counterstatement, which challenges Bell and possibly Lyotard (note 61). Dreyfus insists that the human mind proceeds by quantum leaps and tropes, creating whole configurations that no digital computer can simulate. The issue of Artificial Intelligence, however, remains far from settled.

64 Bell, "Technology, Nature, and Society," in *Technology and the Frontiers of Knowledge,* pp. 54f.

65 Ibid., p. 56.

66 Lewis Mumford, *The City in History* (New York: Harcourt, Brace & World, 1961), pp. 37, 97, 113, 533, 561f., 563–73.

67 Ibid., p. 573. Mumford himself elaborates in many places this theme: "There is another side to this reorganization of the metropolitan complex that derives from the dematerialization, or etherealization, of existing institutions: that which has already created the Invisible City. This is itself an expression of the fact that the new world in which we have begun to live is not merely open on the surface, far beyond the visible horizon, but also open internally, penetrated by invisible rays and emanations, responding to stimuli and forces below the threshold of ordinary observation." (p. 563). Similarly, C. A. Doxiadis and J. G. Papaioannou note: "The changes which are taking place now will end in a completely new system of life, which will be ecumenic in form and will lead us from civilization to ecumenization. Human settlements will have a completely new physical structure, a total global system of linked units of every size." *Ecumenopolis: the Inevitable City of the Future* (New York: W. W. Norton, 1974), p. 394. For further references to this theme, see Ihab Hassan, "Toward a Transhumanized Earth: Imagination, Science, and Future," *The Georgia Review* 32, no. 4 (Winter 1978–79).

68 Scientists seems to have no difficulty in reconciling the One and the

Many. As Werner Heisenberg observes: ". . . we seem to inhabit a world of dynamic process and structure. Therefore, we need a calculus of potentiality rather than one of probability, a dialectic of polarity, one in which unity and diversity are redefined as simultaneous and necessary poles of the same essence." *Across the Frontiers,* trans. Peter Heath (New York: Harper & Row Pubs., 1974), p. xii.

2 /

Toward a Chronography of Change

Claus Uhlig

The phenomenon of change belongs to the few indubitable facts of our existence. We experience it daily, know that we live in a period of rapid transition, and therefore even feel the need to devote an entire conference to this theme. Yet when it comes to finding answerable critical style, let alone accounting for cultural change, our rhetoric seems to fail us, and the very terms of our discourse tend to become blurred.

What I wish to urge at the outset, then, is that we should try to clarify the concepts of our discussion. And for me, if I am permitted to reflect upon the general theme of our conference as a historian, this primarily means to think historically about cultural change: that is, to add the depth of time to our attempts to define a phenomenon that cannot be assessed from the vantage point of the present alone. Thinking historically implies more precisely the search for concepts and generalizations, however cautious and tentative, as possible answers to the problem of change. "The knowledge of the mechanics of historical change is far more profound than it was two generations ago,"[1] writes J. H. Plumb; but I believe that the limits of our knowledge in this matter have not yet been reached.

To be sure, the historiographic concepts I have in mind need to be historicized in their turn because they themselves are subject to time and change and are thus in due course bound to become too narrow or simple in their application to the objects of study. A good case in point would be our much-debated period concept of "postmodernism" itself; for it ought to be obvious that if we continue to discuss the problem in hand mainly in terms of mere chronology, we shall end up with a constant succession of "post-isms." Worse than this historiographic embarrassment, I think, is the apparent lack of distinction within the semantics of our critical discourse, especially with regard to such crucial terms as, for instance, épistémè and change.

Épistémè and change, far from being correlated notions, are diametrically opposed to each other. Épistémè, as used above all in Michel Foucault's archaeology of knowledge, serves to indicate "the total set of relations that unite, at a given period, the discursive practices that give rise to epistemological figures, sciences, and possibly formalized systems";[2] furthermore, it points out the "lateral relations" between adjacent but distinct disciplines, thereby stressing the discontinuities from epoch to epoch rather than the continuities. Through its verticality, however, Foucault's archaeological procedure—which is both unwilling and unable to account for the nature of that epochal change it merely registers after it has happened—can easily be seen as leading to a quite deliberate Nietzschean and Heideggerian destruction of history-writing, whose attempts at establishing any kind of succession it disavows from the start.

Change, on the other hand, as a dynamic notion, while methodologically irreconcilable with structuralist uniformity and static verticality, remains tied precisely to that linearity of the chain of events Foucault's spatializing activity tends to deny. But let us beware of simplistic oppositions like the implied contrast between "static" and "dynamic." "Change," it has rightly been said, "is never complete, and change never ceases."[3] To this we may add William James's observation that "novelty, as empirically found, doesn't arrive by jumps and jolts, it leaks in insensibly."[4] So if nothing ever appears quite new, and change seems to come about gradually, we might indeed experience "a seamless, formless continuity-in-mutability"[5] as the predominant mode of our lives. Yet over against this experience is that of great cataclysmic events which radically mark change as sudden, reveal life as discontinuous, and provide historiography with at least some concepts of form and order by acting as caesuras within the historical process.

Still, our exposition of change, whether we conceive of it as gradual and almost imperceptible or as radical and obvious, has not yet moved beyond descriptive categories. Perhaps there is no need to worry unduly on that score; for, according to a memorable dictum of Michael Oakeshott's, "change in history carries with it its own explanations,"[6] the historiographic inference being that "history accounts *for* change by means of a full account *of* change." True enough, but hardly satisfactory for the historian of culture, even if it is difficult to see how one could proceed from description to explanation. Clearly, a way out of this impasse would consist in breaking up complex historical wholes into their constituent events and then studying the various interrelationships between these particularized events.[7] Apart from its consonance with today's well-grounded mistrust of monistic or even holistic views—witness especially Matei Calinescu's contribution to this volume—[8] such a pluralistic approach would also reckon with Aristotle's insight into the nature of change, whereby an analysis of the phenomenon is said to involve three terms: a subject (unspecified), a field (time), and a final term (result of the process).[9]

Of these terms, I should like to confine myself to the second, and that not for reasons of time and space only. For if, in fact, "all that changes changes in time,"[10] conceptions of time itself must inevitably enter into our discussion of change. Thinking for a moment of Greek terms like κίνησις and μεταβολή, which indicate "movement" and "change" without any bearing on larger concepts of history, and contrasting them with, say, the ideologically charged key-terms of European Enlightenment, which were positively instrumental in channelling ideas and expectations of change into the future and thus in shaping the course of history,[11] we begin to realize that an adequate, historicized discussion of change, while occupying a middle ground between descriptive and explanatory modes of discourse, would seem first to presuppose the establishment of a temporal framework. In what follows, I shall consequently try to deal with my theme in terms of a "chronography of change."

If, then, nothing less than a theory of historical times is needed in talking about the varieties of change, we should inquire how to envisage such a theory, how to understand the transformation of temporal modes of experience into formal categories of chronography. To start with unravelling the complex of experiences in question, the field of historical time as opposed to that of natural time may be said to comprise irreversibility and repeatability — be it in supposed identity, as return of constellations, or in typological and figural coordination — plus asynchrony of simultaneous events, of which anachronism is perhaps the most familiar instance.[12] In order to illustrate further what is meant by these temporal modes, let us recall that historical reversals are definitely impossible after great wars or, to shift the focus from politics to culture, after such decisive developments as atonality in music or self-reflexivity in fictional literature.[13] In contrast, repeatability is a more ambiguous case. While identity might turn out, more often than not, to be the result of optical illusion created by distance in time, a return of constellations could well be discerned in history, provided the appropriate modifications of circumstance are introduced. And as for typological and figural coordination, a method above all practiced in Scriptural hermeneutics, it tries, through accommodating the past to the present in the interest of an eschatologically conceived future, to "sublate" historical time into an ideal timelessness which ultimately erodes the very possibility of historiography as "science."[14] Finally, asynchrony of simultaneous events should be easily acknowledged, by now, as a basic mode of experiencing historical time: we need only ponder the contemporaneous existence, within English literature, of Langland and Chaucer in the fourteenth century, or the coexistence of the heirs of Joyce with those of Wells and Bennett in our own day. One wonders, though, how much is deliberate or endemic in such forms of non-contemporaneity.[15]

Now, even if we view such temporal modes of experience with some skepticism, we can still find them helpful in conceptualizing our observations on an empirical basis. Thus we could develop formal chronographic categories for the critical analysis of phenomena like progress, decline, acceleration, or retardation[16] which, taken together, define the complex historical fact of change in its various temporal aspects. In this connection, it goes without saying that accounts of progress, for instance, would be inconceivable today along nineteenth-century evolutionist lines; any more than decline, despite its cyclical implications, could be depicted in terms of a holistic nostalgia registering change exclusively as decadence, retrogression, or deprivation. Evaluations like these are less likely to affect the way we talk about acceleration; for who can deny that the tempo of human life has increased enormously over the last two hundred years, and that the speed of change within twentieth-century experimental art, aided of late by mass-media technology, virtually devours time by anticipating the future.[17] But since avant-garde art is only one facet of culture, we have to consider acceleration together with retardation, which may be conditioned either sociologically—different strata of society view time differently—or intellectually, seeing that commonplace mentality and conventional morality continue to abide in the face of even dramatic developments in science and politics.[18]

Now, if we combine with all this the methodical organization of historical time as already put into practice by historians of the French *Annales* school—that is, the division of time into *longue durée, moyenne durée, temps court* as well as *conjoncture* —a multiple temporal model, in harmony with today's pluralistic world picture, becomes available to the theoretician of historical times. What is more, owing to such an effort of "balancing particularity against principles of order,"[19] change could then be characterized more fully as the point of intersection, and hence interaction, of two or more kinds of duration.[20] Having thus to speak of changes instead of change might seem a loss; the gain, however, consists in trying to do justice to the multidimensionality of historical phenomena as they appear to us in time.

Let me, in closing, briefly adumbrate how formal categories of chronography could be brought to bear on the critical discussion of historical periods such as "modernism" or, if indeed it is one, "postmodernism." If we are willing to view the present under a historical perspective, as I suggest, we might begin to understand the way in which the various durations mentioned intertwine to form the contours of something like a new cultural epoch. Consider, for instance, the prestige of indeterminacy in present-day critical discourse. Here, a long-term linear process in literature, namely the communication between author and reader, reaching from its playful beginnings in the early novel to the contemporary rhetoric of silence, seems to interact with the relatively "short duration" of the indeterminacy principle in physics to fortify the elements of irrationality and chance in our culture. Another paradigm, involving perhaps a kind of "intermediate duration," tends to point to change as deprivation and decline. I mean the gradual demotion of the literary hero from "eclipse" in the last century to final reduction, via anonymity, to a disembodied voice in our time, as instanced in Beckett or Barth. For such a fate would appear to impress itself on today's critical consciousness in "conjunction" with the "abolition of man" in structuralist thought where language, no longer tied to any form of "anthropo-" or "logocentrism," has come to the fore to establish itself for the time being as a new *proton pseudos*.

In the last analysis, it might well be that this "coming-to-the-fore," this universal "foregrounding," this primacy of the medium over the message so conspicuous in all areas of our culture, more than anything else characterizes our age as a self-transcending metaculture whose very sophistication could soon call for change again and so help to introduce neoprimitivistic attempts at repristination. Fortunately, however, since historians are no prophets, it is not incumbent on a "chronography of change" to devote itself to forecasts which would remain dubious at the best of times.

What matters instead — and I hope to have succeeded in making this point despite the brevity of my discussion — is to avoid lack of conceptual clarity as well as exclusive reliance on the perspective of the present in historiographic activities. That way, artificial oppositions between continuity and discontinuity, or convention and revolt, could disappear from history-writing and make room for the application of chronographic categories grounded, as I have outlined, in a theory of historical times. At any rate, this is in my view the direction in which inquiries concerning the nature of change might be fruitfully conducted.

NOTES

1 J. H. Plumb, *The Death of the Past* (London: Macmillan, 1969), p. 144. Besides, I am generally indebted to Plumb for my introductory remarks; see esp. pp. 57, 106, 143.
2 Michel Foucault, *The Archaeology of Knowledge,* trans. A. M. Sheridan Smith (New York: Pantheon Books, 1972), p. 191. Cf. Michel Foucault, *L'Archéologie du savoir* (Paris: Éditions Gallimard, 1969), pp. 248–51.
3 C. S. Lewis, *Selected Literary Essays,* ed. Walter Hooper (Cambridge: Cambridge University Press, 1969), p. 2.
4 William James, *A Pluralistic Universe* (Cambridge: Harvard University Press, 1977), p. 153.
5 Lewis, *Selected Literary Essays,* p. 2.
6 Michael Oakeshott, *Experience and Its Modes* (Cambridge: Cambridge University Press, 1933), pp. 141,143; quoted and criticized by Maurice Mandelbaum, *The Anatomy of Historical Knowledge* (Baltimore: Johns Hopkins University Press, 1977), p. 110.
7 This approach is advocated by Louis O. Mink, "The Autonomy of Historical Understanding," *History and Theory* 5 (1965): 24–47; quoted approvingly by Mandelbaum, *The Anatomy of Historical Knowledge,* p. 111.
8 Matei Calinescu, "From the One to the Many: Pluralism in Today's Thought," in this volume, pp. 263–88.
9 Aristotle *Physics* 6, 236b5. I owe this and the subsequent reference to Claudio Guillén, "Literary Change and Multiple Duration," *Comparative Literature Studies* 6 (1977): 100–18, esp. p. 112.
10 Aristotle *Physics* 6, 236b20.
11 Cf. Christian Meier, "Der Wandel der politisch-sozialen Begriffswelt im 5. Jahrhundert v. Chr.," in *Historische Semantik und Begriffsgeschichte,* ed. Reinhart Koselleck (Stuttgart: Klett-Cotta, 1979), pp. 193–227, esp. pp. 193–95, 200–227.
12 Cf. Reinhart Koselleck, *Vergangene Zukunft: Zur Semantik geschichtlicher Zeiten* (Frankfurt/Main: Suhrkamp Verlag, 1979), pp. 130–43, esp. p. 132.
13 Cf. Christopher Butler, *After the Wake: An Essay on the Contemporary Avant-Garde* (London: Oxford University Press, 1980), pp. 25–52.
14 For an exposition of the method alluded to, see Erich Auerbach, *Typologische Motive in der mittelalterlichen Literatur,* 2d ed. (Krefeld: Scherpe Verlag, 1964), pp. 12–14; and, for a critique, Plumb, *The Death of the Past,* pp. 68–77, esp. p. 76.
15 On asynchrony within simultaneity, as it is related to the problem of periodization, see Siegfried Kracauer, *History: The Last Things Before the Last* (New York: Oxford University Press, 1969), pp. 139–

63; and, in his wake, Mandelbaum, *The Anatomy of Historical Knowledge,* pp. 22-23.

16 Cf. Koselleck, *Vergangene Zukunft,* p. 133.

17 Cf. Rudolph Wendorff, *Zeit und Kultur: Geschichte des Zeitbewusstseins in Europa* (Opladen: Westdeutscher Verlag, 1980), pp. 550-62, 619-29; and Butler, *After the Wake,* pp. 125-26.

18 Cf. W. H. Auden, *The Dyer's Hand and Other Essays* (London: Faber & Faber, 1963), p. 220; Lewis, *Selected Literary Essays,* p. 7; and Plumb, *The Death of the Past,* pp. 48-49.

19 Geoffrey Hartman, "The New Wilderness: Critics as Connoisseurs of Chaos," in this volume, pp. 87-110, esp. p. 97 f.

20 Most relevant in this respect is Guillén's article "Literary Change and Multiple Duration" (above, n. 9), since it fuses the various *durées* of the *Annales* school with the useful theorems of George Kubler's *The Shape of Time: Remarks on the History of Things* (New Haven: Yale University Press, 1962).

3 /

Intellectual History and Defining the Present as "Postmodern"

Dominick LaCapra

What is involved in the attempt to define the present? It all depends, one might plausibly answer, on the approach taken in responding to this question. Two such approaches immediately suggest themselves — so immediately as to raise suspicion about them.

One approach is to take a distance on the present and, in effect, to treat it as a past — but a past having an almost infinitesimal proximity to ourselves and our current interests. This approach would allow us to acquire some purchase on the present and even to subject it to objective scrutiny. By objectifying the present, we could elaborate a category, such as the "postmodern," and thereby furnish a conceptual "handle" on events which we could envelop, more or less convincingly, with facts both "hard" and "soft." We would also be in a position to utilize the category in a critical way, condemning the present where it had gone astray or applauding it where it seemed promising — variations in praise or blame being of course a function of whether one was for or against the postmodern.

Except for differences of opinion concerning the appropriateness of the latter critical gesture in historiography (or some other "scientific" field), such a treatment of the present would conform to a strategy of understanding that is quite familiar in the study of the past. Its guiding criterion would be the "objective" study of the facts "for their own sake." Its informing mode would often be a restricted, detached, relatively safe, and frequently unrecognized form of irony (even of parody or self-parody) in reporting events or analyzing processes. But at times (at least in prefaces or in authorial asides), it would allow for more direct authorial intervention through the medium of evaluative judgments. In these respects, the historian often seems to write like Flaubert. But unlike Flaubert he is likely to be unaware of the narrative strategies he employs, often using "straight" the techniques or procedures Flaubert used in a parodic way, relying on forms of irony that are less risky and self-incriminating than those of the Great Gustave, and building elaborate documentary edifices upon assumptions that were critically tested, even excavated, by Flaubert and others akin to him. For it is perhaps the hallmark of the historian's craft (or of the understanding of history as a craft) to construct encyclopedically exhaustive and "definitive" accounts upon relatively unexamined assumptions about the use of language.

A second approach is in crucial respects the opposite of the first, perhaps its *frère ennemi* or inverted mirror image. It would assert one's absolute identity with the present and insist upon the "inauthenticity" of abstracting or distancing oneself from it. It would stress subjective engagement in the events of the present and one's empathetic immersion in its currents. An attempt might even be made to valorize or simply to affirm the ecstatic nature of one's adherence to the present as the way to attain one's liberation from the "burdens" of the past. In fact this stance has often been identified as specifically "modern" or even "postmodern" in contradistinction to a historical approach to problems. But here a notion such as the "postmodern" is not intended to serve as a controlling category. It is at best an unfortunately necessary mark of one's identity or of one's difference from the past, indicating one's own existential implication or dispersion in that which can never become a mere object of study or of critique. For here the emphasis would be either upon the intentional subject as the goal-oriented, unifying center of vision or upon the decentered subject as the mobile prism of diffraction in experience

— more rarely upon the interaction between these two tendencies of psychic life.

This second perspective is less familiar in historiography and would probably be condemned as antihistorical. For it would seem to signal the end of historiography as conventionally understood, and it would imply a bewildering version of the historical process itself. The first perspective could be more easily assimilated to what is probably the dominant method of historiographical research, one which identifies historical understanding with the documented knowledge of objectified phenomena set within their specific context.

I already intimated, however, that these two perspectives are closely related. Each would seem to attach itself to one end of a shared subject/object polarity. What would seem even more significant is the tendency of both perspectives to deny or to obscure the role of what may be called (for want of better words) historicity, textuality, and dialogicality in the past and, more notably, in our relation to it. For both are masked forms of transcendence that remove the observer or speaker from problems of language use and eventuate in a monologue about the "other" or the "self." The transcendence in question is, moreover, a fixated or "fetishized" one, for it substitutes for an open-ended and agonistic process of transcending the lure of a state of being itself removed from historical becoming. The position of the orthodox historical observer who knows the past for its own sake and, in knowing, is not implicated in its processes might be seen as a form of conventionalized utopianism. The position of the ecstatic self that identifies itself fully with the present represents a more unconventional utopia. Needless to add, for each the other is the embodiment of dystopia.

The question I would like to raise is whether a different approach to historicity, textuality, and the "dialogical" points to another understanding of the present in its relation to the past. Insofar as this approach is "feasible," it would disclose newer possibilities for intellectual history and at the same time indicate the limitations of attempting to define or to affirm a "postmodern" standpoint. For attention would then shift to the intricate processes of interaction between past and present and the cognitive or existential modes of repetition with variation relating them to one another. Historicity would itself be rethought, not in terms of continuity or of discontinuity, but in terms of interacting continuity and discontinuity. Inquiry into the precise modulations of this process of interaction would involve the historian in a form of research that would supplement documented knowledge with a "dialogue" or conversation with the past having implications for the future. The "present" would be neither a speciously objectified past nor an ecstatically enjoyed "here and now": it would be the "place" for an informed exchange with the past having a bearing upon the future. From the perspective I am suggesting, the continually renewed problem would be that of tradition and its critique.

Before turning to the more concrete issue of the implications of these rather general reflections for the practice of intellectual history, I would like to reformulate the overall point I am trying to make. It is tempting to see the relation among the traditional, the modern, and the postmodern in a way analogous to the processes at work (or at play) in what Derrida terms "deconstruction." The tradition in its dominant form relies on a binary logic of identity and difference, analyzing things into opposites and seeking dialectical syntheses or perhaps ecstatic (and/or deadly) transcendence of them. Yet the "tradition" harbors relatively repressed or silenced tendencies that place its own dominant desires and motifs in doubt. The modern brings about a "reversal" of dominant views or established hierarchies that have become traditional or conventionalized, thereby producing a perhaps necessary "shock effect." But, by this token, it remains within the orbit of tradition, for its own strategies require the terms, oppositions, and procedures that it criticizes. The postmodern might be correlated with the phase or "moment" of generalized displacement of traditional options—a displacement that attempts to "go beyond" simple reversal in its way of posing problems.

But it is important to note that in Derrida displacement never takes place definitively or "once and for all." It is a continually renewed, internally "dialogized," and self-critical gesture that is always threatened by reappropriation or recuperation by the tradition it criticizes and whose repressed tendencies it reworks to enable a more "even-handed" contest or dialogue with dominant forms. Yet transcendence and utopia are not simply denied. Rather they are themselves seen anew as the recurrent hyperboles or forces that disorient existing structures or dominant traditions to give rise to newer structures or traditions. This repeated but changing *agon* is itself the "form" of historicity — one allowing for the hyperbolic quest as a continually resurgent pathos that shifts and rearranges the lines of thought and perhaps of life without itself ever becoming a stable state of being. The appreciation — indeed the emulation and at times the parody — of this pathos, however, requires not the simple forgetting of tradition but its close and careful "working through," its replay or "active forgetting" in a "creation" (Derrida would probably balk at the use of this word) that is never absolute. The less paradoxical formulation of this process would, I think, be in terms of historicity as repetition with variation or change — the process that, according to Heidegger, is most difficult to "think" precisely because it is not one of mere repetition or of simple change.

Let me now turn abruptly to the bearing of these reflections on the field of intellectual history, "illustrate" the argument with two brief "examples," and conclude with a consideration that returns us to the general theme of the conference.

Throughout its modern history, intellectual history has attempted to conform to modes of historical understanding prominent in other areas of historiography. In its various and at times opposed forms, it has been a type of documentary knowledge of the past: (1) treating ideas in intrinsic or formal terms; (2) exploring the contextual "origins," correlates, or impact of ideas; and (3) synthesizing intrinsic and contextual methods (generally through a traditional narrative of "men and ideas"). Other tendencies are at present emerging, but they are in a marked minority position.[1] Indeed the hold of the more established forms upon the profession is indicated by the fact that protests against them often fall back upon a rearticulation of one or more of their variants. The work of Hayden White has, for example, been instrumental in stirring up debate in the United States over the nature and purpose of intellectual history and of historiography in general. But even White's highly self-conscious and theoretically in-

51

formed approach tends at times to oscillate between a "present-ist" demand for utopian liberation from the "burden" of history and the irony of contemporary historiography, on the one hand, and a formalistic way of doing intellectual history, on the other — the two being united in a vision of the historical mind as informed by tropes which poetically shape the field of study.

Virtually all historians would agree that no approach that claims to be historical can dispense with the need for reliable documentation. To some extent, Mr. Gradgrind must always be the monkey on the historian's back, the Socratic *daimon* whispering cautionary injunctions into his ear. One may stress the importance of heuristic fictions in orienting historical research, and one may argue that productive research is a function of the questions posed to the past — questions themselves embedded in one's own "life-world" that can never be fully objectified or known. One may even defend the value of "mixed genres" combining in a militantly or playfully disorienting way documented knowledge and substantive fictions, indeed invented allusions or references. But the more basic issue, I think, is how to confront critically both narrowly documentary conceptions of history and one-sidedly "presentist" rejections of it in defense of an approach that supplements documented knowledge with an active dialogue between past and present that self-critically explores the historian's own historicity.

At least a beginning can be made in elaborating a more "dialogical" approach by conceiving intellectual history as a critical history of texts in relation to various pertinent contexts. The "text" in this sense is a situated use of language marked by a tense interaction between mutually implicated yet contestatory tendencies (such as unification and dissemination or structure and hyperbolic play). The expanded notion of textuality applies to other modes of "symbolism" or "representation" (painting, dance, music), and it construes the context itself as a text of sorts. The value of this strategic move is to indicate that we are always involved in problems of language use even as we attempt to work free of those problems, for example, towards an unmediated vision of the thing itself, an ecstatic enjoyment of radical innocence, or a communal scene of unobstructedly transparent relations. The interaction between language and other "symbolic" modes broaches the general problem of "translation" or transition from mode to mode which always implies both gains and losses. And the "context" is no longer seen as an ultimate, unproblematic reality that grounds all knowledge. It becomes an element or series of more or less unified elements always already implicated in problems of language use and related to texts in the more orthodox sense in a variety of ways that demand investigation. The problem then becomes that of how texts themselves relate to various contexts (or postulate and/or resist referents) and how contexts relate to various texts both written and "lived."

One crucial concern is to see texts as having both documentary (or factual) and work-like (or performative) dimensions that are developed to varying degrees and related in differing ways in specific texts or "kinds" of texts. Given the *"travail du texte,"* no text is a pure document that provides a fully transparent window on the world. The driest document refracts reality in a particular way related to larger social and political processes. At times it is the subdued "voice" of the bureaucratic administration of reality for purposes of efficient organization and control. At the same time no text transcends its contexts to provide pure meaning or untainted fiction that may be recovered in a formalistic reading. Even the insistently self-referential text documents its own mode of production, and it raises the question of the larger role of self-referential activity in a given historical context. More generally, the documentary and the work-like are limiting poles of textuality that texts approximate to varying degrees and combine in multiple ways.

To make these observations about texts is to raise the question of how one is to read them. A purely documentary reading is always open to question, and it is especially dubious in relation to the complex texts that are of special interest to intellectual history. A documentary reading of Hegel, Flaubert, Marx, or Freud is an excessively reductive reading. It is also an unhistorical reading in that it refuses to read the text as a text and to pose the problem of the relation in it of the documentary and that which cannot be reduced to the documentary. To be more precise, an attempt at a purely documentary reading begs a number of questions. What is the relation between the documentary and the other than documentary in a given text or in an established category of texts (philosophical, literary, historical, and so forth)? How should the historian himself use language in discussing texts? Should his language be limited to informational and analytic functions, or should he allow himself to be affected by what he studies to the extent of trying to think about it in more than documentary ways? Should his writing or speaking become more self-consciously work-like and dialogical by employing in more active and responsible ways such "forms" as stylization, irony, parody, self-parody, and polemic? Should the questions posed to the past be both more ambitious and less amenable to seemingly "definitive" answers than those predominant in a restricted informational and analytic framework?

What is, I think, of particular importance in intellectual history at the present time is to stress the problem of reading complex or so-called "great" texts and to pose as an explicit problem the way in which texts are related to contexts. The reason for emphasizing the reading and interpretation of complex texts in intellectual history at the present time is at least two-fold. First, the reading of these texts is underemphasized in historiography in general, and, even in intellectual history, the reading to which they are adjusted tends to be excessively reductive or recuperative. Second, these texts are highly work-like or performative and engage us in an especially compelling dialogue with the past. In other words, one should, I think, stress the need for more intricate and even noncanonical readings of canonical texts. In other fields, somewhat different strategies may be needed, for in those fields the reading of complex texts is the mainstay of virtually everyone's activity. Thus one may want to emphasize the importance of reading "minor" texts in the attempt to provide a more comprehensive understanding of a context or of a prevalent genre. In addition, it is obviously necessary to attempt to reevaluate the relative importance attributed to various works in a canon and to examine critically the reasons for the inclusion or the exclusion of certain texts. Indeed one may want to question certain of the functions the very notion of a "canon" has served. But it is equally necessary to see whether canonical texts can and should be read in other than canonical ways. For what is often surprising is not the fact that certain texts have been selected for special attention but that such texts have been read in certain ways.

In the last-mentioned respect, the question that may be posed is whether any "great" text — and certainly any modern "great" — both tries to establish something — a genre, a pattern of coherence, a unified order — and calls it into doubt. Indeed, is not the judgment of "greatness" at times related to the sense that certain works both reinforce tradition and subvert it, indicating the need for newer traditions that are more open to disconcerting modes of questioning and better able to withstand the recurrent threat of collapse? Are processes of contestation often or typically more powerful in certain kinds of texts, for example, literary or poetic texts in comparison with philosophical or historical ones? How watertight are these higher-order forms of classification in relation to the actual use(s) of language in texts? How distinctive are modern or postmodern texts when compared to more "traditional" ones? Do some of the most informed modern "critics" (Heidegger and Derrida, for example) teach us that assertions of radical disjunction or of newness often conceal subtler differences, thereby obscuring the underground contestation in "traditional" texts and providing an unjustified sense of originality in the present?

With reference to the relation between texts and contexts, the need at present is, I think, to pose as an explicit problem what is often taken as a solution. Thus the concern for inquiry into intentions, motivations, the sociocultural context, or structures, genres, and codes should not be rejected out of hand. What is dubious is the assumption that any one or any set of these "contexts" provides a fully unified framework of interpretation that constitutes a univocal "key" to the meaning of a text. This assumption would seem especially out of place in relation to those texts that explicitly explore the possibilities and limits of making satisfying "contextual" sense of things. The propensity of an uncritical "contextualism" is to fill in the blanks or paradoxes actively explored or more covertly suggested in texts. Usually this occurs through a reliance upon gratuitous "hypotheses" or extremely speculative leaps of the imagination, which may themselves be paradoxical in a rather sterile way insofar as they are proffered to "round out" a basically positivistic explanation. The difficulty is to reformulate "contextual" concerns in more problematic terms that generate newer questions or at least somewhat different conceptions of rather old questions. I shall try to illustrate briefly such a reformulation with respect to the general problem of "carnivalization" in modern culture and the more specific problem of the possible role of the notion of "carnivalization" in the interpretation of Flaubert.

What has become apparent in the modern "period" is the reliance of innovatory "elite" responses upon older and threatened forms of "popular" culture in protesting against what is perceived as the "dominant" sociocultural context. This context separated work from play and the public from the private. Work became serious business, and play was restricted to leisure-time activities, often within a small circle of intimate friends or family members. Play in public life took the form of official parades and spectator sports. In crucial respects, holidays were family affairs with little unofficial activity in the streets or public places. From the fifteenth to the eighteenth century, high culture became divorced from popular culture.[2] And, as one moved from the nineteenth to the twentieth century, popular culture increasingly became a mass culture that was shared by the middle and lower classes. The type of popular culture to which artistic and intellectual elites appealed to oppose this state of affairs often harked back to real or fictionalized modes of carnival activity of one sort or another — carnival itself, marionette theatre, masks and masquerades, the use of frank "marketplace" language, and so forth.

One may note in passing the combination of old and new in the appeal to the carnivalesque in modern art and literature. Mikhail Bakhtin has seen the carnival as the epitome of a broader process of "carnivalization" understood as a critical and regenerative interaction between seeming opposites — life and death, high and low, serious and comic, spiritual and bodily. The carnivalesque is on the most basic level an ambivalent force that relates contending tendencies in a re-creative *agon* of destruction and renewal. On the level of language, it is related to what Bakhtin discusses in terms of dialogue and the dialogical. The mono-logical, by contrast, corresponds to one opposite, split off or dissociated from the other and absolutized—for example, the objective voice of an author telling what pretends to be the un-varnished and uncontested truth about the world. But the actual dialogue in certain circumstances may itself be among the least dialogical of phenomena, for example, when the dialogue con-sists of the quasi-ritual exchange of commonplaces. The dialogi-cal is contestatory, typically in the form of two (or more) strains or uses of language ("voices") tensely cohabiting the same set of words. For Bakhtin, great art and literature (especially the novel) are the primary repository of the dialogical and the carnivalesque in its more restricted modern state. For in the modern "period," the carnival is not, for Bakhtin, the vital social institution it was in Rabelais's Renaissance.

The question one may raise, however, is that of the extent to which the dialogical and the carnivalesque as contestatory forces inform or should inform various uses of language as well as at-tempts to transform social life. The issues Bakhtin himself does not investigate are those of the modulations of the carnivalesque in modern writers and artists and that of its applicability to criti-cism, philosophy, and other fields of inquiry. Indeed, Bakhtin's own style of writing itself tends to remain primarily "monologi-cal" even as it attempts to describe and to evoke, indeed, to re-habilitate, the dialogical and the carnivalesque.

The writing of certain modern figures—and the resistance to them—becomes somewhat more intelligible when one sees in them an attempt to enact a more dialogical and carnivalesque un-derstanding of things. One also comes to see more clearly why, in the attempt to understand these writings, synoptic content analy-sis and the summary of arguments seem excessively restrictive. To limit instances to a few obvious cases, Derrida and Nietzsche, and even Heidegger in significant ways, engage in highly dialogi-cal and at times carnivalized uses of language. Julia Kristeva, in an early article (1966), went so far as to argue that Bakhtin's work itself "suggests the interest of the dialogical principle for a space of thought more vast than the novelistic. Dialogicality, more than binarism, would perhaps be the basis for the intellectual structure of our epoch."[3] Here one has a "definition" of the present that is itself necessarily open to self-contestation, for it appeals to a multivalent "principle" that "institutes" contestation as a critical/re-creative force both allowing for structures and placing them in question.

What about Flaubert, who has often been seen as marking a "turning point" in the history of the novel? Can the "principle" of carnivalization enable us to reopen his highly problematic case? To what extent does "carnivalization" allow us to reinterpret his relation to various "contexts" — say, his intentions, reaction to society, and role in the history of the novel?

What should be apparent at the present time is that the entry for Flaubert in the *Petit Larousse* is itself a fitting tribute to the connoisseur of cliché and serio-comic animator of the encyclopedic quest, for it is worthy of inclusion in his *Dictionary of Received Ideas* (or, more precisely, his *sottisier* of all-too-familiar quotations): "Prosateur soucieux de la perfection du style, il veut donner dans ses romans une image objective de la réalité, mais garde quelques traits de l'imagination romantique." This *juste-milieu* or overly pear-shaped conception of Flaubert is neither quite right nor quite wrong — a status courted by all general characterizations and one which makes them especially suitable candidates for becoming *idées reçues*.

Sartre, with a vengeance, has seen the limitations of this dictionary conception of Flaubert.[4] For him Flaubert is the "idiotic"/genial exponent of a post-romantic ideology of pure art that converts a *trompe-l'oeil* realism and an equally deceptive formalism into masks for a thoroughgoing nihilism. A "knight of nothingness," Flaubert "represents" reality only to negate and transcend it into a deadly sphere of pure beauty or absolute style. His inhuman, sado-masochistic project is to employ a self-tormenting, ascetic practice in writing, demoralizing not only his hated bourgeoisie but man himself.

Jonathan Culler, in a brilliant book, "brackets" Sartre's psychological account of Flaubert's neurotic condition (as a genuine hysteric who feigned schizophrenia) but retains a basically Sartrian understanding of Flaubert's more or less intentional project (demoralization, nihilism, and transcendence through pure art).[5]

Culler inquires more closely into the issue of how this project is stylistically realized in the novels and stories, thereby in effect completing the Sartrian project itself by writing the fourth volume of *L'Idiot de la famille* that Sartre himself never finished. But, in the process, he raises some questions that would seem to depart from the Sartrian framework. Taking certain of Culler's analyses as a point of departure, one might argue that—and here one perhaps finds Flaubert's significance in the history of the novel—Flaubert both "deconstructed" the traditional novel and brought the genre into an impasse or dead end that was challenging enough to prompt successors who were up to the task to hazard a new beginning.[6] Indeed, if one looks at *Madame Bovary, The Sentimental Education,* and *Bouvard and Pécuchet* (putting aside a work like *The Temptations of Saint Anthony* which, rewritten by Flaubert at three different times in his life, would disorient any linear pattern), one seems to trace a progression in the direction of increasing "minimalization" that could be seen as leading up to Beckett.

Culler, however, tends to reduce "pure art" to a formalistic level in his own discussion of novelistic techniques, and he treats the themes of irony and stupidity in a rather abstract way, presenting Flaubert's own quest for a stylistic absolute—notably in *Salammbô*—as culminating in a transcendence of irony (if not of stupidity) through the genesis of a formal-novelistic analogue of the sacred.[7] (One might suggest that the transcendence of irony—itself construed in a subjective, nihilistic, and self-servingly invidious way—is the formalistic problem *par excellence;* the extent to which it was not Flaubert's problem reveals the extent to which he was not a formalist.) Arthur Mitzman in a recent article asserts that Flaubert's notion of "pure art" is itself a "sublimated" version of Bakhtin's carnivalesque, supporting his assertion through such biographical details as Flaubert's life-long fascination with marionette theatre (he first became acquainted with the story of Saint Anthony through Legrain's marionette version at the fair of Rouen) and his strong predilection, especially in his early letters, for ribald bombast and billingsgate.[8] Mitzman simply dismisses the view of Flaubert as an antihuman nihilist and stresses instead his direct criticisms of bourgeois civilization and the indirect ways pure art as stylistic insurrection functioned as a critical force.

At the expense of sounding like the *Petit Larousse* once again, I would note the obvious: there is something to be said for the various interpretations I have mentioned. But the problem is how precisely to say it. All interpretations tend to be reductive or "recuperative" in one way or another but, as Culler himself emphasizes, the self-critical point may be to resist recuperation as long as possible, or at least to suspect premature foreclosures. I would suggest that the overall difficulty in interpreting a writer of Flaubert's complexity is to see how his obvious and his subtle criticism of modern life at times became enmeshed with more symptomatic and escapist tendencies in his work, as he himself became affected by the pressures toward levelling and confusion, which he castigated in the larger society. For at these points he did verge on antihuman self-hatred and nihilism. But it is also necessary to see how his texts at times worked or played toward another level of ambivalence that cannot be identified with simple equivocation—the level, for example, where "stupidity" signified not "bourgeois" complacency and self-satisfaction but forces that were "below" or "above" this commonplace plateau: the inarticulate and almost silent "stupidity" of the good-hearted victim (Félicité in "Un Coeur simple," say, a story in which the apparent ironic meaning is "reversed," through a reversal of the "normal" operation of irony itself, into something sad and serious), or the "stupidity" of the masterpiece that approached natural phenomena in evoking awe "beyond interpretation."

One general problem with interpretations of Flaubert is that they tend to take from Flaubert's *Correspondance* the most unqualified and lapidary formulations of the ideal of "pure art" and unproblematically identify it as Flaubert's project. Then they turn to the novels and stories only to document in one way or another how that project was realized. The stumbling block is that the *Correspondance* itself is often rather qualified in its understanding of pure art. And the novels and stories raise even more pronounced difficulties for it, at times in other than merely negative ways. Indeed one might suggest that the modes of Flaubert's failure in attaining "pure art" attest to the more affirmative accomplishments of his texts.

In the *Correspondance,* pure art is presented as an impossible dream or a utopian ideal — a necessary hyperbole whose point is not to be realized but to punctuate and to agitate the "real." Often Flaubert's own awareness of this "fact" brought him close to despair. But what is perhaps more significant is that he affirmed *both* that art is the most important commitment in the world *and* that in his dedication to it he assumed the role of the clown. In other words, there is in the *Correspondance* a tension between a pathos of belief and self-directed irony and parody. This tension is, I think, explored in subtler ways in the novels and stories. But it is worth observing that this tension, in the *Correspondance* itself, attests to the status of art as more than a formalistic concern of Flaubert. It also bears noting that Flaubert rarely refers to the novel *per se* in his letters; his remarks most often are addressed to the problem of art or of writing prose, the implication being, I think, that his interests are not restricted to the novel as a genre. Indeed, in more ways than one, "novel" is a funny word for books like *The Temptations of Saint Anthony* or *Bouvard and Pécuchet.* (By the time one gets to Beckett's writing, the word seems peculiarly inappropriate or suspiciously conventional.)

According to Sartre's interpretation (which is at times confirmed by Flaubert's own self-interpretation in the *Correspondance*), it would seem that pure art "sublimated" the carnivalesque into the latter's very opposite: a deadly desire for transcendence instead of an ambivalent contestation/renewal of reality. But this is perhaps the place to remark briefly on the subtler modulations of the carnivalesque in Flaubert. In the novels and stories, one has a rather explicit "representation" of the repression, suppression, or stupid, even vicious, distortion of the carnivalesque in modern society. In *Madame Bovary,* for example, one might list: the initial charivari ridiculing Charles in class; the exclusion of the "degrading" gesture of the fishmonger-relative at the wedding of Charles and Emma because it is out of keeping with the "dignity" of a doctor; the bathetic scene at the *Comices agricoles* — the modern provincial analogue of the carnival; the recurrent and uncanny appearances of the Blind Man, a carnival figure "out of season" who evokes only shrill and hysterical laughter at the time of Emma's death; the figure of Homais (as well as that of his clerical *sosie,* Bournisien), perhaps Flaubert's idea of the last carnival man. But with all of this, one finds more complex, self-questioning movements in the texts. What is itself contested, even carnivalized, in the novels and stories is Flaubert's own conception of pure art. The novels and stories, in other words, do not simply realize the ideal of pure art; they render it radically problematic. It is ironized and parodied in at least indirect fashion through Flaubert's treatment of its analogues: Saint Anthony's "temptations," Emma's romantic dreams, Frédéric's amorous obsession, Bouvard and Pécuchet's encyclopedic quest. In more pervasive fashion, the sustained but mercurial medium of Flaubert's highly "unstable" irony is his so-called "free indirect style" — the place where any more extended discussion of his use of irony (or its use of him) would have to begin. Through the multiple modifications in proximity and distance (or the "uncertainty") of narrative voice which it effects, the "free indirect style" makes it impossible to characterize the narrator as a fully consistent identity or a reliable ground for moral judgment. By the same token, it tests and contests the quest for *pure* art, as it problematizes its analogues, suggesting the ideal or the absolute as at best a continually displaced limit. Given the absence of any direct discussion of it in the novels and stories (at least after the *First Sentimental Education*), "pure art" is more protected than its analogues from the work and play of irony. But it neither finds an inviolate sanctuary in some transcendent or formal realm, nor is it totally destroyed or annihilated by its adversary.

This brief and not altogether digressive discussion of Flaubert — through it one finds oneself, as Sartre might say, *en pleine actualité* — may serve as the occasion to raise a concluding problem. One of the most difficult tasks at present is to attempt to distinguish, in works we study or in our own efforts, among the symptomatic, the critical, and the movement beyond these categories to another level of ambivalence. The symptomatic is worrisome when what it incorporates is what one deplores in the larger society, in others, or in oneself. The appeal to the carnivalesque may itself excuse self-indulgence, "media hype," or unjustifiable forms of equivocation. And the over-emphasis upon psychic mobility or the feats of the "performing self" may accord quite well with the planned obsolescence of a consumer society, providing it with one more transient product: the "throw-away" self. (One might even imagine a sinister post-postmodern world in which Beckett's books are assigned to case workers to enable them to adjust more readily to their environment.) However much the idea may be abused, moreover, one must nonetheless insist that the critique of existing practices confront the problem of alternative practices, institutions, norms, and structures having a more viable and acceptable relation to contestation. Here the point, expressed in the most lapidary (therefore "stupid") way, is neither to autonomize contestation or change in the abstract nor to conceive the alternative in the form of perfect authority or community. At the very least, the problem is to investigate texts, and to think or write in terms, actively engaging the question of the relationships among the symptomatic, critical, and more "undecidable" tendencies in language and life.

NOTES

1 See, for example, Hayden V. White, *Tropics of Discourse* (Baltimore: Johns Hopkins University Press, 1978); and the essays in Steven L. Kaplan and Dominick LaCapra, eds., *Modern European Intellectual History: Reappraisals and New Perspectives* (Ithaca: Cornell University Press, 1982).

2 For a treatment of early modern culture (or cultures), with a discussion of the role of carnival, its decline over time, and the withdrawal of the elites from popular culture, see Peter Burke, *Popular Culture in Early Modern Europe* (New York: New York University Press, 1978). See also Natalie Z. Davis, *Society and Culture in Early Modern France* (Stanford, Calif: Stanford University Press, 1975).

3 Julia Kristeva, "Le Mot, le dialogue, et le roman," in *Semiotikè* (Paris: Éditions du Seuil, 1969), p. 173.

4 Jean-Paul Sartre, *L'Idiot de la famille* (Paris: Gallimard, 1971–72).

5 Jonathan Culler, *Flaubert: The Uses of Uncertainty* (Ithaca: Cornell University Press, 1974).

6 The latter theme is explored in Hugh Kenner, *The Stoic Comedians: Flaubert, Joyce, and Beckett* (Berkeley and Los Angeles: University of California Press, 1962).

7 Culler, *Flaubert*, pp. 207–28.

8 Arthur Mitzman, "Roads, Vulgarity, Rebellion, and Pure Art: The Inner Space in Flaubert and French Culture," *Journal of Modern History* 51, no. 3 (1979): 504–24. See also Dominick LaCapra, *"Madame Bovary" on Trial* (Ithaca: Cornell University Press, 1982).

4 /

Crisis Instead of Revolution: On the Instrumental Change of Social Innovation

Paul Noack

I. CONCEPTS AND REALITY

Two statements define at the outset the key concepts of this essay, taken in their most restrictive sense: "What remains of the concept of revolution is basically a metaphor (and that is exactly how the history of this concept began)";[1] and "Crisis is a lay term in search of a scholarly meaning."[2] A closer look at these statements, however, persuades us that every concept is an abstraction which in turn confronts a particular reality. Only abstraction and factual reality together result in a total human reality within time and space.[3]

"Crisis" and "revolution," however, are concepts which, at first glance, lack analytical precision. Yet we cannot dispense with them. We need them not only to reach an intersubjective understanding of political change but also because concepts develop lives of their own, "drives" which turn them and their meanings into an integral part of factual reality. Connotations can turn words into political instruments. This applies to such terms as "class struggle" and "imperialism," "democracy" and "freedom," as well as "revolution" and "crisis." There has never been a revolution without its encompassing revolutionary rhetoric. And it is rightly said today that one can "talk crises into existence."[4]

If we apply this insight — namely that words can become political instruments — to the concept of revolution, we can see that the prestige which this concept has acquired in the course of time has led to its inflation. For revolutions no longer represent a definite, violent form of social change; rather, they have become myths, justifying themselves simply by taking place as incarnations of the Good. In view of this mythologizing, a sobering comment concerning the consequences of revolution seems appropriate: "The difference between before and after is not the difference between this world and another. States which have just recovered from a revolution are often brutal, corrupt, tyrannical, and inept."[5] Such a statement stipulates — rightly, I think — that it is quite possible that the revolution was won by the stronger party, not necessarily the better one.

Nonetheless, the two concepts — revolution and crisis — are entirely different. Revolution is a concept around which myths are woven because it springs from the reservoir of myths. "Myth forms the provisional structure of the political and philosophic interpretations of history and shows the 'inevitable' character of continuity or the will to rupture."[6] Specifically, as *"volonté de rupture,"* the revolution has its origin in the myth of rebirth. Crisis, on the other hand, has to this day never driven people to despair or revolt; the concept is gray and devoid of myth.[7] We must, however, explain the reasons for its present advancement, which can possibly be traced back to the decline of the general belief in progress. (Whether or not belief in the future as progress has been in fact lost must remain unanswered.) Social change takes place regardless of whether a society looks into the future with fear or with hope. Indeed, the less history is considered as progress, and the less the future is considered as a path to a better life, the faster social change seems to take place. Thus what Zbigniew Brzezinski has written seems doubtful: "The fundamental difference between the 19th and 20th century can be described as follows: in the 19th century people's way of life changed faster than their way of thinking; in the 20th century thinking changes faster than the way of life."[8] My reason for doubting this statement is that one of the causes of the crisis confronting our times is the difficulty for the mind to get used to those imperatives which humanity must recognize and obey if it wants to survive. The last part of Brzezinski's statement would be more accurately formulated as follows: Thinking in the twentieth century has become incompatible with life's necessities; it wanders and becomes itself proof of the crisis.

We can already detect a certain blurred relation (*Unschärfe-Relation*) between intellectual and sociopolitical crises; that is, the two types of crises do not necessarily arise from the same root. What does it mean, on the one hand, when Paul Hazard speaks of the "Crisis of the European Conscience, 1680–1715,"[9] and, on the other hand, when we speak of an institutional crisis of democracy as it is practiced in the West? In the first case, Hazard notes a curious change of emphasis of the European intellect which cannot, or can only inadequately, be captured by external dates. In the second case, we refer to pathological changes in the institutional structure of the democratic states, changes in which the relationship between cause and effect is more or less clearly understood by our contemporaries—who may not necessarily know the cure. In the first case we are dealing with the change of consciousness of the individual; in the second with changes in the sociopolitical circumstances in which man lives. The crisis which I envision results from the interplay of these two factors. To show why this is so will be a main purpose of this paper.

My thesis, then, is this: it is not permanent revolution (not even understood as technological revolution) which we confront daily but permanent crisis. The "age of revolutions" seems long past. Perhaps we have missed the beginning of the "age of crises" for the simple reason that "it is difficult to find something that is entirely new." Therefore "one overlooks that which is new when it takes the form of gradual change or is a new combination of long-known facts."[10]

II. CONCERNING THE CONCEPT OF "CRISIS"

Until now, revolution and crisis (just like revolution and progress) have always appeared as twins. Crisis was interpreted as fertilizer of revolution, as the preliminary stage before a revolution.

It was said that the interrelationship was that of cause and effect: because one type of society had reached a "crisis," it therefore was in "revolution." But nowadays situations never reach the stage of "revolution." The "revolutionary situation" (according to researchers of revolutions of quite different orientations, this is the precondition of any successful revolution) does not even occur. The necessary conditions are lacking. Crisis and revolution no longer constitute a continuous entity; they have been irrevocably separated.

Such an interpretation, however, is only acceptable if one disregards the medically and militarily inspired formation of the concept and follows instead the everyday usage of the word. According to this usage, "crisis" is no longer that point between health and death, nor between peace and war, which will decide everything; rather, social crises today are defined by a long, persistent tension which from a certain point onwards fails to sustain itself. Crises have become, so to speak, thunderstorms without lightning, which have therefore lost their cleansing power.

This curious situation of a tension without release has three different elements: (1) social problems are being ignored rather than solved; (2) a social technique has been developed which neutralizes the negative consequences of such strategies of omission, at least for some time; and (3) crises, in order to be resolved, not only presuppose a capability for learning but also initiate learning processes. (It is this third factor which represents the "progressive" or "innovative" aspect of crisis.) Viewed this way, crises not only produce tensions; they also have a deflecting function. If one succeeds in creating a precarious homeostatic balance among these three elements, the crisis can, so to speak, be "eternalized" and tensions reduced so that violent explosion is avoided.

Wolf-Dieter Narr is possibly right when he writes that "A theory of normalcy—be it also a theory of the "not-yet"—is . . . for crisis analysis indispensable."[11] Narr, however, proceeds from a past or future ideal situation to which he then opposes the state of "crisis." According to this tenet, crises arise whenever a society departs from its ideal state. I do not share this opinion. According to my definition, crises originate at a point when the mediating agencies between the postulated values of a society and their implementation fail. In other words, the focus of my thesis is on whether or not state institutions do justice to the changing demands which emanate from society. One can thus speak of a political crisis whenever the state does not do justice to demands made upon it by its citizens and when state and society alike become conscious of this failure.

It seems to me, nonetheless, that in order to speak of a sociopolitical crisis one must be able to formulate at least four preconditions:

1. A society must feel threatened. Fear and threat, therefore, are both aspects of the concept of crisis.
2. The possibility to develop alternatives to the failure of the state must exist.
3. A state in which such a crisis is being diagnosed must be in a condition of transformation. Societies in which nothing can change can, by definition, never be in a state of crisis.
4. A crisis never originates from objective factors only. Each crisis also has its subjective aspect. "I *feel* threatened; I *feel* that the values of my society are being threatened; I *feel* its institutions being threatened"—that also is part of a crisis. I would even go so far as to claim that it is the subjective rather than the objective factor which in many instances is more crucial to the development of a crisis.

In view of these complexities, it is hardly possible for a political scientist to claim more than to study the crises of the Western states in the last third of the twentieth century. The crises for this particular period manifest themselves in two forms: one expresses the objective difficulties that have arisen in the Western states; the other expresses the subjective consciousness of crisis which in turn causes new difficulties for these states.

III. DECAY OF REVOLUTION

Revolution, progress, and innovation have been amalgamated up to the middle of the twentieth century. What, then, has brought about the decay of the revolutionary motivation and argumentation? And an end to radical innovations? Great innovations have always generated still more breakthroughs. No one, for instance, had an inkling of the consequences which the construction of the first steam engine would entail. And the social consequences of the computer age can only be perceived dimly. Still, quantitative changes have always turned into qualitative social changes. These changes found their expression in political, and later social, revolutions in the eighteenth, nineteenth, and beginning of the twentieth centuries.

What has changed since then? Revolutions demand a clearcut pro and con in terms of argumentation as well as social gradation. Shadings and nuances are inappropriate for revolutions. But today we find strong contrasts only in developing countries. In the developed industrial states, however, it becomes increasingly difficult to persuade a majority that a revolution is necessary, that *only* a revolution could lead to the desired political or social goal.

Concerning the history of revolutionary eruptions, the following factors apply: (1) A regime which withholds from me political rights which others possess (e.g., the right to vote) provokes my revolt. (2) Though it is harder to establish the origins of disaffections concerning property, the fact remains that there are the poor and the rich. This provokes revolt, even if the time of incubation is long. (3) On the other hand, the constraints emanating from the technological system produce effects far removed from their source. (Whom do I address when jobs are being rationalized away, when computers replace office workers, when offset puts printers out of their jobs, and robots replace auto workers?) If the cause of the trouble cannot be clearly identified, indignation has little chance to develop; the revolution runs idle, or else aimless revolts occur.[12]

Today, the everyday usage and the scientific usage of the concept of revolution go their separate ways. In view of the prestige attached to revolutions, the everyday usage of the word permits any innovation, any household gadget, to be called "revolutionary." The scientific usage, on the other hand, becomes increasingly selective, sharp. This is due to what I shall call, after Arnold Gehlen, "crystallization theory."[13] This theory propounds the debatable notion that all thinkable forms of human coexistence have been tried in the past. Therefore, those definitions become increasingly outdated which not only hold that a revolution proceeds in fits and starts, using violence and engulfing the masses, but further contend that a revolution must also possess an encompassing progressive idea "which pursues positive goals towards a renewal, a further development or progress of humanity."[14] Even so profound an upheaval as the "revolution" in Iran cannot be grasped completely by such definitions because, in this particular case, it revives the original concept of revolution as return. This "revolution" was not made in the name of progress but, on the contrary, envisioned the restitution of the old order, the return to the "golden age," the abolition of the decadence of history. That is, it was aimed at renovation instead of innovation, at a revitalization of cultural and religious traditions.

My main concern, however, is with Western industrial states in the second half of this century, where crises have replaced revolutions as forces of social change. This transformation has come about through the gradual disappearance of three preconditions for revolution: (1) A world view which had one homogeneous answer to all the important questions of life; (2) the "revolutionary situation" as defined earlier; and (3) the "principle of hope" (Ernst Bloch) projected into the future. From 1688 until 1917, possibly 1947, this principle activated revolutions. It can no longer do so; for the gap widens constantly between what is desired and what may realistically be expected.

IV. EXCURSION: PROBLEMS OF PROGNOSIS

The prognosis for the future of the world will vary according to whether the theoretician has in mind the probable status of the future or its idealistic, normative status. If he interprets the future of the world according to the first, the analysis is bound to be pessimistic; if he interprets it according to the latter, the prognosis will be more optimistic because that which is considered necessary from an ideal point of view is reinterpreted as plausible.

Since this essay is not utopian, what follows will not be an image of the future. For not only do I concur with the view that "it is the general weakness of utopias that they seem to offer less future than the present. One can even state that 'utopia' can be defined as a system without a future."[15] I also believe that by looking at the particular ways in which social change takes place in the twentieth century, we can better perceive the underlying reality. In other words, if we recognize why creeping crises have replaced revolutions as instruments of social transformation, we can better understand those who trigger and suffer crises as well as revolutions.

The tendency of political turbulences to release themselves in crises rather than revolutions is accompanied by another tendency. For three centuries, Europe exported its revolutionary energies to the rest of the world. Today we see a reversal of that trend. If not actual revolutions, then the not so "discrete charm" of revolutionary models drive now from the periphery of the world (having taken over the role of the "noble savage" of the eighteenth century) toward its centers. At the same time, Western capitalism only exports its "crisis of legitimacy," the crises of its own bad conscience; meanwhile, the state socialism of the USSR exports the crisis of the idea of "world revolution," and that is nothing but the crises of socialist internationalism. (Of this, Poland is but the latest example.)

In the concept of crisis management we rediscover the splendor and misery of all these crises in a nutshell. The alternatives which we have nowadays are no longer revolution and counterrevolution. (That alternative, by the way, which sees in the action of thesis and antithesis of human history a constant progress is also invalidated.) The uniformity of the concept of crisis has swallowed them both. Hence, the only alternative for action which remains is crisis management. If we define crisis as a permanent status rather than the climax of a development, then crisis management itself becomes permanent. This means denying the causes of the crisis by breaking it up into less threatening subcrises and thus making it more acceptable. The role of the management is to reduce the *actual* crisis; that is, the temporary forms of the appearance of the fundamental crisis. The fundamental crisis itself, however, remains nearly untouched. Thus, for instance, the management of the Cuban crisis did not do away with the American-Soviet conflict but rather delayed its solution to some time in the future, "resolving" only the actual subconflict. The procedure is to prorate the original conflict into the next crisis — just as the deficit of an account is prorated into the next fiscal year. Neither the causes of the crisis nor the deficit of an account will disappear. On the contrary, if the deficit stays the same year after year, and the symptoms of the crisis accumulate, then one day bankruptcy must be announced.

As I have already noted, I am concerned primarily with highly industrialized states, with an accent as strong on "highly industrialized" as on "states." Such a perspective indicates that, in spite of assurances to the contrary, it will be the crisis of "states" which will determine the near future. Furthermore, "the state will continue to exist for a long time, perhaps one to three centuries or more, under any social system likely to be established in this or that country. The state will retain all its major functions, except that of military conquest, albeit in changing proportions."[16] My perspective for the future, therefore, relies not so much on a fundamental transformation in the conditions of human coexistence (for instance, the advent of classless society or the world state) but rather on those enduring factors which will continue to produce crises within the states and on the directions which these crises will take within social systems. Thus we move from abstract considerations of the term "crisis" to more concrete aspects of it.

V. THE CRISIS AND THE CRISES

In the last quarter of the twentieth century, three factors, primarily, have appeared to cause crises in the West. These are:

1. *The social effects of technology.* In view of what has been said about revolutions, it should be pointed out that the "legitimate" authorities of the state must confront the same difficulties that those who fight the state confront. For nowadays it is as difficult to legitimize the state as it is to revolutionize it; the very same reasons which cause revolutions to appear less and less meaningful lead states into a crisis of legitimacy. A state can establish itself as legitimate by dismantling existing political or legal inequality; by eliminating or diminishing economic inequal-

ity; by protecting the individual against the consequences of the "technological system." However, the state proves itself unable to do just this. The discontent of the individual, the causes of which he is unable to detect himself, leads to the crisis of the state, which in turn is unable to diminish the discontent of those who support it.

The difficulties to which the state is exposed have their roots in the previously determined social and political countertrends in the twentieth century. Industrial growth decreases, and so does the wealth to be distributed. The economic pressure brought about by competition to accomplish production-innovation, process-innovation, and position-innovation, increases at the same time. The consequences of such increased pressure for innovation are felt not only in the social realm. They also make it necessary to push the horizon of action to an ever-increasing distance. (The automobile of the twenty-first century has to be planned today; the weapon systems which are supposed to maintain the precarious balance of powers have to be conceived today.)

Such futuristic planning easily allows developments to become irreversible. These acquire lives of their own which are hard to control. Of course, man has always planned and produced for tomorrow's needs. But now the relationship between present and future changes drastically. What type of change are we dealing with? We are dealing more and more with an overestimation of goods for the present to the disadvantage of goods for the future. The discrepancy between that which *is* and that which is *necessary* becomes increasingly wide. This gravely affects the state's ability to act, which is normally in intervals of four years. And for a politician in a democratic state who wants to maximize his votes, "considerations of long term tendencies are a luxury which he cannot afford, even if he should be interested in the shaping of a long term future."[17] This leads to an unresolvable discrepancy between action requirements and perspectives for the future.

Shaping democratic societies through politics presupposes the maximization of votes. A politician can only maximize votes if he promises a maximum of goods for the present. The crises, therefore, which arise from the discrepancy between unadapted thinking and technological innovation can no longer be resolved adequately. As a result, problems accumulate disproportionately, and this induces permanent crises in the political system. How, then, can the political system react to these perpetual emergencies? Do the crises initiate a process of investigations of their causes, or does the system break apart under their pressure?

2. *Disinformation through overinformation.* The details of the "information revolution" are well known. Less known, at least regarding the social sciences, are the social consequences of the flooding of information. These consist not only in the fact that TV has created new life styles.[18] Equally important is the fact that during the process of creating reality through TV, reality is being distorted, a fact which remains largely unrealized by the viewer. The effect hereby created is called "cognitive dissonance." It originates when news — e.g., the perpetual emphasis of nations simultaneously on their commitment to peace and their arms race — cannot be harmonized in the mind of the viewer. The effect is as divided in the individual as it is in the decision-making apparatus of the states: the flood of information can have a positive as well as a negative effect. If a decision-making apparatus is well constituted, the decisions taken under consideration of as much information as possible will be more balanced and rational. However, if this apparatus is poorly constituted, then despite all the information, decisions will tend to be poor because the validity of the facts can no longer be proven.

A permanent "cognitive dissonance" in social life thus leads to a breakdown of the ability to make judgments. "A mild degree of such a contradiction heightens the curiosity and stimulates the thinking process, but a very high degree of such dissonances . . . leads to a withdrawal into passivity or to fits of rage. A third answer is the escape into some special ideology, special interest group, or the noise screen of a transistor radio."[19] Here, then, is a partial answer to the cause of difficulties in ruling a democracy. The uncertainty of direction, caused by a "disinformed" society, strikes back at itself; bad information erodes the basis of judgment.

3. *Crisis-susceptibility of the individual.* It is possible to relate technical innovation and abnormal behavior. The crisis of

the state is therefore based on the crisis-susceptibility of the individual. Two pictures, one placed on top of the other, reveal the full dimension of the crisis. The first picture is that of a split human consciousness: it has the motivation for a revolution, but no goal for that revolution. "On the one hand, he wants to destroy the society that inhibits him less through the use of force than with temptations and corruption. On the other hand, he feels divided because a part of him belongs to that society. He becomes its accomplice."[20] The second picture is that of the state which can no longer cope with the demands made upon it by its citizens. It is unlikely that a revolutionary consciousness would develop that could fundamentally challenge the state. But the absolute loyalty which provides the state with stability and self-assurance is decreasing. Since it is unable to assert a goal, the state itself, in search for new loyalties, creates those crises which again question its existence. (The struggle for an adequate economic order in states of the Western hemisphere is less a struggle for new orientations than an attempt to make the greatest possible number of citizens their accomplices through high standards of living.[21])

The lack of orientation of the individual and that of the state are therefore interdependent. The lack of orientation of the individual extorts from the state a permanent opportunistic behavior, which also protects the state from having to fear its own elimination in a revolutionary transformation. Thus the necessary opportunistic behavior of the state *diminishes* the number of necessary decisions, but also *increases* the number of crises which have not been mastered.

What differentiates such an interpretation of state action or nonaction from theories influenced by Marxism is primarily this: Neomarxist critique analyzes problem-avoidance strategies, the preventive crisis management of the modern state, as a conscious and cunning manipulation strategy — an insidious deprivation of individual freedom. In short: an increase of power through manipulation. I interpret this behavior as the inevitable reaction to the existence of active citizens in a state; the self-preservation of the state does not allow for any other choice. However, an increase in power is out of the question if—according to Max Weber —one takes it to mean the ability to force one's will upon another.

VI. CRISIS AS LEARNING PROCESS

The picture, however, is not yet complete. I have stated that the consequence of the state's unacceptable fixation on the needs of the present is an increase of the conflict potential. At the same time, it would be wrong to ignore completely its innovative accomplishments, limited as they may be. Without these, our initial thesis, the interdependence of social change and crisis, would be untenable. Crises, then, also foster perception. But what defines the innovative capacities of the state for the resolution of crises which allow social change?

In terms of a system-oriented theory, one could present a series of conditions pertaining to the individual (meanings, desires, values) as well as to the system (identification, the capacity to recognize problems, a highly developed memory capacity and its application).[22] I would like to tackle the problem on a lower, and therefore less complete, level of abstraction. Undoubtedly there is a connection between conflict and crisis: unresolved conflicts create crises. But this negative aspect is not the only one. For conflicts in open systems can be understood not only as causes of loss through social friction but also as "tools for discovery." Often it is a conflict which leads us to perceive a problem and stimulates us to think about it and research it. This allows us, paradoxical as it may seem, to attribute a problem-solving function to the conflict. (Only the settled wage dispute prompts relaxation; the unresolved latent wage dispute could fundamentally threaten a political system.) A settled conflict, with its accompanying learning process on both sides, can, therefore, have a stabilizing effect on the system. Indeed, as will become evident, the acceptance of crises by a political system can actually serve as prerequisite to its survival. At the same time, neither the suppression of the crisis nor its suppression through a pseudoharmony would constitute a solution which would benefit the political system in the long run; for such suppression would lead back to what we have detected as the basic evil of the modern state, the bridging of conflicts through adjournment of the decision.

The acceptance of crises as means for innovation, therefore, signifies the possibility for a system to transform itself through a partial change of its structures without destroying its meaning. It leads to what is known as reform or capacity for reform. Crises, however, which have not been settled do not allow any such learning process, thereby preventing the innovation which the highly bureaucratic systems — not only of the Western world — so desperately require. It is, therefore, necessary to distinguish between the beneficial effect of a crisis and the disastrous effects of an accumulation of crises.

If it turns out that a political system is no longer able to resolve a crisis, the unresolved crisis is carried over into the next one. This as well as any further step in the same direction increases the probability — since the complexity of the cause becomes increasingly great — that the problem-solving capacity of the state is being overtaxed. The flexibility of the system decreases; it is less and less able to adjust to future endangering situations. It then loses credibility in the eyes and minds of its citizens. The already weakened loyalty of the citizens is further overtaxed by the constant decrease of its credibility; the system faces its breakdown.

It is true, then, that conflicts can still be settled. But through the permanent social prophylaxis called crisis management, the individual is no longer able to comprehend the causes of conflicts which are created by the modern situation. He no longer understands why this is done and not that. The tendency in many of our societies to seek that "understanding," which reality does not offer by voting for charismatic figures in whom the impenetrable and contradictory reality seems dissolved, indicates that the very basis of democracy — decision based on reason — is being eroded. The almost messianic hopes which are placed — and not just in the United States — on a new American president is a bad omen. The same applies to those pseudoreligious "movements" which are politically effective because they pretend — through a fundamental transformation of the human being — to be able also to change the state. Both are forms of a "reduction of complexity" (Niklas Luhmann) which works, however, very differently from the way those who consider it as a rational means of orientation or finding of identity can envision.

VII. POSSIBILITIES OF MASTERING CRISES

The question finally arises: "What are the prospects for a future without the 'principle of hope'?" We have to subdivide the question by asking: (1) What should be done? and (2) What will be done? In terms of the "should," one could cite the demands formulated by Bruno Fritsch[23] when he attempts to characterize the "overtaxation of the state." He makes three suggestions to restore the balance between the demands made on the state and its capacity to answer these demands and therefore diminish crisis potential:

1. A selective de-escalation of the increase of disproportions. By this Fritsch means "prolonging the lifespan of consumer- and innovation-goods; the promotion of innovation, not in the direction of excessive growth but in the direction of internal, value-oriented growth. Innovation with value structures and in relation to new institutions."

2. Reduction of complexity through "functional hierarchies." This suggests the creation of "sociocultural" spaces where man can adapt himself to changes; that is, a shortening of the "culture lag."

3. An increase in society's learning capacity. This is meant not in the sense of an intense career-oriented training but rather a "specializing in coherency." Fritsch's reasoning is that "only with knowledge of the continuum can an informed public be taught to adequately limit future development and deal with future problem-solving."

VIII. LEARNING THROUGH CATASTROPHE?

These are the demands. But what is the probability of their realization? This paper is not a quantifying trend analysis, and it does not deny an intuitive element. Therefore I cannot join the optimistic assessments which predict the *result* of an information-society emerging from its *necessity*. ("The liberal traditions of the West lead us to hope that our people can advance into the age of the information society without a loss of identity or freedom."[24]) Though starting from different premises, such trend analyses come to the same conclusion: everything must change because it cannot be otherwise. Because the new society needs the new man, he will have to be different.

To this I would answer: precisely if the "old" society preserves its identity, its perseverance will prevent the necessary transformation of man. Society will change, but not to such a degree that the necessary restructuring from present to future needs can be adequately accomplished. This, however, would be the most indispensable of all changes.

All this leads to the conclusion that the flexibility of the "open" system has undoubtedly diminished. Under pressure to assert itself, the system pursues a kind of crisis management which, rather than increasing, actually decreases the ability of the individual to participate in the process of shaping society. (A good example would be the proliferation of television programs in the Federal Republic of Germany: the explanation is that as long as technological progress cannot be hindered, it can be directed by putting it within a legal framework.) Learning processes seem to be initiated less and less by crises. The result is likely to be further accumulations of crises. It becomes increasingly uncertain whether rationality will actually play a role in the future, when the gap between the necessity of the information society and the reality of the disinformation society grows wider and wider.

The skeptical (and by the way very European) voice of C. F. von Weizsäcker therefore seems to me the more realistic one: "I cannot help it, but I expect that growing crises will culminate in catastrophe." Weizsäcker develops this conviction out of the contrary trends — which I have also observed — of the times: "personal love, cultural activity, meditative receptiveness, and perceptive reason" on the one hand; on the other, "conservative obstinacy, blind or uncritical aggression, inarticulate desire for happiness." All these, according to Weizsäcker, could constitute forms of resistance against the modern penetration of the world by will and science. He welcomes this resistance, but adds: "Its immediate effect is chaotic and can in the short term lead to catastrophe, just as it may perhaps in the long run lead to the avoidance of catastrophe."[25] That is an ambiguous response. But perhaps catastrophe will be a form of social learning for a while, once revolutions and crises have been exhausted as instruments of innovation and renovation. Perhaps we have to go through catastrophe first in order to relearn the social processes necessary to postindustrial society. We may even regress to a wild and chaotic barbarism, as described by the German poet Franz Werfel, in which an overcivilized society confronts a new simplicity:

At the beginning, predominantly at the "edges" of culture, something had erupted which people would describe in vague words tinged with disgust, like "jungle" or "filthy crowd." . . . Inexplicable to science and mocking its resistance, swamps had formed on different parts of the earth's surface which soon turned into blooming wilderness, in emerald green oases, interspersed with hills, fragrant valleys, lakes, rivers, streams, and tall trees. To their horror, the contemporaries were attracted to these blue and dangerous islands looming on the horizon. . . .

From disconnected, hurried words, I learned that these islands were multiplying and that there was even such a jungle right here, close to California, that this disgusting flora and fauna had appeared, or rather re-appeared there, and, even more shocking, a new race, conceived and born from escapees, misfits who had not been able to resist the temptation to revert. They had become apelike beings, midgets or monsters totally unlike the noble mean which humanity had achieved, savage, a filthy crowd who bear their offspring like cats and don't carry it much longer either. . . ."[26]

A "noble mean" will certainly not arise at a time when permanent crisis has supplanted revolution. A "new colorfulness," however, might point to a new goal.

(Translated by Inca Rumold)

NOTES

1 John Dunn, *Moderne Revolutionen: Analyse eines politischen Phänomens* (Stuttgart: Reclam Jun., 1974), p. 229. (*Modern Revolu-*

tions: An Introduction to the Analysis of a Political Phenomenon [Cambridge: Cambridge University Press, 1972].) Here, as in other instances, the situation of the scientific literature necessitated a translation back into English, from where it had originally come.

2 James A. Robinson, "Crisis," in *International Encyclopedia of the Social Sciences,* ed. D. E. Sills (New York: Macmillan, 1968), vol. 3, p. 510.

3 Concerning the history of the concept of crisis, see Reinhard Koselleck, *Kritik und Krise: Zur Pathogenese der bürgerlichen Welt* (Freiburg: Alber Verlag, 1959). Concerning the history of the concept of revolution, see Karl Griewank, *Der neuzeitliche Revolutionsbegriff* (Frankfurt/Main: Suhrkamp Verlag, 1973).

4 For a study of the political function of language, see Karl Dietrich Bracher, *Schlüsselwörter in der Geschichte* (Düsseldorf: Droste Verlag, 1978), p. 9: "Words and concepts not only are an indispensable means for the description and evaluation of historical phenomena; they also form an essential element of political agitation and function as an engine for historical change and as a power factor which has always been used for the implementation and justification of politics."

5 John Dunn, *Moderne Revolutionen,* p. 221. "All revolutions have many followers who, however, would not have opted for these revolutions had they possessed a clear understanding of where these revolutions would lead" (p. 215).

6 André Reszler, *Mythes politiques modernes* (Paris: Presses Universitaires de France, 1981), p. 216. To André Reszler I owe a multitude of hints, which he made at Racine, but which could not be utilized in the given context.

7 It must be emphasized that I consistently speak of a crisis of the political system and not of crises in the international system. See Martin Jänicke, "Krisenbegriff und Krisenforschung," in *Herrschaft und Krise,* ed. Martin Jänicke (Opladen: Westdeutscher Verlag, 1973). An excellent survey of the concept of the international crisis is rendered by Heinz Krummenacher in *Internationale Normen und innerstaatliches Verhalten* (Zürich: Kleine Studien zur Politischen Wissenschaft, nos. 203–4).

8 Zbigniew Brzezinski, "The Technotronic Age," in *Dialogue* 2, no. 4 (1969): 34ff.

9 Paul Hazard, *La Crise de la conscience européenne, 1680–1715* (Paris: Boivin, 1935), p. v: "Quel contraste! quel brusque passage! La hiérarchie, la discipline, l'ordre que l'autorité se charge d'assurer, les dogmes qui règlent fermement la vie: voilà ce qu'aimaient les hommes du dix-septième siècle. Les contraintes, l'autorité, les dogmes, voilà ce que détestent les hommes du dix-huitième siècle, leurs successeurs immédiats. Les premiers sont chrétiens, et les autres anti-chrétiens; les premiers croient au droit divin, et les autres au

droit naturel; les premiers vivent à l'aise dans une société qui se divise en classes inégales, les seconds ne rêvent qu'égalité."

10 Andrew A. Scott, *The Revolution in Statecraft* (New York: Random House, 1969), p. 9.

11 See Wolf-Dieter Narr, "Zur Genesis und Funktion von Krisen: Einige systemanalytische Marginalien," in *Herrschaft und Krise,* ed. Martin Jänicke, pp. 224f.

12 See Jacques Ellul, *Von der Revolution zur Revolte* (Hamburg: Hoffmann und Campe Verlag, 1974).

13 Here is Arnold Gehlen "On Cultural Crystallization" in *Studien zur Anthropologie und Soziologie* (Neuwied und Berlin: Luchterhand Verlag, 1963), pp. 312, 323, 324-25. I deem his theses important enough to quote in some detail:

> I would suggest using the word crystallization to designate that situation in any cultural area which occurs when the possibilities within that area have been fully developed. The counter-measures and antitheses have been discovered and either accepted or excluded, so that changes in the premises or in the fundamental perspectives are increasingly unlikely.
>
> I would expound on this by saying that the history of ideas has been concluded and that we have reached the stage of post-history, so that the advice Gottfried Benn gave to the individual—"depend on your own certitude" —should be applied to humanity as a whole. In this epoch, the earth—as it is visually and factually conceivable—can no longer be surprised; there is no possibility for an event of great significance to arise unnoticed. The alternatives are known, as in the field of religion, and are final in all cases.
>
> The ideologies which have lasted have no viable rivals. They are definite possibilities, like the religions, whose stabilization hundreds of years after they have been threatened by scientific *"Weltbilder"* is one of the most unexpected events. They have apparently passed beyond the danger zone which occurred in the West with the Enlightenment and in Asia with the onslaught of white cultures. Thus it can be said that in the areas of religion and ideology the finality of totally formulated conditions must be taken into account, so that the intellectual energy of man will be manifested in the continued development of details of the great scientific structure.

14 Griewank, *Der neuzeitliche Revolutionsbegriff,* pp. 21f.

15 Denis de Rougemont, *Die Zukunft ist unsere Sache* (Stuttgart: Klett-Cotta, 1980), p. 123. [From *L'Avenir est Notre Affaire* (Paris: Éditions Stock, 1977).]

16 Karl W. Deutsch, "Functions and Transformations of the State: Notes Toward a General Theory," *VG Papers II* pre 80-119. Veröffentlichungsreihe des Internationalen Instituts für vergleichende Gesellschaftsforschung, Wissenschaftszentrum Berlin (September 1980), p. 25.

17 Bruno Fritsch, "Die Überforderung des Staates," *VG Papers II* PV/ 78-24. Veröffentlichungsreihe des Internationalen Instituts für ver-

gleichende Gesellschaftsforschung, Wissenschaftszentrum Berlin (November 1978), p. 2.

18 The literature about the social consequences of media consumption is abundant. See Heinz-Dietrich Fischer and John C. Merrill, eds., *International and Intercultural Communication* (New York: Hastings House Pubs., 1978) and Herbert J. Schiller, *Communication and Cultural Domination* (New York: M. E. Sharpe, 1976). Of interest also is the vision of the future of a former revolutionary. Régis Debray, today an advisor of French President Mitterand, writes: "There actually is a reverse relationship between the informational value of a message and its communicability. The more demonstrative a thought, the more expensive its delivery and the more uncertain its reception. . . . The mass media guarantee the maximum socialization of private stupidity." From *Voltaire verhaftet man nicht: Die Intellektuellen und die Macht in Frankreich* (Köln: Hohenheim, 1981), p. 273. (*Le Pouvoir intellectuel en France* [Paris: Éditions Ramsay, 1979].)

19 Karl W. Deutsch, "Von der Industriegesellschaft zur Informationsgesellschaft," *VG Papers II* pre 80–103. Veröffentlichungsreihe des Internationalen Instituts für vergleichende Gesellschaftsforschung, Wissenschaftszentrum Berlin (March 1980), p. 7.

20 Ellul, *Von der Revolution zur Revolte,* pp. 260ff.

21 See Paul Noack, *Ist die Demokratie noch regierbar?* (München: List Verlag, 1980).

22 See Karl W. Deutsch, "On the Learning Capacity of Large Political Systems," *VG Papers II* RV/77-7. Veröffentlichungsreihe des Internationalen Instituts für vergleichende Gesellschaftsforschung, Wissenschaftszentrum Berlin (August 1977).

23 Fritsch, "Die Überforderung des Staates," pp. 7ff.

24 Deutsch, "Von der Industriegesellschaft zur Informationsgesellschaft," p. 11.

25 C. F. von Weizsäcker, "A Skeptical Contribution," in *On The Creation of a Just World Order: Preferred Worlds for the 1990's,* ed. Saul H. Menlovitz (New York: Free Press, 1975), pp. 111f.

26 Franz Werfel, *Der Stern der Ungeborenen* (Frankfurt/Main: Fischer Taschenbuchausgabe, 1981), pp. 88f.

II / PERSPECTIVES ON

Innovation

5 /

The New Wilderness: Critics as Connoisseurs of Chaos

Geoffrey H. Hartman

The imagination, like certain wild animals, will not breed in captivity.
— George Orwell

Literary criticism, a kind of awareness we carry with us, not only the articulated thing put down on paper and published, but a spirited readiness to discuss, evaluate, and quarrel about whatever is happening in the world of literature — literary criticism as this at once combative and contemplative mix is bound to be in touch with more than literature. Every cultural event butts in and casts its shadow; and the borders once so snobbishly guarded between high art and everything else — journalism, detective fiction, science fiction, soap operas, film, letters — are crossed easily, though they do not cease to exist but haunt the scrupulous critic in subtler, sometimes internalized form. The line between all genres or "orders of discourse" becomes precarious, a fine line; and the very possibility of trespass fades. Is transgressiveness still possible when deviation is the norm? The survival of the fittest invades the realm of taboos, but no taboo seems fit to survive very long.

We can all cite some instances of experiments that blur or transgress boundaries. Robert Lowell's "imitations" efface the distinction between the original text and his translation of it; Truman Capote writes his "nonfiction novel" and Norman Mailer his "truelife novel"; and E. R. Doctorow places real persons and invented characters into the same time frame. Going further back we come on John Hersey's *Hiroshima* and André Malraux's novelistic reportage of the Spanish Civil War in *Man's Hope.* Even biographies are no longer the stodgy things they once were but lively accounts that blend unreserved speculation with stupifying doses of factual detail. Everything tends to be swallowed up, for good or bad, in the "New Journalism," or in the "Maybe" of Lillian Hellman where memory and wishfulness mingle.

When I read John Leonard's typical description of Milan Kundera's *Book of Laughter and Forgetting,* that "calls itself a novel, although it is part fairy tale, part literary criticism, part political tract, part musicology and part autobiography," I feel both encouraged and discouraged. Encouraged, because Leonard recognizes that the issue is not the death of the novel but the freeing up of all kinds of prose. Discouraged, because an amorphous and voracious superprose is emerging, as full of routines and exploits as a circus, and therefore prone to flatten everything into equivalence.

The American novel has scarcely recovered from Nathanael West, when there's Thomas Pynchon with an appetite for comic routines as magical as Moses's rod that devours all others. Under the influence of the media, moreover—described as a "black hole" by certain French sociologists—as push comes to shove, so blur becomes mash. We can still call Al Saperstein's *Mother Kills Self and Kids* a novel, yet it is also an overflow sociological tract (somewhat like Doctorow's *The Book of Daniel*) on the persistence in America of Miss Lonelyhearts; and it is certainly an Anatomy of Melancholy. Saperstein depicts a culture that does everything to inspire a belief in privacy or inwardness, but only the better to rape you. It turns into a grim folktale about a mirror-oriented, self-consuming, necrophiliac society.

Let me continue in this vein, still talking about fiction rather than criticism: about the environment in which criticism presently tries to stay alive. The prose of our best novelists is as fast, embracing, and abrasive as John Donne's *Sermons.* It is polyphonic despite or within its monologue, its confessional stream of words. (There are "sinews in thy milk," Donne remarked of God's style in Scripture.) The interlace of faction and fiction, of some primary source — Scripture or newspaper account or social document — and derived text, that is, novel or artifact, yields the same dimensionality, if not the same authority, as in Donne. In terms of authority, there is only a prophetic sort of clowning or shadowboxing.

Think of Mailer who always puts himself on the line, sparring, taunting, as macho as Hemingway but deliberately renouncing taciturnity. Mailer places himself too near events, as science fiction or other forms of romance place themselves too far. He is always in the bullring, whether it is the six inches of no-man's land between the U.S. Army and the demonstrators in *The Armies of the Night,* or the same six inches between men and women in the orgiastic novels. He is right, though, in remarking that fiction must penetrate the historical account, for events tend to be either too far or too near. "The history is interior . . . ," he says. "No document can give sufficient intimation: the novel must replace history at precisely that point where experience is sufficiently emotional, spiritual, psychical, moral, existential or supernatural to expose the fact that the historian in pursuing the experience would be obliged to quit the clearly demarcated limits of historical inquiry."

John Hersey has recently protested this quitting of clearly demarcated limits: he calls himself the "worried grandpa" of the New Journalism and insists that his *Hiroshima* is documentary reportage and not, in any way, a work of fiction. If we quit the old genre rules, or similar demarcations, how can we escape the situation of those Pulitzer Prize judges taken in by a reporter's fraudulent exposé of "Jimmy," the eight-year-old drug addict? How can we tell reality from reality-fiction? But if Hersey's *Hiroshima* to contemporary sensibilities in a post-Hemingway and journalistic era has the force of fiction as well as the ring of truth, how can we be sure, except through external testimony, such as bringing the interviewees back, or through the proven probity of the writer (his *ethos* in distinction from his *pathos,* the older rhetoricians would say), how can we be sure the events are not, to a degree, fictionalized?

The dilemma becomes more acute when we reflect that the media themselves — photography, film, television — have taught us much about *trucage.* Their realism, like Renaissance picture-space, is an acquired technique. They mean to deceive; and this power of deception is part of the meaning, as it was in the days of Romance. Seeing is only seeing; and the more *see* there is in films, the more color and visual realism, the more conflicted our response. The sophisticated viewer knows too much about technique and *trucage;* while the unsophisticated viewer may experience a similar feeling of unreality coming from the very fact that film must blunt, by its daily iteration, the terrible things it depicts. We sup full of horror when we want; and through countless programs of Action News, even when we do not want. The gulf between seeing and believing has never been wider.[1]

This, then, is our environment, the environment also of the critic; and its confusions are not improved by a conservative reaction that we sense everywhere in and outside the academy. Instead of facing the problem of what criticism can do under these conditions, the conservative reaction makes of literary criticism the last refuge of neoclassical admonitions against mixed genres, against quitting the demaration between criticism and art or criticism and anything else — philosophy, religion, the social sciences.

One quote typical of this mindless conservatism must suffice. In a recent issue of *Novel,* Julian Moynahan calls Northrop Frye and by implication the Yale critics "pod-people . . . many of them dropouts from technical philosophy, or linguistics, or the half-science of sociology," and he wonders how to get us out of "the fair fields of Anglo-American literary study."

Now even I half-sympathize with the man — how nice if criticism were neoclassically separate and pure: fiction here and criticism there and journalism here and social sciences there, and so forth. But this separatism was never more than partial, even in the so-called neoclassical period; and it will prove to be, at most, an episode in the history of art, spurred by a naive view of realism and scientific objectivity. For not only does literary criticism have its own boundary problems today, not only are interesting new kinds of commentary emerging, but the line between original text and critical commentary may always have been precarious, at least not as distinct as the conservative scholar holds it to be. The rabbis and church fathers, as well as the later kabbalists, even when they thought they were honoring the literal sense of Scripture, were producing inventive interpretations, ingenious adjustments to received and authoritative truth under the pressure of daily events that could not easily be reconciled with that truth. They stuck to the text: it was part of their sacred marriage. Gershom Scholem's work has taught us how Jewish mysticism, at least, was an extraordinary "exegetical" response to history, to the harsh contemporary reality that had to be harmonized with the promise in the Bible. Sainte-Beuve puts it most succinctly when he remarked of Ballanche's prose epic, *Orpheus,* based on Vico's reanimation of the dry bones of Roman Law: "The commentary has entered the text."

I am not trying to explain away the offense of modern commentary, of Jacques Derrida in *Glas* or Roland Barthes in *S/Z* (his study of Balzac), of Ihab Hassan's paracriticism or Maurice Blanchot's self-reflective critical narratives, or Heidegger's ruminations or Harold Bloom's "misreadings" or — to add novels that unfold a synthetic poem — Nabokov's *Pale Fire* and D. M. Thomas's *The White Hotel.* These works of scholarship, or fiction based on scholarship, have recognized their affinity with an older tradition of exegesis: they too are crossing the line and merging the expressive force of interpretive commentary with the inspiring, sometimes disruptive, force of the work of art that is the object of the commentary. Whatever distinctions of value and character we wish to make between these writers, they all challenge T. S. Eliot's magisterial pronouncement that there can be no creative criticism.

In *Criticism in the Wilderness* and *Saving the Text* I try to define the symbiosis or tangled relations of literature and literary commentary. I present an argument and tell a story. The argument, to start with that, distinguishes two chief tendencies in criticism. One is comparable to the philosophical method Sartre characterized as a "purifying reflection" and Paul Ricoeur as a hermeneutics of suspicion. This brings to every sacred or received text, to its diction or thought, a scrutiny motivated by the wish to expunge divinity from it, to make literature completely *literae humaniores* — perhaps because only as such is it ours and subject to criticism. The other brings to texts a dangerous enthusiasm, one that allows the possibility of a sympathetic or redemptive contagion between book and reader, to the point where the interest shifts, at least in part, to a new creation: the text about the text, the one produced by critic or commentator.

The story I then tell may be called the historical part of the argument. It shows how the English critical tradition, after the Puritan revolution of the seventeenth century, and by a complex reinforcement that included Jacobinical fears, Popery fears, the impact of French universalism and then of the French Revolution, consolidated itself as a *via media* institution. English critics refused *enthusiasm,* and even smelled it out by a kind of feefofum directed against the non-Englishman: against the esoteric, technical, exhibitionistic, overly earnest — whatever disrupted good conversation. Out of the rigor of that impulse some of the most remarkable British (not only French) literature comes: what is Jane Austen but the flowering of a perpetual reflection on the humane wit of conversation compared to any other form of human display: the dance, duets, cutting a figure, theatricals, the hunt, even reading (in excess)?

There were great energies, there still may be such, in that tradition; but there was also a drift toward gentility; and this gentility, today, so my argument continues, is feefofumming against Hermann the German. I mean the hermeneutic or philosophical criticism that arises in Germany around 1790 and which so greatly tempted Coleridge: that of Schlegel, Hegel, Schiller, Schelling, Schleiermacher.

Nothing divides the two cultures of criticism — Continental and Anglo-American — so much as their attitudes toward "the abominable Hegel."[2] The English tradition, especially, characterizes Hegel as a vampire or bogeyman who sucks facts dry by a "dialectical" method that creates fantastic historical generalizations from a minimum of concrete or researched knowledge. Critics after T. S. Eliot try to save the English mind from such contaminating habits of speculation, or "abstraction" as Yeats called it. But Yeats still regarded philosophies as severe or unconscious poems. Our more academic critics, however, evince a disabling fear of ideas, so that one recent authority actually claims that "most English great poems have little or nothing to say."

As part of my story, I simplify the history of criticism after Arnold by postulating a sequence: first an Arnoldian concordat, which declares that criticism is not inimical to the creative spirit but rather the herald of a new literature of imaginative reason; then a New-Critical reduction of Arnold's position, which agrees that the significant work of art is indeed powerfully and insidiously intelligent but denies the obverse, that there could be a "creative criticism." The critical spirit, Eliot stated, had to be carefully watched lest it usurp upon the creative. Lastly, I claim that we are now in the midst of a reversal that stands the New-Critical reduction on its head by demonstrating that there is such a thing as creative criticism, or a creative element in criticism.

I have to accept the fact, perhaps as a liability, that the concept of a "creative criticism" was circulated in Eliot's time by J. E. Spingarn, who wrote in a well-known essay of 1910 called "The New Criticism" (republished in his *Creative Criticism* of 1917): "Criticism at last can free itself of its age-long self-contempt, now that it may realize that esthetic judgment and artistic creation are instinct with the same vital life. This identity does not sum up the whole life of the complex and difficult art of Criticism; but it is this identity which has been lost sight of and needs most emphasis. . . ." Eliot's testy denial of this "identity" (ultimately derived from Croce's theory of expression) may have been an over-reaction. Let me quote from Mencken's essay of 1919 entitled "Criticism of Criticism." Mencken was for Spingarn, but he glimpsed the truth that creative criticism was hardly a novel concept — it went back at least to the German Romantics. "A professor must have a theory," he begins, "as a dog must have fleas." And he continues, "What [Spingarn] offers is a doctrine borrowed from the Italian, Benedetto Croce, and by Croce filched from Goethe — a doctrine anything but new in the world, even in Goethe's time, but nevertheless buried in forgetfulness. . . ."

Given the swirling polemics of this earlier period, in which

Eliot began his critical career, we have to be cautious and not fall into a propagandistic rather than productive use of what remains a good slogan. Eliot's own criticism, certainly, is larger than his doctrine. Let me clarify, then, without a complex regression to the German Romantics, what is meant by such phrases as "the creative element in criticism."

It is my view that criticism cannot be judged inferior to creative writing unless you accept responsibility for a hierarchic position, a genre theory like that by which the later eighteenth century considered a still life or a Dutch domestic scene inferior to grand historical portraiture. Lowering criticism as a service function, moreover, to practical or pedagogical aims of the most obvious kind, must eventually demoralize us all — if it has not already done so — by allowing the public world, and administrators in our own university world, to view the humanist as a luxury, or at best as the purveyor of a specific skill, that of reading, and (if possible, and it is not always possible) writing. While the English New Criticism still considered literacy as a complex good, among the highest achievements of culture, and while critics like F. R. Leavis even tended to mystify the Cambridge English School as *the* road to literacy, American New Criticism, with a greater though ambivalent respect for science and an imposed commitment to mass education, was gradually forced into a compact that reduced literacy to a technique and the text to a commodity. If, then, the study of literature turned toward France in the 1970s, it was because it had to. This expatriation did not, as with novelists and poets of the 1920s, include England; it turned the European continent against England and tried by this means to recover from the involuntary decline of the gentleman scholar, as from the creation of a corps of amateur technicians, employees of a society that cared less for criticism and culture than for scientific or fiscal accountability.

The result has not been happy. We face an increasingly polarized situation. The genteel tradition, too defensive, has little to offer except the old charges: that this newest criticism is unintelligible and that it will corrupt the prose manners of the young. Arnold lives; but too many Arnoldian epigones cannot conceive that criticism is a comparative and historically varied activity with its own inner dialectic. They are no doubt the moral majority, but they depress themselves — and us — by insisting on a single kind of "conversational" decorum. Yet those who have turned to Continental thought or the *sciences humaines* have also fallen into reductive habits. A new species of coterie writing has emerged, restricted in its range and terminology. It seems unable to open itself to a past, that is, to the Arnoldian tradition still with us; it remains indulgently fixed on a few reiterated texts. Worst of all, it can be scientistic instead of scientific, or is unable to transmit its findings in a form that may be tested — tested, I mean, by a more than mechanical application, tested on art outside the restricted canon, and by criteria that are not only diagrammatic but also, in the broad sense, ethical. Thus the theory and the practice of criticism, instead of moving closer, instead of interacting, collide in a phobic manner.

Practical criticism never grew up. As the university expanded and disciplines proliferated, the old desire for faith and commitment began to reassert itself against the critical spirit. This reaction was inevitable because criticism was denied any creative potential, and because American society shifted the burden of basic education to the literary humanists, who were expected to find the most economical tools to do the job, and therefore became tools themselves.

Science was largely exempt from this burden or charge; not intrinsically, of course, but insofar as it was recognized that science had to have an advanced theoretical component in addition to the applied or practical dimension. That scholarship or critical commentary should have this advanced component, that one might distinguish properly, in this regard, between an Academy and a School, was never denied by a specific doctrine. Yet this combination — the prestige of science, the economic drift that makes even learning a commodity, and secularization, which removed the Bible and then every canonical text as a shared book in the curriculum, a book, like nature's own, whose secrets might be disclosed only by a higher or "scientific" learning — these converging tendencies became, in their very inchoate, inarticulate specificity, the prison whose corner we occupy. Out of this corner I too write; and what I write remains practical criticism, though

I have sought to enlarge it, to insist on a new *praxis* that would not neglect theory or a reflection on the social and institutional context.

Let me now take up in order two objections to this enlarged and more reflective practical criticism. The objections, which often go together, are, first, that it flouts common sense, that its very method of close and rigorous reading dehumanizes; second, that it is a new formalism, avoiding or losing touch with social issues. (A third objection, which impugns the effectiveness and sometimes the good faith of this criticism, charging its practitioners with playing the market rather than truly attacking socioeconomic realities, is a variant of the second. However facile, this charge should be taken up separately, because it entails a longer discussion than I give later about the relation of "high" or university culture to mass culture.)

I. COMMON SENSE

Most of the hostile critics belong to the Common-Sense School. They know when they order a ham sandwich they are going to get a ham sandwich — and should they be served a pastrami special they don't attribute it to the complexities or indeterminacies of language but to getting someone else's order mistakenly. Hence, whatever view they hold about the way literature is written, the Common-Sense School insists that *criticism* should be written as if one were ordering a ham sandwich. They always know what they want, or what literature wants of them. Intentions are clear or should be made as clear as is humanly possible. It is therefore disturbing to this School that critics should wish to have their own styles, let alone that they should claim to be "creative." (Prose standards exist, of course, based roughly on what seems clear to any reasonable person, clear enough to be argued with and eventually reduced to a consensus.) They cannot accept that critics should hunger for something other than ordinary language, that critics should interpose a style of their own and complicate their function, which is to make the work of art accessible.[3]

Instead of thinking about what is being challenged — their

conception of a near-absolute separation between literary and literary-critical discourse, or between literature and commentary —the Common-Sense School goes on the attack. Gerald Graff and Frederic Crews accuse contemporary theorists of wishing to write in a style in which the truth cannot be told, or one that evades argument.[4] Essays that make the readers work too hard, or deflect them from getting their money's worth in the form of the literary-critical equivalent of the ham sandwich, are destructive of an enterprise that intends to keep within the bounds of Common Sense. The stylish critics are merely shielding themselves from being argued with—say those who claim to know what argument is, despite the age-old dispute between *ratio* and *oratio,* or logic and rhetoric.

It does not require a deep look into past history to see that the position of the Common-Sense School is historically naive. Its partisans overlook the era of structuralism, because structuralism was in part a critique of "reasoning" or "argument" based on culture-bound notions of common sense—notions preeminently French and English and going back to British empiricism of the eighteenth century. They forget that structuralism tried to place the "common nature" of man on a new basis, broader than the prestige attached to Western, "enlightened" cultures.

They also forget that poststructural theory is questioning structuralism's reliance on such "universals" as binary opposition. The attempt to forge a new, nonelitist sense of the "common nature" of man—demonstrating the functional similarity of sophisticated analytic thought and primitive classification—is now felt to be reductive as well as redemptive. For the diagrammatic view of literature encouraged by the structuralist method suggests a totalized form of understanding too much like Hegel's Absolute Knowledge, though purged of Hegel's dialectical and historical gymnastics.

Whether there might still be a total form of understanding— modern civilization being fragmentary rather than holistic—is a principle theme in Georg Lukács's *Theory of the Novel* (1920, though written circa 1915). Today the epic, Lukács states, is no longer a viable form insofar as it reflects "Greek" integration. The novel, however, with its large, if unintegrated, scope inherits the epic's strength. Lukács adopts both Hegel's view of the organic, balanced nature of Greek culture and the possibility that our un-Greek, i.e., problematic and unbalanced, world could achieve a holistic perspective at the level of science or philosophical method. "Theory" can have integrity, even if its subject, the novel, cannot achieve cosmic or cultural integration. In *History and Class Consciousness* (1923), totality moves still closer to a crucially utopian perspective: a point of view from which to overcome the fragmentary, fetishistic, and reified nature of capitalist societies. Now totality is clearly a mental need independent of the particular culture, and always retrieving lost unity.[5]

Yet totality as a political scheme—totalitarianism—has made us suspicious of all systematic thought as it rationalizes what is and what is not—I mean as it aspires to the total intelligibility of history or envisions an ultimate order. So Plato and Hegel and every so-called "metaphysical" thinker comes under attack. In England and America, though, this attack too often plays into the hands of an omnipresent anti-intellectualism. We rarely find, in these countries, that merging of philosophical, philological, and political concerns so powerfully exemplified in Nietzsche, Lukács, and Heidegger. We owe something to Derrida and deconstruction, if only because they have kept the scandal of these writers, and even of metaphysics, before us. The rethinking of metaphysics, or what it might mean to make an end of such philosophies, creates tremors that shift the very concept of philosophy toward a denial of the possibility of closure in any sphere of thought. This denial is then exemplified by the method of close reading now known as deconstruction, which keeps metaphysics alive by an interminable reflection on end-terms. Metaphysics, which insists on an end beyond the end, is the joker in any politico-philosophical speculation that wishes to "totalize" thought or history.

Thus the alarmed tone of those who think that poststructural critics are destroying common sense or the possibility of shared and rational discourse may be attributed to their wish to elide history and return to the *status quo ante*—to the empiricism criticized not only by structuralist and Marxist, but by all those who, like Heidegger[6] or Empson, are aware of the complex nature of words. The stones our modern purists cast are those of a reasoning that is supposedly more humane than quasi-philosophical and linguistic wrangling. While no one should object to the preference of the Common-Sense School for one mode of argumentation over another, by exercizing this preference blindly, Graff and Crews, and even M. H. Abrams and Wayne Booth, simplify the historical moment in which literary theory emerges manifestly as theory: roughly the 1920–1970 period, when philosophies of language interact with political and scientific currents that ponder the issue of totality.

An aside. I do not claim that common sense cannot be effective. Only that the Common-Sense School is insensitive to its own vulnerability. George Orwell, to choose an exemplary writer, never abandons common sense in his essays, and he uses every possible weapon against the political lie and the ruthless generalization. Yet he knows that authoritarian pressures may cause common sense to give way. Organized lying can come to seem like common sense, and organized lying is not a temporary expedient for a totalitarianism which demands "the continuous alteration of the past." A schizophrenic system of thought is developed, says Orwell, in which common sense holds good in everyday life and some sectors of science but is routinely disregarded by politicians, historians, and sociologists. Prose especially, he adds, cannot survive when the independent writer is attacked for ivory-towerism or exhibitionism or clinging, against history, to unjustified privileges. In the long view, Orwell concludes, it is not the manipulators of the press, or the film magnates, or bureaucrats that are the worst symptom but a "weakening of the desire for liberty among the intellectuals" ("The Prevention of Literature," 1946).

II. THEORY AND HISTORY

While the Common-Sense School denies, often tacitly, the heterogeneity of discourse, the Social School charges literary theorists with impoverishing the concreteness of human and historical reality. Theory, with the possible exception of Marxism, is taken to be essentially antihistorical. Yet theory, in the period we are considering, is actually a critique of historical kinds of reasoning and branches out in two quite different, if related, directions.

Structuralism may indeed be antihistorical, even antihumanistic, insofar as "humanism" and "history" are imbued with privileged Western ideas. The centrality of self or subject may then be challenged—structuralism is no different in this regard than the "Eastern" world-view presented, for example, in Malraux's influential *The Temptation of the West* or in Heidegger's focus on Being over beings, his overcoming of Western ontology. Malraux interprets history-writing as the West's apologia for missionary and colonizing activities—part of its *Kulturpolitik*. But Malraux adds the wrinkle that Western self-assertion brings on its own fever of self-transcendence: the relentless interrogation, namely, of every concept and institution, until "God is dead" and even "Man" (or ego-centered Western religion) must eventually suffer that fate. This Western form of ascetic self-purgation, Malraux insists—following Nietzsche's *Genealogy of Morals*—is perhaps even more scarring than that of the East.

Theory, then, suspicious of history-writing, wants no truck with rightist or leftist or Hegelian or Marxist philosophies. It knows that historical reflection succumbs to dogma or becomes, willy-nilly, propaganda. But are we not stuck with history in this form? Can we really pretend to leap clear of a situation that has prevailed so long that it is in our language and continues to shape even the most radical political schemes?

Theory therefore also goes in a different direction, and considers the fact that historical claims (genealogical or Messianic) of legitimacy are the way authority is rationalized—that is, talks about itself. Hence the question is no longer, can we deliver truth from propaganda or from propagandistic sorts of history, but rather, can anything function as a corrective for this condition? If the language we live with is both words and the Word (by Word I mean the propagandistic or messianic *logos*), then there is no exit toward pure secularism on the one hand, or toward lost and sacred truth on the other. We must continue to live in the sacred jungle of a heterogeneous language.

Out of this impasse, however, a new consciousness arises.

Theory, also *in* language, is not so much antihistorical as deconstructive: it lives within what it criticizes and tries to isolate certain antibodies. One of these is art, which seems to have the potential to resist ideologies while being deeply immersed in convention. Art may simply become a counterideology, of course. But there are attempts to make theory, especially the theory of art, anti-ideological in essence. We see this both in Malraux and in the formalists. The latter claim that the specific content of art is mainly a "device" motivating the artist's struggle with a world of forms imposed by society or pastmasters. Malraux talks of the lucidity of art in the face of these various seductions and impositions: both modern and primitive nonrepresentational art, for example, is a making rather than a matching, an iconoclastic stylization that breaks with the realm of appearance—with the tyranny of nature or convention. Malraux's achievement is to have recognized a link between art's modern and its ancient function. That function is reticence, cunning, resistance—against whatever is perceived to be fate. And, at present, propaganda or propagandistic versions of history are fate.

In this light, too, the vexed question of the artifact's indeterminacy, polysemy, or even "unreadability" begins to make a kind of sense. These are heavy terms and each is ensconced in its own system. Whatever core of truth may lodge in such terms, their motive is again to defend art against easy types of readerly or ideological accommodation. The "intransigence of theory" recommended by Theodor Adorno, the "A poem should not mean / But be" of the New Criticism, Mikhail Bakhtin's "polyphony," or the various concepts—"pleasure," "bliss," "drift"—shored by Roland Barthes against some ultimate jargon, these very different notions link up to affirm "something both revolutionary and asocial which cannot be taken over by any collectivity, any mentality, any ideolect" (*The Pleasure of the Text*). Each jargon or fiction, Barthes also writes, "fights for hegemony; if power is on its side, it spreads everywhere in the general and daily occurrences of social life, it becomes *doxa*, nature . . . the supposedly apolitical jargon of politicians, of agents of the State, of the Media, of conversation. . . ."[7]

Our experience of modern propaganda methods, their ability to program or brainwash entire nations, is as frightening, in its way, as the modern superweapons. Not accidentally did Malraux and also Walter Benjamin construct a theory that both questioned and asserted art's power to withstand political appropriation. The formalists, encompassed by Soviet ideological pressures, and the New Critics, in the midst of the 1930s turmoil, also tried to save art from ideology without having to fall back on an art for art's sake or aestheticist position. The dictatorship of the propagandists, their manipulation not only of the mass media but also of scholarship, became a reality in Nazi Germany and Stalinist Russia, and is the one historical fact that must not be forgotten in any general consideration of the emergence of literary theory as increasingly anti-ideological.[8]

It was not Malraux, of course, but the Frankfurt School that, in the wake of fascism, alerted us to the basic concepts of art theory in a technological and propagandistic age. (We know Malraux read Benjamin's essay of 1936, "The Work of Art in the Era of Mechanical Reproduction" before writing his *Psychology of Art*.) Often using Hegel against Hegel to evolve a "negative" dialectic, or an unprogressive philosophy of history, these thinkers emphasized the nonconformist character of intellectual and artistic achievement. Art is that which cannot be *gleichgeschaltet* or *aufgehoben*—which cannot have only one dimension. Nor can philosophy, properly understood. The scrupulous sociological analyses developed by Theodor Adorno, Max Horkheimer, and Hannah Arendt did not disconnect the political question: they engaged it at a level where every flat and shallow literalism, every political cliché, was exposed. Political appropriation, they showed, was not forceful in itself; it did not have, to back it up, a special logic, even if "dialectical materialism" came closest: it merely exaggerated the danger of internal conflict and suggested that, at the limit, the only controlling and simplifying force would be . . . War. That leveling tendency, as Barthes suggests, can also assume a deceptively urbane aspect, an insidious intellectual respectability, so that vigilance is required even when no overt political terror is nigh. The tenet of the uniformity of nature, for example, inherited from the Enlightenment, was eventually directed by totalitarian regimes and philosophies to sinister uses—"sinister unifying" is Kenneth Burke's phrase.[9]

The monolingualism that afflicts technologically advanced democracies may also have a sinister effect, especially if it depicts literacy as merely a skill: something teachable without a personal immersion in the literature of the language. Substituting technical or bureaucratic jargon for the imaginative creole that could arise from the jostlings of street language against standard language, or from competing vernaculars learnt through their respective traditions — whether oral or written — this skill-oriented approach leads to fatal political simplifications as well as to a disastrous impoverishment of the culture. For all the great cultures we know of have had a mixed linguistic inheritance and a developed literature that is always revising and recasting its body of variant stories. In these stories, in these literatures, there is no overall unity: their structure is that of a stratified, precarious assemblage whose gloss or consistency is often undone by the grain that continues to show through, by the insubordinate play of language against meaning, by an explosive proliferation of legend and commentary that no treaty can entirely stop. To try to stop it by doctrinal means, whether religious, political, or aesthetic, is an act of repression.

The results of such a repression, even if civilized — that is, performed in the name of democratic concepts of order, assimilation, and educability — are clear. In East London, as in some inner cities of America, we find not hunger strikes but language strikes: the young adults there refuse to speak the dominant tongue. They refuse its passwords however good the latter may be, however socializing and potentially nourishing. The tragedy here is not only that politicizing a language deprives youngsters of an education, of their redemption from inarticulateness in all areas; the tragedy is also that to strike language starves language, making it as instrumentalized as the tyrannous discourse the strikers resist. Nothing is more disheartening to those who know the educative and liberating force of the "school of tongues" we call literature than political types of rhetoric which kill off the possibility not only of agreement but also of vigorously debated forms of speech.

The objections, then, of the Historical School or the Common-Sense School have no cogency. But where there's smoke there's fire; and the real problem of contemporary movements in criticism is that there is too much smoke in the form of a variety of insubordinate concepts, all of which seek to counter, instinctively or methodically, the danger of a dictated language.[10]

What, in closing, can I suggest? Let us recognize that the claims of the Enlightenment, or of humanism, were severely damaged by the two world wars. The gassing, bombing, and desperate trench warfare of the First World War made it clear that the era of individual heroism was in jeopardy, that destiny was passing into the hands of those who held the technological advantage and could use it for purposes of destruction. The rise of totalitarianism, leading to the Second World War and the Holocaust, confirmed our worst fears. "Suddenly it becomes evident," writes Hannah Arendt in *The Origins of Totalitarianism,* "that things which for thousands of years the human imagination had banished to a realm beyond human competence can be manufactured right here on earth, that hell and purgatory, and even a shadow of their perpetual duration can be established by the most modern methods of destruction and therapy." Mastery over nature extended itself to thought-control and to a program of indoctrination so thorough and successful that an entire people was treated not as a part of humanity but as animals — lice, vermin — to be exterminated. Philosophy was powerless before these events, except that social thinkers, fortified by Freud's study of group psychology, saw in Fascism the signs of a displaced religious mania. But this only deepened the perplexity, because now, while humanism had failed as a political philosophy, the return to religion was also cut off. We remembered the bloody history of religious politics which was supposed to have been ended by the "sweet science" of humanist philosophies of toleration, and we saw that the messianic passions were merely channelled into political religions or sporadic evangelical cults. Deconstruction, and similar movements of verbal hygiene, would have arisen, I believe, even without a technical basis in linguistics or semiotics: they mark the crater left by the demise of humanism, and they denounce all quasi-religious rhetoric that rushes unthinkingly into that void. Deconstruction is a theory of language rather than a philosophy of life, not because it is "nihilistic," but because it has seen how language can be manipulated and overdetermined.

And *that* it can be manipulated, for good or bad, is not avoidable: the so-called arbitrariness of the sign points once again to the free will of the users of language, placing the responsibility for the scrupulous reception and production of words on each person, whatever the odds.

This emphasis too is misleading; for language, especially literary language, has its own life, its own way of surviving mechanical or propagandistic impositions. "Poetry is the foreknowledge of criticism," Paul de Man has said: what deconstructionists do is read so closely that a text opens again and reveals both the fearful or joyous energies of language and the tricks closing them off. These tricks may be internal, the artist's own defenses, or external, the premature assimilation of a book by normative commentary. We do not have to be sophisticated theorists to question a text's monologic life, apposing to its pathos irony and distance, seeing through its apparent purity to material or metaphorical residues, countering insidious attempts to homogenize meaning while disclosing, for all to mark, complex resonances, hiatuses, and equivocations.

Our very commitment to literacy and mass education makes it imperative that we respect the labor involved in reading and writing, the stresses and strains of acculturation and of balancing particularity against principles of order. Learning is painful as well as pleasurable; and learning is closely associated with writing and rewriting—with the malaise of never achieving a definitive or more than questioning way of stating things.

If the study of literature remains disputed and problematic, it is precisely because there cannot be an "absolute" but only a "standard" prose, a language of convenience. This language is a substitute Latin, an artificial and ideal diction that masquerades as a vernacular. We need it to purify the dialects around us, to achieve a degree of shared and stable speech, but it has only provisional authority and should never stifle linguistic inventiveness. There must always be a tension between difficult or inventive (including "street") modes of speech, and familiar, conversational ones. This tension between intelligiblity and difficulty, as between ordinary and extraordinary language, may be the only *literary* constant in any age. To repress or deny that tension is to impoverish the past, cheat the present, and cheapen the ideal of literacy itself.

NOTES

1   See Jean Baudrillard on the dominance of simulacra in "Consumer Society," and concerning the media, "Requiem for the Media" in *For a Critique of the Political Economy of the Sign* (St. Louis: Telos Press, 1980); original French edition published in 1972. The most terrifying account of the attrition of concreteness and practical life because of the advertising or consumerist character of mass culture is found in the unpublished continuation of the chapter on the Culture Industry in *Dialectics of the Enlightenment* by Horkheimer and Adorno. This continuation, "Das Schema der Massenkultur," is now printed for the first time in Adorno's *Gesammelte Schriften* (Frankfurt/Main: Suhrkamp Verlag, 1981) 3: 299–335.

2   The phrase, adopted by William Pritchard, was coined by William James.

3   But why is it not accessible of itself? If we follow the logic of the Common-Sense School, critics are expendable. They simply bring the work of art to our attention and make it easier for us to talk about it. If there have been changes in the language or in historical presuppositions, they point them out — they put the work "in context." Yet this perfectly reasonable activity is not as simple as it may appear. For can we, in fact, transcend our own cultural horizon and recover that of the work of art being explained? And can that work be translated into a language not its own and so "opened up"? These very questions, solved in passing or "in practice" by the Common Sense School, are precisely the locus of the more philosophical sort of critic.

Let me grant, nevertheless, that there is a convincing tradition of "practical criticism," one as forceful as pragmatic politics. The achievements of this tradition are limited but they are real; and in this tradition what relation critical style has to literary style is a question that does not have to be raised. Consequently, when the "theory-mad" critic insists that criticism itself should be read closely, as if it had a style, and when, further, some critics allow themselves a style akin to philosophy or to literature, the Common-Sense School is dismayed. Orders of discourse are being mixed. Where will this confusion end?

4   Recent Graff essays, however, have given up sniping at style and recognized one question raised by theoretically oriented criticism. Graff has become sensitive to the issue of protecting ideas from distortive, often propagandistic use (discussed below) because that is an

ethical matter and because he feels at risk in wishing to reach a wide, and not exclusively university, audience. The experiment of mass education has aggravated the problem (first exposed by Plato's comment on written expression generally) that the diffusion of ideas dilutes their context or intent or any form of "immanent" control.

5 A discussion of totality and methodological perspective ("totalization") is found in Fredric Jameson's *The Political Unconscious* (Ithaca: Cornell University Press, 1981), pp. 52ff., 190ff. For a critique of Lukács's theory, see Paul de Man, *Blindness and Insight* (New York: Oxford University Press, 1971), ch. 4. De Man stresses the category of temporality as that which causes the totalizing form to collapse. Cf. also his ch. 2, p. 32: "Understanding can be called complete only when it becomes aware of its own temporal predicament and realizes that the horizon within which the totalization can take place is time itself. The act of understanding is a temporal act that has its own history, but this history forever eludes totalization." A previous critique of Lukàcs, based on his tendency to premature totalization (and his neglect of historical "mediations") is given by Jean-Paul Sartre in *Search for a Method,* trans. Hazel Barnes (New York: Alfred A. Knopf, 1963). It should be noted, however, that the early Lukács was following through Wilhelm Dilthey's "Begriffsbestimmung der Geisteswissenschaften," that is, the attempt to define off the human ("moral") sciences from the natural sciences through, especially, the criteria of a "totality" or "relationality" that remained an experience ("Erlebnis") because of the way historical process creatively built up centers and convergencies. According to Dilthey the study of society and history was the last to be emancipated from servitude to metaphysics. A new concept of totality had to be won. "Nicht die Annahme eines starren a priori unseres Erkenntnisvermögens, sondern allein Entwicklungsgeschichte, welche von der Totalität unseres Wesens ausgeht, kann die Fragen beantworten, die wir alle an die Philosophie zu richten haben," he wrote in 1873; cf. his Berlin Academy lectures (circa 1905-1910) on the "Aufbau" or construction of the historical perspective in the humanities. On Northrop Frye's concept of "total form," see Geoffrey Hartman, *Beyond Formalism* (New Haven: Yale University Press, 1970), pp. 13-17 and 28-31.

6 Critiques of structuralism often evoke Heidegger. He reads closely and relentlessly the Pre-Socratic thinkers on the possibility of a shared logos. Their gnomic and fragmentary pronouncements are set against Plato's dialogues which he considers as deceiving monologues: not truly dialogic, but rather in the service of an ideal sort of totalitarianism. Heidegger discloses the dark verbal passages that lead, or do not lead, from *doxa* to *episteme,* from received or institutionalized opinion to assured knowledge of Being. "Although the

logos holds forever," Heraclitus wrote, "men fail to understand, both before hearing it and once they have heard." "Although the *logos* is shared, most live as if thought were a private procession." The latest editor of Heraclitus, Charles H. Kahn (*The Art and Thought of Heraclitus* [Cambridge: Cambridge University Press, 1979]), tells us in his first note that *logos* may have the following meanings: account, saying, speech, discourse, statement, report, explanation, reason, principle, esteem, reputation, collection, enumeration, ratio, proportion. The word *logos* is no more stable than other words.

Heidegger replays the controversy between Socrates and the sophists to suggest that Plato was a supersophist rather than a savior, and his Heaven of Ideas a vain attempt to create a stability beyond language. The Ideas, we would now say, are just a metalanguage, or wishfully institute its possibility. The Platonic dialogues, therefore, rehearse the condition they deny. They do not get beyond *antilogia,* that is, the Sophists' skill in showing that any statement could have a counterstatement, that in any issue the two sides could be worked up into equally powerful solicitations, so that judicially or controversially an *aporia* would ensue. Plato's effort discloses the abstract force of questioning as such, or the force of rhetoric as such, and only lights up the disastrous schism that divides language from Being and so makes it appear *bodenlos,* ungroundable.

7   There are problems, of course, with theory as a *project* of the sort I have described. It could turn out to be futile or utopian or both. As Kraus suggested of psychoanalysis: is it the illness it pretends to cure? Wishing, for example, to rid language of clichés and slogans, it introduces its own jargon; seeking to be rigorous and purifying, it mimics the "purity" of doctrinaire positions. Even if theory overcomes that verbal deficit, or develops a mode of expression that does not simply add to the burdens of language—can it do more than trace out, again and again, the old ideal of *theoria* as *Anschauung*: the possibility, that is, of attaining a vantage point (a *topos noetos*) from which all mediations become perceptible, and give way to a more primal, now recovered, "unmediated" concept?

8   After writing this I came across Jacobo Timerman's *Prisoner Without a Name, Cell Without a Number* (New York: Alfred A. Knopf, 1981). Both the role of "historical" justification and the mechanism of interrogation he describes show once more how the fantasy of thought-control operates, nightmarishly, in totalitarian regimes. This fantasy, which may be a by-product of messianism, is at once frustrated and exacerbated by the existence of the media. The media, as an arm of totalitarianism, offer the possibility of thought-control; yet the media themselves cannot be totally manipulated, as the case of Timerman and *La Opinión* shows. After reading Timerman I feel

like entitling this essay "The Critic as Jew and Joker," but quote instead the following extracts on the attempt to "rationalize" history, on what happens when that attempt fails and interrogation breaks down, and finally on the ambition of thought-control in totalitarian nations. "While incarcerated in the clandestine prison known as Puesto Vasco, I was asked by an interrogator if I know a (previously mentioned) journalist. The interrogator was proud of having tortured him. He spoke freely, knowing that he enjoyed impunity, convinced of his mission and never doubting that history would justify it" (p. 101). "The interrogator always seems to feel that he can succeed in modifying the will of the interrogated. But in the case of Jews being interrogated, there comes a moment when one can perceive that the interrogator has lost all hope. And that moment coincides with a shift from general topics to the theme of the Jew, the Jewish personality . . ." (p. 68). "The semantics [i.e., the way language is manipulated] of the three governing factions that rule Argentina . . . constitutes one of the oldest processes in political practice. In essence, this is not unprecedented, considering the accumulated experience of fascism and communism with propaganda, slogans, and the structuring of a reality contradicting every step of the way to actual events" (p. 24).

9 Feminist criticism—a large subject—may also be part of this protest against the "uniformity of nature," insofar as the concept denies particularity to woman's experience. The problem besetting feminist criticism is not unlike Lukács's in *Theory of the Novel*. Include, for example, "androgyny" in Lukács's or Hegel's vision of wholeness, and you face the question of the historical suppression and then sidelining of woman's experience. That experience is now as formally fragmented or unintegrated as the world reflected by the novel. It is moving to read in Carolyn Heilbrun's *Reinventing Womanhood* (New York: W. W. Norton, 1979) how recent feminist scholars have "wrestled with the angel of reinterpretation, refusing to desist until they had wrested from the angel the blessing from the female past upon the female future" (p. 94).

Kenneth Burke deserves special mention because of his position that the critic is necessarily a "propagandist" who keeps the fact of propaganda before us in order to contribute to "a change in allegiance to the symbols of authority." See, especially, *Attitudes toward History* (Boston: Beacon Press, 1961), pp. 234ff.; and cf. Cleanth Brooks on Burke in ch. 3, "Metaphysical Poetry and Propaganda Art," of *Modern Poetry and the Tradition* (Chapel Hill: University of North Carolina Press, 1939). This change should come through some sort of "linguistic action" exerted by artist or critic. Burke continually redefines his concept of linguistic action and in so doing produces a large body of engaged social and rhetorical criticism, not only anticipating much in American sociology (itself increasingly influenced by the Frankfurt School) but also creating a freewheeling terminological *oeuvre* as powerful and varied as that of later French writers (Roland Barthes, for example). Yet despite his comprehensive perspective, he remains Coleridgean in being unable to commit his thought to a single theory of linguistic action.

10 Since Heidegger, no one, with the possible exception of Derrida, has succeeded in disclosing a focus to subsume these competing notions. And even Heidegger, in Adorno's view, is guilty of "jargon." (See Adorno's book on Heidegger's "Jargon der Eigentlichkeit.") In the 1930s the "Collège de sociologie" (Caillois, Leiris, Bataille, et al.) began to reappraise the persistence of cosmic feelings and the desire for holistic structures, in religions and after-religions. But the work of that informal group was cut short by the war of 1939. (See Denis Hollier, ed., *Le Collège de sociologie, 1937–1939.* [Paris: Éditions Gallimard, 1979].) Gadamer's magisterial *Method and Truth* is our best propadeutic, from a historical point of view; Hirsch's *Validity in Interpretation* the Urizenic response that reveals how menacing the present, disorderly situation is felt to be. Given this disorder, this wilderness, we are tempted to welcome the purifiers once more, logicians or quasilogicians whose dry or silly wit shames our confusion.

6 /

The Joys and Sorrows
of Literary Theory

Ralph Cohen

I call this essay "The Joys and Sorrows of Literary Theory" because literary theory is a deliberate form of human action, of writing, and all such actions have consequences that range from joy to sorrow for the actors and the audience. My allusion to *The Joy of Sex* and *The Sorrows of Young Werther* is neither accidental nor arbitrary. The pleasures of the text and the anxiety of deconstruction are but two aspects of modern theory, but they do serve to indicate the passion with which theorists write theory. Roland Barthes has described the different pleasures of a text, including those of reading and writing theoretical texts.[1] Such pleasures arouse and express desires with regard to the nature, methods, and aims of writing; no one theory, whether erotic, Marxist, or phenomenological, has come to dominate our thinking about writing. But it is apparent that the multifariousness of theoretical writing has made our time especially cognizant of theoretical formulations.

There are formalist theories, Freudian theories, phenomenological, hermeneutical, historical, semiotic, and genre theories; there are structuralist and deconstructuralist theories, aesthetics of reception, reader response, and speech act theories; there are sociological, anthropological, and Marxist theories; there are affective, institutional, contextual, procedural, archetypal, and Jungian theories; there is a Marxist-Freudian-reader response theory, and there is a hermeneutical-phenomenological-historical aesthetics of reception theory.

I do not take delight in this disorder, but I do wish to suggest that each theory, being an attempt to order some aspects of literature, becomes part of a larger theoretical framework that is far from complete. In this essay I sketch a historical map of contemporary theory, indicating why it has become prominent, what kind of literary studies it has undertaken, what kind of unity or disunity it reveals, what are its triumphs and failures, and what types of exploration we still need to undertake.

Inevitably my map shall be incomplete—not because I do not have time to make it complete, and not because I introduce my biases in drawing the boundaries or formulating problems—but because living among the theories I describe I can only speculate about where they lead, what their dominant features will prove to be, which will be absorbed, which dissolved, which preserved. Human actions, as we know, often have consequences far different from those intended by the actors. But I shall try to minimize my difficulties in this historical account by considering theory not merely as a form of human action but of such controversial actions as are involved in dialogues, arguments, agreements, and disagreements.

I shall try to answer such queries as, why theories which clearly have as their aim the propagation of values about the ends of writing, of interpretation, of literary systems and their relation to other kinds of systems, why such theories which are addressed to all literate members of a society become so technical that they estrange members of the very group they aim to serve. And why it is that literary theories no less than poems are subject to transactions with readers who help construct their meanings. Contemporary theorists have moved from broad questions, such as the nature of interpretation, to narrower questions, such as the nature of the reader or of reading, to help remove the impasses of the original inquiry. I shall conclude, therefore, with directions for what I take to be still narrower but necessary inquiries.

For our time, theorizing may be understood as an effort to systematize interpretation by disentangling the problems that were implicit in formal analysis. For example, theorists raised basic questions about poetic analysis by inquiring not into the specific analyses of particular poems but into the subject matter of literature, which meant inquiring into the shared structure of poems and the nature of literature. Were poems different in kind from biographies or journalistic accounts? Was Gibbon's *Decline and Fall* literature? Ought literature to be confined to self-referential, to imaginative works that were considered "autonomous"? Theorists raised these questions from within the discipline because groups within the profession insisted that the literary canon was the result of an undemocratic aim in teaching "literature," or a consequence of the fact that the human mind operated in certain binary oppositions.

The *desire to theorize* developed from a dissatisfaction with particular empirical analyses, and it moved in two directions. On the one hand, it led to speculations beyond the empirical, speculations that related it to all art. On the other, it led to a more precise use of the empirical, what some theorists identified as a more "scientific" methodology, by grounding it in scientific, linguistic, or psychological assumptions. The desire for theory can be understood as part of a more general search for the origins of our assumptions. Theory has become for us a dramatic spectacle, and Kenneth Burke's dramatistic terms are philologically appropriate because the term "theory" is related to "theatre," to "speculation," to "spectacle."[2] Finally, the desire to theorize was a desire to move beyond the limits of a single discipline, to reach for a literary study that could be made part of a general humanistic inquiry.

Indeed, in other humanistic disciplines, scholars concerned themselves with many of the same problems that led literary critics to turn to theoretical explanations. When Clifford Geertz, the anthropologist, described and analyzed a Balinese cockfight, he was interpreting another culture in his own language; his task engaged a number of the problems that confronted the literary critic, and he recognized this. To what extent did he, as an American anthropologist, distort what he saw because of his Western prejudices, and by the fact that he had to describe behavior in a language that had connotations from a different culture? When

Thomas Kuhn analyzed *The Structure of Scientific Revolutions,* he sought the grounds of periodization in science, and these replicated inquiries by literary and art critics into concepts of literary norms or periods.

My point is that theorists who aim at systematizing literary study are part of a broad group of humanistic scholars who seek to theorize about human actions. Moreover, they agree in rejecting the view that interpreting or theorizing is value-free. They reject the view of a disinterested study of human action, or to put it in literary terms, they reject the belief that the literary work is "autonomous," or self-reflexive, or unconnected with the external world. The procedure, therefore, is to identify the kind of values implied or stated in a text. Such a task results in reconsideration of the writer, the text, and the reader. For the writer is both a member of society and a maker of it; the text embodies his intentions and those of a tradition or genre; and the reader who helps construct the work is shaped by his past readings and his social or group values.

These reconsiderations account for varieties of theoretical hypotheses. The *issue* for theorists is *not a question* of the presence or absence of value, but what literary values are and how they can be located. I take as my first example of a shift in values the case of Paul de Man. In 1963 Paul de Man subscribed to the procedures of the New Criticism, and he contributed to a collection of essays edited by Reuben Brower and Richard Poirier called *In Defense of Reading.*[3] De Man's essay interpreted Wordsworth's sonnet, "Composed by the Side of Grasmere Lake."[4] The sonnet reads as follows:

> Clouds, lingering yet, extend in solid bars
> Through the grey West; and lo! these waters, steeled
> By breezeless air to smoothest polish, yield
> A vivid repetition of the stars;
> Jove, Venus, and the ruddy crest of Mars
> Amid his fellows beauteously revealed
> At happy distance from earth's groaning field,
> Where ruthless mortals wage incessant wars.
> Is it a mirror? — or the nether Sphere

Opening to view the abyss in which she feeds
Her own calm fires? — But list! a voice is near;
Great Pan himself low-whispering through the reeds.
"Be thankful, thou; for, if unholy deeds
Ravage the world, tranquillity is here!"

De Man argued that the poem was unified by tension, and,
he declared, "the juxtaposition of two very different attitudes toward a landscape, [that are] held together by a dramatic progression which constitutes the key to the interpretation."[5] These two
attitudes — of ruthless wars and a peaceful haven held in tension
— underlay the entire sonnet. This emphasis on a single "key" to
interpretation, on the controlling concept of "tension," was the
response of an independent critic whose transaction with the
poem resulted in what he considered a "proper" interpretation.

The social aim of this criticism was spelled out by Reuben
Brower: the essays in the book had as their aim, he wrote, "to get
the student in a position where he could learn for himself. If we
succeed, we have reason to believe that he may acquire a lifetime
habit of learning independently."[6]

The purpose of the interpretation was to teach the student a
"method," one that the student would come to apply by himself.
One can admire the intention behind such an aim — to make the
student independent — but can only regret the neglect of the student or reader as an individual. The kind of learning, training,
and values that the student brought to the class could not make
him independent, only an independent dependent. The student
did not help construct the text, he discovered what was there. The
very concept of independence, as Brower defines it, is a fiction,
for such independence is dependent on another's guidance and
method.

But even more perturbing is how the reader is to respond to
tranquillity as a virtue, to accept a retreat alongside Grasmere
Lake as a form of value which permits him to ignore the sights
and sounds of "earth's groaning field." The practice in which
Paul de Man had engaged took as its aim independence in reading and learning. It attempted neither to understand the nature
of the institutions that fostered this learning nor to ask whether

the canon, including the particular poem of Wordsworth, urged the kind of values that deserved support. The critic-teacher seemed unaware of the social and political values that this fiction of independence nourished. Eight years later, 1971, Paul de Man published *Blindness and Insight*. In the introduction the following statement appeared:

The picture of reading that emerges from the examination of a few contemporary critics is not a simple one. In all of them a paradoxical discrepancy appears between the general statements they make about the nature of literature (statements on which they base their critical methods) and the actual results of their interpretations. Their findings about the structure of texts contradict the general conception that they use as their model. . . . I suggest that this pattern of discrepancy, far from being the consequence of individual or collective aberrations, is a constitutive characteristic of literary language in general. . . . we no longer take for granted that a literary text can be reduced to a finite meaning or set of meanings, but see the act of reading as an endless process in which truth and falsehood are inextricably intertwined.[7]

What took place in the writing of Paul de Man was a shift from construction to deconstruction, from "tension" to "contradiction." He discarded his belief in "the key to interpretation": not only did he find no key, he rejected the possibility that a set of keys could unlock meaning. The act of reading was now an "endless process in which truth and falsehood are inextricably intertwined." De Man's absolute view of language replaced his absolute view of method, and we note the untying of assumptions implicit in his earlier statements.

There was no longer a belief in the possibility of learning from key readings; instead, there was a skeptical view of language, a view that language was an untrustworthy means of communication requiring skeptical readers. Such readers need to familiarize themselves with the varied strategies of mixing truth with falsehood. But does this not imply that the words of Paul de Man are subject to the same deconstruction? Is not this strategy as unreliably transient as all others? Indeed, it is, and he would not deny it.

What he arrived at was a theory suited to a time of public hypocrisy and betrayal. The theory that Paul de Man and other deconstructionists offered was directed at the distrust of language and the reeducation of readers. This distrust, what Hillis Miller calls language as host and parasite, language that undermines itself, is only one of several competing hypotheses about aspects of a text. But this theory and its competitors, despite their many differences, *do share two assumptions: first,* that every text has a subtext, another text concealed in it or implied in it or capable of being derived from it. Whether the subtext undermines the text or supplements it, this hypothesis implies a *second:* every text involves a reader or critic who transacts with it and helps construct it. These two assumptions do away with the earlier limited view of reader independence; rather, they suggest a view that writing and reading involve a *communal* partnership or enterprise, including a way of questioning or testing this partnership. Writing is not a matter of one person issuing a message and another receiving it. The message is constructed by the issuer and receiver. One might say that the linguistic distinction between signifier and signified is undermined by the receiver who mediates or constructs relations between signifier and signified. The situation I am describing implicates sender and receiver in every message; thus betrayal is not the act of another but of oneself, just as partnership is a mutual, not an individual, act.

I quote Wolfgang Iser's phenomenological explanation of the reader-text transaction to convey some of the distinctions involved in his interpretation of this transaction.

. . . The literary work cannot be completely identical with the text, or with the realization of the text, but in fact must lie halfway between the two. The work is more than the text, for the text only takes on life when it is realized, and furthermore the realization is by no means independent of the individual disposition of the reader—though this in turn is acted on by the different patterns of the text. The convergence of text and reader brings the literary work into existence. . . .[8]

The distinctions between "text" and "literary work," distinctions among "text," "realization of the text," and a convergence of the two, confirm the point I made earlier—that theory proceeds by refining or untying concepts taken for granted. Thus for the formalists, the subtext is a series of expectations that the text defeats or alienates. For Freudians, the subtext consists of the nonconscious conflicts submerged in the text. For the phenomenologists the subtext is the realm of Being, the open space implicit in the text or the gaps and indeterminacies which the reader must fill. For the Marxists—or at least for some of them—the subtext is the description of social oppression which the text conceals.

I wish to focus on the Marxist position—or Fredric Jameson's version of it—in order to discuss not only the concept of reader as a collective figure but the concept of reading as a historical dialectic. Jameson writes:

> We must try to rid ourselves of the habit of thinking about our (aesthetic) relationship to culturally or temporally distant artifacts as being a relationship between individual subjects (as in my personal reading of an individual text written by a biographical individual named Spenser or Juvenal, or even my personal attempt to invent an individual relationship to an oral story once told by an individual storyteller in a tribal society). It is not a question of dismissing the role of individual subjects in the reading process, but rather of grasping this obvious and concrete individual relationship as being itself a mediation for a nonindividual and more collective process: the confrontation of two distinct social forms or modes of production. We must try to accustom ourselves to a perspective in which every act of reading, every local interpretive practice, is grasped as the privileged vehicle through which two distinct modes of production confront and interrogate one another. Our individual reading thus becomes an allegorical figure for this essentially collective confrontation of two social forms.[9]

The forcefulness of this argument is impressive—not only because Jameson is conducting a dialogue with other contemporary critics but because he is absorbing and redefining their arguments. He does not dismiss "the role of individual subjects in the reading process," but restates the relationship as a "mediation for a nonindividual and more collective process: the confrontation of two distinct social forms or modes of production." He finds the individual to be both an individual and a part of a larger cultural process, and he conceives of a text as a social form or a mode of production.

This is a subtle procedure for reintroducing the concept of collective behavior into theory; still, if each individual reading is an allegorical figure for collective confrontation, are we not left, once again, with multiple distinctions in reading, only this time *within* a single trope — allegory? And has not Frye argued that all interpretation is allegorical because it constructs its own meaning from another text, and does not Jameson's claim lead to the same dilemma as Frye's?[10] When critics move from individual readings to analyses of the nature of reading, are we necessarily involved in the same type of collectivism or cultural process? In fact, does not the introduction of mediation create a special dilemma because mediation as criticism or theory is itself a form of writing, which creates values as well as describes them? What becomes problematical is the act of confrontation between two modes of production. What sort of historical relation is involved? How can the critic control the perspective through which he sees the modes of production? What does the term "mode of production" conceal? Is not "mode of production" as collective a term as "individual critic"?

The hermeneutical critic (I refer to Heidegger here), who also assumes (with some Marxists) that texts interrogate each other, adds a belief in their "immanence" and "truth"; these further assumptions are necessary for his text to speak for itself. For example, David Hoy writes: "On the hermeneutic account . . . immanence and truth must be seen not only as properties of the text, but also as assumptions granted to the text by the reader in the process of letting the text speak for itself. The text does not exist except in a dialogue between test and interpreter."[11] But we must be wary of the dialogue metaphor because the dialogue is conducted through a monologue. The critic who speaks for the text is the same critic who speaks to it. The dialogue is filtered through one mind; what we have is a partnership; but the thoughts and words of the silent partner are filtered through the mind of the vocal one. "Truth" and "immanence," therefore, can be filtered out as well as permitted to drip in.

If the hermeneutic theorist and the Marxist critic both wish to avoid total relativism, they at least realize that this act cannot be performed by returning to Kant and to value-free objectivism. The alternatives to relativism may prove complicated, even insurmountable, involving questionable questions and answers. But these critics are aware that the questions they ask are conditioned by their own culture, not released from it. I would, however, be an inadequate guide to contemporary theory if I did not inform you that there *still* are critics who argue that value-free judgments exist in literary study. Gerald Graff has declared that "we all become value-free objectivists to some extent when we attempt to make sure our value judgments rest on an unbiased understanding of the object. In other words, value-free objectivity is a necessary first stage of making value judgments—the descriptive, disinterested determination of what it is that is to be judged."[12]

But is it precisely the assumption of selectivity—"what it is that is to be judged"—that governs canon-making. The establishing of the subject matter is governed by what theorists take to be the aims or ends of a discipline, the values they want to convey. I do not claim that there exists only one set of values—there are, after all, personal as well as public values. But the selection of a subject matter is tied to the values that those in control believe are best for the discipline. Even the language of literary study—such terms as "literature," or "belles lettres," or "genre," "novel," "poem," "narrative," are value-laden. Does it help to claim, as Graff does, that "value itself is objective in that it rests on prior understanding"[13] since "prior understanding" is no more than a term for values established at some prior time by an institution, class, or group?

Gerald Graff's *Literature Against Itself* is a historical study of contemporary criticism and theory, but its version of "history" is one that the theorists I have been discussing earlier would reject. Graff maintains that there are indeed certain objective truths that need to be accepted despite the fact that the very process of arriving at them marks them as relativistic and transient. But why do theorists continue to hold fast to theories that are being undermined, that are being dissolved or untied? There is the desire to maintain stability, to cling to views that are familiar. There is the belief that the overthrow of authority, literary or otherwise, includes the overthrow of logic and reason even though the newer theories are based on accommodations to logic and reason and, indeed, call for "rational inquiry."

I have introduced Gerald Graff not because he opposes what Michel Foucault or Jacques Derrida do, but because the reasons he gives exemplify the disjunctions they describe. His objectivism belongs to an earlier time frame, and the point of some contemporary theoretical writing is that a *period* contains within itself contrary theories from different time frames, and that this awareness is one of the characteristics of modern writing, including the writing of theory considered as "modern."

Graff's literary history, based on his version of logic and objectivism, does not describe the kind of "reality" to which Foucault, Derrida, and others point. It is not surprising that modernist writing, of which recent theory is an example, develops a series of rhetorical traits that, according to David Lodge, reflect the breakup of earlier forms. Lodge writes:

Now the characteristics . . . of modernist writing in particular, have been often enough described: formal experiment, dislocation of conventional syntax, radical breaches of decorum, disturbance of chronology and spatial order, ambiguity, polysemy, obscurity, mythopoeic allusion, primitivism, irrationalism, structuring by symbol and motif rather than by narrative or argumentative logic, and so on. And it is easy to see how these strategies and themes reflect the sense that the modern period has a special historic destiny, perhaps to abolish history itself.[14]

David Lodge's irony in writing a modern historical account suggesting that "the modern period has a special historic destiny, perhaps to abolish history itself," reveals that the "history" which is being abolished is not the "history" written by Foucault or Derrida. Their "history," like contemporary "literary theory," invents or redefines the vocabulary of discourse. Foucault declares:

We must also question those divisions or groupings with which we have become so familiar. Can one accept, as such, the distinctions . . . between such forms or genres as science, literature, philosophy, religion, history, fiction, etc. and which tend to create great historical individualities? We are not even sure of ourselves when we use these distinctions in our own world of discourse, let alone when we are analysing groups of statements which, when first formulated, were distributed, divided and characterized in a quite different way. . . .[15]

So, too, Derrida's substitution of "text" for "work" is a deliberate effort to remove the metaphysical implications of linearity and succession inherent in the earlier term. But "text" and "history" are words with their own pasts, and the effort to erase this fact and rebaptize the terms creates deliberate disjunctions of meaning and equally deliberate hostility to such disjunctions.[16]

One can appreciate the desire to start anew; to begin with a vocabulary constructed by the critic and to provide a series of relations among works that are the result of uncontaminated concepts. But if a theorist conceives of his theory in terms of new beginnings, we find that all theorists who stress their novelty *share* a search for differentness. If we consider our time as disjunctive with explanations of previous events in history, we can understand this disjunction only by knowing previous explanations.

Can there be a complete rejection of the language that deals with history, with past actions — a complete rejection of the expressions of past events? If a text is a form of human action and human actions undergo change, some continuity is essential to define any action. If a text is identified with a genre, then any particular text can only be understood in terms of past traditions or examples of its genre. If a text is understood as a series of conventions, history is necessary to explain these conventions. But what if one believes a text is constituted by a self-referential language? Is not such a text to be understood only in its own terms and without any past conventions, traditions, or actions? What use would historical procedures be in understanding such a work? But even as one asks this question, the answer is self-evident: how does one know a language if one has never used it? How does one know a poem if one has never seen or heard a poem? How does one know what "understanding" is if one has no prior understanding of "understanding"?

The issue is not, "Are historical procedures necessary for the understanding of theory?" but "What kind of historical procedures are necessary for such understanding?" Contemporary theory that accepts disjunctions and discontinuities is inevitably confronted with how past meanings can be recaptured. The hermeneutic circle suggests that the critic interprets past texts in terms of present premises. It is only critics who, like Gerald Graff, urge ideal objectivity by denying empirical objectivity, who can overlook the hermeneutic paradox in interpretation. Others, like Hans Robert Jauss, Stanley Fish, Wolfgang Iser, have undertaken to circumvent this dilemma by providing restraints on subjectivity. Jauss's aesthetics of reception is one of the most comprehensive attempts to reduce individual subjectivity by tracing the subjectivity of past critics.[17] Jauss sees any response to a work as part of a historical series which begins with the generic nature of the text. Each response is then related to responses to other works of the same time. Responses to the work are thus controlled by synchronic as well as diachronic texts. The consequence is that the modern response is not unrestrained but defined and delimited in terms of prior historical awareness. Of course, the subjective element is never eliminated. But at least it is brought to consciousness and is confined by the frame that has been historically traced.

Such a historical theory offers contemporary critics an opportunity to redefine key terms; for example, what a "genre" is and how "genre" is part of a series and a literary system. It also leads us to consider the relation between popular writing and sophisticated or elite writing, for, surely, there is writing which consciously supports the prejudices of bourgeois readers, as there is writing which attacks or subverts these prejudices. A novel by Judith Krantz may fit uneasily with a novel by Thomas Pynchon, but a theorist would have to explain the interrelations of such different works within the same genre.

But theorists are not always ready to engage the problems that empirical acts impose or to make such inquiries accessible to the common reader. Theory in our time has had to face the charge that it has become all too often a technical study. On the one hand, theorists seek to relate their study to human values and concerns; on the other, they must render their study highly technical in order to accomplish this.

The argument against the scientific or technical vocabulary of contemporary theory is, I believe, misdirected. There is no reason to assume that theory need or need not be simple: different theoretical inquiries have different ends. What needs to be simple and clear is the explanation of the value that theoretical study has for any layman, because such discourse is addressed to laymen. The practice of theory requires a special competence, and theorists recognize this. One of the practitioners of institutional theory, Charles Altieri, puts it this way:

> . . . The essential properties of literary response are created by education and exposure rather than by necessary and sufficient conditions in the object. . . . When we read a text, we have implicitly operating a history of other texts and of questions we put often without being self-conscious about them. The competent reader is like a trained athlete, whose skills far outweigh his explanatory powers and whose actions combine required moves with a continual possibility for free improvisation.[18]

The practice of theory requires a special competence, but every human being is engaged in one way or another with interpreting language and other social forms. The need to possess this competence is what should be made clear to all thinking human beings: to learn which verbal actions to trust, which to distrust; to recognize the value-laden qualities of such actions, to distinguish between the continuities and discontinuities of value (between a living and a dead tradition).

But it is all too easy to admire so seductive an institutional theory, especially for scholars who are themselves members of an institution. If readers learn by imitating teachers and critics, the importance of these acts may elevate our pride but not always their knowledge. For such theories are subject to the same objections that were levelled against the statements of Reuben Brower. Students do not come naked into the classroom; they bring values and attitudes. And they select aspects of a teacher to imitate that do not necessarily duplicate his values: Paul de Man can stand as such an example. Moreover, an institutional theory that does not explain why or how an institution changes cannot offer an adequate explanation of its value structure. In a sense, an institutional theory addresses itself to the collective nature of the individual, but it cannot adequately define the institution without placing it within a context of other societal institutions: those of religion, politics, the family, the law, and science.

I wrote above about Clifford Geertz and Thomas Kuhn, writers who deal with institutions other than that of literary study. And I suggested that the approach they had to human problems resembled that of literary theorists. For purposes of institutional study, I want to note now that a number of critics from other disciplines use literary criticism and theory as models. Indeed, in the sociology of Robert Brown, in the anthropology of Dell Hymes and Victor Turner, in the history of science of Gerald Holton, literary theory has become a model. Its analysis of interpretation, of writers who are readers and readers who are writers, of the relation between text and critic, have all served to establish not only a concept of communal responsiveness in verbal actions but a closer relationship among the different disciplines and institutions.

I want to conclude my study of contemporary theory by examining two examples – one of which aims at scientific precision and the other which deliberately avoids it. Both are open theories: they await and invite evidence and confirmation. And they display the joys of invented vocabularies that are meant to encourage humanistic discourse. The German theorist and concrete poet, Siegfried J. Schmidt, in "Empirische Literaturwissenschaft als Perspektiv" argues that *rational inquiry* can and should be applied to literary study. Ihab Hassan, in "Desire, Imagination, Change: Outline of a Theoretical Project,"[19] among other essays, seeks to illustrate that literary and scientific discourses are indeed interrelated.

Schmidt seeks to do away with speculative, imaginative theorizing and offers as an alternative an empirical, "scientific" literary theory based on a series of propositions for which evidence still needs to be assembled, but which, he is convinced, can be assembled. Schmidt explains that he uses "empirical" in a special sense: "the empiricity of a statement cannot be decided in relation to reality as such, but only in relation to a model of reality consensually adopted by a community of investigators. The value of methods used to prove the empirical contents of statements or arguments can consequently only be judged by the interpretation of this model of reality."[20]

As for "theoreticity," he declares, "The fundamental theory predicate must be identifiable; the logical structure of problem solving strategies must be explicit or at least explicable; the theory must be empirically interpretable (or: the empirical content of the theory must be expressible)."[21] The three preconditions that Schmidt finds essential for a proper *Literaturwissenschaft* pertain to the kind of intellectual activity that is to be performed in the framework of theory; the classification of the concept of literature; the aims and functions of theoretical investigations and the social relevance of such activities. His text includes references to historians of science, to theorists of science and literature; it includes formulae — T = (K, I), where T = Theory; K = Kernel; I = Intended Application — it includes diagrams, different type fonts. It is also composed of sentences and sentence fragments. In his critical writing, he seeks to bridge the gap between the verbal and the visual, between the word and the nonverbal formula, and his literary theory includes elements of scientific and of linguistic (diagrammatic) notations.

There is an element of pseudoscience in Schmidt's formulas; they can, after all, be written without the equational mystique. And the precision that he calls for requires evidence not yet assembled. But his plea for "rational inquiry" is another version of the contemporary communal enterprise shared by those who participate in a method of arguing or a manner of writing or a procedure for thinking. His argument for the empiricity of a statement makes the communal element clear: "The empiricity of a statement" can be judged only in relation to a model of reality" consensually adopted by a community of investigators." Different investigators do adopt different reality-models, and Schmidt leaves unresolved the conflicts between such models.

Schmidt's model for literary theory is coherent and consistent, but can the evidence for it be assembled? Can the classification of the concept of literature be defended on rational grounds when it is selected for historical rather than rational reasons? Does the term "rational" activity take account of the learning that is done by imitation or — to be paradoxical — by model following? Is not Schmidt's theorizing speculative and imaginative rather than scientific and experimental? Is not his theory constructed as an imaginative whole prior to the data that are to fit it?

The kind of theorizing that he rejects is the speculative intertextual writing that Ihab Hassan practices. Hassan's text offers quotations from A. N. Whitehead, J. D. Bernal, William Blake, Nietzsche, Freud, Heisenberg, Haldane, etc., and organizes them into an inquiry about interrelating the systems of science and art. He asks, "Can the gnosis of science and the prophetic dream of art converge on some idea(s) of change that criticism has yet to acknowledge, let alone explore?" Hassan does not argue for a thesis; rather, he is intent on provoking the reader to consider or reconsider certain theoretical issues. Because of this, he and some other contemporary theorists have been accused of competing with literary texts. But ought we to be guided by Matthew Arnold's hypothesis that criticism must prepare the way for creative writing or be the handmaid of such writing? If writing is a form of human action, then at some times types of verbal action such as Plato's *Symposium* or Nietzsche's *The Birth of Tragedy* or Shelley's *Defense of Poetry* can be, and indeed have been, considered by critics as works of art. What constitutes "literature," "works of art," or "creative" writing depends upon the values and functions one attributes to these. In our time theory is causing us to rethink the nature of past texts; as such, it is initiating a rewriting of past poetry and prose; it leads us to new responses to old poetry.

It used to be considered a devastating attack upon criticism — and even theory — to declare that there would be no criticism or theory if there were no literature. The idea was that theory was parasitical upon literary texts. Whether or not it was the theorists' revenge, the Russian Formalists began, and some contemporary theorists continue, to argue that every literary text is a form of theory. Each text exemplifies certain principles of composition and is, by example, an instance of theory. Thus the argument can be reversed — there can be no poetry without theory.

This interpretative reversal leads me back to the nature of a text, for if a text includes a subtext, both include principles of composition. The term "text" needs further division and analysis; the concept of intertextuality — the inclusion of quotations from and references to other texts — in a theoretical work indicates one possibility of dealing with the multiform character of a text. This is, therefore, one of the three directions we can take in theory: an investigation of the collective, combinatory nature of a text; a study of the nature of literary value—its kinds and functions, especially in relation to other kinds of values; and, finally, a study of the nature of and reasons for literary change—of styles, subjects, genres, periods, and so forth.

Hassan posits quotations from a variety of thinkers, and he designs the printed page with numerous typological innovations. Many of these prove trivial and unsuccessful, but the aim of his text is to challenge the imagination of the reader to cooperate in the construction of theoretical ideas. When a text includes quotations that come from different times, it urges the reader to interrelate them, to make unexpected and unanticipated temporal connections, to reconstitute tradition. The fragments of time embodied in such quotations urge readers to compare a fragmented quotation with the whole of which it is a part and with the new whole of which it has become a part.

I began by indicating some of my own literary presuppositions, hearing in my ear the voice of Geoffrey Hartman: "Interpreter: define thyself."[22] I then explained why theory had become prominent in our time both from the demands of the discipline and from the external recognition of inquiry into human actions. This was followed by the study of a specific example of a critic, Paul de Man, who turned from criticism to theory. It was a theory that answered, I said, to certain public needs, and I then illustrated that a body of contemporary theorists agreed upon certain formulations expressing shared values. I focused in detail on two specific statements dealing with theoretical issues involved in reading and introduced a standard opposition to the formulations. I sought to show that this opposition was based on a misconception and explained how this misconception could arise from the ambiguity of theoretical language. I then illustrated several theories that sought, not always successfully, to restrain relativism without succumbing to untenable claims. No theory has yet proved entirely satisfactory, but the impact of theorizing and criticizing has affected disciplines other than literary study and has called into question the conventional assumptions about theory.

Theory has, for us, been freed from its subservience to literature, and it now appears as a genre on its own. In this respect, its history has not yet begun to be written, and we have before us a challenging and provocative task. Confronting it, we can envision once again the disturbing joys and pleasurable sorrows of literary theory.

NOTES

1 Roland Barthes, *The Pleasure of the Text,* trans. Richard Howard (New York: Hill & Wang, 1975), pp. 16–17.
2 Kenneth Burke, *A Grammar of Motives* (New York: Prentice-Hall, 1945).
3 Reuben A. Brower and Richard Poirier, eds., *In Defense of Reading,* (New York: E. P. Dutton, 1963).
4 Paul de Man, "Symbolic Landscape in Wordsworth and Yeats," in Brower and Poirier, *In Defense of Reading,* pp. 22–37.
5 Ibid., pp. 22–23.
6 Brower, "Reading in Slow Motion," in Brower and Poirier, *In Defense of Reading,* p. 8.
7 Paul de Man, *Blindness and Insight* (New York: Oxford University Press, 1971), p. ix.
8 Wolfgang Iser, "The Reading Process: A Phenomenological Approach," in *New Directions in Literary History,* ed. Ralph Cohen (Baltimore: Johns Hopkins University Press, 1974), p. 125.
9 Fredric Jameson, "Marxism and Historicism," *New Literary History* 11 (Autumn 1979): 69–70.
10 Northrop Frye, *Anatomy of Criticism* (Princeton: Princeton University Press, 1957), pp. 89–92.
11 David Hoy, *The Critical Circle* (Berkeley and Los Angeles: University of California Press, 1978), p. 145.
12 Gerald Graff, *Literature Against Itself* (Chicago: University of Chicago Press, 1979), p. 86.
13 Ibid., p. 87.
14 David Lodge, "Historicism and Literary History: Mapping the Modern Period," *New Literary History* 10 (Spring 1979): 550.
15 Michel Foucault, *The Archaeology of Knowledge,* trans. H. M. Sheridan Smith (New York: Irvington Pubs., 1972), p. 22.
16 Jacques Derrida, *Of Grammatology,* trans. G. C. Spivak (Baltimore: Johns Hopkins University Press, 1976), p. 18.
17 Hans Robert Jauss, "Literary History as a Challenge to Literary Theory," in Cohen's *New Directions in Literary History,* pp. 11–41.
18 Charles Altieri, "A Procedural Definition of Literature," in *What is Literature?,* ed. Paul Hernadi (Bloomington: Indiana University Press, 1978), p. 70.

19 Ihab Hassan, "Desire, Imagination, Change: Outline of a Theoretical Project," *Studies in the Literary Imagination* 12 (Spring 1979): 129–43.
20 Siegfried J. Schmidt, "Empirische Literaturwissenschaft as Perspective," *Poetics* 8 (1979): 560.
21 Ibid., pp. 560–61.
22 Geoffrey Hartman, "The Interpreter: A Self-Analysis," *New Literary History* 4 (Winter 1973): 219.

7 /

Renewing the Medium of Renewal: Some Notes on the Anxieties of Innovation

Wayne C. Booth

I. WHY WE ARE ALL TEMPTED BY INNOVATIONISM

Our age has been characterized as the age of novelty, the age that above all others has pursued the new and devalued the old. Though many modern thinkers have deplored the pursuit of novelty for its own sake, the number of people engaged in that pursuit seems to increase, and some thinkers have even claimed that it is the most prominent mark distinguishing ours from all previous cultures. European critics have long claimed that Americanization threatens civilization, and Americanization for them consists in a frenzied pursuit of whatever is new, for the sake of the novelty.

Some have claimed that we Americans pursue not only what is new *now,* but that we are in love with what will *be* new *later*—that is, with the future. We are a future-oriented society,[1] not to say a future-shocked society. We ask—these critics claim—not whether a trend or a novelty is good or useful or beautiful or true, but simply whether it moves us rapidly toward the year 2000. In this view everything gets reduced, in practice, to the clichés of the world of fashion: our intellectual leaders are those who can set or spot a trend, and we followers prove our worth by our alacrity in jumping on or off bandwagons at just the right moment.

So far as I know none of us attending this conference has yet come out of the closet as a confessed futurologist. We are perhaps a bit too sophisticated to profess a nondiscipline that only Americans could have invented, the one discipline in the world whose results are sure to be wrong, the study not of what was, not of what is, not of what should be or even of what we ought to hope for, but of what will be. But though we may be smart enough not to call ourselves futurologists, though we reject conference titles like "Future Shock and What To Do About It" and resist organizing our predictions under names like "The Club of Rome," we still spend much of our intellectual lives haunted by futurism. We worry a great deal about strangely resistant questions like "Is modernism finally dead?" or "Has post-modernism finally arrived?" Many critics, philosophers, historians, and social scientists seem to share a shimmering, fluid, sometimes hopeful but often anxious view of what is most worth knowing: namely, *what is the new thing*?

It takes no great depth of prophetic vision to see why. No matter how much we may analyze or deplore or even mock innovationism, its roots run so deep that we all must be tempted to grow *that way*. I shall mention only five causes that I find working within myself, try as I may to deny them.

First, innovationism is an American habit. The United States of America was a grand innovation, promising—as had the colonization effort in earlier centuries—a new heaven and a new earth.[2] Our myths almost all suggest that we fulfill the Lord's will by starting over, by repudiating the wicked and depleted past, by building a new order. Whatever disappointments our quest for a perfected society has encountered, the habit continues to run deep.

Secondly, perhaps as a by-product of such habits, many of us have founded or joined or inherited millenarian sects claiming to offer in "what's new" the fulfillment or redemption from a past that is by definition old hat. Many of these, like the Mormons who gave me my own deepest beliefs, have been fundamentally, ineradicably protestant, in the root sense of urging a discovery and affirmation of an individual truth that the rest of the world has either lost or never even had. And the Mormons, like many other groups, have stressed the "principle of continuous revelation." God has not laid down all truth for all time, but He issues it in ever new forms. He Himself is progressing; like the rest of us, He is in process, moving up an inclined plane toward perfection.

A third reason, following in part from these first two, is the one that I find perhaps most compelling in myself: All of us know that we are radically imperfect, that we need to improve, and thus that our hope lies in finding something new, outside us or within us, to make us new. The habit of critical introspection runs deep in Western culture, and especially deep in American experience. But it is not just habit that reveals our need for the novel: every clear view of ourselves reveals that to be completely satisfied with *who I am now* is to succumb to a kind of death. Different Western societies have expressed this universal truth in different ways. A good Greek warrior-king like Agamemnon, knowing that he ought to be an even better warrior to accomplish his goal, may decide to sacrifice his daughter to the gods in exchange for assistance in becoming a better warrior. A Christian might say, "I know that I am deeply and originally sinful, and that without thy help, Oh, Lord, I shall eternally remain so." In our own time we are flooded with programs for self-improvement, promising to cure us if we will just follow this or that novel method of meditation, or group counseling, or family therapy, or sexual liberation. And of course these programs are not confined to the West. This week I am promised, in an ad in *Time* magazine, that the sexual program of one Bhagwan Shree Rajneesh will "surprise me, enrich me and benefit me," enabling me to "tumble upon" my "spirituality" and "become free," and that my future will be "totally different," with "more fun, more joy, more friendship." Anyone who answers that ad, as of course I am deeply tempted to do, is thereby acknowledging dissatisfaction with the present self. Lord, please just jack up this old soul and run a new one in under it.

Political failures provide a fourth good reason to hope for, nay long for, something new. We have an acute sense that the old ways have been working out badly in the political domain, and it just may be that the reasons are not merely political. We are faced daily with evidence that unless our race can find some new way to manage our planet, unless we can find new political forms, we shall surely die—not just each of us individually, as we have always known enough to expect, but the whole human project. It is true that many previous generations believed that the human project was doomed. But they had a comfort that is denied to most of us here: they believed in a miraculous redemption at the end of time, an ultimate future renovation when God will salvage all that is salvageable from the human experiment. We find ourselves believing, in this secular age, that unless human beings can build a life that redeems itself in the living of it, there will be no redemption. The result is that what's new, what's happening now, seems more important to us than ever before: what's happening *now,* is what's happening *finally,* not just a prelude to what will *really* happen, the working-out of a drama written by the great playwright, God.

For some this sense of a desperate clinging to the only thing we have, this secular life, has gone so far that even the past is no longer thought of as in any way a value that might help to redeem or mitigate what happens now—or tomorrow. The past thus becomes less real than the future, as unreal as eternity. The primary reality is the forward-pointing arrow of the present moment. And unless a great many prophets are wrong, that arrow points downward toward doom. Our various Clubs of Rome predict total disaster within fifty years. Optimists tell us it will not come for a century or so. All agree that we are doomed—doomed *unless* we can find novel ways of running our affairs. Is there any wonder that we all succumb to a lust for novelty?[3]

Finally, I think we long for novelty as a proof that we are free, that we are not the charted, determined—and therefore dull—automatons that some pictures of human behavior suggest. For many of us, the loss that would outweigh all other losses would be the sense that we are essentially no more than complicated robots, enacting roles that are as determined by the past as if we could actually trace the springs and wheels and sprockets that make us tick. And what better proof is there that we have escaped determinism than to unveil something genuinely new under the sun? In this respect, we who live in Western democracies exhibit anxieties not felt by writers in totalitarian countries. They clearly value freedom at least as much as we do; they often say that we undervalue what they would give their lives for — the simple right to say what we think. But since to fight, however subtly, for that freedom is more than sufficient as a lifetime project, those writers do not worry as much as we do about finding other means of innovation: to say something freely, under the threat of suppression, is already sufficient proof of one's being undetermined.

Beneath these differences, most of us, regardless of our political setting, seem to see the possibility of freedom as the defining feature of our lives as human beings; the essential ingredient of our intellectual pursuits is the freedom to move beyond the constraints imposed by others, whether by present dictators or by past thinkers, and to discover — well, to discover what is to be discovered when freedom is practiced. And that must surely be something new, mustn't it? It can hardly be something old, predetermined, fixed?[4]

What we also know, living in this culture in this century, is that it is not only in totalitarian countries that constraints on freedom threaten. Though Western complaints about lost freedoms have sometimes looked a bit absurd to writers in Moscow or Argentina or Cuba, who envy us the freedom we have, we are quite justified in our sense that something, somehow, constrains us as well. Something in our society prevents our growing as we would like to grow; something drives us and our children into stunted patterns, repetitive patterns, uncreative patterns, deadly patterns that look liberating when we first meet them but that finally destroy us; something turns our cultural products into a level of repetitive shoddiness that makes us ashamed of what we ourselves are and do.

What is more, wherever we look we seem to find enemies who would impose constraints upon us. We find proponents of scientific world views that threaten us with ever more "proofs" that we are simply products of impersonal and stochastic forces that we cannot hope to understand, let alone to control; and we find an increasingly computerized industrial society closing in upon us with ever more evidence that as individuals we count for nothing in the statistics either of politics or of commerce. Finally, the lines between our personal wills and any results in the world that might really matter seem more and more tenuous.

II. EFFECTS OF THE FIVE REASONS ON THEORY AND PRACTICE OF INTERPRETATION

If as scholars and intellectuals we feel constrained, patterned, charted, if as heirs to traditions of innovation we feel our powers to innovate denied, we naturally seek evidence that we can become the free creatures we had hoped to be. If for the most part we have lost our faith in political solutions, and if the very notion of expressing our freedom by perfecting our souls has long since been lost, where are we to turn but to expressions of intellectual freedom as we practice what used to be called our "disciplines"? Surely in the study of history, of philosophy, of criticism, of linguistics, we can find freedoms that are distinctively human.

Yet we find in those *disciplines,* especially as traditionally practiced, rules and conventions that seem further to threaten our freedom. Instead of theories that would liberate me, I seem to discover hidebound traditions and authoritative canons, telling me that my duty as a humanist is to enslave myself to what other people have thought. In my most clearly humanistic activity of interpreting human discourse I ought — so I seem to be told — to be constrained by codes of interpretation that bind me to what has already been said. I find the New Critics and the Chicago Critics and Northrop Frye and E. D. Hirsch and a whole host of historicists and linguists trying to construct modes of interpretation or sciences of discourse that would bind my own thoughts.

Can there be any wonder that at the end of a century full of such stuff, all hell should break loose, that chaos should be asked to come again, that theorists of new freedoms should emerge everywhere, in every discipline?

And so, even in disciplines where we thought ourselves least free to invent, the physical sciences and mathematics, we seek to convince ourselves that we are in fact not constrained by nature, or by a proper method of studying nature, or by the nature of number, but are freely inventive of systems that are more like poems than like scientific conclusions. And if this is so of disciplines traditionally thought constrained by some sort of reality, how much more obviously true, we can now say, in the arts of communication and interpretation.

These arts have been threatened by various scientisms that would constrain their natural freedom. The rhetoric of criticism and hermeneutics has been co-opted by people aping the rhetoric of science and of positivist philosophy, aspiring to the condition of certainty about necessities. Our obvious move in response surely must be to recover the natural freedom of a rhetoric not bound by false norms. We shall go to the very roots of rhetorical freedom, the free use of language itself, and we shall invent modes of interpretation that are—at last—really free. But to do so we must develop intellectual systems that practice liberation as a supreme value, systems in which to be free is more important than to be sound or right or justified. We must innovate by revolutionizing the very medium of innovation, the language in which it is carried out.

But how do I do that? Well, I have been told, by certain hidebound, scientific-minded critics, that my chief, perhaps my only task is to perform an objective recovery of what has already been said, to reconstruct the author's intentions and surrender to them. Not on your life, not by a long shot will I succumb to any such totalitarian demands. Here is the one place in my life where I can still exercise freedom, where *my* mind and *my* will and *my* desire and *my* bliss can still count, count not just for a little but, if I so wish, for everything. I can say what I damn please, about Chaucer, about Flaubert, about Goethe, even about Shakespeare. I can, if I will, look into my heart and write, and I need not—indeed I should not—write what other men and women might, in similar circumstances, faced with the same text, choose to write.

In doing so I shall at the same time perform an important

political act. The promised revolutions of the sixties and early seventies may have been aborted, but there is one revolution that I can still carry on with: the final revolution of the word, the freeing of our words from the dictates of an absurdly constraining bourgeois notion of reason and responsibility and referentiality, those three old "Rs" that add up to one logocentric, stultifying notion—to be *sound.* To be sound means to be tested by somebody else's constraining notion of what's sound. It means, surely, the surrender of one's freedom to the impositions of conformity.[5]

Listen for a moment to a letter from a young critic, proposing a paper for a conference on criticism.

I propose a paper entitled, "Righting Communal Discourse: Graff, Hassan, Lyotard." In my talk I will link Graff and Hassan as strategists of a new right whose aim is to silence the disparate voices of poststructuralism by asserting the legitimacy of one communal discourse. . . . While Graff dismisses poststructuralism, Hassan attempts to diminish what he fears as its terrorism: the utter difference (and indifference) of its many textual modes, plays, and ideologies. . . . Hassan's goal of a unifying imagination—a new gnosticism—endorses the "pluralism defined by a community of debate" sought by Graff. And both plead for a decharged, gentile [*sic*] discourse somehow avoiding the ideological incommensurability of "terroristic" language. I will suggest, however, that these gestures towards centrality, towards the making common of legitimate marginalisms, are discussed by Lyotard (and Blanchot) as the performative substance of the sort of terrorism they repudiate. For by changing the rules of critical performance, Graff and Hassan deny texts the right to speak for and by themselves, to have spaces and positions on the margins of (and unconcerned with) the center.

What could possibly motivate such passion? I submit that when this young man pleads for the right to be on the "margins" of discourse, when he insists on the right of texts to "speak for and by themselves," and when he accuses Graff and Hassan of secret "terrorism," what he is really fighting for is his rhetorical freedom. If he must submit to someone else's notion of a central code of interpretation, especially if that code suggests a community of those who share an interpretation, how can he consider himself free?

III. WHY THE SEARCH FOR INNOVATION IS ITSELF OLD HAT

As in all efforts at innovation, the innovation that would give us freedom by revolutionizing the word is by no means new. The structures of thought it yields are in fact found in many earlier intellectual revolts. I am especially interested in the relations it offers between communal norms and private discoveries. In effect, I am told that my freedom will be found by pursuing a sincere new reading of my own, regardless of whether or not it conforms to notions of soundness imposed by my community. Those notions are after all merely inventions by other readers — or, what is even more likely, hypocritical dead copyings of what originally may have been alive. Established communal readings may be *sound,* in the sense of according with what an author consciously intended. But is it not better to discover one's own free reading, however idiosyncratic, than to achieve soundness by following some established pattern or procedure?

I repeat the structure of thought here to underline the striking similarity between this view of how idiosyncrasy and communality relate and that of many earlier Romantics of how we find individual salvation. Throughout the nineteenth century — to go no earlier — many expressions of individual integrity in the face of the church's doctrines stated quite bluntly that it would be better to be damned for a sincere embrace of a private falsehood than to be saved for submission to someone else's truth. Nor were these expressions as inharmonious with ancient Christian traditions as their speakers generally thought. One major tradition that we all share, either in high literary form, as in Milton, or in popular forms exhibited in various current fundamentalist denominations, holds that Satan offered to God a plan that would have saved everyone by demanding conformity to the truth. Christ, in contrast, offered His Father a plan that allowed free choice. In doing so, He fore-ordained that some sheep would be lost.

Note that while individual salvation in this myth comes only for those who choose God's preestablished paths, the plan itself bestows the badge of supreme approval on individual choice, since those who *are* saved clearly receive a higher form of salvation than would have been attainable in the totalitarian plan of Satan. It is only a short step from the view that individual choice for all is so valuable that it is worth the damnation of some to the view that true salvation lies in individual choice per se: God will honor me more for an honest choice of erroneous novelty, as He honors Faust at the end of Goethe's Part II, than for a slavish or insincere acceptance of established ways. Not only for the plan but for the individual as well, it is better to have independence with error than dependent truth.

It is a scarcely discernible further step to the view that to be novel is more important than to be right, because after all, if you are not novel, you are in fact showing dependence on someone else's earlier view.

We have by now a fair number of powerful literary heroes — to say nothing of their flesh-and-blood counterparts — in whom the drama of the supreme choice is enacted. Perhaps the most wrenching portraits, for me, are those torn creatures of Dostoevsky who would elect what is unreasonable just because it *is* unreasonable and therefore free.[6] When I was a young man, working out my own rebellions against what I considered a singularly repressive upbringing, I read such moments — or so it now seems to me — in an entirely uncritical spirit. That is, I did not really look closely at the terms of the Faustian bargain: the sacrifice of salvation for the sake of a private knowledge, privately pursued. I knew, or rather I *felt,* what it was that I sought, and that seemed to me precisely what had been sought by various heroes from Socrates through Byron to James Joyce, who had fought my battles long before I was born.

To show that our quest for interpretative novelty is itself a mere reenactment of exhausted habits of Romantic thought, it should prove useful to look closely at one of the finest portraits of a hero making the Great Bargain: "Rather *my* truth, however impoverished or even damnable it may prove to be, than salvation through a received truth." I am thinking, of course, of Stephen Dedalus.

Portrait of the Artist as a Young Man moves — no critic has, I think, questioned this view of its structure — through a series of temptations or possible deflections of the hero, Stephen, from what is finally to be his elected fate: to become an artist. To become an artist he must repudiate the appeals of all communal values or established vocations and embrace simply and absolutely his true vocation: that of the honest artistic seer, pursuing a private vision never before known or dreamed of.

I must leave to one side the vexed question of how much distance there is between the bargain as viewed by the character, Stephen, and that same bargain as viewed by Joyce at the time of creating that character. Clearly Joyce sees it as the kind of bargain young people like Stephen had made and would make. What is important to us is the combination of seven ingredients in the choice. To trace them in Joyce will be to see just how traditional our own more recent efforts at innovation have been. Most of ours have revealed six of the seven ingredients that were, by Stephen's time, long since standard in "modern" innovations.

First, Stephen's bargain entails great personal risk; it is a choice among ultimates, a choice between spiritual freedom and damnation: "I am not afraid," Stephen says in his final conversation with Cranly, "to make a mistake, even a great mistake, a lifelong mistake and perhaps as long as eternity too." In Pascal's time it had made sense to face the ultimate risky choice and grasp the infinitely less risky alternative, the side of the wager that custom and traditional and social sanctions also favored. But for Stephen, it seems clear that the only honorable way to face that wager is to grasp the far riskier alternative.

A second ingredient shows why the rebellious choice is the more honorable: it demands absolute, total honesty about Stephen's doubts, and results in a kind of integrity or wholeness of spirit that accommodation to traditional beliefs will preclude. Explaining why he dares to risk the wrath of God, Stephen says to his friend, Cranly, "I fear more than that [wrath] the chemical action which would be set up in my soul by a false homage to a symbol behind which are massed twenty centuries of authority and veneration." A chemical reaction can take place only when the soul is divided into conflicting elements. A modern spirit like Cranly who clings to traditional beliefs is inevitably torn, as Cranly admits, pulled in conflicting directions. To submit to such a state is not only to show lack of integrity in the sense of unity-of-soul but in the more modern sense of the word: it is to be insincere, dishonest. Traditional views of the soul or of "character" saw each creature as inevitably a composite of elements, not a clearly unified, single force in the universe; no classical hero was troubled by his multiple roles. But like many another modern, Stephen will no longer tolerate such division: he is willing to be damned, if necessary, in order to achieve sincerity or authenticity.

Third, as is already evident even in these brief quotations, the ultimate value for such a soul is freedom, liberation. ". . . I will try to express myself in some mode of life or art as freely as I can and as wholly as I can. . . ." (It may be significant that Stephen seems divided between the language of souls and the language of selves. Later rebels would avoid the word "soul" like the plague.)[7] He talks of seeking "unfettered freedom." Later in his journal he dwells on the word free: "Free, yes. . . . Soul free and fancy free. Let the dead bury the dead." Explaining why he will not become a Protestant, Stephen says, "What kind of liberation would that be to forsake an absurdity which is logical and coherent and to embrace one which is illogical and incoherent?" Note that the word "liberation" is his only argument: if it is not some kind of liberation, it will not do, regardless of whatever else might be said for it.

It is important, fourth, that such integrity or honesty in pursuit of freedom be exhibited in a negotiation primarily with a private self, only incidentally by honest dealings with others; the risky choice can be made honestly only by a single, isolated, even lonely person or self — not a soul made in the image of God and thus inherently more like other souls than different from them, but a soul that is unique. The choosing self is a single lonely atom that cannot but be its own most precious possession, once that Pearl of Great Price, the Good Word, the word of the Other, has been repudiated. Words like "my self" and "alone" recur throughout the conversation. Cranly remembers Stephen putting the choice like this: You seek "to discover the mode of life or of art whereby your spirit could express itself in unfettered freedom." Cranly presses him about what it will mean to be alone: "Alone, quite alone. You have no fear of that [?] And you know what that word means? Not only to be separate from all others but to have not even one friend[?] . . . And not to have any one person who would be more than a friend, more even than the noblest and truest friend a man ever had[?]" And Stephen answers, "I will take the risk."

Just think of what that means, not only as a rejection of the Catholic Church but as a rejection of almost all that makes human life possible anywhere at any time. The expression of the supreme value of the isolated atomic self has never been more forceful. There is no hint from Stephen, though the artist Joyce provides plenty of hints from Cranly, that in surrendering to or embracing the Other or Others one might find support or healing or instruction, let alone freedom. There is indeed no hint, even in Cranly's words, that Stephen's picture of his "self" is radically suspect — no such isolated self could ever exist — or that his picture of the self he serves is a Romantic inheritance from his own immediate past and thus dependent on others.

In fact, Stephen's values are in no sense his own; they are inherited. All of them are by his time commonplaces of revolt, and this seems most evident of the value of the self placed in opposition to society. Already one hundred years earlier Jane Austen could parody the notion that the isolated self can discover its own values — not only in an antiromantic novel like *Sense and Sensibility* but even in her juvenilia, where she has great fun with independent characters like the young lover who draws himself up to his full height and proclaims, "No! Never shall it be said that I obliged my Father." (See the whole marvelously funny episode in "Letter 6th" of *Love and Freindship.*) In short, the enemy of Bright Young Rebels for more than a century had been other people; there is not yet in Stephen any awareness of what many critics since then have stressed — that each of us has met the other and, as Pogo might put it, they is us.

The battle is not, however, only with others, in loneliness; it is especially with those others who stand for the past. Cranly, young and already threatened by doubts similar to Stephen's, must be at least argued with. But no older person in the book — no teacher, no priest, no parent, no companion — is shown as really worth talking with, let alone as worthy to offer advice. (I admit that this is not as strong a point as it might be if other *young* people were not—except for Cranly—treated with almost unfailing contempt.) The true enemy to liberation of the soul is "twenty centuries of authority and veneration," the past and those who stand for the past. "I will not serve that in which I no longer believe whether it call itself my home, my fatherland or my church. . . ." Fetters from the past threaten. One seeks a "defence," in a proud choice of arms that protect oneself from intrusions from the past: "silence, exile, and cunning." It is true, of course, that Stephen is an unusually learned young man, and he is quite willing to make use of fragments from the past in fighting his battles: bits from Aquinas or Aristotle or Bruno, bits of Greek myth. The past can lend him hints and examples; but it cannot grant him an inheritance of credible beliefs.

Implicit in all this and explicit at several points in *Portrait* is a sixth mark, an insistence that liberation will be found, if at all, only in some original mode, as yet unforged—in some innovation, some form of creativity that will break with everything that has gone before. The lonely, bravely honest battler for freedom, breaking the fetters of a hostile past, does so by seeking what is truly new, what has never before been conceived. Since his "self" is unique and new, his freedom will be found in a lonely expression of novelty. Stephen repudiates Michael Robartes's embrace of the "loveliness which has long faded from the world," desiring instead "to press in my arms the loveliness which has not yet come into the world." Seeking finally to "learn in my own life and away from home and friends what the heart is and what it feels," he goes on, in what is surely one of the most representatively modern moments in modern literature, "to forge in the smithy of my soul the uncreated conscience [n.b.: the as yet *un*-created conscience] of my race."

IV. WHAT RECENT INNOVATORS LACK THAT STEPHEN STILL HAD:
A SENSE OF A POSITIVE VALUE THAT IS NOVEL IN ONE'S TIME.

All of these six ingredients of innovation can be found in current efforts at intellectual novelty. There are variations, of course, perhaps the most notable being the radical critique of the atomic self that some deconstructionists have recently offered. What is most strikingly different, however, about all sophisticated efforts to innovate in our own time is their lack of Stephen's seventh ingredient: some strong, supremely desirable value in addition to freedom itself—a value that is worth the cost of all that must be cast off, a value that is turned *toward* as the past is rejected.

For Stephen that value can be only art. Like many others facing the death of God, Stephen turns to the domain of the aesthetic as the one value that the past has not shown to be hollow. The forging of the uncreated conscience of his race is to be done by creating great works of art; there is no hint of skepticism about the possibility of such works, and no hint of the possibility that works of art are not worth every conceivable sacrifice. Everything that is rejected is rejected because it would prevent—not just the freedom to innovate or be creative—but the freedom to create the one thing in the world of unquestioned value, something of such ultimate worth that a total sacrifice of everything else in its service makes sense.

I do not see any such ingredient in current programs of innovation, and I suspect strongly that there can be none. Remember that the ingredient must be something both supremely valuable and something that has never before been worshipped *as* the supreme value: otherwise its worship will not be genuinely novel. And the painful truth that all would-be innovators must face in the 1980s is that, so far as anyone can now tell, there are no such novelties left.

To make sense of such an implausible claim, we must distinguish between what might be called grand innovations and petty innovations. Petty innovations abound, and no doubt they will continue to abound: brand new views of the age of the universe, or of the true anthropoid ancestor of our race, or of the nature of black holes or charmed quarks; exciting new miniaturizations of computers; new games to stave off the boredom that threatens all hedonisms. But *grand* innovations—new underminings of past ultimate values combined with new stabilities worth fighting for —these depend on our finding some undeconstructed value that we can turn *to,* as we turn *away* from whatever becomes outmoded. We are privileged or cursed to live at the end of a long, long line of grand innovations. Possessed of the habit of grand innovation, convinced that what our past offers us just won't do, we open the barrel labelled "Grand Innovations" and find it empty.

Grand innovations are religious conversions, turnings toward a new set of ultimate beliefs that provide, as a capstone and justification for life, a reason for rejecting the old gods. A totally secular age would be one with no stable beliefs remaining of any kind. Obviously most people in our society do not yet live in a totally secular age; most people at least believe in Success and Mammon; and there are no doubt very few, outside limited academic circles, who are aware of just how thoroughly the rhetoric of negative innovation has done its work. It has done its work only for those who have attended to the history of critical underminings, of last-ditch stands against the steady march of what we can call, leaning on Paul Ricoeur, the "rhetoric of suspicion." That history has at last shown that innovation-by-casting-off simply cannot be an infinite progress: it comes to the end of the line, an end signalled by the lack of anything further to be cast off.

Such statements are risky; they smack of the futurology I have scoffed at. I am aware that innumerable thinkers throughout modern history have seen themselves as individually at the end of that line, in a *cul de sac* that required a total rethinking of who we are and of where we might go in our innovations. Again and again since Descartes, thoughtful people have shown how systematic doubt can lead to total skepticism, and they have then shown how some fresh start, some reconstruction or renovation, could not be undertaken. In each case until the present, later thinkers have been able to show that the desperate turn itself still depended on some faith that was as yet unquestioned: Descartes relying on the unquestioned ego; Hume relying on a referential language; everyone until recently on the assumption that at least the truths of mathematics were certain. When I say that we are at the end of the line, how am I to know that we are all not relying on some unspoken, unconscious substance or presence that has never yet been uncovered and subjected to the melting fires of systematic doubt?

Well, all I can know is that every conceivable solidity that anyone here might mention would be rejected by someone else in this room, *on the basis of a systematic critique that some major philosopher has already made.* "There is no such thing as a self, but only a shifting chain of illusory signifiers for various selves, characters, identities, figures, persons never unified into a single stability." "There is no such thing as a substantive unified work of art of the kind Stephen sought to create carrying the authority of its own quality; all we have is an infinitely open invitation to interpretation." "There is no such thing as language that refers to any nonlinguistic reality, but only an intertextuality, allusions alluding to allusions in another infinite chain." As people are fond of saying these days, at last in our time everything is in question. But everything.[8]

It is important to see that the point is not whether you or I have some faith that we cling to — most of us do, I hope — or whether the majority of thinkers in the world have come to a dead end. The point is whether any one of our faiths has still not been systematically undercut, by someone, somewhere, using in a responsible way the methods of questioning and criteria of evidence long taken as standard for responsible inquiry. If you can think of a value for which this claim does not hold, I shall be delighted to look at it closely with you. But I shall not hold my breath while waiting.

Note that in constructing this paper so far I have myself relied on one remaining value as the defining feature of human existence, namely freedom. Even the most radical of critics claim still to be serving this ultimate value. But even as we rely on it, we know one deeply disturbing fact about our service: freedom has long since been subjected to radical critiques of the kind I'm talking about. No one of us can claim to be able to prove that we are free, against those philosophers who have "proved" that we are not. We know too much, by now, to pretend that freedom is invulnerable to the question: Do you *know* that you are free, according to the criteria of genuine knowledge accepted by all tough-minded inquirers since, say, Descartes? I think the answer is obvious: we do not know our freedom, we cannot prove that we have it, according to those criteria of demonstration.

V. WHY THE EXHAUSTION OF NOVELTIES NEED NOT IMMOBILIZE US

Where are we to turn, if indeed all stabilities have been undermined, all novel grand-values tried and found wanting, including our confidence in our freedom? One possibility would be to embrace what Stephen Pepper calls "utter skepticism" and simply shut up shop. Another possibility is to follow certain existentialists and absurdists and say, "I do not *know* my freedom. But I can *affirm* it, against reason. Reason has failed, but action is still somehow possible." What we cannot say, I think, is that we have a reasoned case for seeking further intellectual innovation. With all platforms bombed out of existence, we are forced to give up our tired old quest for novelty and take up with some serious efforts at *re*novation.

No such efforts can succeed, however, so long as we forget to "deconstruct" the modes of reasoning that led to our impasse. Only if we can find a method of reasoning together that is not itself discredited can we hope to renovate any of the platforms that the march of "reason" destroyed. But on the other hand, if we *can* develop such a method or methods, then "everything is put into question" in a sense radically different from what is usually meant by the formula these days: every value that we thought we had lost might now offer itself for reconsideration—for a kind of "reconstruction."

We could not know, in advance, which of our former repudiations would now have to be repudiated. But we could know that the whole history of thought, with its seeming account of refutation after refutation, is now itself put into question.

To some this turn will seem backward, reactionary, because every competent historian will be able to show "old-fashioned" precedents for every move we make. To others it will seem innovative, because they will not know that the turns have been forced upon the human enterprise (though on a lesser scale, I believe) many times before. But to some of us the turn will seem inevitable and self-justifying; as professors of rhetoric or communication or philosophy of language, we have for millennia been trying to tell the world that all knowledge is only probable at best, that the most important knowledge is least subject to absolute proof, that—as Vico put it—we really know only what we have ourselves made, and even that knowledge is rhetorical knowledge. It depends on chancy human inferences, and it is mediated by consensus established in rigorous but necessarily ambiguous verbal exchange.

But once the return to reliance on rhetorical proofs has been accepted as inevitable, once we have recognized that the search for the absolutely indubitable has reached the end of the line, vast new—or rather *re*newed—enterprises open themselves before us. Every past stability that we had thought taken from us can now—indeed *must* now—be taken seriously again, the grounds for and against relying upon it carefully reconsidered: God, Nature, Law, the self, character, history, justice, political progress, knowledge of causes, knowledge of persons, love, friendship—all are suddenly possibilities once more; all of our previous questionings are now in question.

Hints of this exhilarating renewal have been in the air throughout the century, all of them based on an attempted renewal of the language of renewal. Pragmatists like Peirce, Dewey, James, and Royce attempted a final deconstruction of the private, atomic self, and—with a new *social* psychology and a new logic of action—effected what Dewey called a *Reconstruction in Philosophy;* in *acting* we *think,* and in joining thought to action, instead of divorcing the two as Descartes and his heirs had done, we come to know truths that are invulnerable to positivist underminings. Wittgenstein and his followers, in a surprisingly similar move, began with a special kind of action, our indubitable ability to talk together, and they renewed philosophy by showing that when we speak we know much that we cannot prove in the old ways; we speak value judgments that we *know* in *speaking,* and scores of Wittgensteinians have by now shown why the scientific tradition was wrong when it sharply separated knowable fact from merely assertable, unknowable value.[9] Michael Polanyi, reconstructing the philosophy of science, demonstrated that all of our knowing, even the most positive, depends on a kind of tacit knowing, a *Personal Knowledge* that can be called neither subjective nor objective but intersubjective; as knowers we are inescapably "convivial." Rhetorical theorists like Chaim Perelman have shown the total inadequacy of modern proof-paradigms in accounting for rational procedures in law, politics, and everyday life. In my own view, no doubt absurdly biased, the revival of rhetorical studies since about 1950 may prove to be the most important of all the steps in the renaissance I am tracing. Finally, I should mention—though they do not fit the list as neatly as I might wish — the Neomarxists, who have never surrendered their beliefs that we can know a good deal about injustice and inequality, and that we should not let our scientific inquiries on old models obscure the possibility of knowledge about the matters that concern us most. (The way in which they do not fit is this: they began their critique earlier, and in a sense the twentieth-century advocates of a science of political values, like Fredric Jameson and Raymond Williams, are just a touch too predictable in the values they discover.) And there have been many others who, like Suzanne Langer, would develop a *Philosophy in a New Key,* based on looking closely at our modes of symbolic exchange — at what I am calling our rhetoric.

None of these is entirely new, though each one packages its "novelties" in distinctively modern — or should I say post-modern? — ways. Each of them revives values, and modes of discovering values, that have been effectively employed — and "disproved" — in the past. Each of them depends on one simple innovation, itself really only a renovation: the rejection of paradigms of proof, which is to say standards of systematic disproof, that were seemingly established once and for all by the scientific revolution. What they share is a sense of how absurdly imitative we are if we try to find our freedom by innovating in acts of sheer critical doubt or rejection of what has been done before. To show, one more time, that everything is questionable, by any questioner who decides to play Socrates's game of repeating the question "Why?" and insisting on hard proofs in the answers — to perform one more act of undermining — is not to be free but merely to act out, in a final twitch, the habits of centuries.

VI. FREEDOM OF INTERPRETATION RESTORED THROUGH A RHETORIC OF RECONSTRUCTION

What does all this suggest about freedom, and especially freedom of interpretation of the kind sought by the young critic I quoted?

In the traditions of modernism, freedom became more and more commonly defined as freedom from restraint — not freedom *to* act but freedom *from* constraints on action. In this view, free interpretation became simply freedom to avoid error, and it was exercised by ferreting out error wherever doubt could discover it. Once doubt had discovered that error could be found everywhere, since every reading could be shown to be wrong from some other perspective, freedom was radically threatened. The only direction to turn was to abandon the notion of error altogether and to find freedom in the discovery of sheer individualized novelty, freed from the author's intent. In his will is not my peace but my slavery; it is his intent to constrain my freedom.

But if freedom is defined not as the absence of restraints on action but as the capacity to act, we get a different picture. My freedom in this view is the sum of what I am able to do. It will of course depend for its employment to some degree on lack of restraints, but its true limits will be established only by whatever *in me* limits my capacity to act. And that is more likely to be some kind of privation, some kind of inexperience or lack of practice than any imposed compulsion. The more choices I am in fact qualified to make, the freer I am; indeed, in certain traditional views that I am echoing here, the more I can act the *realer* I am.[10]

Without pushing into the metaphysical speculation that is almost too tempting here,[11] we can see that if I want more freedom, I will seek whatever ways there are for increasing my capacity to act, which is to say my range of choices for action. Immediately, my view of texts and their demands upon me shifts radically. Instead of a general warning to "myself" to exercise "my" freedom upon all texts, because they will enslave "me" if they can, I must now begin to discriminate. I must choose among texts and among degrees of influence, because quite evidently some texts, and their authors, would diminish *our* choices if they could, and others would increase *our* capacities by adding possibilities *we* could never have thought of on our own. (I am temporarily concentrating only on range; but the argument applies equally to quality, though in more complicated form.)

Suddenly, with this view, all of our easy division of texts and criticisms into traditionalist (constraining) and avant-garde (liberating) breaks down. "Enslavement" to some texts—those that will in any way enlarge my power to act—will in fact free me, free me to *become* as free as that text. The range of choices, actions, feelings, "worlds," friendships and enmities offered by some texts is immensely broader than what I am likely to bring to them: let's make things easy and think only of *The Iliad, The Divine Comedy,* and *King Lear.* The range of others—let's say *Love Story, M*A*S*H,* and Agatha Christie's *Curtains*—is so narrow that it is hard to think of any interpreter who would profit from a *total* surrender to the vision they proffer. I have enjoyed all of these texts and will enjoy them or others like them in the future; but my freedom is best served by dealing with their invitations to me as at best starting points, and quite possibly bad ones at that.

You will note that this view of texts as resources for freedom is based on a reversal of Rousseau's dictum about our being born free. The truth is that humankind are everywhere born in chains, capable of exercising less freedom than a newborn calf. The human baby, potentially so much freer than the lilies of the field, is in fact almost totally dependent for the direction of its growth on those *others* it is fortunate enough to *take in.* The lily of the field has only one possible path to its full expression of an extremely limited freedom: to become arrayed, without toiling or spinning, more gloriously than Solomon. Though freer to express itself than is a stone, the lily's freedom lies simply in its recognition of a necessity to become one patterned thing: an adult lily that will bloom, fade, and die. The only other possibilities are stuntedness, disease, monstrous bypaths: freedom from the one genuine path is invariably disastrous for all lilies except those that happen to innovate in the direction of some viable new species.

What we human beings did in becoming human was to open up vast ranges of potential action, potential freedom—at the cost of being relatively helpless until, by *taking in* more-or-less free models, we have become capable of action. Everyone is talking these days of the peculiar human version of neoteny, the capacity of the human cranium, unlike all others, to increase its size, and thus its brain cells, by very large amounts, *after* birth. Those billions of new brain cells added after birth are all infected, as it were, with cultural experience, and that infection will be either in the direction of freedom or slavery. But the difference between freedom and slavery is not determined by whether the baby invents totally new ways of growing; for the baby, unlike the off-spring of all lower creatures (who are all "lower" in this respect), freedom is found in following the right models, not in being genetically determined like the lilies of the field.

Perhaps by now my negative analogy with other creatures is clear: unlike the rest of creation (except as Creation itself includes us), we find our freedom not by pursuing an "internally" determined pattern of growth (though that no doubt plays a part for us too) but by picking and choosing among many possible "external" invitations to grow or wither on the vine.[12] Feeble at birth, we imbibe our strength from the thought and experience of whoever enfolds us. Viewed according to one definition of freedom, we are increasingly enslaved to others as we grow—conditioned to social patterns that would have been entirely different from those we would have received in any other time or place. But if freedom is the freedom to act, not the freedom from constraints, then it is found not in breaking free from influence but in learning modes of choice from those who have learned them before us.

If we accept something like this picture of freedom, we can see at once the folly, for any human creature facing the task of interpreting a text, of the attempt to produce an innovative reading at all costs. If my freedom is the product of all the choices I can make to act or not to act, then the test of whether a given reading frees me (and in consequence frees those who read *me* in turn) is not whether it is the same as or different from what the author intended but whether I have expanded or contracted the range or quality of possible action—including, of course, the action of imagining worlds I could not imagine before. To surrender to some imagined worlds will diminish me; to surrender to others will augment my soul by removing previous limits on my powers to act, to do, to imagine. Innovation as such is thus the last thing I need worry about, as I attempt the never-perfected task of distinguishing those encounters with texts that will liberate from those that will enslave. Indeed I shall innovate, whether I want to or not, because my own specific inheritance of voices from the past, speaking to the voice of the text, will produce novelty of the only kind I need care about—a new conversation impossible in any other moment in history. But the novelties I produce will be either stunted novelties — my peculiar, precious, but blighted version of what seems new to me — or real moments of growth; the difference will depend partly on what I bring to the text (my inheritance of past voices, past texts) and partly on the potential in the text, itself coming to me from the past.

It is not possible, in any brief statement here toward the end, to illustrate the act of finding one's freedom with a text by succumbing to it. The clearest example I know of from my own experience is that of rereading any fully wrought work carefully after having read it badly. Most of you have had the experience, and I invite you to incorporate it here — that moment when you said to yourself, "I can't imagine what was wrong with me when I first read this work. I thought it was saying or doing such-and-such, a silly or vicious or obvious job. But now I see that it is doing thus-and-so, and what a difference that now makes." It can happen in a small way with a single word. We read a silly sentence from the *Federalist Papers,* silly because the word "imbecile," meaning "idiotic," sounds like petty name-calling against *idiotic* governors; someone then suggests looking up the word in the *OED,* and that older word, *"imbécile,"* is discovered, turning the point into a serious argument about governmental *weakness.* Who is freer, the readers who thought that Hamilton was calling the governors idiotic or the reader who has discovered that the subject is power and impotence in the state?

Perhaps the best brief examples of freedom-through-surrender might be the discovery of humor in texts that originally appeared solemn, or of irony in texts that are dull or repugnant or meaningless when taken straight. I have described elsewhere a favorite graduate student of mine who declared that Mr. Bennet in *Pride and Prejudice* must be quite stupid, because he decides that Wickham is his favorite son-in-law. As soon as we looked at the text together, he saw how much he had missed: "I admire all my three sons-in-law highly," Mr. Bennet says to Elizabeth toward the end of the novel. "Wickham, perhaps, is my favourite; but I think I shall like *your* husband [Darcy] quite as well as Jane's."

What kind of freedom was it, to be free to overlook Mr.

Bennet's teasing? It was of course the freedom to remain unable to practice and enjoy such teasing and its creation by a great novelist; in addition it was the freedom, as I learned in further conversation, to reduce a highly amusing and stirring text to a rather banal discussion of freedom and necessity. For the student it was the freedom to remain where he was. Jane Austen managed to violate that nonfreedom, with a slight nudge from me; surely it is in such "violations" that our most important freedoms are released.

There are plenty of puny works around that might serve as contrasting examples; to surrender to *their* demands will be to reinforce whatever is puny or inattentive or frozen in our souls as we come to them. Even with the most powerfully freeing texts— as you would expect, they are usually but not always those that other people before us have found to be liberating, namely the "classics," the "canon" that is so often deplored these days—even with the greatest works, we will want to come to a moment when the effort to *under*stand changes to a stance of *over*standing.[13] "Great as you are," I may want to say to Dickens, "you do risk reinforcing my native male chauvinism."[14] "Exciting as you are," I may want to say to many modern works, "I do want to resist your elitism." To others we may acknowledge their powers but still say, "Stand back a bit. You're trying to reinforce my blindness to this or that political or philosophical issue, or my complacency about my class biases, my culture, my profession." But the quality of such judgments will in every case depend largely on the depth of initial surrender to *this* text (how otherwise can I discover what it is trying to do to me?) and of my past surrender to other great texts (where otherwise am I to discover standards superior to these before me?). The standards of taste that I can bring to bear, in any act of overstanding, will be derived only from what I have previously tasted.

The freedom to act as what one is—that is surely the gift beyond all other gifts. And for human beings, that inevitably entails the freedom to expand the range and quality of act, because if I am not taking in nourishment from others, I am no longer fulfilling my nature.

The whole question of innovative interpretation thus boils down, like every other question of freedom, to the question of the kind of freedom we seek. If we seek to continue as what we already are, and to express that stability and integrity as forcefully as possible on the world, then of course we will have more anxiety about being influenced than about failing to be. But if we seek to become in any sense better or larger or more mature or more *anything,* then we will find humility our surest guide.

Some few of us do, on occasion, discover something genuinely novel. That's very nice when it happens—or so I must assume, since I am fairly sure that all of the moments when I thought it was happening to me were illusory. In any case, we should never forget that every genuine novelty brings with it novel problems and pains. When Descartes and others revolutionized the medium of inquiry, insisting that we believe only what we can prove in well-defined ways, they ensured centuries of emptying and a final facing of the void. As we join thinkers in all disciplines who now labor at renewing the medium of *re*newal, we cannot predict all of the problems and pains that lie ahead. But at least *we* are freed of that most destructive of all illusions, the romantic notion that *I* am travelling alone into entirely uncharted territory, doomed to failure unless I can innovate.

NOTES

1 The best single discussion I know of America's futurism is Yehoshua Arieli's *The Future-directed Character of the American Experience* (Jerusalem: The Magnes Press, 1966). Whatever is distinctive about the American experience, it is obviously related to fundamental trends in Western culture. To put our hopes in the future-as-new is not essentially different from the traditional eschatological faith of Christians, or the Utopianism of some Marxists and of some capitalists trusting to technological progress. See John Passmore's sadly neglected *The Perfectibility of Man* (London: Duckworth, 1970).

2 See Sacvan Bercovitch, *The American Jeremiad* (Madison: The University of Wisconsin Press, 1978).

3 The most forceful summary I have seen of our apocalyptic anxieties is that of Jonathan Schell, published long after I wrote this paper: *The Fate of the Earth* (New York: Alfred A. Knopf, 1982).

4 Obviously we cannot say that everyone in fact agrees on a common formulation of this value. When a B. F. Skinner, for example, writes a plea that we move *Beyond Freedom and Dignity,* he may appear to be repudiating human liberty in the name of determinism. But even

superficial analysis of his stated goals for us as conditioned creatures shows that what he would serve is what *we* might call a "higher freedom" of the kind I shall describe below: not the *freedom from* external constraints but the *freedom to act* effectively in the world. The excitement one observes in Skinner's followers looks exactly like that seen in other twentieth-century liberation movements: at last we have found *the* system that liberates us from past compulsive repetitions of error and opens the future to a genuinely constructive — that is, free — innovation.

5 My shifty use of the first-person here gave some trouble to some readers at the conference. There are many hidden dangers in using the free indirect style in intellectual discourse — sliding from one's own words into the words of others, without clear lines of demarcation. But it is the only way I know of entering fully into the plausibility of alien positions: though I do not feel tempted by the theories I describe here, I can imagine myself into a position of feeling so tempted, and that is what I have tried to do. But I can see how my style could have led readers, most notably Professor Jane Tompkins, my official respondent, to see radical inconsistencies between what "I" say of "myself" here and what *I* say later on. See Werner Cohn's excellent analysis of the dangers of what he calls "free indirect citation," in "The 'Aryans' of Jean-Paul Sartre: Totalitarian Categories in Western Writing," *Encounter,* December 1981, pp. 86–91.

6 Many of Dostoevsky's characters — Ivan Karamazov, for example, or the narrator of *Notes from Underground* — express something like this view; critics debate about whether their author agrees with them. The hero of Butler's *The Way of All Flesh* provides another echo of this one version of Byronism.

7 For an excellent sorting out of various notions of what a "person" is, see "Literary Postscript: Characters, Persons, Selves, Individuals," by Amelie Oksenberg Rorty, in the volume that she edited, *The Identities of Persons* (Berkeley and Los Angeles: University of California Press, 1976).

8 In another talk at the conference, "No More Darwins, With a Little 'd,'" I developed this tracing of exhaustion in detail, attempting to show that the deconstructionist critique of recent decades constitutes a final turn of that particular screw. Some auditors were surprised to find me "talking like a deconstructionist"; I seemed to be saying that the critique of logocentrism offered by Derrida and others is a successful and final undermining of "presence." On another occasion one might show that rhetoricians have many times before deconstructed all presences, in the effort to defend a rhetorical reasoning about probabilities and possibilities, as against a scientific or philosophical search for certainties.

9 Eight years ago I offered, as an appendix to *Modern Dogma and the Rhetoric of Assent,* "Two Score and More of Witnesses Against the

Fact-Value Split. " By now the list would run to hundreds, among which the most ambitious witnesses would perhaps be Alan Gewirth's *Reason and Morality* (Chicago: University of Chicago Press, 1978) and Alasdair MacIntyre's *After Virtue* (Notre Dame, Ind.: University of Notre Dame Press, 1981).

10 A fuller account of the distinction between *freedom-from* and *freedom-to* that I am relying on here is given in "Freedom of Interpretation: Bakhtin and Feminist Criticism," forthcoming in *Critical Inquiry* 9, no. 1 (Autumn 1982).

11 One of the most interesting revolutions occurring in the thought of "hard scientists" centers around the consequences for cosmology of beginning our thinking with human beings as the center, rather than seeing them as accidental epiphenomena. See George Gale, "The Anthropic Principle," *Scientific American,* December 1981, pp. 154–71, for a development of how "the anthropic principle" uncovers specific, literal consequences for scientific decisions about how the physical universe works. See also Gale's "On What God Chose: Perfection and God's Freedom," *Studia Leibniziana* 8 (January 1976): 69–87.

12 Some versions of evolutionism have indeed tended to value only the neoterics that lead to a new species, as if the one monstrous genetic freak that leads to a new species of lily and finally (along another genetic line) to the glorious bloomings of humanity were more worthy than the full representative of the species. Toiling and spinning with his eye on the future, the monstrous New-Non-Lily innovates, expressing freedom by departing from the pattern. But at the same time she loses freedom, too, the freedom to be a lily. Surely it is a strange philosophy that would see more value in the freedom of innovation than in the simple freedom-to-act-as-non-toiler-and-spinner — to act as that simple, glorious, pattern-fulfilling bloomer.

Our subject leads us here, obviously to current debates among anthropologists. I am clearly siding with those who, like Marshall Sahlins, would repudiate simple functionalism in favor of seeing us as essentially creatures of symbolism; we do not "serve" easily discerned functions but rather enact roles in elaborate cultural dramas. Peter J. Wilson (*Man, the Promising Primate: The Conditions of Human Evolution* [New Haven: Yale University Press, 1980]) sees us essentially defined as "promising," in a double sense. Because we are the first creatures capable of making promises (forming cultural bonds by the exchange of symbols) we both tie ourselves to a past and open up unlimited possibility in the future. He is concerned not with literary texts but with the initial act of the mother in making a promise to both mate and offspring, thus creating the family and simultaneously a kind of relation that can be abstracted and applied in many patterns. What interests me is the analogy with our treatment of texts: *my* freedom to do anything worthwhile in the face of any text will always depend on some fulfillment of responsibility to *it,* not just on my *willing* to be independent from it.

13 See my *Critical Understanding: The Powers and Limits of Pluralism* (Chicago: The University of Chicago Press, 1979), ch. 6.

14 I face the great Rabelais in this way in the work cited in note 10 above. To me feminist critics offer us the most interesting models today of renovation through new applications of old values.

8 /

The Remission of Play

Herbert Blau

"We had lost all pleasure in this game of chase, and we weren't children any more for that matter, but now there was nothing else we could do."

— Italo Calvino,
"Games Without End," *Cosmicomics*

Since the radical impulse of performance is inherently reactionary — dancing back the tribal morn or, like Artaud's actor, signalling through the flames — I am somewhat embarrassed to say that my own concern for innovation arose from less ecstatic progressive tendencies in our liberal tradition. My convictions about the theatre were formed in a period when the prospect of a repertory theater with *continuity* — a cultural rarity in the United States — seemed an aspect of the emerging struggle for Civil Rights. Through the political inertia of the fifties, in the first fallout over the Bomb, it was necessary to revive a case (it had actually been made in the thirties but was dismantled as "creeping socialism") for the relevance of theater to society. It's something you appear to take for granted, with whatever grievances, in England, France or Germany; and in societies where the theatre seems even more naturally grounded, as in Bali or Senegal, performance is both aboriginal *and* contemporary, and innovation seemed irrelevant until the dancers came out of the Bush to go on tour, and the attritions of world travel, with thousands of curious eyes, started to adulterate those seemingly Eternal Forms. So, to begin with, the issues of innovation or renovation in performance are relative to where you are, historically, and what sort of continuity you have.

In America, it wasn't until they started to think the unthinkable in the Pentagon that we started to think about permanence in the theatre. The radical thing was survival, in both theatre and society. But activism was—as Winnie says of love in Beckett's *Happy Days*—in "the old style," and experiment was tentative—with a little *Verfremdungseffekt* and increasing dosages of the Absurd—until all continuity was disrupted in the sixties, when reality took on the character of a performance. As the dissidence thickened with the unthinkable, it was soon something of a non sequitur to ask whether the theatre is relevant to society, but whether—in a world of pseudo-image and after-image, identity crises and new life-styles, demonstrations and Happenings, role-models and play therapy, the improvising of confrontations and the staging of cover-ups, as well as the convergence of the Biomedical Revolution with the *mise en scène* of the Unconscious and other cybernetic fantasies, like the play-within-the-play, feedback and freakouts, transplants (the first one, by the way, reversing Clytemnestra, a woman's heart in a male body) and transformations: genetic management, doctored sound, permutated sex and programmed dreams—we were really getting the message of the media (Deep-Throated and beamed by satellite), that society may be nothing but a scenario after all, with Total Theatre at the living end.

Over the global village falls the veil of Maya. Amazement sits upon the brow. We are not only talking about play, but in the galaxy of the Imaginary, the immanence of World-Play. If we follow the play of thought—the whole planet thoroughly imaged—we encounter a paradox: through the shimmering display of signs, we are in the service of the imageless. The play of surface is the measure of an invisible exchange. There are eyes everywhere. What we now call spectacle is the reflex of surveillance. The world that was a stage—even the old two boards and a passion—seems to have been deconstructed and whittled into the world. There is nothing that we see, not a single gesture made in the psychopathology of everyday life, which is not an assignation with an invisible power. This is doubly true of the theatre, doubling upon itself, and unsuspectingly in the service of what it reveals. The place where three roads meet is the place where "prayers cross" (*Measure for Measure* II.ii.159) or where, the charm wound up, we encounter the three witches and look into "the seeds of time" (*Macbeth* I.iii.58). It is an array of inquisitive mechanisms, put into operation by the ingenuously self-seeking Oedipus, the instruments of a vast apparatus of surveillance—as in the scabrously mirrored fantasies of Genet's brothel, an almost demonic structure of watching and being watched—of which the CIA and the SAVAK and the GPU are merely the top, not the bottom, of the iceberg; or, as Genet would have it, the mausoleum, in which the Police Chief would be reflected to infinity. The rest is less magnificent and more insidious because part of the documentation of everyday life and the "docudrama" of historical life, in which, as Shakespeare had warned in *Measure for Measure,* "millions of false eyes / Are stuck upon thee; volumes of report / Run with these false" (IV.i.59–61), on every bill we pay, every breath we breathe: procedures, records, traces, verifications, punchcard lines of force, and a whole relational system of surrendered power in which—as Michel Foucault repeatedly points out—far from being denied individuality, we are granted it outright, by number, status, code, file; signed, sealed, and delivered to our distinction.

When, during the Vietnam War, the delivery system became demonic, some were scared to death and simply took to the hills; or, in that homeopathic magic whereby conspiracy subverts conspiracy, went underground, with lethal consequences we saw later in Europe, in the Red Guards or the Baader-Meinhof group; and aesthetic consequences, such as the nomadic paranoia of The Living Theatre or the para-sitical homesteading of the Hungarian group Squat, which is living now and performing in the United States. It seemed a kind of poetic destiny and part of the conspiratorial pattern when, in 1979, the documentation of the outlawed performances given by Squat in their apartment in Budapest was destroyed by a fire in their storefront theatre in New York. The members of the company—acquisitive as squatters in their survival techniques—say with arch irony that they "highly appreciate happenings 'by accident'"; they seem to like the idea of only partially readable remnants of their past, like the charred palimpsest of a legend, which "give some meaning, some sense, of that time."[1] Now they develop pieces for our time out of an obsessional personal mythology in a Pop-porno-Surrealist form which is the ritualized liminal outgrowth of the life they collectively live, which may—in one of their recent works—be watched through the plate glass window. Sometimes, their lives may spill out onto the street, where they may even pick up performers from among the indigents passing by, in a catatonic parody of social identity, the dubious achievement of which remains —through the equivocal narcissism, a tradition of shock tactics, and a surfeit of indeterminate play—the unsettling recidivist mission of the postmodern and a major source of innovation.

Like the Théâtre du Soleil—a post-Brechtian collective born in Paris of the Days of May—Squat is a further mutation of the communitarian anarchy of the sixties. In its works, activities have ranged from washing the dishes and taking care of the baby (who was almost born on stage, and symbolically knifed), to transvestitism and vein-cutting, and the politically saturated sequence in which a dwarf uses Zen archery to combat King Kong who—before his phallus is bloodily ripped out by a New York vamp—responds to the attack with quotations from Blake's "Proverbs of Hell." After an early phase of avant-garde self-inquiry, the work of the Théâtre du Soleil was determined to be less insular and more legible, and more specifically historical—though positioning itself as far as possible outside the conventional theatre system. The production of *1789*—subtitled *The Revolution Must Continue to the Perfection of Happiness*—was performed in an abandoned munitions factory in a suburb of Paris, where the crowds were moved around with giant puppets as at a carnival, or at one of Robespierre's pageants as it might have been staged by a proletarianized David. It is a work of considerable scale as compared to that of Squat which—for all its exhibitionism—is more furtive, self-enveloped, and encoded. As older politicized groups disappear, Squat is now part of a growing circuit of "private" and "solo" performances extending—sometimes arcane, sometimes ribald with political residues, like a fusion of *Samizdat,* Gurdjieff, Joseph Beuys, and Lenny Bruce—

all the way from lower Manhattan across the Atlantic Alliance through unaligned Europe to the Theatre on Chekov Street, where young actors brought up on Stanislavski are performing clandestine "rituals" which might have been staged by Grotowski, who is currently seeking liberation (about which, more later) by retreating to the Source.

While the more desublimated illusions of liberation, abraded by politics, seem to be in hiding, our concepts of performance, (re)sublimated in theory, are still modulating or consolidating the liturgy of the sixties. First of all, the primacy of the *staging*, dominion of the performance itself. Datum: subversion of the authoritarian Text and the system of ideological support. As the demonstrators said in the charges against Jean Vilar at Avignon in 1968, when The Living Theatre was forbidden to perform in the Cour des Papes, the theatre must be freed "from the censure that annuls it" as "the unconscious is liberated from the regime that negates it."[2] Behind that insistence was a view of the actor's old relationship to the Text as a form of servitude or a Faustian pact, in either case the actor conceding the autonomy of his body to the exigencies of the Text in exchange for the illusion, to the spectator, that the *character* being played is real. That is a social contract with an ideological subtext inscribed, as the feminists now say, in the Name of the Father, with all the vertical articulations of power in that formerly resistless and invaginated Name.

When I came into the theatre, that was orthodoxy. We used to speak, as if it were gospel, about being "faithful" to the Text, "*line perfect*," doing "what the playwright wants," which was very rarely questioned, and then only with the finest discretion about a variation. When the playwright was not present, or dead, what he wanted was a problem, but that—the actors were always told (I told them myself)—was apparent in the Text. In the European theatre this allegiance to the Text had its institutional embodiments, like the Comédie Française, which at the time we envied, though it entailed a servitude to the classics to which there could be no equivalent in the United States, where we were, as a result, even more slavish to the idea that the final arbiter of all desire in the act of interpretation was (as in the New Criticism) the indelible word on the page.

After Brecht, we started to ask the actor—that former ventriloquist's dummy—if he could *agree* with the words; if not, he might strike that part of the Text as an assumption of freedom. Abruptly, we turned the Stanislavski Superobjective upside down, like Marx turned Hegel, asking not what the character wants but what the actor wants, however blasphemous to the Text. The blasphemy was intensified by Artaud, whipping his "innateness" and passing it on to the actor, while reasserting the imperial claim of the Director, with the *mise en scène* emerging as a nearly autonomous force. In that process, the staging was to be a transgression of the Symbolic (in the Lacanian sense), an erotics of performance (in Barthes's sense), an infinitely curving field of parabolic play, further disempowering an already disappearing Origin; and there are presently young directors in France, like Mesguich or Gourville, who think like Althusser or sound like Derrida. The philosophical intricacy of Derrida—the arcanum and transparency of the "Writing before the Letter"—was synchronously spelled out in their studio exercises by the intervolving bodies of American actors in their uncontrollable mysteries on the bestial floor, and *literally* by The Living Theatre in the corporeal writing of PARADISE NOW. Simpleminded as some of them were, those "psychophysical" exercises—along with the occultations of the Counter-Culture—turned on the Europeans, who have been busy ever since giving them intellectual dimension, fortified by all the theoretical depredations on the signifying Word.

While there was a (sluggish) restoration of the Word onstage during the decade that followed, there are still repercussions of that short-circuiting of the normal conduits of discourse whose power is invested in the invisible. In short, who had the power? and where was it situated? and if it couldn't be discerned, then *displacement* would become the strategy of innovation, if only in self-protection. Performance would move out of the duplicitous "privileged space" into other arts and other disciplines, which were meanwhile using theatre to disenfranchise themselves. Secular prey to the specular, the old laws of theatre were dematerialized into the unruly speculations of a shifting subject which performs by echolocation. If it sometimes resembled the action of urban guerrillas with scrambled walkie-talkies, it was also the manifest destiny of subversion *within* the historical evolution of the form. One can imagine the gasman Antoine in the Théâtre Libre transformed into Genet's gasman in the Brothel by way of Jarry's debraining machine and Pirandello's *Six Characters in Search of an Author,* who were in turn divided up by Brecht's Alienation and broken down by Artaud's Alchemy, with its "unremitting pulverization of every insufficiently fine, insufficiently matured form . . . through all the filters and foundations of existing matter."[3] into an almost onomatopoeic alphabet of physiological signs.

This apocalyptic radicalization came out of the almost compulsive historical assault on representation. The theatre was asking not only *what* was being represented but *who* was doing the representing and by what suspect means. That in part accounts for the shift away not only from the established theatres but from the word/idea of theatre itself to the idea of *performance.* For there is no way to resolve what theatre is, a *sui generis* event or a tautologous representation of something other than what it appears to be. That it *appears* to be, or appears in *order* to be, is one of its troubling aspects, even when—with nontheatrical candor—it is denying representation by the representation of its own denial; no matter what, a representation represents itself either *as* itself or something other, with infinite combinatorial possibilities for that other, making for degrees and inversions of illusion, as well as renewals of the age-long desire to abolish it.

Cross-eyed representation: the problem is that it is somehow bisected in its *appearance* by what the American Method actor, with a heavy psychological bias, dismisses as *indication* (or untruth), forgetting that he is inevitably indicating what *that* psychology—a compound of oblique Skinnerism and popular Freudianism—prescribes as truth; just as the eighteenth century —drawing on a faculty psychology going back to the Ancients— designated as truth the precise indication of appearance, apparently as prescribed in its articulations (with Garrick or Betterton) as the *mudras* or eye-rollings of the Kathakali, which had an *un*inhibiting influence on our ideas of acting over the last generation. The running argument in acting about indication is an argument—going back to Diderot and Delsarte even before

Saussure—about the arbitrariness of the sign. To anyone in the theatre who thinks about it, Structuralism is a high theorization of the discourse on acting, as we can see (though his theory of discursive practice rejects the label Structuralism) in Foucault's remark that representation is "in its peculiar essence always perpendicular to itself: it is at the same time *indication* and *appearance;* a relation to an object and a manifestation of itself. From the Classical age, the sign is the *representativity* of the representation in so far as it is *representable.*"⁴ And in so far as it is representable, there is potentially the high melodrama of complicity that Derrida (in a quite Augustinian way) warns against, the promiscuous and illicit redundancy of reflections which deny reference and disperse origins in the narcissistic reflecting pool—like the "Private Moment" of the old Method actor, like Marlon Brando in the Studio, or the equally private moment of the newer Conceptual Artist, like Vito Acconci in *Seedbed,* who is not only on the bestial floor but regressively *under* it, masturbating over an amplifier. *Last Tango in Paris* is the French connection.

In the spilled seed, still-breeding thought; in the unwatched eye, the look of something that is looked at; speculation doubling and braided, expelling all thought of identity, since "What can look at itself is not one. . . ."⁵ And the noise which comes over the amplifier is an insufferable static, like the voiced ubiquity of repressed history, which sticks in the thorax like velcro. Which gives some justification to the redundancy, since we know from cybernetic theory, as from postserial music, that redundancy is required in a system to get through the noise, which is most deeply perceived in silence. No wonder, then, that performance went, with all the public outburst, nonverbal or antiverbal or spastically verbal for a while; or flooded, like a burst blood-vessel of engorged thought, into a logorrhea of abuse, as in Handke's *Offending the Audience,* in which we also feel the self-mocking babel of the actor's double bind as he tries to get out from under the false bottom of mimesis by not-performing, and the falsifying pathos of fictive time, where something was always happening which tries to hide and expose itself at on(c)e, as if there were no eyewitness to the event which never occurred until *now,* a perpetual present moment which he knows is all a *pre*tense.

The break with established discourse and the extension of theatre into other conceptual space led to a reconstrual *in* the theatre of every aspect of performance: subject matter and subject, language, audience, playing space and duration, play itself, techniques of production (against the "production ethic" and in the spirit of *bricolage,* not productions but "pieces," "events," "activities"), operational principles in a troupe, questions of ownership and property, amateurism or expertise?; in the disputed provenance of the Text the issue of a presiding presence, problems of depth and surface, duplicity and doubleness, imitation and metathesis (in the uninterrupted middle, the question of beginnings and ends), the acting body and the Body Politic, the issue of participation and the nature of power (restoring production with the repossessed means), the conduct of rehearsal (Fr., *répétition:* in the confusions of anamnesis, the dangers of the returning Same), acting methodology, improvisational form, standards of credibility (as inscribed on the price of the ticket, or with no tickets at all), scale and privacy, confession, the disappearance of the Chorus in the murmur of history, the "deep structure" of voice (*sounding:* the original plenitude and the *phōne*), ideographical or behavioral notation, theatre as therapy or ritualization, masking, solipsism, "Seeming, seeming" (*Measure for Measure* II.iv. 50) and polyseming, *theatricality* itself as it seems irremediably attached to representation, and thus subject to obscurantism (curtains? screening? tormentors? teasers? white light?), the illusion that sustains the discourse that, *in appearance,* seems to be exposed.

There was also serious thought for a while—in France (with the shaken but durable presence of the Comédie) and in Germany (with its heritage of State theatres) and in England (with no intention of giving up Shakespeare to the Germans, who think they own him)—to the place reserved for *tradition* and for the institution of theatre in society. This was, as I've suggested, not a question that could really be debated in America, where the theatre was belatedly spawned in an anti-intellectual atmosphere of no-theory which persists to this day, and there is no similar tradition to protect. *La mise en pièce et contestation du Cid,* a "collective creation" under the guidance of Planchon, addressed itself to this issue in 1968, and the debate continues about the Centres Dramatiques. For a while, as in the animosities surrounding Günter Grass's dialectical assault on Brecht, another question had to be entertained: why bother, as in *Le Cid* or The Berliner Ensemble's *Coriolanus,* with fake fighting on stage when there are pitched battles in the streets? We may think the question has disappeared with guerrilla theatre, but it is revived anywhere in the world where an insurrection arises, as in Colombia, and Americans have an almost absurdly peculiar perspective on it right now, as we watch the weird proceedings in Iran through images provided by our own television cameras, while German actors read from the stage a letter from Günter Grass to Chancellor Schmidt asking for a break with American foreign policy. Innovation in Iran or Rhodesia or Nicaragua is, even when the fighting stops, an altogether different affair; and we haven't yet heard of experimental theatre activity in Cuba, certainly not of the formalist kind (the Bolshevik Revolution ended that with Meyerhold), though it may be sufficiently innovative in some parts of the world to bring theatre of the simplest kind to people who've never seen it. Or, as Peter Brook and Eugenio Barba have done, used such expeditions as a possible pretext for a later formalism, in Brook's case with a polyglot group of carefully chosen performers who speak in their separate languages to people who don't understand the words at all.

That a sort of world community might be achieved by means of theatre—by rolling out a carpet in an African village or performing on a raft down the Mississippi or by immemorial incantations in the air over Persepolis, crossing the barriers of culture and time—is a notion which still has some currency against and within that other tide, the closure of representation, or the eddies of small voices distributed in solo performances all over the world, some of them (coming up from the Gulag) barely making a sound at all. For the distance between underground performances is as great as that between a maximum security prison and Broadway or between Soho and Moscow, never mind Persepolis (where Brook's *Orghast,* drawing on *Life Is a Dream* in the language of Zoroaster, was financed by the Shah). When the Theatre on Chekov Street does a ceremony in which a live carp is cut apart and cooked in a congested space with no ventilation for the smoking oil, the high solemnity and the political risk rise in the inhalations as they simply do not in the lofts, bistros, and apartments of lower Broadway, where fellow artists perform for each other and congenial visitors, with more or less paranoia or solipsism, but little secrecy—and ambivalent feelings about *not* being watched.

Assessing the scattered energies of innovation after the sixties, Julia Kristeva wrote in 1977: "Modern theater does not exist —it does not take (a) place—and consequently its semiology is a mirage."[6] As we might also expect, Kristeva argues that the theatre does not exist outside a Text, so what we are dealing with is not so much a failure of representation but of *demonstration* (or, to lend a reproachful piety to the showing, a *remonstrance*), as if, like Othello, the theatre wants ocular proof of the existence of a communal discourse for play which, if it existed, we would reject, since it would be supported by the Sacred in which we cannot believe without the mirage. Without the Sacred, a communal discourse is for all profane purposes insupportable. What's left? only private fantasies, as Mallarmé predicted. The withdrawal of the Sacred into language made it possible to sustain fantasies for private consciousness—assuring the theatre of a public of *one,* but *one divided,* as we've seen, that audience enlarged by the exponential fractures of Original Division, as in the solo performance of the broken King Richard in Pomfret Castle.

Kristeva is not the only one who believes that every attempt by an avant-garde to reconstitute a space of play for collective representation is necessarily illusory or short-lived, and more or less evasive of the central issue: that if a space of theatre were to exist at all within the supersaturated spectacle of World-Play, it would be in displaced and imaginary circles of individual consciousness, where no-time *is,* as in the *mise en scène* of the Unconscious. The liability of the contracting circle, contracting the actor to his own bright eye, is that performance may just barely exist, or not at all, in the objective world, and only as a vanishing into thought, the nature of performance becoming the destiny of performance. (Exactly this possibility was the *subject* of my own work with the KRAKEN group, putting the liability aside.) Or it might regress in another direction and attach itself to *things,* like the string tying an actor or an orange to a chair, coequally, in the theory behind the "landscape plays" of Richard Foreman. The actual landscape of his Ontological-Hysteric Theatre is indebted (and the term) to Gertrude Stein; and like her prose it is a species of performance which thinks of itself *as thought,* but beginning all over again, which seems to be — with every de-definition of art — what innovation has become. But there are definitions to be made within the de-definitions.

Foreman is one of those who has wanted to drain out of play the old *expressivity* of the drama. His theatre pieces are like an exegesis in motion of the phenomenological reduction of Minimalist art, cooled down originally by an affinity with Brecht. In the semiotic atmosphere of the Human Sciences, Foreman has been admired in Europe for these clinically surreal and cerebral plays which he virtually conducts from the lighting console, barking out cues and blowing the whistle for changes in tempo as the actors go through a disjunct puppetry of acutely choreographed paces on a stage rigged out like a Chinese puzzle box. Foreman's manifestoes are somewhat cribbed from Merleau-Ponty, but the performances — like the umbrella and sewing machine on the surgical table — are nothing like a phenomenology of the body. As with certain forms of contemporary dance, or the more gregarious pageants of the Bread and Puppet Theatre, almost anybody can perform in one of these plays, though certain actors are by now identified with them. The more rigorous training of the body in the sixties left us, however, with a reservoir of actors who would be put off by the slapstick asepsis of such a form. They are not only able to take physical risks we could never have asked of actors a generation before, but they can also *think* ideographically and insist on doing so, as if it were "a matter of *confession,* no more," as Marx put it in his letter to Dr. Ruge calling for a *"ruthless criticism of everything existing. . . ."*[7]

In the obsession with "body language" in the sixties, there was, however, an almost purely uncognitive phase where the theatre seemed to be groping toward a primal unity with dance. Much of the groping — olfactory exercises, touch therapy, and ass-to-mouth connections — was rather brainless, only suggesting in the effort to break down the "mental hang-ups" of God's frozen people, that there is a limited wisdom in the unlocked body. We used to think of dancers as brainless, too, but when dance began to think, after Martha Graham, it eventually did so with a vengeance. "I don't have ideas, exactly," said the elliptical Merce Cunningham, who gave plenty of ideas to Yvonne Rainer, who once did a piece named, as if from Nietzsche, *The Mind Is a Muscle.* "If my rage at the impoverishment of ideas, narcissism, and disguised sexual exhibitionism of most dancing can be considered puritan moralizing," she wrote in the program (1968), "it is also true I love the body—its actual weight, mass, and unenhanced physicality." [8] The dance itself was strenuously unmimetic and encapsulated: the dancers never even gazed at the audience, in order to avert the solicitations of performance, its "problem," in favor of commensurate motion, equilibrated to *task* or *movement-as-object.* The labor input is not disguised but registered. You are supposed to see the dancers sweat.

Rainer's performance-*work* has always had an autobiographical base. But it was, in the register of the time, cannily or wittily distanced, on a wobbling pivot between the severest of tasks, *like* formal requirements, and a sort of exhilarating free play, as a decoy for constructed fictions. (I once saw her break arbitrarily from an improvising ensemble and walk a manic gleam of hallucinatory purpose over the heads of the audience.) These fictions, as in *Lives of Performers,* became more openly feminist and, abandoning dance, are now being choreographed into film. *The Mind Is a Muscle* was performed with the Vietnam atrocities on her mind, but Rainer insisted then that ideological issues had no bearing on the work, which nevertheless felt "tenuous and remote" from the world crisis. The body was still "the enduring reality," [9] but she could foresee a time when the remoteness had to end, as it has been doing through the withdrawal of the body into the cinematic image—with its paradoxical impression of immediacy. Very recently—during the filming of *Journeys to Berlin/1971*—she was living in West Berlin and had direct contact with victims of surveillance. Aroused by the climate, and language, of repression written into law—in reaction to the Baader-Meinhof violence—she revised the end of her film to put on record what the head of the BKA called "*the State's monopoly of force* [Rainer's italics]." [10] She was careful to indicate, remembering repression at home — and with the "gentle *semi*-urgy" (Jean Baudrillard) of "friendly fascism" (Bertram Gross) in the industrialized world — that it is not only Germany that concerns her.

As the power of the cinematic industry has grown, it has appropriated powerful energies of performance and, in America especially, most of the major talent that might once have been in the theatre, where the devalued dollar is not so available, nor jobs. But for women artists, turning to film is, politically, the first step toward expropriating the expropriators who control the image repertoire and, psychically, like following the thread back to the Minotaur. There are numerous feminist theatre and dance collectives, but film is the lair of feminist theory, with its assault on phallocentrism and the much-belabored doxy of presence-as-absence, projected in the female Body-as-Object. Most dance, however, continues in Europe and America, with whatever feminist impulses, in the other apolitical tradition. The tenuous distance between the two is a possible measure of what you consider to be innovative.

Whether political or not, the rhetoric of the New Dance is now as easy to define as the paradigmatic dance it displaced: unencoded and quotidian movement, with maybe a parodistic obeisance to the broken barre and the remembered step; if things are there, there sparsely, no impediment to the body's presence; the music arising (via Cage's noise) from the order of Silence, in the spaces between — the frequencies of discovered sound or the scansion of randomly or serially moving feet: separate, additive, cyclical, or reversed. Reservations, of course, about the degree of randomness, as with Meredith Monk, who has also wanted a more *expressive* theatricalized space, refusing to leave things to chance. "John Cage would say there's enough structure and I would say there's enough chance." [11] Most companies now take their chances with structure, but among the many techniques the astringency of Cunningham's is dominant. Even when everyday occurrences are explored for emotional content, as by Pina Bausch at Wuppertal, it is within the *Zeitgeist* of *indeterminacy* which possesses the arts and literature. Along with the disjunct reflexions of the untellable tale and the splitting subject, there is a theodicy of *interruption,* and the sovereignty of *the recursive principle.* The repetitions of rehearsal, like the *vers libre* which is not *vers,* have always had to do with the *measuring* of redundancy. In the old dramaturgy, we always worried about how long and repetitive the behavior of a scene should be, as appearances kept slipping away. Has the audience seen *enough?* Enough for *what?* What I once learned as simple timing turned out to be a metaphysic in a time-serving form, as the system transposes gestures, words, happenings, thought, in the rhythmic interplay through space of light, sound, color, and behavior, human and otherwise. In the conventional system of drama, there was the calculated deterioration of forms, the metonymies of representation. But in *Einstein on the Beach,* Robert Wilson plays with a sort of particle physics of that problem, including the long slow petrification of motion in high-energy states. In over two hours of repetition, the first two letters of the alphabet become a code which, once established, can be permutated for several hours more. But the question remains: how long do the repetitions need to occur before the code is established? In the alternations of order and disorder within the structure of a work, or within an artistic tradition, the issue becomes one of controlling what, to use Robbe-Grillet's term, one may think of as *slippages,* the displaced continuity of decentralizations: "it is never a question of replacing the Tsar's statue," says Robbe-Grillet, "by a statue of Stalin. It is a question of never placing any statue in position, but continuing to slip."[12] The unexpected outcome of the slippage is not that, instead of a statue, you will be putting a (soon conventional) mobile in place, but a slippery slope.

There may be, then, as in the Serial Threshold Theory of cell *regeneration* (e.g., if a worm is cut in two, why does one part grow a head and the other a tail?), some limit to the process of recurrence where (as is already happening in performance) a distinct message is transmitted through the noise, an (undeniable?) act of communication (aesthetically unorthodox but a matter of survival) in that ecliptic moment before reversal begins (as in the instant of the worm's severance) — as if deciphering in the redundancy, through the signifying chains of the DNA, the originary code of the Eternal Return.

Which brings us back to the prison-house of language where, in the profusions of desire, there is still the desire for meaning. In the sixties, the kinesthetic intensity of the most innovative theatre, largely without words, *looked* like dance, where words, if they occurred at all, were objects or impulsions or random expletives of air, as they still are in the spectacles of Wilson. Across the gulf of language, one of the important rediscoveries of the period was the inseparability of actor and dancer in the theatre forms of the Far East, which are entering the structure of innovation even while some are trying to renovate the classics, not through daring new conceptions but by redressing them as Kabuki, Topeng, Jatra, or Saraikella Chhau. If recent theatre was chastened by this conspicuous memory of a common source with dance, bringing words back to the body, there is still in the theatre that other reflex, from the engrailed memory of our dramatic literature, that wants to bring the body back alive to the words, words, words, and wants them, moreover, to amount to something, for "Nothing will come of nothing" (*King Lear* I.i.90). That, too, as we learned from Beckett can be *done;* and the wonder of it was an immense reversal of theatrical entropy from the holding action of the Cold War into the synergies of the sixties. The release took place at the last articulate margins of thought where, in our avant-garde tradition, we have come to expect the real energy of innovation to come forth. That is not, however, at all the case in the German theatre today, which was early on hospitable to Beckett and has a long investment in the classical drama of words.

Despite its equally long investment in bureaucracy and the industrialization of theatre skills, the huge governmentally sponsored apparatus in Germany is apparently more active with innovation than small groups trying to survive outside the system. In a collaborative form, there's an experimental advantage in established continuity. There's also the anxiety that liberation by subsidy makes for the kind of experiment that is technocratic, replaying the bourgeois Text on the electronic turntables and computerized switchboards. Theatre activity started up in the ruins of World War II even before public transportation and the newspapers, but what Brecht said at his first rehearsal in East Berlin seems to linger on as a recurring suspicion: "The state [East and West] gives off a strange aura of harmlessness . . . as if Hitler had also used up the meanness of the Germans. . . ."[13] I don't pretend to be an authority on the degree of meanness revived in the German theatre of the last decade, but I was in Frankfurt last year on the night when the radical theatre TAT did its farewell performance, right after the general election, when the CDU came in and closed it. At the time we were told by our German friends that only the classics could carry the burden of experiment anymore because, through long familiarity, they were considered harmless, however renovated.

Nevertheless, I also saw in Frankfurt—on the black box of a nearly empty space, with a scrimmed fluorescent cube suspended menacingly above, like a block of Euclidean thought or the reflexive negative/positive of the white geometry of the corporate structure across the street (it might have been a bank), in turn reflecting in plate glass and plastic skin the Mies-en-same of the theatre building itself—a version of the Sophocles/Hölderlin *Antigone,* which included a long-haired Creon in black jeans who evolved (like student leaders of the sixties) into a business suit, and a punk-rock chorus from an S/M cabaret, who humiliated Antigone to death. Over a lowered trestle on the forestage, like a customs barrier (*"I can't go to Europe without a passport!"* American actors screamed in the sixties, though they went to Europe), an incriminating arc of white light splayed over the audience, who argued loudly in the lobby afterward both the charges of collusion and the issue of political censorship. Again, equivocal feelings. The staging was presented as an alternative to the one-dimensional thinking about a politics otherwise controlled by the media, which hardly allows a single coherent thought. Who could doubt that it was an intelligent and valuable performance? Who could doubt that the media-controlled politics was going about its business as usual?

If I've been backing away to the sixties for perspective on what's happening now, the reasons are all palpable in that offbeat production on an affluent stage in Germany, where the repercussions of that period are still being played out, as they are in Squat, organized as a commune in still-affluent America, and living from hand to mouth. As compared to Squat, the young director of *Antigone,* Christof Nel, was in a compromised situation, with all those technological resources contradicting his politics, though he tried to minimize the resources to avoid it. Some German directors—like Ariane Mnouchkine with the Théâtre du Soleil in France—shift the resources to other sites, like factories or movie houses. But there is also in certain German directors, as in Patrice Chereau at Bayreuth, the desire to use resources extravagantly to compromise the situation, like the Pop Art grotesqueries of *Bühnenraum* or the production of *The Winter's Tale* with Mattel (the toymaker's) slime all over the stage. Chereau's postindustrial version of *The Ring of the Nibelungen* (1976), with Pierre Boulez as musical director, saw in the divided Wotan an abyss between the music and the drama, in which the music disavows the ideology of Wagner's text. It seems an easy way of letting Wagner off the hook though quite consistent with the program of deconstruction, undoing the threads of the illusory fabric, letting the components have their say not in concert but in contestation with each other. The anecdotal score—overpowered by its own insurgency—culminates in a concluded music and an indeterminate drama, which causes Boulez to feel a cyclical impulse where everything begins again, with a Wotan 2 and a Wotan 3,[14] in a sort of Fibonacci spiral that might have been scored at the electronic music studio at the Beaubourg. At Bayreuth, where the Text is nearly Sacred, the supernal Wagnerian Myth was shown to be biodegradable, recycled as bourgeois melodrama. There was an uproar. But elsewhere, the spectres of Myth and Archetype also linger in contemporary performance, as at the Jungian doors of perception.

If the sixties were a time when the technocracy was rabidly assaulted, they were also a time when, against the power of the technocracy, the technological was also occulted. Marshall McLuhan was the shamanic voice. In "the mosaic world of implosion," we were told, video invokes "archaic tribal ghosts of the most vigorous brand."[15] It was in an American tradition of cranky prophecy. "See, they return," wrote Ezra Pound years before, but not for the sixties the "tentative/Movements" and "slow feet"[16]—rather the polymorphous clamor of Love's Body and high decibels, from which the Chorus of the Frankfurt *Antigone* was derived, like the murderous Altamont Festival from the Love-In at Woodstock. In the Age of Aquarius there were contradictions in the acoustics as in the communes, and a dream of Eden in computer feedback. Embracing stimulus with stimuli, we would conduct "transactions" with the means of regimentation. Or, taking vows of poverty, plunge into the accelerating dance of Shiva. Whether with oscillators, amplifiers, and light projections, or chanting pyramids of doctrinaire flesh, as in The Living Theatre's *Frankenstein,* the senses were assaulted until illusion took over, disabling the boundaries of art and life.

The boundaries still stand, of course, as stubbornly as the Berlin Wall. There were, in the sixties, other more beguiling versions of that disabling tendency, in the tradition of Duchamp and Cage. The landmass relocations (over the transcontinental telephone) and moveable feasts of the Fluxus group, who performed everything from the making of salads to mixed-media variations on the Cageian Silence, were also epistemological conundrums. Ubiquitous, domestic, and cosmic, an overflow of the fifties, they were the jetset of World-Play. If not apocalyptic, they were still iconoclastic; and in the performances of Dick Higgins or Nam June Paik could also be manically aggressive, as when Higgins sped through a crowd with a (poisonous?) uroboric snake in the air, or Nam June smashed up pianos. The after-images of Fluxus are still influential, though there was also something effete about it—too aesthetically riddling—for the raw political fervor of the sixties, with its "self-help" auxiliary of crash therapies, mass arrests, decision-making processes, Encounter groups, and karate. These tendencies have in turn influenced the new performance Activities of charter members of Fluxus, such as George Brecht and Allan Kaprow, who did the first memorable Happening and a transitional event in which a Wall made of iceblocks was constructed and melted, proving that art can do what the world can't.

In the eighties, whatever's left of the Movement has grown tentative again as, at the level of World-Play, inflation dances grotesquely with recession, and politics drags its feet. And none of this might mean much to our theme if the spin-off hadn't found its dizzy way, like the aftermath of Sufi whirling—the long diminuendo of which we see in Wilson's operas—into advanced performance theory, experimental practice, and conventional theatre, as into the circling stylistics of postmodern thought, which thinks of itself, vertiginously, *as* performance, "a whole carnal stereophony," as Roland Barthes embraces it in *The Pleasure of the Text.*[17]

Eroticizing the Text is to make of it a graph of intensities arising from a libidinal source moving over a surface that has no interior, a labyrinth of excitations without signals. If an intensity has a shape, it has no future. It is not a project. Intensities are unnameable because anonymous. In this view, the theatre is a space of intensities with no other presence but itself, atemporal, neither the movement of an a priori nor the incursion of nothingness upon the inaugural moment, only the intrinsic contours of the libidinal flow, with its glandular displacements in the acting body. But if the intensity is anonymous, it is also—for reasons beyond knowing—*amortized,* and it is the space of amortization which is the theatre that *remembers,* staking out identities and slowing down the intensities. It's these slowed-down intensities that Jean-François Lyotard perceives in artists today who are, like Daniel Buren, engaged "not in the destruction of significations but in extending the limits of sense perception: making visible (or audible) what now goes unobserved, through the alteration of sense data, perception itself."[18] That's undeniably so, and a modest proposition for art as compared to the short time ago when the analogy between "language-games" and "art-games"—asserted by Lyotard *as* analogy, but still assuming the *games*—was suspended with other distinctions, as if in the pure hegemony of play there could be the path of an excitation without memory.

So it was thought, or desired, in the sixties. And if not, why not? In the theatricalizing of everyday life, the choice seemed to be for those with half a heart: *play, or be played upon.* In the politicizing of theatrical life, there seemed to be no choice—as in the anti-oedipal seizure of the Odéon in 1968 and the pathos of Jean-Louis Barrault, who tried to mediate things with the students and ended up being fired by Malraux. You all remember the specific intensities, the spectacles and farcical *lazzi* of the time, from the levitation of the Pentagon by the Yippies to the mortification of Che Guevara by the Bolivian generals. The repertoire was catalogued in a rather exultant issue on "Politics and Performance," in the summer of 1969, by the leading theatre journal in America. Judging the photographed exposure of the dead Che as a repressive spectacle that failed, the overview was that "we seem to have entered an era in which the human dramatic potential is to be realized foremostly in life and for life. The stage once again follows along."[19]

But follows to what end? Life, as the theatre well knows, mystifies the demystifiers. An irony of our reflective distancing from the period is that what appeared to be superficial or became faddish also acquired ideological force. Take one apparent fad, virtually named in the passage quoted above: the Human Potential Movement. As it developed and diversified, from Esalen and EST to Deleuze and Guattari—even appropriating Grotowski, paratheatrically, on behalf of life—the drama dropped out of "the human dramatic potential" along with the oedipal narrative, and the human seemed to be following after, dropped by theory, a mere fissure in the anonymous order of things, the ultimate bourgeois illusion, concussively figured in the duplicities of language, with its seemingly impermeable calculus of representations. Which is how we came, in theory, to what is desirably left: the intensities of the *pure potential.* There was an intimation of this dispossessed energy of disjunctions in the jubilatory discourse —the "divine apathia divine athambia divine aphasia"—of the prophetically berserk Lucky in *Waiting for Godot.* That demented plainsong of love's bereft body, rejecting figuration, is also the topological model for the unmediated presence of the aphasic (Christopher Knowles) in Robert Wilson's *The Life and Times of Joseph Stalin* and the subsequent conversion of various types of dysfunction into a communal energy in Wilson's theatre compositions, with their stunning deployment of outer space as a Moebius strip of *in*-determinable life—which is not the surface of a depth.

What has been sought for in experiment under the name of

Artaud is a new volumetrics of theatre, in the space of the spectator who is permeated by what, then, is admissible as representation. In this seizure of a space (within), the volume unfolded cannot be reduced by speech, nor reduced *to* speech. It is a *spacing* produced by the incitation of a time which disobeys the Word and its patrimony of phonic linearity, like aphasia, a resonance of the subject in the space of words between culture and the inner ear, a voice without rhetoric. The end or closure of representation is, in this vision, "original representation," according to Derrida, "autopresentation of pure visibility and even pure sensibility."[20] Wilson's imagination appears to close upon this state. The aphasic, with the virtue of pure sensibility, has not only been given a consecrated space in the performance, but the performance gathers itself around him as a structuring force. That there is therapy in the process is a purely coincidental by-product of the aesthesis, and the therapy is mutual. What has been done is to bring into performance for the sake of performance something like the post-Laingian dispensation of Deleuze and Guattari, a strain of thought still drawing on the radicalized "politics of experience" and the ethos of disjunction. Beckett's mouth, Artaud's body without organs, and the breasts of Tiresias on the naked torso of the hallucinating Judge Schreber act together — like images out of Wilson, Squat, Zadek, Ronconi, or Terayama — to describe an autoerotic delirium that is "an intense feeling of transition, states of pure naked intensity stripped of all shape or form. . . . Nothing here is representative; rather it is all life and lived experience: . . ."[21]

We keep circling back to the intensities because, despite the slowing down, they are still being sought. Another approach to the pure naked experience — more specifically atavistic — is the recent quest of Jerzy Grotowski for a "Theatre of Sources." In the celebratory paratheatrics of *Holiday* and *The Tree of People,* Grotowski seems to be after a more elitist version of the participatory utopianism of the sixties, by which he was stricken when he first came to the United States. Is it theatre? What he is doing sounds, through the rash of skeptical and rapturous reports — torchlight processions in the forest, honey-dipping meditations, and the laying on of hands — like a Gothic renascence of Gestalt therapy. But Grotowski has been, and may still be (though I distrust the messianism) one of the more seminal artists of our time; and the theory for what he is doing may be found in Derrida's essay on Artaud, to whom Grotowski was originally indebted, in the hermetic formalism of his early work.

In the essay, Derrida speaks of the higher politics of the Festival, a return through the initiatory trace to the abrogation of all binaries and the disappearance of theatre into itself. Since the spectator is impregnated with the spectacle, he cannot project it scopically, which is a way of warding off the reality of those powers which, threatening in life, are celebrated in the Festival, which "must be a political *act*. And the *act* of political revolution is *theatrical*." [22] It is important to realize, in the de-definitions of art, that not all circles are the same circle, as this revolutionary circle back to theatre is not quite the circle of *The Eighteenth Brumaire*, from tragedy to farce (which requires parallax rather than impregnation), because it is a conception projected outside of history, where the theatre exists only in a perpetual present. In that scene, what appears to be repetition is not, and that's what we want destroyed. For the Enemy *is* repetition, the life-denying force of a cadaverous return, where the present holds on for dear life, coming into Being, the Enemy of the libidinal body, negativity incarnate, ungenerous, since it refuses the present to death, wanting to preserve its illusion. The Festival would consume it at once, leaving nothing to be repeated, *not a trace* — "expenditure without economy, without reserve, without return, without history." [23] The power of theatre is an *abandonment* — both the wildness and the discard — a politics with neither property nor propriety, where "the origin," already *within* representation, "is always *penetrated*." [24]

We can only anticipate the time with what Henry James, a stylist almost as labyrinthine as Derrida — abandoned *by* the theatre to the specular intricacies of the Novel — called somewhere "a reflective gape." Meanwhile, *in* the theatre that we know, in the immediacy of its wildest new forms, there is the pressure of old compulsion. Whether consciousness pretends to cosmic proportions or contracts to a needle's eye, it must certainly see the pretense in the performance.

Where's the action? they were asking, as everybody was making a scene or putting a body on the line. When we looked around, however, to check the line, it seemed to have disappeared, going through a series of indeterminable behaviors from action to activism to atavism, while the overdeterminations of emergent French Freud gave theoretical grounding to the idea of disappearance as the subject of performance, the self-consuming thing itself.

It may have been something of a coda to the period which haunts us like those archaic tribal ghosts, when a young man with self-cancelling propensities, who had previously had himself crucified on a Volkswagen, took up the proposition of disappearance as a cue for performance and, after duly publicizing his intention, literally vanished. His real name is appropriately Chris Burden, and I believe it was for three days. It was not entirely clear, when he returned, *the degree to which* that was the Same — the anamnestic horror of the repetitive play of disappearance, like the follicles of the *Fort/Da,* not the play but the *remission* of play — the critical problem of performance, along with the problem of *Who cares*? For if the Enemy is repetition, the repetition is *in* the play, both a limit and a spur (*éperon*) to innovation, to which performance wants at *its* limit to put a stop. We see that, literally, in Alan Sonfist's conception of a *rigor mortis* whereby he would deed his dead body to a museum. When I say, Who cares? I mean that in the declensions of performance from the public scene and the magnitudes of political action to the autisms of Body Art and the new modes of confessional performance, we are once again reconceiving, as with the aphasic, the idea of an audience, its prerogatives, propriety and scale, and the old question of wisdom in numbers. Sonfist's performance of his last will and testament, his naked body on a glass-enclosed slab, is the absolute inversion — in the body Artaud detested — of the naked streaming sonorous realization he discerned in Plato's allusions to the Orphic Mysteries.

If there is anything to be concluded from this dispensation of ceaseless beginnings, it is that there is something lethal in a pure physiology of performance — a desideratum of material murmurs that speak of forgetfulness and death. In the imagination of Artaud, it comes with equivocal reverence for the holiness of the acting body. The metaphysics through the skin would just as well, in a ceaseless sparagmos, tear the body apart; or there is a kind of fierce tumerous gloating over the progressive accompaniment of death, as over the bubos of the Plague, as if the time of theatre were a kind of Veronica-dance over the already-bled eyeballs of the *other* time, which we'll never forget.

Trying to forget is perhaps the most painful theoretical problem with which we are still wrestling in performance. The sixties took up, as if it were canonical, the "active forgetfulness" of Nietzsche and tried to enact it into being until, in the intensities of the resistance, it felt legislated. The agency of the desire-to-forget was the self-estranging subject of the play-within-the-play, denying where it came from and starting all over again, until the action we were looking for, just as it came into focus, seemed to pass out of sight. The disappearance of what we sought is the function of a longing for an unimpoverished plural, the full benison of a life pushing beyond representation, a Text which, like a field of gazing grain, extends *"as far as the eye can reach . . ."*[25] (Barthes). But the reach is also deadly, and we can't forget that, as the theatre never does, desiring *less* theatre in its crucial difference from life.

In the eighties, the outward appearances are less apocalyptic, but we are by no means free of the suffusion of life with theatre. We can see it in politics, fashion, poetics, therapy, reception theory, ethnography, and advanced critical discourse, where the terminology of performance is so prevalent we are likely to think of innovation as *nothing but* performance, taking *absolutely for granted* that you can't tell, for instance, the dancer from the dance—which was always an open question. As for the politics of performance and the performance of politics—and the shift in authoritarian modes—we see in the prolonged negotiations for the hostages in Iran a spectacular demonstration (*and* remonstrance) of that structural indeterminacy that was the participatory ideal of the sixties and the deconstructionist ideal of the seventies, a paradigm of uncentering authority, heterotopic, polyvalent, and tape-looped for speculation, where in the field of the subject there is no referent, like an avant-garde text described by Barthes, whose specific nature is *uncertain* and which can neither be classified nor judged nor — in *Le chantage à la théorie* — its immediate or eventual future predicted. "Yet this quality," as Barthes understood, "is a blackmail *as well* (theory blackmailed): love me, keep me, defend me, since I conform to the theory you call for; do I not do what Artaud, Cage, etc., have done? — But Artaud is not just 'avant-garde'; he is a kind of writing *as well;* Cage has a certain charm *as well* . . . — But those are *precisely* the attributes which are not recognized by theory, which are sometimes execrated by theory. At least make your taste and your ideas match, etc. (*The scene continues, endlessly*)."[26]

And so it does in Iran, asking our aesthetics to put up or shut up in political terms, matching taste to ideas as we helplessly observe the ceaseless deferrals in practice, outwardly masculine, but labile, feminine, veiled, a metonymic miracle of shifting power — from the militants in the embassy to President Bani-Sadr to Foreign Minister Ghotbzadeh to the Revolutionary Council to the Ayatollah Khomeini, who purportedly has the last word about which we can't entirely be sure, like a sybilline echo of the instituted trace. In this situational ethic where no answer is prefigured, we have a suggestion perhaps that structures which are alluring and supportable in art may be simply intolerable in life, depending on what game you're playing on which side of the demon of analogy, and whether or not you are the hostage, as you are to theory, where we are at a semiological loss to make distinctions about the indeterminacy. It may seem insufficiently theoretical, but it is also tempting to think — at this turn of the Viconian gyre of performance — that our next major innovations are likely to come from those who absolutely *refuse* to play games, upping the ante on illusion and thereby improving the quality of the play. The risk is clear in politics which is, so long as you *see* the illusion, an object lesson to art.

NOTES

1 Quoted by Jim O'Quinn, "Squat Theater Underground, 1972–1976," *The Drama Review* (T84) 23, no. 4 (1979): 8.
2 Quoted, from the *Treize questions aux organisateurs et aux partici-*

pants of the Festival of Avignon, by Josette Feral, "1968-1978. Theater in France: 10 Years of Research," *Sub-Stance* 18/19 (1973): 10; also in E. Copferman, *La mise en crise théâtrale* (Paris: François Maspero Éditeur, 1972), p. 68.

3 Antonin Artaud, *The Theater and Its Double,* trans. Mary Caroline Richards (New York: Grove Press, 1958), p. 51.

4 Michel Foucault, *The Order of Things: An Archaeology of the Human Sciences* (New York: Vintage Books, 1973), p. 65.

5 Jacques Derrida, *Of Grammatology,* trans. Gayatri Chakravorty Spivak (Baltimore: Johns Hopkins University Press, 1976), p. 36.

6 Julia Kristeva, "Modern Theater Does Not Take (A) Place," *Sub-Stance* 18/19 (1973): 131.

7 Karl Marx, *The Marx-Engels Reader,* ed. Robert C. Tucker, 2d ed. (New York: W. W. Norton, 1978), pp. 13, 15.

8 Yvonne Rainer's entire "Statement" is printed in *Work 1961-73* (New York: New York University Press, 1974), p. 71.

9 Ibid., p. 71.

10 "A Letter from Yvonne Rainer," *October* 10 (1979): 131-32.

11 Program note to dance concert at the Billy Rose Theater, New York, in *Playbill,* 3-8 February 1969.

12 Alain Robbe-Grillet, "Order and Disorder in Film and Fiction," trans. Bruce Morrissette, *Critical Inquiry* 4, no. 1 (1977): 16.

13 Bertold Brecht, quoted by Arno Paul in, "The West German Theater Miracle: A Structural Analysis," *The Drama Review* (T85) 24, no. 1 (1980): 7; from Brecht, *Arbeitsjournal,* Zweiter Band 1942 *bis* 1955 (Frankfurt/Main, 1973).

14 For Boulez's commentary on the interpretation, see Jane Boutwell, "Chereau's Ring," *Performing Arts Journal* 2, no. 1 (1977): 84-90.

15 Marshall McLuhan, *Understanding Media: The Extensions of Man* (New York: McGraw-Hill, 1966), pp. 294, 301.

16 Ezra Pound, "The Return," from *Ripostes* (1912), in *Personae* (New York: New Directions, 1966), p. 74.

17 Roland Barthes, *The Pleasure of the Text,* trans. Richard Miller (New York: Hill & Wang, 1975), p. 66.

18 Jean-François Lyotard, "Preliminary Notes on the Pragmatics of Works: Daniel Buren," trans. Thomas Repensek, *October* 10 (1979): 67.

19 Lee Baxandall, "Spectacles and Scenarios: A Dramaturgy of Radical Activity," *The Drama Review* (T44) 13, no. 4 (1969): 53.

20 Jacques Derrida, "The Theater of Cruelty and the Closure of Representation," trans. Alan Bass, *Theater* 9, no. 3 (1978): 10.

21 Gilles Deleuze and Felix Guattari, *Anti-Oedipus: Capitalism and Schizophrenia,* trans. Robert Hurley, Mark Seem, and Helen R. Lane (New York: Viking Press, 1977), pp. 18-19.

22 Derrida, "Theater of Cruelty and the Closure of Representation," p. 14.

23 Ibid., p. 15.
24 Ibid., p. 16.
25 Roland Barthes, *S/Z*, trans. Richard Miller (New York: Hill & Wang, 1974), pp. 5-6.
26 *Barthes by Barthes,* trans. Richard Howard (New York: Hill & Wang, 1977), p. 54.

9 /

News, Sex, and Performance Theory

Richard Schechner

I

It's as hard to *write about* performance, theory, or practice, as it is to put ideas, *as such,* on stage. For the writing is always indirect, representative, the map not the territory. And the stage always is there, physical first, a howling territory only vaguely pointing elsewhere. But both writing and performing create negativity. Emily Dickinson: "Wonder is not precisely knowing, / And not precisely knowing not, / A beautiful but bleak condition."

Performance theory, when well done, takes into account both the beauty and the bleak condition. As well as the negativity, full of the Japanese *Mu,* pregnant pause, full emptiness, that the stage so totally is. Because, as I said, the stage is first a physical space waiting to be filled; and then a full physical space. But at the same time that the stage is full, it is filled with propositional emptiness. Quoting myself,

All effective performances share this "not — not not" quality: Olivier is not Hamlet, but also he is not not Hamlet: his performance is between a denial of being another (= I am me) and a denial of not being another (= I am Hamlet). Performer training focuses its techniques not on making one person into another, but on permitting the performer to act in-between identities; in this sense performing is a paradigm of liminality.[1]

And what is liminality but literally the "threshold," the space that both separates and joins two other spaces: the essence of in-betweenness.

This in-betweenness, thresholdness, too is emphasized by poets as having something to do with performance, with the flow and evanescence of human life (as consciousness of itself). "But tell me," Rilke asks, "who *are* they, these acrobats, even a little more fleeting than ourselves?" Rilke has no answer until, maybe, the Ninth Elegy:

Threshold: what does it mean to a pair of lovers, that they should be wearing their own worn threshold a little, they too, after the many before, before the many to come, . . . as a matter of course! *Here* is the time for the Tellable, *here* is its home. Speak and proclaim. More than ever things we can live with are falling away, for that which is oustingly taking their place is an imageless act. Act under crusts, that will readily split as soon as the doing within outgrows them and takes a new outline.

I feel that way: the theatre I know, for all its activity and visual splendor, has become an imageless act. But also my seismograph detects that *Mu* stirring beneath. The tilted jugs under the Noh stage, reverberating the stamping that summons the ghosts.

Thus the theme for my "aspects." In-betweenness, thresh-olds: the creative negativity, the double negative that when multiplied yields only positive sums.

II

There are two main realms of performance theory: (1) looking at human behavior—individual and social—as a genre of perfor-mance; (2) looking at performances—of theatre, dance, and other "art forms"—as a kind of personal or social interaction. These two realms, or spheres, can be metaphorically figured as interfacing at a double two-way mirror. From one face of the mirror persons interested in aesthetic genres peep through at "life." From the other side, persons interested in the "social sciences" peep through at "art." Everything is in quotation marks because the categories are not settled. The very activity of peeping through unsettles the categories. Or, as Erving Goffman slyly remarked in 1959: "All the world is not, of course, a stage, but the crucial ways in which it isn't are not easy to specify."[2]

Sometimes, I would say almost always, people peeping through see not only what's on the other side but their own image too. The interface between realms is a mirror. Only by willingly disregarding that image of themselves are they able to "see through" to the other side. But this willing suspension of disbelief has become too costly. Many prefer to see things tainted by the consciousness that one is seeing. Thus the reality of the perceived event — as art, as life — is a reality of both what is seen and the seeing of it. So much has this experience of seeing myself even as I see the event I am looking at become central, even obsessional, that I run back and forth from one side of the mirror to the other, looking first at art from the life side and then at life from the art side; always seeing myself from either side.

This activity — trying to see all there is to be seen, including seeing oneself seeing; trying not to use conventions to block out what is there — leads to the development of "meta" theories: theories that take into account what people experience not only on each side of the mirror — within the sphere of art or of life — but also what they experience moving back and forth from side to side.

The reports of those dealing with "meta" — performance theorists all — are complicated. Even confused. Because so many levels or modes of seeing, of experiencing, are present simultaneously. A person sees the event; he sees himself; he sees himself seeing the event; he sees himself seeing others who are seeing the event and who, maybe, see themselves seeing the event. Thus there is the performance, the performers, the spectators; and the spectator of spectators; and the self-seeing-self that can be performer or spectator or spectator of spectators.

It is this *layering* of seeings that radically distinguishes animal play, animal art, animal ritual, animal symbolism, animal communication, animal thought, from their human counterparts.

This layering can also be called playing. It is not all that playing is, but a very strong part.

III

Bateson got at the relationship between play and theatre:

We might expect threat, play, and histrionics to be three independent phenomena. . . . But it seems that this would be wrong, at least so far as mammalian communication is concerned. Very brief analysis of childhood behavior shows that such combinations as histrionic play, bluff, playful threat, teasing play in response to threat, histrionic threat, and so on form together a single total complex of phenomena. And such adult phenomena as gambling and playing with risk have their roots in the combination of threat and play. It is evident also that not only threat but the reciprocal of threat — the behavior of the threatened individual — are part of this complex. It is probable that not only histrionics but also spectatorship should be included within this field.[3]

But what is play?

Now this phenomenon, play, could only occur if the participant organisms were capable of some degree of metacommunication, i.e., of exchanging signals which would carry the message "this is play."[4]

This message is transmitted by means of the play-face, the play-mood, the eyebrow flash, the slack lower jaw: signals given in milliseconds. Such signals can be transformed and socially encoded; they may even be faked. Once they are socially encoded — understood as conventions belonging to this or that specific culture — they can be used to signal "this is play" across a broad spectrum of activities.

Buying tickets is one such signal in our culture. When I reserve seats at Madison Square Garden to see the Rangers play hockey I am prepared to witness mayhem, but within a controlling play frame. When I go to that same Garden for the circus I am prepared to see danger, but also to be tricked about what is dangerous. And if I go to the theatre, on Broadway or off, I may even see feigned death. If I were a Roman attending the Circus Maximus I would see real death, but death still bounded by the play frame. It is not simply a matter of consequences (does the actor die or not?) but of context. The gladiatorial combatants need not be enemies of each other to kill each other, any more than the player performing Hamlet need hate the person who performs Claudius. But the conventions of the Circus Maximus dictated, usually, death for the loser, while the conventions of Shakespeare's theatre asked only that, in Hamlet's own words, the mirror be held up to nature "to show virtue her own feature, scorn her own image, and the very age and body of the time his form and pressure." The difference between the Circus Maximus and the Globe is the difference between Spanish and Portuguese bullfighting. Surely the difference speaks of nontheatrical differences within the societies, and I prefer peaceable to bloodletting drama. But still I tune into professional football each Sunday afternoon. So if I announce for peace I still enjoy, if not the death of entertainers, a sport that has its fill of broken bones.

And even in New York today there is some theatre — not sport, not licensed combat like boxing — but authentic theatre where the "real" is mixed in with the fantasy. This theatre includes live acts and episodes on television. Before this essay is over, I will be saying a good deal about television reality. For the moment, let me speak of Belle de Jour, a sado-masochistic theatre on West 19th Street in Manhattan. It costs thirty dollars for men, five dollars for women, to attend Belle's. Belle herself welcomes the audience and takes them on a tour of her place. Before the theatrical presentation begins, we see a woman stretched on the rack (obviously pretending to be hurt), a man burned by a candle, a woman urinate into a man's mouth. Then the audience is seated on bridge-chairs opposite a small raised stage of gloriously polished wood. It reminded me of a Noh stage. As part of several skits, some of them comic, some meant to be scary, a variety of sado-masochistic actions take place: whipping, breast pinching with pliers, testicle tying, dripping of molten wax on a woman's breasts and body. One of the climaxes of the performance is when Belle herself drives a three-inch nail through the penis of her "toilet slave." This is no Grand Guignol trick. In fact nothing at Belle's is like the Grand Guignol where we, as spectators, expect to be tricked. Belle thrives on giving her audiences, as much as she can, the real thing.

After the skits Belle invites spectators onto the stage to spank or be spanked. About fifteen of the audience of fifty respond. It usually takes some coaxing to get people on stage. More men than women accept Belle's invitation. The participants spank or get spanked. One or two of them are given a heavier workout. I saw a man get stripped, hung upside down by his ankles, and be heavily spanked until his buttocks were very red. Participating spectators don't work on each other. They work over Belle's people, or her people work them over. It's all very carefully controlled. And most people are new for each performance; a few are regulars. When the participation segment is over, Belle announces that "private sessions" will be offered until 2 A.M. These sessions actually occupy Belle and her staff most of the week. The big money is in private sessions where clients propose scenarios that are acted out with/for them. Belle's theatre is actually doing very much what Genet proposed in *The Balcony*. I asked Belle: she never heard of Genet or his play.

Talking with Belle I found out that much of her artistry, theatrically speaking, came accidentally. She was the owner of a small clothes boutique specializing in the kind of garments sadomasochists like to wear. She designed the clothes herself. She describes herself as a "dominant." One day she moved into a new loft on 19th Street. It had a stage in it. "I didn't know what to do with that in the middle of my living space," she said. After about a year it dawned on her: stage = theatre, and so she started Belle de Jour. It's been very successful. She talked to me about a new idea she has: opening a small dinner theatre specializing in S & M acts and featuring a cutesy menu with items like "humble pie" for dessert.

Belle wants to take acting lessons. I wouldn't advise it. Her stage presence is strong just because it is so unstudied. She mumbles, she looks spectators straight in the eye, she actually gets angry when something goes wrong. In her fifties with straight gray hair cut short, Belle is not pretty. But she is very convincing in her black leather miniskirt, high heels, net stockings, and riding whip. An original. Hers is an authentic folk theatre.

Is it decadent? If decadence means what happens when cultures "decline" (itself a shady concept), I caution against labelling

Belle de Jour. I'd guess that activities like hers have been around a long time, in many different circumstances and cultures. And compared to what I've seen in gay bars, bath houses, and at punk clubs, the audience at Belle's is very bourgeois, dressed mostly in conservative suits and ties, or sweaters. I wouldn't go labelling the bars, bath houses, or clubs decadent either.

The people at Belle's—players, spectators, and spectator-participants—are playing and they are not playing. Or, if you prefer, their play takes on an intensity, a concentration, a seriousness that we do not often see in the "real theatre" where we have been accustomed to a flabby pretense. The concentration I felt at Belle's was like what I've seen in professional sports, or at a black church I attended in Harlem, or at my own parents' family celebrating Passover seder.

Intensity, passion, concentration, commitment: these are all part of the play mood. But this alone is not what makes play play. There is also the quality of acting out, of becoming another, of displaying a normally hidden part of yourself. And of becoming this other without worrying about consequences. Play implies getting away with it. Or as Bateson puts it succinctly,

These actions, in which we now engage, do not denote what would be denoted by those actions which these actions denote. The playful nip denotes the bite, but it does not denote what would be denoted by the bite.[5]

Or, as Belle put it, if someone really hurts someone in her theatre she knows something is wrong. Nips are "pretend" bites, and even if they hurt they are forgiven (usually) if framed in play. But even these pretend bites remind us that nips are a "kind of" bite, and can, if the play frame is destroyed, become "real" biting.

Where does this leave the bleeding gladiator, or even the authentic sado-masochist at Belle's? Their condition, theatrically speaking, is very different. The Gladiator doesn't want to play. He is not playing. He is a spectacle for the spectators. He is one with the animals: brought in under guard to be used as entertainment. The spectators are "at play," but the gladiator is a slave given only the choice of death now or death later. But still his own situation, which is not play, is presented within the play frame. If this seems strange, even obscene, I will show that it is not too different from what NBC presents each night on its local Nightly News 6 O'Clock Report on Channel 4 in New York.

As far as the man who gets his penis nailed at Belle's, he is in "real life" a mechanic. He likes getting his cock nailed. He is not paid for it. He also likes Belle urinating into his mouth. It is a matter of psychological opinion whether or not this man is more or less free than the ordinary actor who also likes his work which may involve simulation of some pretty gruesome situations. One fact is clear: the man at Belle's is not physically coerced as the gladiator is.

But are the foregoing actions themselves — which I pick as extremes to test Bateson's propositions concerning the play frame — mere nips denoting the bite, but not denoting what would be denoted by the bite? In other words, is the death of the gladiator any sure indication of enmity between him and his opponent, or even between him and a wild animal? Is the man at Belle's being "hurt" by the nail? Is she punishing or torturing him?

However these questions are answered, it is certain that Belle de Jour is a "liminal" theatre. Its performances are not advertised (yet) on the theatre pages of the *Village Voice,* but in a quasi-classified section near the back titled, "Adult Entertainment." There a great number of "fantasy" entertainments are listed. Many of these are thin masks for prostitution; others, like Belle's, comprise a genre of performance of the "not — not not" category. Places like "Fantasy Manor" where, the ad promises, a person can "experience decadence & delight in a new unique concept in sensual, bizarre, & unusual partying — plus all facilities of an on-premise swing club for singles & couples." On Thursday at Fantasy Manor there are "live onstage 'unusual' performances."

Although this kind of stuff is not reviewed in the *Voice* or *New York Times,* it has been written about in *The Drama Review,* the nation's leading scholarly theatre journal. The March 1981 issue was devoted to "Sex and Performance." Most of the articles concerned legitimate theatre, both mainstream and experimental, that have used sex or sexual themes. Obviously, this can include a lot of items since sexuality has been one of the major preoccupations of theatre throughout history and in many cultures. But one article was specifically about the kind of theatre presented at Belle de Jour's. Catherine Burgheart's article begins:

One need only open a copy of the *Village Voice* or *Screw* to become familiar with the wide variety of sexual performance available today. Along with the peep shows on 42nd Street and the private "on-the-premises" clubs, there exists a little-known network of four or five establishments in lower Manhattan offering sexual entertainment in the form of theatre. Sex theatre deals almost exclusively with sado/masochism (S & M), bondage and discipline, and dominance and submission.[6]

Burgheart's article goes on to detail the "network of sex theatres" which, she claims, "form a small and intimate community." In other words, these theatres — and the people who run them as well as the audience that attends — are not yet part of the entertainment world, competing with each other; but they are "not not" part of that world either. Just as the activities inside the theatres — what goes on on the stage, in the "private sessions," with the participating audience — cannot be strictly categorized as belonging either to theatre, prostitution, ritual, economic exploitation, community sharing activity, or any other single category, so the theatres themselves are also "in between."

But liminality is a quality that is found not only in performances that stand between the "legitimate" and the "illegitimate" theatre but also something that experimenters in the theatre have been playing with (is there anything comparable in literature? or in so-called pornographic writing?). In experimental theatre, the limen is between "life" and "art," and, relatedly, between "chance" and "fixed" structures. Because much of this work dates back to the Surrealists and includes, more recently, the work of John Cage, and is therefore well known, I won't linger on it. Instead, I will present a more recent example from a theatre still working in New York, a theatre whose very history is liminal.

I am talking about Squat, a performance group residing and performing on 23rd Street, just west of the Chelsea Hotel. This group has received a lot of attention in New York and is considered one of the city's leading experimental theatres.[7] Squat, as the name implies, is a theatre of exiles, a bunch of squatters, people of several families who began work in Hungary, were forced to

197

leave, worked in other places in Europe for a few years, and then came to America in 1977. They first performed here at the New Theatre Festival in Baltimore in 1977. Shortly thereafter they moved to New York. The ground floor of their rented building is a store-front theatre with room for about 65 spectators sitting on risers facing the window. On the other three floors are small performing spaces (sometimes used, sometimes not), a lobby, and living quarters.

Almost all of Squat's shows exploit the window fronting on 23rd Street. This window actually is a model of that two-way mirror I was talking about at the beginning of this writing. On the 23rd Street side there is "life"; on the inside there is "art." And Squat plays with moving back and forth from one side to the other. Let me give examples from *Pig, Child, Fire!* (1977) and *Mr. Dead & Mrs. Free* (1981). For much of *Pig* the street is a backdrop offering some gags: passersby doing doubletakes as they see something strange going on behind the window, like a goat eating vegetable scraps as a family sits at table, or a little girl parading around in falsies; and the audience laughs at passersby, as they would at Candid Camera. That's because the audience inside knows that *Pig* is a "play" (however offbeat) while the passersby can't decide what they are seeing. So the audience sees people who are unable to locate in terms of genre what they are seeing, and the audience inside enjoys watching the incidental audience outside. Later in *Pig,* a TV camera is focussed on the audience inside the theatre. At that point the paying spectators can watch themselves watching.

It even happens that some knowing persons, having seen *Pig* from inside the theatre, return later to watch it from outside. At that point there are three audiences: insiders, outsiders, insiders who are outside. Sometimes the street is used to stage *coups de théâtre,* as when a man strolls by, his arm ablaze. (He wears a special kind of plastic coating that flames at relatively low temperatures.) I won't discuss the overall flow of actions of the five parts of *Pig.* These are not significant as drama, narrative, or social commentary. (That itself is a problem, the problem of meaning or content, and I will deal with this problem in relation to contemporary experimental performance later.) What the actions of *Pig* do is evoke and illuminate the system of transformations relating the "art" side of the performance to the "life" side. Again and again, Squat points up the differences of these realms and then questions those differences. Examples follow:

1. A large puppet hangs upside down. From out of its anus protrudes the head of a man whose face is identical to that of the puppet. Around this man's neck is a noose. For 20 minutes or so this man stares unblinking at the audience. The large puppet is removed so that the man appears to be born from the puppet's asshole; and as he is born so is he hung. Then, slowly, he removes his "face" (a very cunning mask that conforms precisely to his own features). This mask = both his own face and the face of the puppet. The face under the mask is identical to the mask. This confounds the audience's expectations concerning the mask. For what is a mask if it is not a concealment of, or at least different from, the face? One might say that this performer was wearing a mask that had been drained of its maskness. Or, to apply the categories I began with, the puppet is art in reference to the man who is coming out of its anus; but the face of the man is = to his own mask and cannot be categorized either as "art" or "life." I cannot "place" either the mask or the face on either side of my "life"/"art" double mirror. For some time I thought the unblinking mask I was looking at was actually a face. That's because I checked it out against the face of the puppet, which was more "art," less "life," than the mask. Squat gave me a proper lesson in relativity.

2. A taxicab drives up outside the theatre. A man gets out of the cab and draws a gun. Across 23rd Street another man, a pedestrian, stops, kneels by a street light, and draws a gun. Between them the actual traffic of a busy Manhattan street flows. A few drivers and passengers duck as they see men with drawn guns on either side of the street. In typical New York fashion most cars don't stop but drive through this battle zone. Inside the theatre, a woman performer draws a gun and takes aim at the gunman who had arrived by taxi. She shoots, he falls, but the glass between them is not shattered. Again a system is revealed. The taxi = "life," and belongs to 23rd Street. The gunmen in the street are ambivalent. They belong both to the realm of art and to what we

have increasingly become accustomed to as life in the streets. To passing pedestrians and motorists, the gunmen are "life." Then the woman drawing her pistol and shooting from inside the theatre makes clear that the two gunmen outside are "art." The blank shot that drops a person proves the point. But to whom does it prove it? The people just passing by on 23rd Street see a man with a gun fall. Maybe, they think, we didn't hear the shot. Or maybe, they assume, a movie is being shot. Or maybe they don't think anything but just move through minding their own business.

3. In *Mr. Dead and Mrs. Free,* a jeep drives up on the sidewalk and stops close to the glass door adjoining the storefront window. Two soldiers in battle dress unload a bloody passenger from the back seat and carry him through the door into the theatre. They put him in a hammock. A priest and nurse attend him. Spectators gather outside the theatre, peering in and staring at the jeep on the sidewalk. Soon a police car arrives. It is an actual New York City police car. Why did it arrive? Did someone in the theatre call for it? Or did a passerby? Do the police come every night? Don't they know that a "play" is going on? *Dead/Free* had been running more than a month when I saw it. Does Squat have permission to use 23rd Street? To drive a jeep onto the sidewalk? Two cops get out of the car and talk to the performers next to the jeep. Then the cops enter the theatre through the glass door. The audience laughs. They laugh some more, and gasp, when a city ambulance, with all its lights flashing, drives up nose-to-nose with the police car. The cops confer with the performers in the theatre; one cop writes in his notebook. They leave. The ambulance leaves. The cop car drives off. Then the jeep drives away. The cops and the ambulance are "life" — but when the cops enter the theatre they are also "art." The jeep on the sidewalk is "art," but to some passersby it is "life."

Squat intentionally confounds these categories. Squat makes me ask: what's the difference? enjoy what is. The performances of *Pig* and *Dead/Free* expose these categories as not being dynamic or flexible enough to handle today's experiences. The audience inside is not shocked. Neither are the passersby. Somehow popular aesthetic sensitivity is better able to handle the situation than orthodox aesthetic theory. Audiences and passersby, even the cops, can cope. But there's no performance theory to explain their being able to cope.

A closer examination of the spheres of space used for *Dead/ Free* (and *Pig* too) reveals five separate areas. There's a lot of communication among these five.

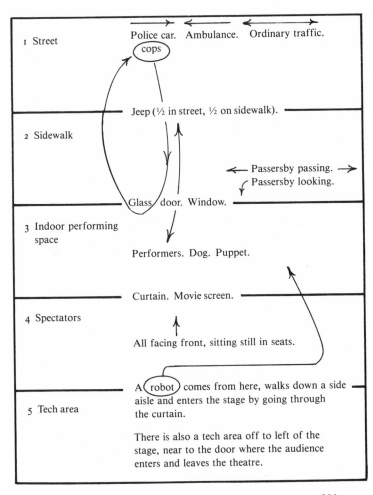

1 Street	Police car. Ambulance. Ordinary traffic.
	cops
	Jeep (½ in street, ½ on sidewalk).
2 Sidewalk	
	Passersby passing. Passersby looking.
	Glass door. Window.
3 Indoor performing space	
	Performers. Dog. Puppet.
	Curtain. Movie screen.
4 Spectators	
	All facing front, sitting still in seats.
5 Tech area	A robot comes from here, walks down a side aisle and enters the stage by going through the curtain.
	There is also a tech area off to left of the stage, near to the door where the audience enters and leaves the theatre.

Between each sphere is something that both separates and connects spheres. The jeep is of the street, but driven onto the sidewalk. The cops come from their car in the street, across the sidewalk, and into the theatre. The glass door and window both separate the indoor from the outdoor spaces and unite the two because of the see-through quality of glass. The movie screen and curtain (a film is shown as the first part of *Dead/Free*) mark off and connect the spectator and stage spaces. On several occasions the curtain is used not just as a barrier or as a mask for the stage but as the link between the stage and audience spheres. Near the end of the performance a robot emerges from the tech area behind the audience and makes its way down a side aisle, turns in front of the audience and disappears through the place where the two halves of the curtain meet. Just after that a man with a violin and a female singer emerge from behind the curtain. She sings, he accompanies. It's like an *entr'acte,* except that nothing is being prepared behind the curtain. When it opens the play is over.

Such back-and-forth movement—police, spectators, performers, robots—and inversions—the police entering the theatre as part of the entertainment rather than as those who halt the performance, the final curtain opening to signal the end of the play rather than closing to signal it (or opening to signal the beginning)—draws attention to boundaries, frames, the interfacing of the various performative realms. Also it invites the investigation into rules—formal and categorical as well as experiential and pragmatic—that govern the relationships among the realms. In other words, Squat's performances are an invitation to make performance theory.

What remains questionable at Squat, what doesn't yield easily to interpretation, is meaning, content. The performers of Squat do what they do extremely well. But what are they doing? Or rather, what does it mean, what they are doing? Squat confounds orthodox categories, providing a field day for theorists. Although the audience at Squat is immobile, sitting quietly in theatre seats that all face forward—the most orthodox of the Western audience orientations—what the audience witnesses violates many basic modern Western theatrical conventions. But what's it all about? This question of content, pushed aside during the period of intense experimentation in performance from the late fifties through the mid-seventies, now once again is important.

IV

The question that Squat's performance puts to its audiences is the same one that Goffman asked in 1959: How can you distinguish between performance and nonperformance, between art and life? I'm not sure that it's an important question as such. The artists of Squat assert that what is "art" depends on the frame surrounding the actions. When the cops walk into Squat's stage they have positioned themselves "as art," regardless of what they may intend to be doing or how they themselves feel about it. In an epoch of information media—I mean TV, movies, radio, the microchip, the satellite hookup—when "authenticity" is often a highly edited, refined, idealized (or brutalized) version of "raw" experience, people wonder exactly what is "raw" and what is "cooked." Is there any such thing as "human nature" understood as unmediated, direct, unrehearsed experience? And if there isn't (there isn't), how can understanding the whole theatrical process —rehearsals, training, warmups, preparations, as well as the show itself—help us grasp social process: how lives are lived ordinarily and in crisis?

These questions too have a "content" and "value" dimension to them. Cooking the news is preparing it in such a way as to support particular social and political positions. There is no neutral information.

V

Clifford Geertz, anthropologist, "reads" behavior as if it were literature. He says of the Balinese cockfight,

Like any art form—for that, finally, is what we are dealing with—the cockfight renders ordinary, everyday experience comprehensible by presenting it in terms of acts and objects which have had their practical consequences removed and been reduced (or, if you prefer, raised) to the level of sheer appearances, where their meaning can be more powerfully articulated and more exactly perceived. . . . What it [the cockfight] does is what, for other peoples with other temperaments and other conventions, *Lear* and *Crime and Punishment* do; it catches up themes — death, masculinity, rage, pride, loss, beneficence, chance — and, ordering them into an encompassing structure, presents them in such a way as to throw into relief a particular view of their essential nature.[8]

To interpret a Balinese cockfight "as if" it were a conscious art form is to treat the cockfight the way Squat treats 23rd Street. Such a treatment by Geertz tells us more, probably, about the emerging way of looking at experience typical of "postmodern consciousness" than of how the Balinese themselves think of cockfighting.[9]

I mean, granted that the Balinese "use" the cockfight the way Geertz says they do (and not all those who have lived in Bali and experienced cockfighting there agree with Geertz), do they "interpret" the cockfight the way he does? That is, even if the cockfight is like *Lear,* do the Balinese believe it is like *Lear*? And if they do not, how much should we pay attention to the Balinese, and how much to Geertz? And is this question any different from wondering who knows more about my dreams, I the dreamer or a skilled dream interpreter? Even Pharoah preferred Joseph. But Geertz has not written his interpretation at the request of the baffled Balinese driven to understand their cockfights. The Balinese are perfectly happy with things as they were *ante* Geertz. Also he is writing in what is, to them, a foreign language. His interpretation is addressed to people who cherish *Lear,* not the *topeng pajegan* play, *Jelantic Goes to Blambangan.*[10] So, even though I agree with Geertz that the Balinese cockfight functions "as if" it were *Lear* in Bali — "catching up themes" of great importance to the Balinese — Geertz's perception that this is so finds no native place in Bali.

Ought Geertz, therefore, abandon his project? His position is liminal, in between Bali (where his "raw" material is) and Euro-America (where his "cooked" or "manufactured" product is distributed). Is his work leading to a better understanding among peoples, or is it a further imposition of alien categories on Third World cultures?

Victor Turner goes even further than Geertz. Turner sees as the motor driving all kinds of social conflict everywhere a four-phase sequence of action: breach, crisis, redressive action, reintegration (or schism).[11] Geertz himself has summarized Turner's scheme:

For Turner, social dramas occur "on all levels of social organization from state to family. They arise out of conflict situations—a village falls into factions, a husband beats a wife, a region rises against the state—and proceed to their denouements through publicly performed conventionalized behavior. As the conflict swells to crises and the excited fluidity of heightened emotion, where people feel at once more enclosed in a common mood and loosened from their social moorings, ritualized forms of authority—litigation, feud, sacrifice, prayer—are invoked to contain it and render it orderly. If they succeed, the breach is healed and the status quo, or something resembling it, is restored; if they do not, it is accepted as incapable of remedy and things fall apart into various sorts of unhappy endings: migrations, divorces, or murders in the cathedral. With differing degrees of strictness and detail, Turner and his followers have applied this scheme to tribal passage rites, curing ceremonies, and judicial processes; to Mexican insurrections, Icelandic sagas, and Thomas Becket's difficulties with Henry II; to picaresque narrative, millenarian movements, Caribbean carnivals, and Indian peyote hunts; and to the political upheaval of the sixties.[12]

This is what Turner calls a "social drama." It works itself out the way a dramatic plot works, and is strictly analogous to modern Western drama. Again the problem is whether or not Turner is projecting onto a number of social and aesthetic genres the shape of one particular form. Or, as Geertz says, "This hospitableness in the face of cases is at once the major strength of the ritual theory version of the drama analogy and its most prominent weakness. It can expose some of the profoundest features of social process, but at the expense of making vividly disparate matter look drably homogenous."[13] But lest we fall with Geertz into the fallacy of heterogeneity, it is not necessarily a mistake to find some rather simple universal processes underlying all the elaborations and diversity of human social behavior. I am suspicious mostly that Turner's four-phase sequence conforms so nicely to what is modern mainstream Western dramatic convention. It doesn't suit what happens at Squat or, for that matter, Aeschylus's *Seven Against Thebes*. And some social processes, at least, seem to emphasize not the resolution of crisis but their prolongation and their segmentation. Social life may be as much like a soap opera or a serial as it is like Ibsen.

So there is theatre in the theatre; theatre in ordinary life; events in ordinary life that can be interpreted as theatre; events from ordinary life that can be brought into theatre where they exist both as theatre and as continuations of ordinary life (the cops at Squat). For some, drama is the motor underlying social process and crisis management. For others, like Goffman, all human behavior has a strong performative quality.

A theatrical performance or a staged confidence game requires a thorough scripting of the spoken content of the routine; but the vast part involving "expression given off" is often determined by meager stage directions. It is expected that the performer of illusions will already know a good deal about how to manage his voice, his face, and his body, although he—as well as any person who directs him—may find it difficult indeed to provide a detailed verbal statement of this kind of knowledge. And in this, of course, we approach the situation of the straight-forward man in the street. Socialization may not so much involve a learning of the many specific details of a single concrete part—often there could not be enough time or energy for this. What does seem to be required of the individual is that he learn enough pieces of expression to be able to "fill in" and manage, more or less, any part that he is likely to be given. The legitimate performances of everyday life are not "acted" or "put on" in the sense that the performer knows in advance just what he is going to do, and does this solely because of the effect it is likely to have. The expressions it is felt he is giving off will be especially "inaccessible" to him. But as in the case of less legitimate performers, the incapacity of the ordinary individual to formulate in advance the movements of his eyes and body does not mean that he will not express himself through these devices in a way that is dramatized and pre-formed in his repertoire of actions. In short, we all act better than we know how.[14]

As Goffman explains, "the details of the expressions and movement used do not come from a script but from a command of an idiom, a command that is exercised from moment to moment with little calculation or forethought."[15] What then separates acting in the strictly theatrical sense from behaving in the ordinary sense? From Goffman's point of view—like that of John

Cage—nothing. The theatrical event is theatre only because it is framed as theatre, presented as theatre, received as theatre. Just as the message "this is play" identifies play behavior, so the message "this is theatre" identifies theatrical behavior. Inside the frame "this is theatre," every conceivable kind of behavior—from the most calm and mundane to the most intense and exciting—is presented. And some genres of theatre—performance art, happenings—specialize in the undramatic, while some kinds of presentations of ordinary life (framed as "not theatre but real life") specialize in the dramatic. Newspapers and magazines have long done this with their photographs and headlines. But TV news has made the theatre of ordinary life its special province.

TV news seems to me to be a paradigm of that peculiar kind of in between or liminal performance genre we are getting more and more of. It connects the theories of Goffman, Turner, and Geertz, while offering a kind of performance akin to that of Squat. Despite its apparent frame of "this is real life," TV news presents a format that proclaims "life is theatre, and this is it."

There are two kinds of regular TV news ("specials" are something else again): the local and the national network news. Some items usually overlap; and the late local news usually repeats a lot of the early evening news. Thus there is, at the outset, some kind of ritual repetition of items. (In this, the news coverage itself is like the commercials that depend upon repetition, a form of incantation, to get their messages across.) But what's dealt with on national news is often more threatening than anything seen on the local program. Nuclear weapons, invasions of nations, mass starvation, refugees, great natural disasters— these items are framed calmly, presented reassuringly. A domestic tragedy on Staten Island may affect me, but it doesn't directly threaten me. The subways of New York may be unsafe, but I can choose not to ride them. But a nuclear war? Local news is close, hot, forcefully dramatized and personalized. The national news is cool, under control, rationalized. What's interesting from the point of view of performance theory is that these different kinds of news follow particular formats based on theatrical conventions. The local news is a kind of modern, Ibsenian naturalistic drama contained in a burlesque or variety show format surrounded by certain ritual formulae. The national news is more directly cinematic, connected to those weekly newsreels of the thirties and forties, and the kind of documentary film that overlays the visuals with soothing narration. I can't hide my admiration for the skill with which the news department has put together a mini-drama: event, heroine, victims (unseen except for something wrapped in black plastic on a stretcher being carried from the burned-out house), villain, chorus, and storyteller. And, yes, the storyteller promises a *deus ex machina*, an investigation. It is all framed as "news"—and it satisfies our society's demand for facticity—but it actually is soap opera tragedy.

It is said that too much of this kind of thing deadens public responsiveness. I don't know about that. What I do know is that the framing on TV news is very sophisticated. Both the message "this is theatre" and "this is life" are broadcast simultaneously. All the quick cuts, editing to the second, mixture of news and commercials, appearance of regulars, mix of new items and familiar ones, like sports and weather, tell viewers that the news program is theatre. But the content of the items themselves, the facticity of the reports, the excitement associated with the items being "new" (not reported before), tell viewers the program is life. And even the "this is life" aspects have a ritualized, repetitive quality: this fire is followed by the next and the next; this international crisis by the next and the next. Thus, if I were to diagram the frames of TV news, it would look like this:

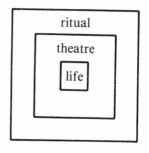

This scheme is like nothing so much as the Hindu theory of *maya-lila* where all experience is both authentic and playful, real and illusionary.

Back to Emily Dickinson and her "beautiful but bleak condition" of not knowing and not knowing not that started me off. I've tried to show that performances take place increasingly between "art" and "life." That these kinds of performances — TV news, Squat theatre, Belle de Jour — and many more that I have not specifically cited — call into question classic Western aesthetic categories. The categories remain useful only inside quotation marks, quarantined.

I think that there will be more and more "in-between" performative subgenres: between literature and recitation, between religion and entertainment, between ritual and staged shows. Also the in-between among cultures: events that can't be easily located as belonging to this or that culture but which appear to extend into several cultures, like the national news, which is neither national nor news.

NOTES

1 Richard Schechner, "Performers and Spectators Transported and Transformed," *Kenyon Review,* n.s. 3, no. 4 (Fall 1981): 88.
2 Erving Goffman, *The Presentation of Self in Everyday Life,* (Garden City, N.Y.: Anchor Books, 1959, p. 72.
3 Gregory Bateson, "A Theory of Play and Fantasy," in *Ritual, Play, and Performance,* ed. Richard Schechner and Mady Schuman (New York: Seabury Press, 1976), p. 70.
4 Ibid., p. 68.
5 Ibid., p. 69.
6 Catherine Burgheart, "Sex Theatre," *The Drama Review* 25, no. 1 (March 1981): 69.
7 Among the articles on Squat, I suggest the following: Adele Edling Shank and Theodore Shank, "Squat Theatre's Andy Warhol's Last Love"; and Richard Schechner, "Anthropological Analysis," both in *The Drama Review* 22, no. 3 (September 1978). Also, Richard Schechner, "The Natural/Artificial Controversy Renewed as Seen in *Rumstick Road* and *Pig, Child, Fire!*," *Bennington Review* 1 (1978).
8 Clifford Geertz, *The Interpretation of Cultures* (New York: Basic Books, 1973), p. 443.
9 Lots has been written about postmodernism, most of it obscure. But there are a few good things. I recommend (some of the entries in) *Performance in Postmodern Culture,* ed. Michel Benamou and Charles Caramello (Madison, Wis.: Coda Press, 1977). Also, Douglas Davis, "Post Performancism," *Artforum,* October 1981, pp. 31-39. My own view of the matter, still unsettled, is contained in two

articles: "The End of Humanism," *Performing Arts Journal* 4, nos. 1 and 2 (double issue) (1979); and "The Crash of Performative Circumstances," *TriQuarterly* 52, Fall 1981.

10 For anyone interested in this *topeng* play, it is translated and appears in *The Drama Review* 23, no. 2 (June 1979): 37-48. *Topeng* is a masked dramatic form of Bali and very popular there.

11 Turner is a prolific writer, and he has enunciated his theory in a number of places. The one I recommend is the essay, "Social Dramas and Ritual Metaphors" in *Dramas, Fields, and Metaphors* (Ithaca: Cornell University Press, 1974).

12 Clifford Geertz, "Blurred Genres," *The American Scholar* 49, no. 2 (Spring 1980): 172-73.

13 Ibid., p. 173.

14 Goffman, *The Presentation of Self in Everyday Life,* pp. 73-74.

15 Ibid., p. 74.

10 /

Theatre/SIGNS/Performance: On Some Transformations of the Theatrical and the Theoretical

Régis Durand

Let me begin with a celebrated remark on the theatre:

What is theatre? A kind of cybernetic machine. When it is not working, this machine is hidden behind a curtain. But as soon as it is revealed, it begins emitting a certain number of messages. These messages have this peculiarity, that they are simultaneous and yet of different rhythm; at a certain point in the performance, you receive at the same time six or seven items of information (proceeding from the set, the costumes, the lighting, the placing of the actors, their gestures, their speech), but some of these remain (the set, for example) while others change (speech, gestures); what we have, then, is a real informational polyphony, which is what theatricality is: *a density of signs* (in relation to literary monody and leaving aside the question of cinema). What relations do these counterpointed signs (i.e., at once dense and extensive, simultaneous and successive) have among themselves? They do not have the same signifiers (by definition); but do they always signify the same thing ["mais ont-ils toujours le même signifié"]? Do they combine in a single meaning? What is the relation which unites them during an often very long interval to that final meaning which is, one may say, retrospective, since it is not contained in the last speech and yet is not clear until the play is over?

Further, how is the theatrical signifier formed? What are its models? We know that the linguistic sign is not "analogical" (the word "cow" does not resemble a cow), it is formed by reference to a digital code; but what about the other signifiers—let us call them, for simplicity's sake, the *visual* signifiers—which prevail on the stage? Every performance is an extremely dense semantic act: the nature of the theatrical sign, whether analogical, symbolic, or conventional, the significant variations of this sign, the constraints of linkage, the denotation and connotation of the message—all these fundamental problems of semiology are present in the theater; one can even say that the theater constitutes a privileged semiological object since its system is apparently original (polyphonic) in relation to that of language (which is linear).[1]

As always, a quotation from Roland Barthes (here from a 1962 essay) is a tribute to his extraordinary intelligence of signs. The observation here still has, after twenty years, the same programmatic value; for the semiotics of theatre has not progressed as decisively as that of narrative or cinema. But quoting this passage is also paying homage to a grand and perhaps obsolete fiction of the theatre, a "*récit majeur*" in Jean-François Lyotard's phrase, a dominant fiction of the theatre which set its mark on a whole generation. In the essay from which I quote, which is really not on the theatre at all, Barthes begins with the remarks above as if he saw in the theatre a paradigm of the constitution of signification and of the "science" of semiotics which was supposed to interpret, in fact to constitute, it. This was written in the wake of Barthes's Brechtian period, and if he never wavered in his admiration and his instinctive, affective affinity for Brecht, Barthes did at any rate "traverse" his semiotic phase and move on, as we know, to radically different things. "The theatre," "the theatrical," are used here as *index* and instance of a theoretical interest, which is not primarily centered on the stage. Indeed, it would almost be possible to write a history of the transformations of theory in the last twenty years by following the slender thread of references to the theatrical or theatricality.[2] I am not, of course, proposing to do this here. Were I to do it, I would summon Barthes, Derrida, Lyotard, and a few others, and come quickly to a double conclusion: first, that the theatre and the theatrical occupy a metaphorically pervasive but in fact *marginal* place in contemporary theory; second, that "theatricality," like "literarity" (*littérarité,* the *literaturnost* of the Prague Formalists whose rediscovery in the late 1950s triggered the Structuralist movement), is one of those ungraspable abstractions, an essence whose main purpose is to allow the deployment of critical discourses which often have a quite different objective.

This displacement of a concept pressed into the service of polemics and theoretical (de)construction is particularly in evidence in an article well-known in art criticism, and which is essential to an understanding of the transformations of performance in the last twenty years. I am referring to Michael Fried's "Art and Objecthood,"[3] to which I now turn before moving on to Lyotard and Artaud.

Fried's article is written from the point of view of the ebbing "modernist" aesthetic in painting and sculpture and as a last stand against innovation, the innovation then represented by what he calls "literalist" (i.e., minimal) art. The resistance to change is brilliantly articulated around the notion, precisely, of theatricality, so that a careful reading of this essay becomes necessary for our own discussion, which bears on theatricality and change.

The first point at issue is that of the *objecthood* of the work of art. If the work of literalist or minimal art can be seen as an *object,* it implies (in the literal sense) the beholder as *subject,* and therefore a *relation* between the two as a constitutive element, a *situation.* That, in the modernist credo, is anathema, is alien to the artistic experience itself:

. . . The literalist espousal of objecthood amounts to nothing other than a plea for a new genre of theater; and theater is now the negation of art. Literalist sensibility is theatrical because, to begin with, it is concerned with the actual circumstances in which the beholder encounters literalist work.[4]

Why is the essential "theatricality" of minimal art, of its objecthood, seen as a wholly negative factor? The answer is complex and holds the key to the nature and the discourse of innovation in the years that followed. In Fried's words, it is primarily a moral question, a matter of deepest sensibility and conviction. The language here is one of righteous indignation, of a crusade against the abomination of the theatre: "Art degenerates as it approaches the condition of theater."[5] There is a war going on between modernist sensibility and "a sensibility *already* theatrical, already (to say the worst) corrupted or perverted by theater."[6] "It is the overcoming of theater that modernist sensibility finds most exalting and that it experiences as the hallmark of high art in our time."[7]

Beyond the purely passionate plea, the assertion of belief, a few theoretical elements can be pieced together. If "literalist" art is theatrical, it is first of all because of the way it turns the beholder into an *audience,* by confronting him and forcing him to keep his distance from the work. Distance becomes foremost, problematized; it creates "a more extended situation" because of the *size* of the work, or of its *endlessness,* in which physical participation becomes necessary. Not only is it a question of distance, space, but also of time. Here again, Michael Fried's description of a factor inherent in the theatrical experience is extremely interesting:

The literalist preoccupation with time—more precisely, with the *duration of the experience*—is, I suggest, paradigmatically theatrical: as though theater confronts the beholder, and thereby isolates him, with the endlessness not just of objecthood but of *time;* or as though the sense which, at bottom, theater addresses is a sense of temporality, of time both passing and to come, *simultaneously approaching and receding,* as if apprehended in an infinite perspective. . . .[8]

The theatrical, then, through the manipulation of space and time, brings to the fore the concept of *presence* as the infinite play of space/time, their variability, and the foregrounding of all the variables of the situation, including the beholder's body. This presence is distasteful to modernist sensibility because it is seen as abject complicity, as something that the work "extorts from the beholder." Fried opposes it to the concept of *presentness,* which is the pure and instantaneous assumption and apprehension of the work of art, an experience which has no duration because "at every moment the work itself is wholly manifest"![9]

I shall return to this condition of "presentness," to this continuous and timeless present as a kind of grace. But I want to underline first a remark which concerns the theatre itself (and not merely theatricality in general), and which shows how Fried uses it to deny and subvert innovation at every stage:

The success, even the survival, of the arts has come increasingly to depend on their ability to defeat theater. This is perhaps nowhere more evident than within theater itself, where the need to defeat what I have been calling theater has chiefly made itself felt as the need to establish a drastically different relation to its audience (the relevant texts are, of course, Brecht and Artaud).[10]

But as we know, the import, the innovative thrust in Artaud and Brecht, was precisely to make of the relation between the work of art (here the theatre) and its audience something in the nature of what Fried condemns in reference to "literalist" art as theatricality. I return to this further on in discussing Artaud, but I think the case could be made with Brecht as well.[11] One wonders, in other words, what model of the theatre Fried could have had in mind, what decayed version of the commercial theatre in America, in order to remain blind to the fact that theatre itself had effected its own transformation in the direction he denounces, in the direction, that is, of "presentification," of the introduction of the complex "situation" of space/time/spectator. But of course Fried's quarrel is really with the fact that theatre is inextricably bound up with an audience, is precisely an art of relations in presence. This repression of the theatre, although somewhat hysterical, is so detailed that it provides in fact one of the best descriptions we have of minimal, postmodern art (albeit a wholly negative, inverted one).

But if we now add to the aspect I have just analyzed—the question of the necessity of an audience and the problems of space, time, and presence that it brings into play—two other aspects which the critic raises in succession, we have the basis of an early and fairly comprehensive description of postmodern performance.[12]

The next aspect concerns the interaction of the different arts, the "disparate variety of activities" that go into literalist art and which have become a characteristic of postmodern performance. Fried deplores the loss of "real distinctions" between music and theatre (Cage), painting and theatre (Rauschenberg). His vision of the arts is an apocalyptic one, bringing with it the loss of all values and identities. Innovation here is seen as the displacement of specificity, essence, or convention by an illusion, "the illusion that the arts themselves are at last sliding towards some kind of final, implosive, hugely desirable synthesis." [13]

The third aspect follows from this: "The concepts of quality and value — and to the extent that these are central to art, the concept of art itself — are meaningful, or wholly meaningful, only *within* the individual arts. What lies *between* the arts is theater." [14] Beyond the statement of a conservative aesthetics, what is interesting here is the identification of theatre with an interface, an in-between. It is a place which postmodern performance has been willing to occupy and explore. But it is also a locus which postmodern performance has more recently challenged and displaced — the very question of *a* place itself becoming problematic, as Julia Kristeva has pointed out, and the nature of innovation no longer conceived as a "reaction against," which was a typical modernist way of framing it.

What Fried attacks and outlines, then, with a clarity which made a classic of his essay, is the innovative trend of a period, the early and middle sixties. And as he writes, he knows that change cannot be opposed, and that the question is not one of fashion, decadence, ideology, or even chronological succession, but rather of synchronic, dialectical rhythm. "Theatricality" is a constitutive factor of our consciousness:

> In these last sentences, however, I want to call attention to the utter pervasiveness — the virtual universality — of the sensibility or mode of being that I have characterized as corrupted or perverted by theater. We are all literalists most or all of our lives. Presentness is grace.[15]

But we cannot quite leave it at that. The historical process, the repression of which lies at the heart of the essay under discussion, cannot be allowed to become diffused in some universal form of sensibility. In fact, when Fried's essay was written, performance was already in the process of embodying different features of "literalist" art and sensibility; since then, it has further evolved new relations to the theatrical.

However, in addition to its undeniable origin in minimal art (in its "theatricality"), contemporary performance has other historical sources, other forms of connections. There is the sort of performance, for instance, which is massively grounded in *one* art or medium, and one only, and which becomes performance by exploring the conventions and the codes of the medium, "theatricalizing" them, staging them as "dispositives" (*dispositifs*). This is in contradiction with Fried's restrictive view that the division is between an art which stays within its conventions and an art ("literalist," "theatrical") which ignores or subverts them in the interplay with other forms. Contemporary performance has shown us that attention to the conventions, if intense and rigorous enough, leads to another form of theatre, not a theatre of dissolution, but a theatre of intensity, a theatre of materials and codes and affects, grounded in one medium, but heightened, made fabulous. Think of Joan LaBarbara's art, "pure" music undoubtedly (i.e., not involving other forms of art), yet performance nonetheless because of its uncanny exploration of the medium (range, pitch, electronic reproduction of sound), because of the passionate relation between voice and the electronic apparatus (amplifiers, loops, speakers), and through that, the space and those present in it. Or think of Daniel Buren's paintings, as "painterly" as they come, yet quite as clearly performative because of the way they problematize the place of painting in its urban space, in its relation to institutions, to time, to perception, etc.

And lastly, there is the kind of performance which is grounded in the theatre itself and which, after Artaud, takes as its material the actor, the subject himself in his/her physical and psychic actuality. This has given birth to performances in which the performer explores himself as material, a bio-theatre which ranges from the crude versions of body-art to the subtleties of the theatre of memory of Spalding Gray and Elizabeth LeCompte. The distinction does not escape the arbitrariness and the insufficiencies of all such distinctions. Nevertheless, it must be reiterated because it has tended to be forgotten. Art criticism (following Fried in that) often considers the reference to the theatre as a theoretical weakness and traces the origin of performance too exclusively to minimal art.

But I want now to examine certain aspects of theatre in the "imaginary" of postmodern performance, and in order to do so (re)turn briefly to Artaud. To refer to Artaud today is somewhat problematic, distinctly not in fashion. There is, it is felt, something almost embarrassingly vociferous, personal, and metaphysical about him. Besides, too many pretentious epigones have given him a bad name. Yet a return to his writings seems in this context inevitable.

It is best, perhaps, to introduce our rereading (brief as it will be) a little circuitously. It will be by way of a remark by Lyotard, which connects what follows with my opening observation on Barthes. With the latter, we came in contact with a dominant fiction of the theatre — that of the cybernetic machine destined to produce signs loaded with meaning, of codes piling up and harmoniously resolving themselves in the final meaning. But one of the characteristics of postmodernism is precisely the suspicion which affects the notion of signs. Ten years after Barthes, Lyotard remarks, with the theatre again in mind:

The theater places us right in the heart of what is religious-political: in the question of absence, in negativity, in nihilism, as Nietzsche would say, therefore in the question of power. Both the theory and the practice of theatrical *signs* (whether it be writing, directing, interpretation, set designing, etc.) rely on the acceptance of the nihilism inherent in the act of representation, they even reinforce it. For a sign is, as Peirce said, something which stands for something else in the eyes of someone. To conceal/ to reveal: such is theatricality. But modernity today is characterized by the fact that there is nothing to replace, no "being in the place of" [*lieutenance*] is legitimate, or else anything is. Replacement, and therefore meaning, is itself only a substitute for displacement.[16]

Lyotard shows how the theatre, "being where displacement becomes replacement, where the flow of drives becomes representation, hesitates between a semiotics and an economics." I would like to take up the idea of this hesitation and show that it is characteristic, at least in one of its aspects, of contemporary performance as well. This leads me to examine briefly what Lyotard says about Artaud in the context of the essay I am discussing, and also to what Artaud himself says about signs in his writings. I am not concerned here with the question of influence or filiation, but simply with remarking the analogies between contemporary performance and the theatre according to Artaud, and with examining what theoretical background and gestures, what contradictions and ambivalences, make this possible.

Artaud defined his theatre as "unperverted pantomime," as the effort "to break up language in order to reach the quick of life," provided that, he added, "when we speak the word 'life,' it must be understood we are not referring to life as we know it from its surface of fact, but to that fragile, fluctuating center which forms never reach."[17] But to say that it is untouched by forms does not mean that the dominance of signs has miraculously vanished or failed to take hold. Rather, it means, as Guy Scarpetta has shown, that the theatre is "to unfetter its inarticulated, nocturnal side" in order to allow the "unconscious body" to surface and to ascend toward "the surface film of signs."[18] When Lyotard, speaking of what he calls "a theater of energies," says that what is needed is

. . . not the concordance of dance, of music, of mimicry, of speech, of season, of time, of public, and of nothingness, but rather the independence and simultaneity of sound-noises, of words, of body-figures, of images, which characterize the coproductions of Cage, Cunningham, Rauschenberg, . . .[19]

he is defining an aesthetics close to the one negatively outlined by Michael Fried (with the emphasis here on discontinuity rather than on theatricality). This is undoubtedly a correct description of certain features in the performances of the late 1960s and early 1970s; but I do not think that it invalidates "the sign-relation and its depth-effect," nor that by implication "the *power* relation (hierarchy) [is] made impossible." The question of the relation to signs and power remains more than ever present, even though it may have been displaced and fragmented.

In many ways, then, the theatre of the future which Artaud describes and anticipates is a blueprint of contemporary performance (in spirit and theory, if not literally). Consider, for example, the question of the organization of the different materials of expression. Over Roland Barthe's dream of a harmonious layering of signs leading up to a unified meaning, we could superimpose another narrative which runs through Artaud's texts and treats the different constituents of performance, not as bits of information to be received and decoded, but as energy transmitters and transformers:

[The theater] recovers the notion of symbols and archetypes which act like silent blows, rests, leaps of the heart, summons of the lymph, inflammatory images thrust into our abruptly wakened heads. The theater restores us all our dormant conflicts and all their powers, and gives these powers names we hail as symbols: and behold! before our eyes is fought a battle of symbols, one charging against another in an impossible melée. . . .[20]

Of course Lyotard is right to point out in Artaud the desire for "re-territorialization," for taking command of what Artaud calls "symbols" in order to bind them and order them in a "hiero-glyphic" language. But it should be seen that for Artaud it is only one moment in a dialectical process, and also that it is perhaps the vanishing point in his system, a sort of utopia of signs, the metaphor precisely of a paradoxical thought: that of a nonverbal writing which would *at the same time* have the "frenetic gratui-tousness" of drives *and* the rigor of syntax. Contemporary performance, in its most achieved manifestations, is still confronted with this dual exigency.

But what, really, characterizes signs in performance? The fact that they are no longer "bound" by homogeneity and continuity. Once freed of the great narrative continuum which rules over Western performing arts, signs become floating, polyvalent elements, capable of entering into polymorphous combinations according to the energy they are charged with (what Richard Schechner calls "multiplex signals"). The major change in recent years has been the passage from an essentially narrative art to various practices based on different modes, such as description, inventory, montage, documentation, chance, effectuation, etc. The organizing forces are no longer narrative impetus and coherence but rather superimposition or "layering," "tracking" (Lee Breuer), quotation, repetition, tracing and erasing, doubling, "ghosting" (Herbert Blau), translation, transference, etc. This is not so much a rejection of narrative as a displacement of its status. And if many performance artists are again showing interest in narrative, it is not in deference to its ideology of representation but in recognition of narrative as one possible (and indeed powerful) operator of performance, a variable "dispositive" (*dispositif*) through which transformations may be generated. But with these artists as with Artaud, each dispositive operates only through its particular connection with the subject of the performance. Not only is a dispositive a source of energy in itself, but it also summons and liberates energies in the subject's "unconscious body."

We now reach a point of controversy which concerns what Artaud calls "the metaphysics of signs." I shall simply make three observations concerning his metaphysics in the theatre and its relation to performance work.

1. There is in Artaud's writings, as in performance art, the desire to "make of every spectacle a kind of event." This raises the question of the *use* of such spectacles, of their relations to place and audience. It will be remembered that Artaud in "The Theater of Cruelty (First Manifesto)," under the heading "The Public," merely noted: "First of all this theater must exist." The question is in fact mostly that of the relation between two desires, that of the performer and that of the spectator.

2. Artaud calls for an end to the aesthetics of conflict in the theatre (even if he proposes, in a quite different sense, to give back "the conflicts which are dormant in ourselves"). Performance art, similarly, offers nonconflictual scenographies, and substitutes ritual for narrative, indeterminacy for causality, and variability for deliberate hysteria.

3. All this can perhaps be summed up in one of Artaud's central ideas:

To derive, then, the most extreme poetic results from the means of realization is to make metaphysics of them, and I think no one will object to this way of considering the question. And to make metaphysics out of language, gestures, attitudes, sets, and music from a theatrical point of view is, it seems to me, to consider them in relation to all the ways they can have of making contact with time and with movement.[21]

The "metaphysical" intention, taken out of context, might be objectionable to contemporary practitioners. Yet it is an integral part of Artaud's dialectics of renovation of the stage; it is, in fact, its innovative edge, with a technical, physical particularity to it. Indeed the word "metaphysics" is, like "signs," used in the performative mode: "*faire la métaphysique,*" "*faire signe,*" "*aller jusqu'au signe.*" The ambiguity of the phrase "*faire signe,*" in particular, accurately captures the dual nature of performance. "*Faire signe*" must be understood as both to make a sign out of something ("to carry," as Artaud puts it, certain elements of performance "to the point where they become signs") *and* "to signal to someone." This raises a number of fundamental problems. These include the question of the *form* of performance, for instance, of form as the end of process, as aesthetic stasis; also the question of the connection between the signs of performance and what lies outside of it, other signs and their referents, including those "others" who may be receiving the signs, out there. Again, in the celebrated preface to *The Theater and its Double,* Artaud shows himself consonant with innovative thinking today:

Furthermore, when we speak the word 'life,' it must be understood we are not referring to life as we know it from its surface of fact, but to that fragile, fluctuating center which forms never reach. And if there is still one hellish, truly accursed thing in our time, it is our artistic dallying with forms, instead of being like victims burnt at the stake, signalling through the flames.[22]

To substitute for a traditional semiotic organization notions such as indeterminacy, citation, etc., cannot change the fact that signifiers will not remain pure signifiers. Quite the opposite: the principle of displacement, so much in evidence today, is itself cause that signifiers are constantly becoming signifieds for other signifiers. And those reluctant signs tend towards, or produce, referents, even if these are in a fragmented, anguished or imaginary form. Artaud sometimes names this referent *life.* We have seen some of the implications of the word for him as well as for contemporary performance. Those implications could be pursued much further, if we were to listen to the reverberations of such phrases as "a secret psychic impulse which is Speech before words,"[23] or the "concrete conception of the abstract,"[24] which is another version of an infinitely reversible metaphor that Wallace Stevens named "an abstraction blooded." But it is well perhaps to pause on the challenge which lingers in the last words of the preface: what sign does a victim make as he is being burnt on a pyre, and to whom? Who is watching those signs, through the smoke and the stench of burning flesh, and what goes through his mind?

NOTES

1   Roland Barthes, "Literature and Signification," *Critical Essays,* trans. Richard Howard (Evanston, Ill.: Northwestern University Press, 1972), pp. 261–62.
2   The reason I use both words will become clear, I trust, as I proceed. But the problem of terminology remains. "Theatricality" does not, in English, connote quite the same thing as the French *théâtralité,* a relatively "purer" abstraction.
3   Michael Fried's article originally appeared in *Artforum,* June 1967. It is reprinted in *Minimal Art,* ed. Gregory Battcock (New York: E. P. Dutton, 1968).
4   Fried, "Art and Objecthood," *Minimal Art,* p. 125.
5   Ibid., p. 141.
6   Ibid., p. 136.
7   Ibid., p. 140.
8   Ibid., p. 145.
9   Ibid., p. 145.
10 Ibid., pp. 139–40.
11 Brecht's *V-Effekt* is of course intended as a way of distancing, of breaking the "abject proximity" (Maurice Blanchot). But the distance achieved is certainly not intended as the crystalline assumption of the work of art in its pristine, immediate "presentness." Quite the contrary, it is intended to make possible the interplay of factors such as time and space (*history*) and to make possible the construction of the final meaning.
    Fried's only comment on Brecht comes in a footnote and appears as a disavowal both of Brecht's Marxism and of the fact that his plays were written with the audience and their effect on it in mind — both elements are essential, as everyone knows, to Brecht's theory and practice. Here is the comment in question, a striking example of (probably unconscious) disavowal and repression of a theory which would of course ruin Fried's development on theatricality:

    The need to achieve a new relation to the spectator, which Brecht felt and which he discussed time and again in his writings on theater, was not simply the result of his Marxism. On the contrary, his discovery of Marx seems to have been in part the discovery of what this relation might be like, what it might mean: "When I read Marx's *Capital* I understood my plays. Naturally, I want to see this book widely circulated. It wasn't of course that I found I had unconsciously written a whole pile of Marxist plays; but this man Marx was the sole spectator for my plays I'd ever come across" (*Brecht on Theater,* ed. and trans. John Willett [New York: Hill & Wang, 1964], pp. 23-24).

Brecht's plays, then, had no audience, were untainted by one . . . until the encounter with Marx and the fall into the abject relation!

12 For a detailed examination of those aspects of performance, see Thierry de Duve, "Performance Hic et Nunc," *Performance, Text(e)s, & Documents,* ed. Chantal Pontbriand (Montréal: Parachute, 1981), pp. 18-27, as well as my own "La Performance et les limites de la théâtralité," ibid., pp. 48-54.

13 Fried, "Art and Objecthood," *Minimal Art,* p. 141.

14 Ibid., p. 142.

15 Ibid., p. 147.

16 Jean-François Lyotard, "La Dent, la paume," *Des Dispositifs pulsionnels* (Paris: U.G.E., 1973), p. 95, (my translation).

17 Antonin Artaud, *The Theater and its Double,* trans. Mary Caroline Richards (New York: Grove Press, 1958), p. 13.

18 Guy Scarpetta, "La dialectique change de matière," *Artaud* (Paris: U.G.E., 1973), pp. 263-96.

19 Jean-François Lyotard, "La Dent, la paume," p. 103.

20 Artaud, *The Theater and its Double,* p. 27.

21 Ibid., pp. 45-46.

22 Ibid., p. 13.

23 Ibid., p. 60.

24 Ibid., p. 64.

11 /

The Death and Rebirths
of the Novel:
The View from '82

Leslie A. Fiedler

More than thirty years ago, I declared in print boldly, unequivo-
cally (as I declare every new insight, my not-so-secret motto being, "Often wrong but never in doubt"): THE NOVEL IS DEAD. I can
still remember the immediate occasion. I had undertaken—being
still young enough to know no better—an "omnibus review" of
the year's crop of fiction; and after slogging my way through six
or eight particularly banal books, none of them even bad enough
to be interesting, I fled (as I also confessed for publication) to the
movies—returning sufficiently refreshed to write an obituary for
the genre whose death it seemed to me those books betrayed.

I was well aware, of course, that long prose narratives would
continue to be published long after I myself and the posthumous
novelists who had so dismayed me were dead. And I was sure
that such narratives would also continue to be read by a perhaps
steadily diminishing, but surely respectably large number of
readers, to whom the novel would seem still the reigning genre, as
it had since the middle of the eighteenth century, when it achieved
its classic, bourgeois form and (I know, I *know*) critics first began
announcing that it was dying or dead.

What I must have meant then—it is hard to be quite sure at the distance of over three decades—was that the kind of novel written in response to the social and aesthetic exigencies of the eighteenth and nineteenth centuries, what my poor reviewees still trying to write in the mid-twentieth, and what most ordinary readers still think of when they hear the word "novel" (fat, realistic fictions with recognizable plots and characters, plus comfortably lofty ideas about love and marriage, gender and race, society and the nature of man), would disappear from a radically changed, late industrial world, in which the sensibility to which that kind of novel appealed had become as obsolete as the modes of production which had originally helped determine its form and function. At the very least, it must have seemed to me, attempts to re-create this kind of novel, with its archaic aspiration to "verisimilitude," its demand for the reader's total "suspension of disbelief," would no longer be taken seriously; but would have been remanded long since to the underworld of Low Literature, trash beneath even the contemptuous notice of serious critics.

But the howls of execration which greeted my obituary notice, the insulting letters from certain writers who took themselves quite seriously and, though young enough to know better, were committed to resuscitating the sort of novel I was trying to bury, soon made it clear that not everyone agreed with my diagnosis of the state of fiction. Not surprisingly, in their attempts at refutation, they alluded over and over again to the achievement of Saul Bellow—who, they insisted, despite his allegiance to the traditional novel, clearly could not be lumped with more popular and disreputable practitioners of the form like, say, Herman Wouk or James Gould Cozzens. The latter they would have agreed with me in classifying as (it was then a still fashionable term of condescension) "middle-brow," *schlock* in High Art's somewhat demodé clothing.

But Bellow's work was quite another matter, as I myself, they reminded me, had acknowledged in my rather adulatory reviews of his earlier novels. Indeed, it was not until I confronted the protests of his epigones that I began to realize that Bellow must be in some sense a posthumous writer. But in *what* sense? I was then driven to ask; as I have been asking ever since, attempting to come to terms with the fact that in the following years he has gone, with books in what I had defined as a defunct mode, from triumph to triumph. Moreover, he has succeeded not only with the mass audience but with the critical establishment as well. He has produced, that is to say, if not quite best sellers, at least near misses, while simultaneously winning all the most prestigious literary prizes, from the National Book Awards to the Nobel Prize itself.

In part this is because, I am convinced, Bellow is politically in tune with our regressive times, representing a backlash against almost everything considered advanced or progressive at the moment he began to publish, movements with which, indeed, it was possible for a while to identify him. Was he not a Marxist, a Freudian, an heir of Modernism? But *Mr. Sammler's Planet* made quite clear where he had really stood all along, establishing him as the literary mouthpiece of the intellectual wing of the "New Right" whose house organ is *Commentary* magazine, and the darling of certain aging ex-radical readers whose other preferred novelist at the moment is V. S. Naipaul. Like the latter, Bellow managed to combine reactionary politics and late Victorian aesthetics without seeming an outright yahoo or a flagrant philistine.

It is not finally possible, however, to explain Bellow's status with so simpleminded a political equation; because almost all of the Jewish-American writers with whom he is typically lumped (and justifiably so, despite his own objections), even when they do not subscribe to his reactionary politics, tend to share his fondness for the traditional novel. So, indeed, do other parochial or programmatic writers, including the most radical, who think of themselves or are considered by their most ardent fans as spokesmen for stigmatized social groups, ethnic or sexual. Consequently, the Black American novel, for instance, or the feminist novel is still by and large written in the form which I long ago declared dead. Nor is it a matter of generational taste, since an overwhelming majority of the favorite books of the young, the makers of the "Cultural Revolution" of the sixties and their latter-day heirs, are, from the *Rings* trilogy of J. R. R. Tolkien to the *Dune* tetralogy of Frank Herbert, written in the same old-fashioned mode.

To whom, then, (besides me) is this kind of novel dead?

Most especially, I think, to certain readers in the academy, both young and old: not only many students learning to write the kind of novel which will be prized—and taught—in the twenty-first century, but also many of their "creative writing" teachers. Both such students and such teachers either do not read Bellow at all, or respond to him unsympathetically—lumping him with other obtuse American writers (Sinclair Lewis, for instance, Pearl Buck, and John Steinbeck), honored by equally obtuse Nobel Prize Committees, in part *because* they betrayed no awareness that the traditional novel might be dying or dead. Certainly these Committees had never given the coveted literary award to an older generation of writers like Jorge Luis Borges or Vladimir Nabokov, much less to such younger ones as John Barth, Donald Barthelme, Thomas Pynchon, or William Gass, who had introjected into their fiction the critic's awareness of the death of the novel.

Some of the latter, in fact, particularly John Barth, wrote me after the appearance of my infamous little review to say so; making clear in the course of doing so that for them not only were the works of pseudomodernists like Bellow examples of what should and could no longer be emulated, but that the masters of High Modernism were in this sense also defunct. However they might respect the achievements of, say, Proust, Mann, or Joyce, they considered them no longer useful as models for living fiction.

Though a novelist like John Barth is clearly indebted to the example of James Joyce, he uses Joycean techniques not developmentally but terminally; that is to say, though a work like *Giles Goat Boy* may seem at first glance merely one more late Modernist Art Novel, it is in fact an anti-Art Novel, a kind of autodestruct device. Read properly, it serves to undercut the posture of the novelist as elitist "artist," as well as the reader's sense of himself as a self-congratulatory connoisseur of what is unavailable to the popular audience; so that finally it blows up the very notion of *avant-garde* experimental fiction.

In light of this, I was convinced for a long time that what was really dead in our culture was not the conventional novel at all, but *only* the kind of anticonventional long fiction which asked of the reader a constant awareness of its own artifice—and a concomitant admiration of the virtuosity of its artificer *as* artificer, as well as his ingenuity in making the death of the genre he purports to write its central subject. Clearly, it seems to me, such terminal fiction could not be written over and over without becoming an intolerable bore to its writers as well as its readers. But, alas, under the aegis of "post-modernism," it has continued to be practiced to the very verge of the twenty-first century—and is still read by a tiny audience of a very special kind, whose nature can only be understood in terms of a radical change in the way long fictions have come to be consumed since the 1950s.

At that point it became evident that though some contemporary novels were still being borrowed from libraries or bought on impulse from book stores or the display shelves in railroad stations, airports, and supermarkets, others were being read on assignment in high school and college classrooms where their consumption was, as it were, redefined as a duty or a chore rather than a diversion, an escape, or a refreshment of the spirit. This has been true for a long time of "classics," i.e., books by dead authors, preferably in "dead languages"; but only with the growth of the mass university did it become true for any recent literature.

At the same time, for quite another, extra-academic audience (the two developments are linked by factors explicable in socioeconomic rather than literary terms), some novels were being translated from words on the page to images on the screen, made into movies or TV series, like *Gone With the Wind* or Alex Haley's *Roots.* In such postprint media they became available to those who lusted for stories but were incapable of assimilating print with ease or pleasure: an audience considerably larger than that reached by any fiction between covers, hard or soft, and infinitely greater than that which reads in the classroom novels without "stories."

Occasionally these days, the same books make it both ways (Ken Kesey's *One Flew Over the Cuckoo's Nest* would be an example, along with Nabokov's *Lolita,* Kurt Vonnegut's *Slaughterhouse Five,* and in the misty mid-region of the neomiddlebrow, Doctorow's *Ragtime*), these being simultaneously or consecutively transmogrified into classroom material and popular films:

the stuff of the academy, on the one hand, and "Show Biz," on the other, what movie makers like to call "the Industry." But by and large, novels tend to fall into one or another of these categories — not just after they are written and published and have been sorted out by critics and/or the blind mechanism of the marketplace, but in their very conception. More and more writers in the last decades anticipate falling into one or another of these mutually exclusive categories, and they tend to write, therefore, *as if* for the classroom *or* Hollywood: write in order to be taught and explicated, or to be packaged, hyped, and peddled. Many, if not most, novelists of both kinds, I am suggesting, seem in the initial avatar of print oddly transitional, either embryonic movies or potential diagrams on the blackboard.

But it is, of course, only the writers of books intended for or doomed to classroom use — let us call them Elite Novels, Art Novels, Minority Novels, Required Novels — who realize that they are in even this limited sense dead. And they are likely, in their loneliness and pride, to believe that only the kind of fiction they do *not* write — Pop Novels, Commodity Novels, Majority Novels, Unrequired Novels — are in print embryonic. To be sure, as I have already observed, while "post-modernism" was still a protest movement rather than a new academy, an ironical awareness of the provisional status of their own work hovered just beneath the surface of certain novels by refugees from the academy like Thomas Pynchon and even academics like John Barth; but in their mandarin successors that awareness has been lost. Indeed, the most naive and ghettoized among the latter are likely to believe that they have broken out of the trap, that for them the novel is not, in this sense at least, dead — so long as, and to the degree that what they write is nothing like what the mass audience continues to think of as a "novel": i.e., a book which exploits plot, character, and dialogue without irony or shame; or which asks of its readers a belief in the reality of its fictions rather than that of its intrusive and self-conscious maker.

It never occurs to writers of novels intended for translation into film and television that the translatability of their twiceborn works from print into postprint media means that they are merely embryonic, since they consider the latter not a substitute for the former, but a way of creating larger audiences for both. Certainly, some such conviction is suggested by the hopeful slogan typically affixed to new paperback editions of pop novels after success at the box office: YOU'VE SEEN THE MOVIE, NOW READ THE BOOK. Their writers remain, moreover, blithely unaware (they are at least desperately eager to pretend so) that the traditional novel is dead or moribund or even ailing. Yet they cannot help knowing that some of their most respected and critically praised, if not financially successful, colleagues believe so: writers of the kind of novel which they tend to think of as stillborn, since it is not twice-born like their own.

If they have not attended elitist classes in literature themselves, their children are likely to have ended up sitting at the feet of the minority novelists who teach such classes in the Ivy League schools to which their own success has enabled them to send their children. In a way, the plight of these writers resembles that of present-day Born-Again Christians and backwoods Baptists, whose very self-definition depends on ignoring the Death of God; though He did indeed die for a minority of intellectuals (small but important enough also to be taught in university classes) some two hundred years ago, just as the novel was beginning. And who is to say where the truth lies? For some the Novel is dead, and for some it is not.

But this difference—which separates not just majority and minority writers of fiction but majority and minority readers as well—is evidence that the Novel is in yet another sense dead for both audiences. It is dead, that is to say, as a single, unified form: the only literary genre since the invention of printing and the democratization of literacy able to provide the satisfaction of literature to all elements in a society otherwise ever more divided, no longer simply by class, but by differences in ideology and taste cutting across class lines. How likely is it that in the foreseeable years between right now and, say, the mythological 2001, any novel will appear which, like Harriet Beecher Stowe's *Uncle Tom's Cabin,* will be, in the words of Emerson, "read with equal pleasure in the nursery, the kitchen and the parlor"?

Yet such novels did appear with fair frequency from the middle of the eighteenth century to the end of the nineteenth. It seems possible, indeed, to argue that the Novel became the reigning genre of the bourgeois and postbourgeois world of Mass Culture. (At the moment its status is least problematical in those totalitarian "socialist" states, which, by edict, are able to extend nineteenth-century taste indefinitely.) This is precisely because the novel has subverted the distinctions which had separated written High Literature, whether Humanist or Courtly, from aural-oral Folk, thus creating at least the momentary illusion of an ad hoc community (what we have come to call "the audience") in which rich and poor, male and female, young and old, white and nonwhite, naive and sophisticated, uneducated and educated, however otherwise alienated from each other, are moved by the same plots and characters, images and myths.

We are likely these days to think of the post-Gutenberg media as the source of such communal myths; and this has become in fact more and more nearly true. Not only are figures central to what universally shared culture we still have, from Mickey Mouse to Archie Bunker, created for us on the screen; but even those originally invented in books, like Scarlett O'Hara or the Wizard of Oz, do not really enter our collective consciousness until they have been recreated in films and "immortalized" — in a context of commercials and station breaks — on television. Yet the novel was the first form which provided waking dreams capable of possessing the psyches of everyone, regardless of gender, generation, or class. And it continued to perform that function for a long time, even after certain "modernists," the culturally upwardly mobile sons of the bourgeoisie, were driven to abjure this levelling function for their "art." Think of the series of books which begins with *Gulliver's Travels, Robinson Crusoe, Pamela,* and *Clarissa,* and includes much of Scott and Dickens, plus most of R. L. Stevenson and H. G. Wells, along with a good deal of Balzac, Dostoevsky, and Tolstoy, as well as Americans like James Fenimore Cooper, Harriet Beecher Stowe, and, most notably Mark Twain.

From the start, however, university-educated critics, whose standards of literary excellence were derived from the study of classical epic and tragedy, were baffled by the mass-produced and mass-distributed novel. That essentially popular form (resolutely prosaic and shamelessly "vulgar") seemed less the product of individual talent and devotion to the Muse than of technology and subservience to the marketplace. Only begrudgingly did they grant it the status of "real literature" at all. But not merely did the Novel refuse to go away; it became, over the dead bodies of those critics, the dominant genre of the literary world: what young men and women dream of writing in their lonely chambers, whether they aspire to make it to "greatness" or only to get rich and famous. Particularly in the United States, where literary culture began with the rise of that bourgeois form, it has not been the Great American Epic but the Great American Novel which the most talented and ambitious of our artists have sought to write — or at least have pretended to (think of the novelistic camouflage of that essentially epic work, *Moby Dick*) in order not to lose the mass audience.

"If you can't lick 'em, join 'em," even the most hardline members of the critical establishment finally decided, belatedly convinced that prenovelistic narrative forms were dead. But even as they ceased dismissing all novels as subliterary entertainments for the half-literate, chiefly girls and women, they began to discriminate, as most readers did not, between two *kinds* of novel. One kind, they insisted, was worthy of being preserved in libraries as a new sort of "classic"; while the other was fit only to be consumed quickly and thrown away — like one more disposable commodity. Most readers of popular novels, of course, did not trouble to read such critics, but some writers of them did, and a great debate ensued, best represented perhaps by the interchange between Robert Louis Stevenson, in an essay called "A Humble Remonstrance," and Henry James, in a piece he entitled, "The Art of Fiction," which is still reprinted in school texts. Expectedly enough, the former's fiction has been largely remanded to the nursery; while the latter has come to be regarded as the founder for England and America of the tradition which was to culminate in the work of Modernist masters like Proust, Mann, Kafka, and Joyce.

But James, of course, thought of himself as European rather than American; and this seems only fair in light of the fact that the majority of eminent American novelists who succeeded him, though sometimes they began by flirting with "modernism," like Hemingway or Nathanael West, ended by rejecting it. Yet most American critics, both inside and outside the academy, have refused to come to terms with this disconcerting fact, proposing year after year (and always in vain) certain homegrown candidates for Highest Modernist Honors; then falling back in despair on the European founding fathers of Modernism and their less inspired "post-Modernist" epigones. Meanwhile, they have consistently ignored or dismissed out of hand not only popular American novelists, like Edgar Rice Burroughs, L. Frank Baum, and Margaret Mitchell, but their immediate transatlantic predecessors, like Bram Stoker, Rider Haggard, and H. G. Wells.

It has somehow seemed to the critics irrelevant that *Tarzan of the Apes, The Wizard of Oz, Gone With the Wind, Dracula, She,* and *The Time Machine* have never been out of print from their moment of publication to the present. Nor are they moved by the fact that such books continue to be familiar to a reading audience which may never even have heard the names of *Remembrance of Things Past, Ulysses, The Castle,* or *The Magic Mountain,* and to an even larger group of story lovers who, having rejected full literacy, know only what has been translated from bound books to comics, movies, and TV specials, i.e., what can be "read" as images on the screen.

What seems important to the critical establishment is, in any event, not the longevity but the analyzability of novels. They tend to esteem not what has pleased many and pleased long, but what is most amenable to exegesis in terms of methodologies fashionable at a given time. They are at a loss, therefore, before works which the mass audience prizes not for their elegance of structure, precision, and grace of expression, much less subtlety and nobility of thought; but for characters, turns of plot, images capable of surviving changes of medium without loss of authenticity or effect. Such books are not merely read by a different audience than that which finds its deepest satisfactions in the Art Novel, but they are read differently by whomever reads them, including the most hidebound elitists, many of whom do in fact turn from time to time in private to what they publicly condemn.

I remember reading a year or two ago a statement by Elizabeth Hardwick, I think, in which she declared that not only had she herself never read a "best seller," but that she knew no one who ever had; and while I would not presume to doubt the truth of her assertion as regards herself, I am reasonably sure that it could not possibly hold true of her whole circle of acquaintances, no matter how restricted. Certainly, I myself know few people, sophisticated or naive, who have *never* picked up a detective story, a science fiction novel, a Western, a woman's romance, or resisted the temptation to slip off to a movie or flip on the TV and see some version of such *schlock*. Perhaps such elitist readers do not think of themselves as properly *reading,* however, even when they seek this kind of escape between bookcovers, hard or soft; and maybe, after all, it is wrong, misleading, to use the single word "read" to describe the different ways in which we experience the two reborn forms of the dead classical novel.

We respond to Pop Novels, typically, not as we have been taught in school to respond to what we have learned there to think of as "literature," but more as we respond to movies and TV — which we have never been taught anywhere to "read" — which is to say as secular scripture, quasi-religiously. But this is appropriate enough in light of the fact that Pop Novels are the source of the myths which most deeply move most of us, even those of us who still go to the churches of our forefathers. Such disreputable, uncanonical figures as Frankenstein's Monster, Superman, and Popeye, I am trying to suggest, along with Rhett Butler and Dorothy's dog Toto, have effectively replaced the official mythologies of our culture, whether Judaeo-Christian or Greco-Roman, thus fulfilling the prayer of Walt Whitman who more than a century ago invoked his modern American Muse to "Cancel out please those long overdue accounts to Greece and Rome . . . place 'to let' on the walls of Jerusalem. . . ."

Why then are we critics, who purport to love Walt Whitman (I include myself in their number, since for a long time I echoed their distress), so unhappy with the event he so joyously invoked? In part, surely, it is because we had imagined more noble deities than these replacing our old gods; but in part also because the most ardent worshippers of those deities of mass culture tend to despise the kind of criticism which derides their holy books. I know I was myself dismayed by the response of their most articulate spokesmen among my own students, who in the sixties began to urge on me their own favorite fiction and nonfiction (the distinction had begun to blur for them for obvious reasons): Tolkien's *Rings* trilogy, for instance, Heinlein's *Stranger in a Strange Land,* Kurt Vonnegut's *The Sirens of Titan,* and the unspeakable *Jonathan Livingston Seagull,* which they ranked with newly revised pop classics like *Frankenstein* or *Dr. Jekyll and Mr. Hyde.*

When I objected that the "best" of their beloved books were marginal by any respectable literary standards, and at worst abominations, they answered, "Don't give us that standards crap. Man, *Jonathan Livingston Seagull* changed my head, changed my life. . . ." I had an answer then, I am sure, but what could I really say, I, for whom literature had replaced religion, to them, for whom religion had replaced literature. My response would have been as irrelevant as pointing out to a Fundamentalist the "contradictions" in the Creation Story of *Genesis.*

Nonetheless, I have continued the argument in my own mind ever since, especially as it has become clear to me that those former revolutionaries could not have been wholly wrong, since in fact their passionate mythology has changed literary standards, opening up the canon to certain works once dismissed out of hand. This seems to me, indeed, one of the few lasting changes wrought by the Cultural Revolution, which promised, like all revolutions, so much more than it achieved — or maybe more than it really, *really* wanted to achieve. At any rate, it is possible now, from the vantage point of the eighties, for me to see what these novels or quasi novels have in common with the most popular novels of the last two hundred years, and how they differ from Art Novels, particularly since the triumph of Modernism.

They are neither avant-garde nor experimental in technique, nor are they mimetic or psychological in mode. By and large naive or downright simpleminded, insofar as they are self-conscious at all, they are self-consciously fantastic. Moreover, whatever meaning the uses of fantasy may have had for their authors, to their readers it seemed a kind of revolutionary protest, since most of those readers were members of a generation deprived in childhood of the pleasures of the fantastic by repressive, self-righteously "liberal" and "reality"-oriented parents. Consequently, they turned to such material in adolescence with all the thrill of rejecting authority and breaking a taboo. Moreover, the very naiveté of the texts they loved seemed a similar holy transgression against their English teachers.

Such works are in this sense, despite their resemblance to older pop fiction, something new under the sun, a new subgenre of the best seller, the Youth Best Seller. That subgenre had first begun to emerge in America as early as the fifties with J. D. Salinger's *Catcher in the Rye* and Jack Kerouac's *On the Road.* Its high point, however, was not reached until some twenty or twenty-five years ago with the coming of full awareness of a generation of readers who were, on the one hand, affluent and independent enough to buy whatever they wanted, and, on the other, convinced that their culture, their values, were radically other than those of their parents. They believed therefore that they needed a new subvariety of Pop, a new kind of secular scripture whose mythology was congruous with their dissident politics and deviant lifestyles.

Such fiction had to be different not just from the Art Novels required by a school system they distrusted but from the kind of best sellers which the Book Clubs brought their bourgeois mothers: novels of domestic sentiment in exotic settings and of impetuous passion verging on soft porn, the so-called "bodice-rippers." Nor could it be too similar to the masculine protest Pop which pleased their fathers: adventure stories, spy thrillers, mysteries, Westerns, and (less openly, to be sure) hardcore porn. There was, however, among their fathers' favorite genre, one kind, science fiction, which escaped their scorn; and which, indeed, they made so firmly their own, that as they themselves have become fathers, they have helped make it the reigning pop form of the late twentieth century.

The *macho* values and conservative politics of an old SF hack like Robert Heinlein are scarcely distinguished from those of a professional detective-story writer like Erle Stanley Gardner, who was until the end of the sixties the most bought and read author in the world. But the makers of the Youth Revolution despised the latter, at the same time that they kidnapped the former for their own purposes, making him a *guru,* a presumed mouth-piece for causes he utterly abhorred. Nor did it faze them when he declared publicly, "I hate even my adult readers!" After all, the science-fiction genre of which Heinlein was a founding father was also being used by writers who came closer to actually shar-ing the world view of the young (the early Vonnegut, for instance). Moreover, SF was the youngest of all pop forms; not merely the last invented, but one typically produced by authors scarcely older than their youngest readers and possessed by similar ado-lescent fantasies. Finally, its mythological center has always been "the Future," which the young quite properly think of as their special province.

In any case, as the taste of the sixties has come to prevail in the marketplace of our culture, SF has, like blue jeans, become modish. But, of course, the Youth Best Seller has no more driven out adult best sellers, male or female, than jeans have driven out polyester stretch pants—or, for that matter, than the drugs espoused by the young have driven out booze and beer. In the Great American Supermarket, where it is always possible to open up next to the old a new department to satisfy a new consumer demand, and whose motto is not either/or but both/and—all these continue to exist side by side, more complementary than competitive.

Years ago—in "Cross the Border, Close the Gap," an essay born of the euphoria of the late sixties, which, despite my indur-ated ambivalence, I briefly shared—I mistakenly predicted that an upwardly mobile mass audience would eventually merge with a downwardly mobile elite audience. But as I have already sug-gested, the latter, instead of blending with the former, has split into two wings, each condescending to the other and both to Pop. For one wing, the only true Art Novels are those which as-pire to the tradition that begins with Flaubert and James and cli-maxes in Samuel Beckett; while the other esteems as properly highbrow long fictions which bypass or ignore what they con-sider "faddish" modernist/post-modernist models, and emulate, say, Dostoevsky and Tolstoy.

So also the middlebrow camp (I find myself obliged to re-turn to a term which years ago I forswore, since no other word can describe what still continues to exist) has split. On the one hand it has divided on political lines into Feminist Middlebrow, Gay Liberation Middlebrow, Black-is-Beautiful Middlebrow, etc. — most didactic fiction tending to seek that level. On the other hand, it is separated by the different obsolescent highbrow or pseudohighbrow models it strives to emulate into Paleo-middlebrow (imitations of imitations of John Galsworthy or J. P. Marquand), Mesomiddlebrow (imitations of imitations of Saul Bellow), and Neomiddlebrow (*kitsch* with a veneer of Modernism, like the novels of E. L. Doctorow and John Irving).

Similarly, Pop has become ever more atomized as its sub-genres grow more various, more specialized, more parochial, each embodying a mythology congenial to its fans and anathema to those of other forms. Indeed, in recent days this conflict has eventuated in full-fledged religious wars as indignant parents, who still find scriptural satisfaction in old-fashioned best sellers of the school of Lloyd Douglas's *The Robe,* attempt not merely to ban from class reading lists but to burn in schoolyard bonfires such pop favorites of their own disaffected children as Kurt Vonnegut's *Slaughterhouse Five.* This has distressed not only certain disinterested defenders of First Amendment rights, but commercial publishers as well, to whom all books, High or Middle or Low, are commodities rather than secular scriptures of "great art." They seek, therefore, to legitimize every one of the manifold forms of the contemporary novel, defending some against the book-burning moralists, others against contemptuous aesthetes.

It was surely with something like this in mind that the Association of American Publishers, in a document dated August 6, 1979, announced that henceforth they proposed to give in place of the single prize for fiction, hitherto bestowed under the aegis of the National Book Awards, several separate prizes for "Science Fiction," the "Juvenile," the "Mystery," the "Western," the "First Novel," and "General Fiction." The last two categories were ambiguous, but all the others are pop genres which the self-perpetuating board of critics chosen in the past had always insisted on excluding from consideration. I learned this one year when I myself was such a judge and tried to nominate for the award a work of flagrant science fiction. The well-mannered scorn with which my colleagues greeted my suggestion dismayed me a little; but it prepared me for the howls of execration which were directed against the Association of American Publishers for theirs.

Not only did individual writers, including old comrades and friends, send letters of protest to the press, but petitions were circulated by professional organizations like PEN, especially after it was learned that judges would be selected in the future by a process which seemed to gurantee that "journalistic hacks" would outnumber proper academic critics. The Association of American Publishers, however, since it wants to be respectable, i.e., accepted by the spokesmen for the minority audience, as well as rich, i.e., patronized by members of the majority audience, in the end hedged and equivocated, working out a compromise which pleased no one, not even me, who had, in any case, never managed to register my opinion publicly. I did not, of course, sign the petition of PEN, of which I am a member in good standing, nor did I send off the letter I had planned. Far from protesting the inclusion in the list of Book Awards of unworthy genres like the Western, that letter was going to ask why the publishers in their collective wisdom had not thought to add to their list either the most ancient and dishonorable of all lowbrow forms, Hardcore Pornography, or the most ancient and honorable, the Woman's Romance, which was not only the first best-selling genre in America but is today once more the most popular of all, outselling even science fiction.

But maybe, it has occurred to me since, the publishers were true enough sons of their mothers to have thought that the latter genre fell under the rubric of "General Fiction"; so that (I find it an intriguing thought) it might well be possible that in the near future the latest novel by Donald Barthelme will have to fight it out for the award in that category with the newest book (surely, she will produce at least one more) by Taylor Caldwell. And if the judges chosen by the new method, it tickles me to surmise, turn out to be as crass and vulgar as my less crass and vulgar colleagues seem to believe, they will end up choosing her over him. It will not matter, I want to assure them, in any case, because the Art Novel will continue to be honored elsewhere, especially by the more prestigious Nobel Prize Committee, which—to make matters even better—has been very kind indeed to our own Art Novelists.

Ironically, however, the two authors whom that august body has most recently honored, the Jewish-American novelist, Saul Bellow, and the American-Jewish one, Isaac Bashevis Singer, both write as if the Death of the Novel has never occurred, or at least as if the trauma of Modernism had somehow not touched them. Both, that is to say, continue to publish novels in the tradition of nineteenth-century "serious" narrative before it had abandoned all hope of reaching large segments of the mass audience. I am not suggesting that they are identical in this regard. Singer blessedly grew up in an East European community where even relatively sophisticated writers were not yet alienated from naive readers who still turn to novels for the "story"; while Bellow, who came of age in metropolitan American centers where Joyce and Kafka were the preferred models of the young, has had to reject alienation by a deliberate act of the will, reactionary in essence if not quite perverse. Both have, however, ended up in the same place: a mid-region verging on, though not really the same as, that cultural no-man's land inhabited by the middlebrows.

They tend, therefore, (especially Bellow, perhaps, since Singer is redeemed for some readers by his taste for the demonic and his folk roots) to be distrusted by younger "experimental" novelists at the same time that they are spurned by the producers of hardcore Pop, who may be even richer than Bellow but aspire in vain for the literary honors which fall on him like rain. Whatever his status in America, moreover, in Europe, East and West, Bellow is in all quarters the favorite art novelist; while in the Third World—from India and Japan to Argentina and Brazil—scores, even hundreds, of Ph.D. dissertations are being written on him at this present moment.

It is not mythological post-modernist France, celebrated by our own last-ditch defenders of genteel High Culture, which kindles the imagination of scholars and aspiring writers in countries still trying to make it culturally in the late Industrial world, but our, to them, even more mythological America. From that Promised Land of triumphant vulgarity, they eagerly import—along

241

with other mass-produced products of a levelling technology like blue jeans, pop music, shameless B movies, TV sitcoms, Kentucky Fried Chicken, McDonald's hamburgers, Pepsi-Cola and nuclear power plants — the classic bourgeois novel, which they have not heard (or cannot afford to believe) is dead.

12 /

Rehearsal: An Alternative to Production/Reproduction in French Feminist Discourse

Didier Coste

I visited Algeria for the first time in 1966; there were still barbed wire, miles of it straddling the heights of Algiers, and French concentration camps at the foot of each hill of Kabylia where the original Berber villages had been shelled. There were also the incomparable light of newly acquired freedom and *their* belief that I could not be guilty of my national past if I visited their land then, travelling fourth class onboard an old, twice-converted troop carrier.

The comparison expires at this point because I can only wish I visited feminist thought as a member of the male nation, personally liberated by the defeat of male logos. As it is, I am only a traitor. I will be suspected of being a double agent, and I am perhaps finally unable to detach visibly this "I" I am using from the subjective implications of an inescapably male heterosexual position.

The most constant and characteristic claim of feminist thought in the last few years has been, it seems to me, the need for women to speak themselves. Their object position, their being spoken by men who pretend to speak to them but actually reject interlocution, is no longer seen as just another means of domination but its essence: the shapeless form of female alienation. This shapelessness of the object/other in male discourse vitiates this discourse as much as it motivates it; it is the necessary counterpart of the obsession of the owners of the means of representation with the reproduction of their capital. More deeply, representation, the distorted form of male imagination, is reproductive in essence: capital and cattle become confused. As they try to escape the "law" of reproduction, contemporary feminists no longer aspire to a takeover of male discourse; they want to deconstruct the phallic structure of language and, more specifically, "*écriture*"; they want to spread out the ruins of their Imaginary and let the puzzle tell its story, a story of not-yet, since all past, all history, belongs to the proprietors of phallic language. In this process, feminist textual practice, whether poetic, polemic, or psychoanalytic, has indeed developed much more than just a new style. It has invented itself as antistyle, antilinear nonstyle, and de-definition, thus constituting the only avant-garde of today and bringing to fruition, unexpectedly and well beyond itself, a long exhausted Modernism.

> Thus I dream for each body
> of bi- or multifaces which would break the poverty of this
> single face . . .
> and permit the simultaneous superposition of all the marks of
> one durable or fleeting state.[1]

Without abusing the well-worn simile of body and text, itself denounced as an instrument of oppression by other feminists (A.-M. Dardigna), it is possible to say that Michèle Causse proposes here not only a model of physical presence opposed to the one-dimensionality of a "Ladder" but also hints at a new type of textual practice which would do away with all kinds of linear "progression" (whether temporal, logical, or rhetorical). To a large extent her own work, the highly metaphoric "autobiographical fable" *L'Encontre,* keeps the narrative thread to a minimum and aims, with the later and best Beckett, at a radical spatialization of verbal (re)presentation (cf. *Le Dépeupleur*).

Similarly, Luce Irigaray and other feminist psychoanalytic

thinkers intend to reclaim the totum of female sexuality against the one-track evolutionist schema leading to reproductive genitality (of which the "normal" adult male would be the sole achieved specimen). On the one hand, they oppose a genetic model of successive differentiation which discards more "primitive" phases, represses early partial drives, and presents female sexual specificity as a transcendence of polyvalence for the sake of masochistic submission; they are very close to Lyotard's attitude in his *Économie libidinale,* but they tend to perpetuate the notion of the female body as a totally erotic surface. On the other hand, they may treat this body as the material support of a lexicon from which each individual woman should be able to *select* freely her own vocabulary, exploring her territory without being subjected to any external pressure. In both cases memory is a provider which does not restrict future/present possibilities; the not-yet is in no way dictated by a frozen historical interpretation of the past; the past is as plastic as the future: it is a set of possibles, and memory must be content to make it available to the present.

In a very real sense, feminist liberation is the liberation from the dictatorship of time. Time the divine, the unyielding, unconquerable rule of all things and way of all flesh, is relegated to the darkening gallery of romantic myth; but time, the tool of speculation, the accomplice of surplus value and masquerade of reproduction, can be conquered and abolished. The role of *Erinnerung* as it is reinterpreted by Marcuse at the end of *Eros and Civilization* reappears here with a new aspect: the promises of female childhood (rather than those of maternal memory) are to be kept by the text of the female Imaginary against the male alliance of time with repression in the guise of historical or biological determinism.

I cannot recover from such an ending. And I flirt with the conditional mood. I rewrite history.

I invent a possible for us.

A voice, the Adventurer's makes up some impossible for me with warmth and persuasion

/ we'll live it out unreasonably
as possible or even certain, thus reserving the conditions of
the so-called fatal misunderstanding /

The voice works in
inmediacy.[2]

It appears that today's feminist textual practice, however
utopian in the reading gymnastics it requires and the set of human relations and psychological attitudes it exposes, remains
quite distinct from all classical types of utopia, whether positive
or negative, in that it refuses to legislate. And it does not present
its array of possibles as a *future* possible, possible only at a certain point along a given historical continuum. This practice,
which I am going to illustrate and analyze further in a moment, is
primarily deconstructive and situates itself precisely in the secret
"no-man's land" of a present which is still actually, in its social
practice and power structures, all-men's and no-woman's land.
The Ladder System in *L'Encontre* allegorizes the institution of
socioeconomic verticality (hierarchies, accumulation, growth)
duplicated by historical rigidity (including the Marxist and
Freudian versions of evolutionism, sharing the myth of the similarity between phylo- and ontogenesis). But we are told that history can already, here and now, take the radically different form
of an unbounded surface variously occupied by beings with
fluid, moving outlines; it can be remade into a curvilinear and
playful stage for each female self.

Monique Wittig's quasi narratives have constantly endeav-
oured to evoke the possible aesthetics and the efficient form of
such a complete rupture. Her *Les Guérillères,* probably the best
known recent feminist utopia and, in 1969, one of the earliest,
departed very markedly from the lyric tradition of Anaïs Nin, departed as well from the preciosity, the grammatical psycholo-
gism, and the masterminded Newnovelism of the *Opoponax*
which French critics had acclaimed five years earlier. Yet *Les
Guérillères* builds on the partly deconstructed material of the
lyric short story; it has not renounced Surrealist profusion or the
initiatory wonder (*émerveillement*) of the childhood novel in
which magic and the reality principle are fully interchangeable

means and ends; and it retains a measure of Newnovel-like emphasis on overt enunciation. What we must not forget, however, is the theoretical program, the undertaking of a particular process of semiotization, formulated and illustrated prephatically in its very form, then expressed throughout the novel at a number of levels:

ELLES AFFIRMENT TRIOMPHANT QUE
TOUT GESTE EST RENVERSEMENT[3]

"TRIOMPHANT" is at first "misread" as an adverb, then restored to its status of adjective, modifying GESTE, as we proceed: any triumphal gesture is a reversal (or an upsetting) and this, in its efficiency, is made iconically perceptible by a bold inversion. The circle found on the next page (a left-hand page) reappears on page 71 (right-hand), then finally on page 138 (left-hand), thus completing a symbolic rotation or revolution and a "translation" by repetition. It also divides up the volume in three parts of roughly equal length but does not occur again at the end, which must be interpreted as negation of circularity, the upsetting of the cycle. The format of a "poem" of three verses in capitals is taken up on the third from last page, but with the clear difference that the latter is largely a collage of Mallarméan fragments, including the central evocation of CONSTELLATIONS; the last words are GESTE RENVERSEMENT, pointing at a text traversed by the figure of reversal as the "*Coup de dés*" is traversed by the magisterial tautology. This taking of a male voice into the she-text should not be read as her defeat or the cannibalistic devouring of the male by a praying mantis, or yet an insemination in extremis; rather, it coincides with the peace which puts an end to the war of the sexes, with the synthetic moment when, without conciliation or abolition of difference, the differences are rethought, transferred to another plane, and become cooperative.

But this last reversal, the victory of women over the power structure of sexual difference, operates on an initial situation which is itself a reversal of present historical conditions. The presented world of the tale is from the beginning one in which women exist in a self-constituted, self-produced, self-spoken group ("*elles affirment,*" "*elles disent*"). They are never isolated, confined individuals separated from the herd for the sake of individual male ownership, or an indistinct mass relegated to collective existence. The *"on,"* one, subject of *The Opoponax,* now takes on the new function of marker of self-awareness; *"on"* is neither singular nor plural, neither masculine nor feminine, neither you nor me, but both and both and both; it is not indefinite, it is multiple, changeably defined, or rather de-fined.

In the first phase, *elles* revaluate their own sex, assert its positiveness, its concreteness, the universally powerful metamorphoses of the ("full") circle implicitly opposed to the Freudian-Lacanian concept of phallic absence, lack, castration. In the second phase, *elles* are able to contest their sexual symbolism itself; it is useless, it depends implicitly upon an imitation of phallic symbolism (cf. Colonna's *Hypnerotomachia*); it is bygone insofar as women have started to fight actively for a nonphallocratic, egalitarian world whose shape is yet to come. In the third phase, with the victory of the *guérillères* over oppressive phallocracy, with the alliance of the nonsexist young men, the truth content of the new world has become actuality; implicitly again, the reproduction of the species has become possible with the freedom of the she-birds and production of aesthetically meaningful signs with the exaltation of a fruitful past. In this process, that which undergoes a reversal is not only the given world as backdrop and material (in a mimetic perspective) but negation itself, which is always negation of the negative, always finally affirmative even in its moment of annihilation (the man-hunt, which retains a festive overtone).

The future, the other of a patriarchal world, was always there in the childhood of girls (*The Opoponax*) in certain pagan rituals, in the feminaries, no matter how imaginary:

I say that that which is, is. I say that that which is not, is also. When she repeats the sentence several times, the duplicated, and later triple voice superimposes uninterruptedly that which is and that which is not. The shadows lying on the lake move and begin to shiver under the vibrations of the voice.[4]

The defeat of the narrated in the order of fact is thus necessary, and it is never final (it changes object):

They say that, to judge by what they know of the history that followed, the quests of the Grail have not been fulfilled, they remained of the order of narrative.[5]

The apparent contradiction of a future-oriented narrative is no more or less than that of a future-oriented past; if past futures are the stuff history is made of, its unwriting (strategically solidary like the sheets of a book, the letters on the printed page, and spaced out to take over its own space) will make itself of future pasts:

They say that any symbol which extols the fragmented body is temporary, must disappear. So was it once; they [*Elles*], bodies complete prime principal, advance marching together into another world.[6]

It is in *another* world that machines are destroyed, miraculous weapons used, and the Female Proletariat Revolution celebrated. Because of the already contained in the not-yet, repetition is but repeated negation; it discovers itself on the side of the Novum, to use Ernst Bloch's terminology. But the rehearsal which takes place is more than *Vorschein:* it upsets or reverses radically the spatio-temporal code of recording, neither production nor reproduction but repeatedly final actuality of the elsewhere.

The quasi nonperformance of the utopian artistic text is not the already possible model of a future life; it is its actual repetition, just beside itself, just beside performance. Monique Wittig says this, very crudely perhaps, in 1969: the pamphletary crudeness helps to uncover the disallowed crudeness which also moves other contemporary and later utopian (or rather rehearsive and reversive) tales, among them:

Duras, *Détruire dit-elle,* 1969
Hyvrard, *Mère la mort,* 1976
Cixous, *Ananké,* 1979
Derrida, *La Carte postale,* 1980
Mallarmé, *Un Coup de dés,* 1897.

"And if we do not destroy all the traces, we are saved, that is to say lost."[7] From the pasts, futures alone can be retrieved, but what else would be worth saving or rescuing now?

249

The very title of the conference in which this paper accepts to be framed in powerless gratitude for a womb, a *vase clos,* seems to be caught, arrested, on the brink of an effort to question itself. I was at first tempted to imagine long passionate debates about the semantic status of the stroke between Innovation and Renovation; then I realized how aesthetic the title was in its desire to combine the *bougé* effect of the stroke with the breath of humanistic relief offered by the *vista* of the colon and reconcile them under the spell of a lullaby: in-re-re-re. . . . We are thus given a fair icon of the average state of Western thought in the early eighties, a state of post's and neo's in which novation is still considered to be valuable for its own sake even though it is a nostalgic ideal, and a cumulative notion of knowledge still prevails. Novation in terms of concepts is a kind of wish-fulfillment, which goes more than half way to meet the demands of repression, to salvage an order which is always preconstituted in language as a given. But even this kind of novation must be more than the reproductive need of philosophical discourse can take, since its report is regularly subjected to a labor of secondary revision of an aesthetic nature; hence the "*bougé*" technique common in expressionist and post-expressionist painting. One of the conceptual tensions which have become especially vexing in the last 15 years is precisely the production/reproduction pair whose *bougé* similarity/dissimilarity continues to plague any number of fields of reflection from ecology to semiotics.

Feminist thought, too, has been confronted by this situation in which change is inscribed by default. It seems there is as yet no way out of supercoded speculative discourse or the Modernist aesthetics of *bougé,* and their practice proves nothing that we do not already know: by thinking itself as topic, utopia can do no more than illustrate its given definition and reveal the forced procrastination of radical social change, without which procrastination the concept of utopia would point to its referential other, the present, the given. Moreover, under the circumstances, it is not possible to say whether a way out of supercoded speculative discourse or Modernist aesthetics is desirable, and this undecidability does no more than confirm the prevalent "oppositional" definition of desire as that directionality of psychic forces which has

no given direction, which has no object other than the unappro-
priated, the unchosen, the nonobjectifiable. In order to rebel
against this imposed definition of desire as supreme contradiction, we can perhaps do no better than perform it tentatively,
right to the tragic extreme of a perennial deferral of catharsis.

It remains that the "matter-form-composition" (Michèle
Causse's term for the various bodies or subjects of actional predi-
cation in *L'Encontre*) of the male paraphilosophical discourse
which tried to come to grips with the sliding wall of production/
reproduction is greatly at variance with feminist textual practice.
First of all, Baudrillard's fierce critique of political economy at-
tracts our attention:

> Revolutionary imagination [*imaginaire*] is haunted by a ghost; the fan-
> tasy of production. It sustains everywhere an unbridled romanticism of
> productivity. The critical thinking applied to the *mode* of production
> does not touch on the *principle* of production.[8]

Baudrillard is grappling with the metaphysical aspect of historic
materialism, a vicious circle of teleology and necessity well exemplified by Ernest Mandel's inaugural anthropological statement:

> Of all the species, man is the only one that cannot survive by adapting to
> the natural environment; he must try instead to bring this environment
> under his own requirements.[9]

This is meant as the foundation of a Marxist (political) economy.
While Mandel projects this original "truth" on the rationale of
historic development and equates progress with a numeric
growth of the species founded on the growth of material products, Baudrillard goes on to denounce productivist ideology in all
areas of human behavior, including the construction of theories,
hermeneutic and critical. The holy conceptual trinity of western
humanism — need, signification, and value — is assaulted as a result of combined attacks on binary dissociations such as subject/
object, signifier/signified, and use/exchange, all reducible to the
CODE, or products of the CODE which produces them to reproduce itself. Ultimately, just as in orthodox Marxist economics
mirrored by the morality of orthodox Communist parties, there
is no valid distinction between production and reproduction; but

whilst both are good for the Communists, both are bad for Baudrillard, since they do nothing but perpetuate a "logic" of appropriation, a logic of measurement by and for division, instead of the uninterrupted continuum of symbolic exchange, which constantly compensates lack not by things but by the reciprocity of dispossession itself.

We may be wary of the strategems, terrorist in essence, used by Baudrillard to shelter his (anti-)theory from criticism or even discussion. He resists evaluation by suggesting an immeasurability which is beyond rather than beside measurement: "The fantastic power of challenge cannot be measured."[10] Thus no one is welcome to inquire about applications or effects, since Baudrillard's thought, like the challenge he formulates, is "intransitive" and carries no direct object. There is a tinge of mysticism in all this, as we can expect wherever oxymoronic structures prevail, and it is always relatively easy to contest the sincerity of such denials of power; but the importance of Baudrillard's radicalism can only be fully appreciated in the face of the persistent vicious circles and sly assertions of Marxist, liberal, or conservative theories of production and reproduction.

Thus, for instance, Gerald Graff theorizes a new "decadence" of textual practices as follows: capitalist or more generally industrial society has made *reality* elusive and *life* in it alienating by subverting the old order which was supposed to be reality. Modern art and modern thought, so threatened, turned their backs on *reality,* condemned representation or mimesis, affirmed their autonomy, their irresponsibility, flew forward into the shelter of marginality where this same *reality* wanted to confine them. Experimental literature, for example, by abandoning a reference frame of normality and an ideal of truth, would only *add* to the prevalent meaninglessness instead of criticizing it; by denying the possibility of reference to a nonlinguistic reality, it would assert (within the world of discourse at first, and especially in academe) the power of powerlessness. In fact, paternalistic repression has vanished, and Post-Modernism only pretends that this repression is still active in order to promote aims of desublimation that are precisely those of the industrialist-consumerist apparatus. In brief, since mimesis (as reproduction) is inevitable, it should be carried out consciously and submit to the guidelines of a reasonably open code of recognizability rather than occur under the guise of self-determination (production).

The contradictions are all the more obvious because they are dissimulated: reality is no longer reality, but art should remain realist, and in order to achieve this goal, it should treat unreality as if it were real; art is not reality, but its productions can add to reality more of something that is part of it (meaninglessness). In the further stages of Graff's reasoning, the fallacies of the underlying equations (of consciousness with intentionality and morally adequate action, of true representation with thematization, of thematization with communicated content or message, etc.) are easy enough to detect. Graff, like his adversaries, considers production as the capture of pleasure, a *fait accompli* which does not require the participation of anyone other than the producer; but unlike his adversaries, he finds production obscene, unchaste, unless it takes place under the authority of given reality. Production and the accompanying pleasure should be the bonus paid by the reality principle for the submission of the pleasure principle. Critical thought is incidental to conformity. The dynamics of change, if any, would sprout from fact finding.

Unfortunately, this attitude is not specific to the rear guard of bourgeois empiricism. For Macherey, the work of art reflects willy-nilly the world of its conditions of production, but it cannot make its own theory; critical understanding, reserved to the Marxist theoretician, is separated from representation; the artist predigests the worlds and offers a medley of signs which will constitute excellent material to exhibit the efficiency of a theory of contradictions. No wonder that deliberate realism is demanded of the artist: the inherent contradiction of mimesis supports the given division of labor which makes the critic a specialist, hunter, and connoisseur of contradictions. Macherey claims the profit of production, derived from a reproductive activity that he leaves to the unlucky artist; as a pimp, he actually reproduces the imperative of reproduction, without which his own "function" would have no *raison d'étre*.

But, we may ask, would reproduction be really necessary if we stopped thinking in terms of profit? And, on the other hand, is it not the sole fact that it is *forced* reproduction which makes it bad? Reproduction subsumes three different notions: imitation, multiplication, and mechanicity. It is thus opposed to the old individualist values of originality, authenticity, and divorce from the past which served the rise of a bourgeois industrial society and, paradoxically, the later development of a consumerist society. Reproduction is wrong because another given than our given remains unthinkable. And production is wrong because it is under the spell of this cult of difference which we all share, which makes us all unknowingly similar. The quest of *identity* is exactly that. The largest sector of Modern art has been so persuaded that objectification, conceived as the affixing of identity, is both inescapable and dutiful that, taking it literally, it has fled into the ultimate reification: non-art, non-work, non-object, coupled with supersignature, superlabelling, thus paying the greatest homage yet to the "work" as extension of the producer. The result, in the words of Terry Eagleton, is that "the writer's production is merely the *appearance* of a production, since its true object lies behind or within it."[11] A "real" production would be something like the old "creation," with its object before it! If women have, as they say, nothing behind them but the long curtain drawn over their oppression and the mutilated remains of a silent body, must they then renounce to produce, or must they give themselves the impossible task to create?

Perhaps we should try to think ungrammatically for a moment. Who will help us to think production as the operation of positing that which will never be here, objectification as the operation of positing the unself of self? Can we turn for help to Lyotard, for example?

Lyotard does not think the ungrammatical; he thinks that kind of grammaticality in whose context Fontanier could state that "to be" was the only true verb. It is the theology of presence, the poetics of tautology that Romanticism and its sequels have endlessly repeated in the vain and insincere hope of circumventing it. The quest of a theory is condemned because it is a fantasy of internal coherence, a fantasy of the complete body, strikingly similar to the projected completion achieved by death. But is it not another kind of death to live one's incompleteness in a state of fascination? Is it not to seek and to *offer* masochistic rewards? The yes of Lyotard, like the yes of Molly Bloom, is still an echo: it expresses desire in the language of another who is supposed to be the absolute presence of demand; it repeats the language of Death, or the language of God.

Death has become fashionable again in recent years. I see this theme as a direct counterpart of unsuccessful or half successful efforts to come to terms with the production/reproduction dilemma or get rid of it altogether. In other words, it is often the last recourse, the metaphysical refuge of failed, disenchanted utopian or radical critical thought. There are nevertheless significant differences between its role in male radical *Weltanschauungen* and in recent feminist literature.

Jeanne Hyvrard's thought appears to be essentially engaged in negation; it relies on the now-conventional view of woman's predicament in a male-dominated society as caused by male fear (of castration?). In such a society women are appointed to represent a threat, not only to the genital emblem of power but to reason, law, and order. Equated with the powers of darkness, women, the maddened ones (*les enfollées*), are symbolically deprived of a tongue, a mother-tongue, and some counterpart to the male logos which could be pitted against it. Confronting a male definition of femininity as madness, nonsense, the inscrutable, no alternative can be found in a "return to reason" or to the real, in the cure or survival; a cure is just renunciation, abdication, defeat, and servitude; what is sought is "the end of madness. The imaginary which [would] violate the real and save my life."[12] But it is unclear whether such liberation *is to* take place historically, in a remodelled reality at some future time, or whether it has always been potentially available or even actualized in the form of an inner emancipation or escape: the very inscrutability and elusiveness of women to men. Within the Freudian-Marxist perspective implicitly adopted, the danger certainly exists of the usual shortsighted shortcut by which the specific forms of alienation are claimed as an autonomous or oppositional mode of being, the counterculture of the oppressed. In fact, we know how easy it is to step over the thin line between counterculture and subculture, between self-reaffirmation and acquiescence to domination and segregation; and the line is more difficult to cross the other way around:

They want to cure me. Of what? Of the death they have put into us? Of the confinement in which they keep us? Of the madness into which they throw us when we rebel? . . . But look. I escape them. We escape them. The sea breaks the dike in which they confined her. We are the sea and the storms. We like the ships of their nakednesses crossing our infinites. But they will never circumnavigate them.[13]

In a sense, it is the Romantic and Post-Romantic ("Symbolist" and "Decadent") revolutions all over again, with the oppressed on the side of Nature and Nature a model of Freedom. But death has two faces really; we could label them respectively paternal and maternal. One kind is artificial, instilled, which takes the form of the internalization of codes of behavior and grammar, rigid instruments of torture in need of a host to reproduce only themselves; the other kind is a habitation where the self is not questioned, an at-oneness with all the unruly demands, losses, and flows coming from within. All the attendant paradoxes of the avant-garde as well as those of proletarian culture lie in wait; we are requested to believe that their presence is the solution rather than the problem, if reason is in essence phallic power and femininity the principle of uncertainty, the destructuring principle rather than an alternative structure.

Hyvrard uses, both in denunciation and nunciation, a terminology very similar to that partly shared by Lyotard, Baudrillard, and Deleuze-Guattari—for example, the distinction between *pouvoir* and *puissance* and the opposition of *contraire* to *négation*. Some of their anticoncepts or metaconcepts are also involved. But against death as control, cloning, endless reproduction of the Code, Hyvrard does not contract, like Baudrillard, any alliance with superfluous, gratuitous, or violent death in order to force the restoration of symbolic exchange; her solution is completely contained in a poetic deed, in the solution of an aesthetic problem. At the same time that she abandons the elegiac discourse, she proposes the themes of love, voyage, and cosmic

fusion as the motors of an unlimited narrative; and this gift, perhaps naive, of a newly discovered tongue coincides with a specific offer, a generous program of *transgression:*

> We shall go toward them with our bleeding wombs. We are marching to-
> ward them, all these years that they have been killing us and we lie to our-
> selves. We shall free them from their anxiety, for love has no end. We
> shall release them from their jealousy. Our wombs are large enough to
> contain all their nakednesses.[14]

Echoing back through Cixous, Wittig, and even Duras, a
shock wave of idealistic nihilism points at the limits of utopia in
current feminist textual practices, but it does not pervade them.
This is because they have invented, against production and reproduction, a new time structure which protects them relatively
well against the bouts of Golden Age syndrome to which other
radicals are usually prone. I will call this structure rehearsal (in
French *répétition,* 2nd sense).

Rehearsal is this type of behavior which is never its own
model, which cannot duplicate itself because it steps over itself,
having its model in a "not yet" as an improved image of a "before." Rehearsal belabors the not-yetness and the no-longerness
of the present. Rehearsal is not a concept; it only holds together
insofar as it disperses and as much as it disperses. Rehearsal has
an oxymoronic structure: it is the memory of the future. As such
it is not subject to the principle of equivalence; its value is the
minus (*the manque à être*) of another which negates it and will be
negated in turn at the next rehearsal; such value cannot be circulated; it can only be translated with the translation of reversibility which is the dynamic form of reversible time (that is *not* any
form of "intemporality"). Rehearsal is the practice by which we
cannot drink *once* water from the same river. It is to repetition
what sameness is to twins: that which prevents each from being
the other *or* himself. Rehearsal is opposed laterally (*en décalé*) to
performance; it occurs by interpretation of repetition, as the
given is defeated by its lack of self-coincidence betrayed by repetition. Rehearsal is the practice of utopia which denounces the
given as already future and thus as already past, always super-
seded by its actualization. There is little theory of repetition, per-

haps because of its incestuous vicinity to rehearsal (rather than regression). There can be no theory of rehearsal, because rehearsal cannot be reduced to a model; or rather a theory of rehearsal can only be a special kind of practice, a rehearsal itself, an untheory which can only see and enunciate itself as *bougé,* unsettled theorization.

In Duras's *Détruire, dit-elle,* Max Thor teaches the history of the future; there is nothing there, he says nothing, his students sleep; but among them was Alissa, the mad one, the forerunner. Alissa was eighteen, she will always be eighteen, because she shares the determination that Elisabeth Alione-Villeneuve be eighteen too, for ever and ever, like the mad one in *L'Amour.* But if S. Thala, anagram of sea, is everything and is also all those who receive their name from being looked at, if S. Thala extends even beyond itself in the dimension where man is sometimes lost and from which he will return, what kind of rehearsal is this? Is there any possibility of a no-longer, any space for a not-yet? If, for *Détruire,* human figuration is superfluous, what kind of rehearsal is this, and does it take place in the land of the living or the land of the dead? Are we dealing with anything else than a mirror image, a passive duplication of the given?

The answer is a clear negative. From *Lol V. Stein* to *L'Amour,* Duras's narrated world has acquired a much more intense presence (by simplification, reduction, and repetition, or reharrowing), a presence which is in no way characteristic of the world in which we live, whose reality is never quite real, always screened by the act of valuation. The world in which we live is never given for what it is; it is a screen to itself, and no naming within the code will lift the screen. We remember this statement of Cixous: "to write is always primarily a way of not managing one's mourning work for death [ne pas faire son deuil de la mort]."[15] But though Duras's progressively greater economy of presentation parallels the evolution of Samuel Beckett's work, it has a completely different function: in Beckett the near vicinity of silence is the threat of aphasia, the grip of oblivion, while in Duras it is a sign of immediacy and intimacy, the privacy of an unlimited collective, the proximity of physical communion, the imminent reign of desire, a spreading of certainty such that all the difficulties on its way are conquered. The temporality of Duras is the time of extreme expense which precedes orgasm or parturition:

Elle vient quand même de la forêt, dit Stein. Quelle peine. Quelle énorme peine. Que c'est difficile.
— Elle doit traverser, traverser.
— Oui. Tout.
La musique recommence. Cette fois dans une amplitude souveraine. Elle s'arrête encore.
— Elle va y arriver, elle va traverser la forêt, dit Stein, elle vient.
Ils parlent entre la musique et la musique, à voix douce. . . .[16]

The "elle" that comes is both the music with which voices may be no longer discordant and Elisabeth Alione who has gone, who *can now come* through the forest that she would not enter. Elisabeth, the chosen collective object of love, the catalyst of life in her very apparent banality ("she is beautiful; it is invisible"), may no longer absent herself from where they are all together. The sovereign music is a fugue, its going is forever a coming: reversal and rehearsal. One terror is left behind (i.e., on the other side of totality, of S. Thala); Derrida gave it its appropriate name: "the fear of being the last to keep what I wanted to entrust you with, my love."[17] Stein, Max Thor, and Alissa are on this hither side of totality (the thither side of the given) where they no longer need to will their desire and thus no longer wish. Effects of language play the same magic role as the miraculous weaponry of Wittig. Distances are not abolished, but they are all very short and almost equal; they are the precise stuff of our relationships, the ability of availability, a presentation such that the other does not have to keep her/his otherself to receive the gift of existence.

A theoretical justification or rationale of utopian/rehearsive proceedings could be found in a certain vision of femininity, suggested by Cixous, as contradiction assumed and affirmed. Women under the law of the father are pure (speculative) currency, simulacra of a power-to-enjoy; womanhood is thus an everdeferred goal, something unattainable which becomes in itself the object of their masters' perverted desire; but by being subjected, alienated to this position, women would manifest the unfinished state of the human species; their lack (the *manque à être* projected on them by men-the-fathers) would be at the same time false consciousness and the signifier of an actual specific lack from which men would be separated by false consciousness. Femininity would then be at one and the same time what we are all deprived of and the completeness built from the negative image of loss or the cognition of complete loss. If I am not unfaithful to the thought of Hélène Cixous, summarizing it as I did, I perceive here a movement toward the perpetuation of the given, not very different from that denounced by Baudrillard in Marxist political economy and the post-Hegelian dialectic spiral.

Although the direct line of death which Hyvrard, Wittig, and Cixous either claim or aspire to hold can be read as anti-production or counterproduction, as radical rejection of mechanicity, there is perhaps an inherent trend in theoretical thinking which seeks the ineluctable for the foundation of a previsional continuum. The order of masculine sexuality is then reputed to have introduced conceptual discontinuities in order to achieve reproduction. Uninterruptedness, whether of symbolic exchange, erotic dialogue with oneself, or poetic excitability, becomes a goal in itself which risks to defeat the discontinuity of rehearsal.

Fortunately, neither Cixous nor other recent feminist writers have fallen in the same trap as Baudrillard: to confuse the visible with appearance, to reintroduce in the place of value a symbolic mediation which fulfills exactly the same role, the institution of one-directionality. Rehearsal and psychoanalysis, if they are well understood, have these two features in common: they are arts of making visible that which is only apparent, and they are not one-directional. To produce may thus acquire a new sense: to bring before itself everything that hides behind itself. Psychoanalysis, and more particularly the psychoanalysis of psychoanalysis (as it is practiced for example by François Roustang and Monique Schneider), may help feminist rehearsers in a futuristic task which is a bit better than *bougé* insofar as it answers now the age-old challenge of the displacement of castration. If the sex of woman is not (yet) one (L. Irigaray), women are less castrated by being denied the phallus than they are castrated of *their own* sex, which is "reduced to ashes" (M. Schneider), socially defined as undefinable, or pinpointed in a sad parody of the ready-made definition of the phallus. If this is so, men are at least equally castrated of that same sex which they misread as absence and on which they project their own absence to themselves, their wish-to-fullness.

What we have to learn to make both production and reproduction meaningful, in the practice of language as in the practice of eros, is to consent to otherness in ourselves in the first place. In fact neither production nor reproduction have occurred yet, for fear of objectification. To objectify is nothing else than to consent to otherness and, yes, there is never enough imagination, if imagination is that activity by which we cease to be other-blind:

In truth, that invisible tongue which still wrapped me not long ago and dictated my steps, I have torn it away, the old knotty tongue which sheathed my breath, I have taken it out. . . . My internal country my climate. Let the young tongue tell it to me! I have borne it in the womb of my mouth. This is the seed of the world tied to my door. This is the moment of its release! Now it is born! It hovers like a bird, it comes down the air it has ascended, it veers, it turns, it settles on my bow. . . ."[18]

As Alissa says: "it is too late to die." In the same labyrinth where Baudrillard and Lyotard were going crazy and praying for the soul of Nietzsche, where Macherey and Eagleton were holding a Critics and Related Industries Union meeting in a corner, threatening to strike against a world which threatens not to mirror itself in words, I also met Gertrude Stein and the young Marx escaping from protective language:

> Write and right.
> Of course they have nothing to do with one another.[19]

NOTES

1 Michèle Causse, *L'Encontre (fable autobiographique)* (Paris: Des Femmes, 1975), p. 53.
2 Ibid., p. 91.
3 Monique Wittig, *Les Guérillères* (Paris: Éditions de Minuit, 1969), p. 7.
4 Ibid., p. 17.

5 Ibid., p. 62.
6 Ibid., p. 102.
7 Jacques Derrida, *La Carte postale de Socrate à Freud et au-delà* (Paris: Flammarion, 1980), p. 38.
8 Jean Baudrillard, *Le Miroir de la production, ou l'illusion critique du matérialisme historique* (Paris: Éditions Casterman, 1973), p. 7.
9 Ernest Mandel, *Traité d'économie marxiste,* 4 vols. (Paris: U.G.E. 10/18, 1962), vol. 1, p. 19.
10 Jean Baudrillard, *Oublier Foucault* (Paris: Galilée, 1977), p. 77.
11 Terry Eagleton, *Criticism and Ideology* (London: NLB, 1976), p. 97.
12 Jeanne Hyvrard, *Mère la Mort* (Paris: Éditions de Minuit, 1976), p. 36.
13 Ibid., p. 147.
14 Ibid., p. 154.
15 Hélène Cixous, Madeleine Gagnon, and Annie Leclerc, *La Venue à l'écriture* (Paris: U.G.E. 10/18, 1977), p. 44.
16 Marguerite Duras, *Détruire, dit-elle* (Paris: Éditions de Minuit, 1969), p. 136.
17 Derrida, *La Carte postale de Socrate à Freud et au-delà,* p. 212.
18 Hélène Cixous, *La* (Paris: Des Femmes, 1976), pp. 112–13.
19 Gertrude Stein, *The Geographical History of America,* as quoted by William Gass in *Fiction and the Figures of Life* (New York: Alfred A. Knopf, 1970), pp. 84–85.

13 /

From the One to the Many:
Pluralism in Today's Thought

Matei Calinescu

I. THE NEW PLURALISM: FROM ABSOLUTE STRUCTURES
TO IMPERFECTION

Innovation? Renovation? These are (fortunately) not unambiguous words. In any case, as far as the theme of this essay is concerned, both are relevant and even mutually reinforcing. It is almost a truism to say that modernity was a period dominated by various monistic models of thought, some of them drawing on the cultural prestige of science, and particularly on the materialist-physicalist versions of science, with their built-in passion for reductionism. Perhaps more interestingly, if we see it as an "anti-traditional tradition" (Harry Levin) or as a "tradition against itself" (Octavio Paz), modernity also was, in some of its major philosophical and aesthetic formulations, sharply critical of its own visions of unity, often in the name of a "lost" or "forgotten" or "hidden" or "unrecognizable" Truth. With curiously few exceptions, modernity's movements of radical skepticism confront us with the striking inconsistency that they were premised on monistic assumptions. Would it then not be the case that even modernity's critique of monism was in fact little more than a search (patient or impatient, darkened by despair or illumined by strange millennial hopes) for a new, all-embracing and all-explaining monism? From this vantage point, the contemporary flourishing of pluralist thought has a definitely innovative dimension.

On the other hand, if we abandon the "logic" of linear time, which characterizes modernity's secularized version of Judaeo-Christian eschatology, we immediately realize that the recent trends away from monism belong to the realm of renovation rather than innovation. After the One, after its largely absentee reign in the modern period, we are witnessing a return of the Many. The thought of plurality in Western culture goes back straight to antiquity, both religiously (Greek polytheism) and philosophically (was not Empedocles a full-fledged metaphysical pluralist?). Furthermore, pluralist views, although they often had a marginal existence, never completely disappeared — not even in the midst of the modern intellectual crisis, whether this crisis looked for solutions in the direction of a positive (often positivist) monism, or whether it favored a temporarily more fashionable negative monism of absence and derealization. The continuity of pluralism becomes evident if we consider, as far as modernity is concerned, the line of thought that goes from the mid-nineteenth-century reaction against Hegel, through Fechner and Lotze, to William James and his school, not discounting such philosophers with strong pluralistic leanings as John Stuart Mill, C. S. Peirce, Henri Bergson, or John Dewey, to name only a few.[1] In a way, each of these thinkers has paved the way for to-day's pluralistic renaissance.

In considering innovation or renovation or both (and per-haps the word "both" should be stressed here), the fact of the matter is that most recent Western attempts at defining the major paradigms of today's cultural consciousness show a particularly intense concern for the question of pluralism. This concern can obviously take many forms; but the important thing at this point is simply to take stock of an issue that is, often quite explicitly, at the center of such different works as Ihab Hassan's two latest books, *Paracriticisms* (1975) and *The Right Promethean Fire* (1980); or Paul Feyerabend's *Against Method* (1975); or *Performance in Postmodern Culture* (1979); or the essays by Ihab Hassan, David Antin, Julia Kristeva, Wallace Martin, Matei Cali-nescu, Marjorie Perloff, and Charles Russell, included in the

Bucknell Review special issue on *Romanticism, Modernism, Postmodernism* (1980); or, last but not least, the papers printed in this volume.

It may be noteworthy that the return to pluralism in contemporary thought is by no means confined to authors who identify themselves with, or are sometimes characterized, as "postmodern" (an admittedly confusing but not unuseful label). Advocacies of pluralism often also come from more "traditionalist" quarters. (Parenthetically, I employ the term "traditionalist" in a sense that is both positive and new; this novelty reflects the whole new attitude toward the past that is emerging as a characteristic of our time, an attitude that will be discussed more specifically in the concluding part of this essay.) Chaïm Perelman, for instance, has provided the pluralism of his predecessor at the Université Libre of Brussels, Eugène Dupréel, with a new and highly sophisticated basis by returning to Aristotle and rediscovering the philosophical meaning of rhetoric, then developing his own theory of argumentation and founding the school of *"La Nouvelle rhétorique,"* whose major historical landmark is the publication (with L. Olbrechts-Tyteca) of *Traité de l'argumentation* in 1958. The significance of Perelman's doctrine of pluralistic argumentation, within the broad context of what I would call "cultural symptomatology," is brought out by the fact that, completely independently and deriving mostly from the post-Wittgensteinian Anglo-American analytic tradition, Robert Nozick, in his *Philosophical Explanations* (1981), asks himself questions and arrives at conclusions that are sometimes similar and often complementary to Perelman's. Thus, to give an example, Perelman's opposition between possibilistic reasoning and demonstrative conviction becomes in Nozick's different language the opposition between "explanation" and "proof," implying a rejection of "coercive philosophy" based on "argumentative bludgeoning."

Closer to the concerns of literary criticism and hermeneutics, however, is Wayne Booth's *Critical Understanding: The Power and Limits of Pluralism* (1979), whose focus is both theoretical and practical. The latter consists of an attentive and discriminating discussion of the work of three quite distinct pluralist critics, Ronald Crane, Kenneth Burke, and M. H. Abrams.

Like Crane, a representative of the "Chicago School," Booth clearly arrived at his pluralistic philosophy of literature via Aristotle and a revaluation of the Aristotelian rhetoric of *persuasion* along lines that, although independent, cannot help but remind one of some of Perelman's insights. Booth's central questions deal with both "methodological pluralism" in literary study and with what could be called "hermeneutical pluralism" (is there only one "correct" interpretation of a given text or are there several "valid" or "admissible" interpretations? and, if so, how many? and what are the criteria for distinguishing between an "admissible" and an "inadmissible" interpretation? and what are the criteria for establishing an order or even a hierarchy among the numerous, possibly countless, "valid" but ultimately incompatible interpretations?). These are not perhaps the exact terms in which Booth poses the questions; but he addresses them all in one way or another, and his general stance of "limited pluralism" emerges enlighteningly from the unfolding of his dialectic of "understanding" (submission to the text) and "overstanding" (intentional but "just" violation of the text).

This is, not unintentionally, a list of quite heterogeneous names and works. However, there is a not-so-hidden characteristic that is common to them. These and other authors, irrespective of ideological or philosophical commitments, share a certain hostility toward monistic or "totalistic" solutions, however refined and tempting. Not all of them, as we have seen, are complete pluralists; but their implicit table of values is largely pluralist, or at least compatible with pluralism. In the words of one of them, Ihab Hassan, "To think well, to feel well, to read well . . . is to refuse the tyranny of wholes; totalization in any human endeavor is potentially totalitarian." And then, raising the question of models (social but also more general), the same writer goes on to formulate a series of questions that are highly relevant to the theme of this essay: "Model, anti-model, without model? Is a model-in-the-making still a model? Can a model convert, subvert, or pervert its own versions, and so keep itself incomplete? What if various models were set against one another, without dominance of a single model? [One recognizes here the pluralistic-dialogic alternative that will receive more attention later.] How does an under-determined model (anarchic) suddenly become over-determined (totalitarian or utopian)? Or is every model of 'perfection' really an image of the void?"[2] If perfection is indeed "an image of the void," then the poet, Yves Bonnefoy, should be right when he states, bluntly but how suggestively: "L'imperfection est la cime." The brief poem bearing this title may serve as an introduction to the (postmodern) spirit of our time:

Il y avait qu'il fallait détruire et détruire et détruire,
Il y avait que le salut n'est qu'à ce prix.

Ruiner la face nue qui monte dans le marbre
Marteler toute forme toute beauté.

Aimer la perfection parce qu'elle est le seuil,
Mais la nier sitôt connue, l'oublier morte,

L'imperfection est la cime.[3]

II. MONISTIC VERSUS PLURALISTIC AXIOLOGIES AND THE QUESTION OF DIALOGUE

How many worlds are there? How many kinds of worlds? What types of relationships can one establish between the world—if there is only one world—and the plurality of apparent worlds that are its manifestations? And if there are many (actual and possible) worlds, according to what criteria is one to judge and assess them? And is not the mere fact of adopting uniform criteria by which to appraise them a way of positing the existence of a superworld, or a universal model, which would subsume the many worlds? In which case, would such worlds not deserve to be called worlds, but simply aspects, or parts of a larger whole, whose meaning could be understood only in terms of the totality to which they belong? Even from the formulation of such questions we can see how complicated the issue is between monism and pluralism.

The monist says: there is only one real world. The dualist postulates the existence of two worlds or two heterogeneous kinds of reality, separated by an unbridgeable gap. The pluralist says: there are many irreducible principles, and therefore many worlds. The difficulties of each position appear as soon as one tries to "explain" it (in Nozick's sense) with consistency. And these difficulties are only compounded by the highly complex, often contradictory, and almost always overlapping axiological assumptions that are implicit in each of these stances. The monist's assertion of ultimate unity is clearly a value-laden statement: it is based on certain choices of demonstrative strategy (deduction, reduction, and analysis are valued not merely as instruments of truth but also as weapons against multiplicity and complexity, which are supposed to bow in humility before the final triumph of the One). The monist may welcome the fight and may revel in its tension, insofar as overcome tension gives significance to the victory. In the monist's implicit scale of values, unity, totality, simplicity, and universality obviously rank higher than multiplicity, fragmentation, intricacy, or diversity. The scale of values of the pluralist will be tipped naturally in the opposite direction. But not necessarily so. As suggested by Booth in *Critical Understanding,* the mere assertion of plurality does not preclude the possibility of introducing some kind of hierarchy among the many interpretations (or worlds) whose irreducible existence is recognized. And clearly, with the introduction of hierarchy, axiological monism can creep even into ontological pluralism. If, from whatever perspective, one or some worlds are superior to others, there is no reason for not focusing attention on the first to the detriment or even the exclusion of the latter.

This brings us to one of the great issues raised by the relation between monism and pluralism. There are monisms which are axiologically pluralistic; there are pluralisms which are axiologically monistic. These possibilities are best illustrated in the case of dualism. The ultimate ontological dualism of Plato, for instance, presents us with one of the most clear-cut versions of axiological monism. The world of movement and flux apprehended by our senses is, in Platonic philosophy, in absolute contrast with the world of changeless and perfect Ideas known by pure intellect. True values can be defined *only* in relation to the latter, and from this exclusive perspective Plato's axiology is of necessity strongly monistic, "totalistic," and, if we accept Karl

Popper's argument in his *Open Society and Its Enemies,* even plainly "totalitarian." To deal meaningfully with the perplexities brought about by the distinction between monism and pluralism (including the particular case of dualism), we need therefore a further distinction that would account not only for *what* is stated about the world or worlds and their reciprocal relations, but that would also account for *who* makes such a statement and *why* (for what purpose and in whose interest?), and *how,* and on the basis of what kind of *authority.* Such a distinction is recommended by certain religious philosophers (most prominently, Martin Buber) or literary theorists (most prominently, Mikhail Bakhtin) as a distinction, on the level of the discourse, between *monologue* and *dialogue* or, more broadly, between a monologic type of consciousness and a dialogic type. By and large, monologism may be seen as having natural affinities with the monistic view and dialogism with the pluralistic view. But under closer examination, this "rule of thumb" allows for outstanding and unexpected exceptions. Thus, Buber's philosophical dialogism is articulated within the framework of the monistic (monotheist) theological tradition of Judaism. And Bakhtin's aesthetic and ultimately religious dialogism, while hostile to the institutionalized forms of "ideology" (including Christianity), is not only compatible with but actually derived from some of the major tenets of the Christian tradition. As Michael Holquist has convincingly pointed out, Bakhtin's unpublished *opus magnum, The Architectonics of Answerability* "contains in embryo every major idea Bakhtin was to have for the rest of his long life. The whole conception of the work [is] a kind of phenomenological meditation on Christ's injunction to treat others as you would yourself be treated."[4] The fact that Bakhtin's major philosophical-moral work remains unpublished in the USSR (and will probably remain so for the foreseeable future) explains why many of Bakhtin's readers, familiar with his published works (on Dostoevsky, on Rabelais, on the philosophy of language, and on the formalist method in literary scholarship), are generally unaware of the relation between his pluralistic dialogism, rooted in a "heteroglot view of language,"[5] and Christ's fundamental injunction (which may be understood as a formulation of the principle of dialogic equality).[6]

No one summarizes better than Bakhtin the linguistic-stylistic consequences of the consistent monistic-monologic world view: and no one argues more convincingly about the need to focus attention at long last on the "centrifugal forces" in the life of language, on the "dialogized heteroglossia" which has marked the evolution of the novel. Predictably, Bakhtin gives the novel a philosophical dignity that it has traditionally rarely enjoyed. What he has to say about the "centralizing" monologic tendencies in the history of Western linguistics and poetics can be easily generalized to other areas of knowledge (including the knowledge of knowledge, that is, epistemology):

Aristotelian poetics, the poetics of Augustine, the poetics of the medieval church, of 'the one language of truth,' the Cartesian poetics of neoclassicism, the abstract grammatical universalism of Leibniz . . . , all these, whatever their differences in nuance, give expression to the same centripetal forces in socio-linguistic and ideological life. . . . The victory of one reigning language (dialect) over the others, the supplanting of languages, their enslavement, the process of illuminating them with the True Word, the incorporation of barbarians and lower social strata into a unitary language of culture and truth, the canonization of ideological systems, philology with its methods of studying and teaching dead languages, languages that were by that very fact 'unities,' Indo-European linguistics, with its focus of attention directed away from language plurality to a single proto-language—all this determined the content and power of the category of 'unitary language' in linguistic and stylistic thought. . . .[7]

And Bakhtin adds, with specific reference to dialogue: "One might even say outright that the dialogic aspect of discourse and all the phenomena connected with it have remained to the present moment beyond the ken of linguistics."[8] We might note that the phenomena Bakhtin is citing have remained not only beyond the ken of much of modern linguistics and the philosophy of language, but have also been neglected by modern epistemology and philosophy in general. The recent attention that has been devoted to them, and that Bakhtin was recommending as early as the mid-1930s, when he wrote his "Discourse in the Novel," may be a sign that the pluralistic dialogism which lies at the heart of fictional discourse could not be discussed seriously, that is, taking into account its larger philosophical and axiological implications, before both the positive monism of tradition as well as the negative monologism of modernity had run their course.

III. TRUTH AS LYING: NEGATIVE MONOLOGISM AND
THE ALTERNATIVE OF PLURALISM

The age of truth "with a big 'T' and in the singular," to which William James opposed his pragmatism and "radical pluralism" toward the end of the nineteenth century, has never since managed to come back in a philosophically credible fashion. The subsequent critical age, marked by doubt and crisis, led to a refinement of earlier strategies of demystification and to a triumph of the "hermeneutics of suspicion" as defined by Paul Ricoeur in his study of Freud. According to Ricoeur, the three masters of the "school of suspicion," Marx, Nietzsche, and Freud, share a general approach to "truth as lying" and a "decision to look upon the whole of consciousness primarily as 'false' consciousness." We remember that "false consciousness" is the standard Marxist definition of "ideology." Eventually, though, Ricouer believes "all three [masters of suspicion] clear the horizon . . . for a new Truth, not only by means of a 'destructive' critique, but by the invention of a new art of interpreting."[9]

Needless to say, this "new reign of Truth" has never come about. The attempt to revive truth "with a big 'T' and in the singular" by means of absolute suspicion has resulted not merely in failure but, wherever it was pursued along the lines of large-scale "utopian engineering" (to borrow Karl Popper's phrase), in the creation of new, arbitrarily imposed, and rigidly dogmatic forms of "false consciousness."

We also note that the modern ideologies of anti-ideology, including the philosophy of antiphilosophy, whether directly or indirectly, tend to view truth primarily in terms of power. And this applies both to old versions of truth (whose mendacity must be exposed) and to the new "liberating" truth that such ideologies always strive to attain and often proclaim. Interestingly, the terminology of power is all-pervasive and almost obsessive in the discourse of the "masters of suspicion": economic power relations, exploitation, and class struggle in Marx; psychological, ultimately biological power, "censorship," and "repression" in Freud; the paradoxical power of the weak, *"ressentiment"* as the basis of "slave morality," the "will to power," and the advent of the "overman" in Nietzsche. Not surprisingly, the "art of interpreting" invented by suspicion is bound to be, at least potentially, paranoid. This underlying trait of the modern hermeneutics of doubt was noticed and perceptively described by Michael Polanyi in his *Personal Knowledge*.[10] More recently, André Glucksman has attempted from a similar point of view to bring out the common "project of mastery" that forms the obsessive core of the theories advanced by the *maîtres à penser* of modernity (from the German romantic philosophers, particularly Fichte and Hegel, to Marx and Nietzsche).[11]

Elsewhere, I have characterized the major critical doctrines of the modern age as expressions of "negative monologism."[12] This negative monologism can be translated philosophically as "negative monism." I am aware that this phrase is not unequivocal. It may mean the kind of monism that is attained primarily through a critique of one, or several, or all of the prevailing versions of monism at a given point in the history of philosophy. But it may also mean the special kind of (admittedly metaphorical) "monism of absence" which is implicit in the "deconstructionist" philosophy of Jacques Derrida and his numerous imitators or epigones. The method of deconstruction uses the sometimes loose philosophical equivalents of scientific "demonstrations of impossibility" and explicitly assigns itself the task of discovering and dramatizing the *aporias* of the "metaphysics of presence" and of the "logocentrism" of the whole Western philosophical tradition. This negative monism appears therefore as a monism of negation and of radical agnosticism: to deconstruct is to decenter, displace, dislocate, disseminate, disperse, derealize, fracture, fragment, and to consistently refuse to think in terms of "origins," "originality," "truth," "authority," "authenticity," "legitimacy," "hierarchy," etc. True, the highly sophisticated negation of the idea of unity (in even its minutest aspects and remotest consequences) may in certain respects appear to be close to the recognition of plurality. Furthermore, the very notion of plurality is frequently resorted to, but exclusively for purposes of subversion and disruption of the One, and never for the *affirmation* of the Many. Negative monism in this sense is not inconsistent with a kind of negative pluralism or a pluralism *"en creux,"* in which the apparent "pluralization" or "proliferation" of theories and countertheories is used as a polemical device. The multiplicity that is posited by such pluralism (sometimes with a great display of philosophical imagination) is clearly an empty one: a "doubling" and "redoubling" of absences, an endless repetition, an infinite regress of frames that frame nothing.

But there are, in today's culture, increasingly numerous signs that modernity is rapidly approaching its end (or has it already ended?). One sign is the "pluralist renaissance," a phenomenon whose manifestations are themselves, as we have seen, extremely diverse, indeed so heterogeneous as to frustrate any attempt at generalization. Incidentally, the near-certainty that the effort to unify multiplicity will fail and will eventually be confronted with irreducible "facts" or "fictions" or "worlds" does not mean that such effort should not be undertaken. On the contrary, monistic or reductionist assumptions should be constantly tested and retested against an irreducibility that, in the process of being assailed from all sides, is as open to change, revision, and enrichment as are the hypotheses that challenge it. Authentic pluralism, which is possible only in a dialogic context, has the following remarkable and paradoxical characteristic: it takes monism, in its various versions, quite seriously; not only does it not dismiss but it also welcomes and even encourages it, knowing that the strength of its own theories is conditioned by the strength of those it opposes. Pluralist philosophies can be judged by the degree to which they live up to the great dialogic principle: one must always argue against the strongest case. That is why we should not be surprised to discover that while there is obvious tension between pluralism and monism the two views are not ultimately incompatible. This lack of any fundamental incompatibility can be best understood in terms of dialogy: whatever the specific opinions they want to articulate and test, the participants in a dialogue must observe certain rules if the dialogue is to be pursued in a meaningful and enlightening fashion; mutual respect and the search for a common ground of comprehension—

comprehension even of incompatibility or "incommensurability" — is one of these rules. Thus, even the most incompatible ideas or theories are *dialogically compatible* by virtue of simply being presented as alternative solutions to similar, although never quite identical, problems.

Students of pluralist thought have not failed to notice the striking fact that most of the philosophers that can be defined as pluralists are in certain important respects monists. Discussing William James's ambiguous title *A Pluralistic Universe,* a title that taken by itself is not only equivocal but plainly a *contradictio in adjecto,* a declared pluralist like Nelson Goodman points out in his recent book, *Ways of Worldmaking* (1978), that "the issue between monism and pluralism tends to evaporate under analysis. If there is but one world, it embraces a multiplicity of contrasting aspects; if there are many worlds, the collection of them is one. The one world may be taken as many, or the many worlds taken as one; whether one or many depends on the way of taking."[13] One should add that this is so when the issue is analyzed by a pluralist and not, as Goodman puts it a couple of pages later, by his "typical adversary." That adversary is

the monopolistic materialist or physicalist who maintains that one system, physics, is preeminent and all-inclusive, such that every other version must be reduced to it or rejected as false or meaningless. . . . But the evidence for such reducibility is negligible, and even the claim is nebulous since physics itself is fragmentary and unstable and the kind and consequences of reduction envisaged are vague. (How do you go about reducing Constable's or James Joyce's world to physics?) I am the last person likely to underrate construction or reduction. . . . But reduction in any reasonably strict sense is rare, almost always partial, and seldom if ever unique. The pluralist's acceptance of versions other than physics implies no relaxation of rigor but a recognition that standards different from yet no less exacting than those applied in science are appropriate for appraising what is conveyed in perceptual or pictorial or literary versions.[14]

The last part of the foregoing quotation may serve as a broad introduction to one of the major themes encountered in today's pluralist thinking, namely, the relation between scientific worlds and aesthetic worlds. At long last, the "traditional" conflict between science and art seems to have come to an end, an end that had been not seldom intimated over the last century or so by quite a few great scientists and philosophers of science, as well as by artists and aestheticians, but that somehow failed to be fully recognized. In part, this recognition was prevented by the remarkable stubbornness of "physicalism," the last positive form of monism in the context of the critical or negative monisms that become more and more numerous and sweeping as modernity runs its course. In the meantime, pluralist thought, while accepting science, felt the need to justify and even borrow models from certain types of activity and experience—religious, moral, legal, political, and increasingly aesthetic—which modern scientism had ignored or dismissed as irrelevant to the search for objective truth.[15]

IV. EPISTEMOLOGICAL MODELS: THEIR "FIDUCIARY" AND
ULTIMATELY AESTHETIC BASES

Once the assumptions and goals of scientism (as distinct from the development of the sciences themselves) came under question, once it became clear that such requirements as total reducibility, absolute uniqueness of truth, total predictability (even in the ideal case represented by the fictional "demon of Laplace"), or perfect linguistic consistency were, even as working hypotheses, untenable, it became possible to discover that the differences among various kinds of human experiences are unbridgeable only within certain frames of reference, and that such frames are not intrinsically preferable to others. There are, then, postcritical and more broadly postmodern frames of reference within which, say, mathematics, religion, and the arts, while preserving all their irreducible differences, can be seen as having highly significant common features. We note that the recognition of such features, rather than being the starting point of a new attempt at reduction, renders possible the resumption of an *intracultural dialogue* that modernity had abandoned. With respect to the relationship between mathematics, religion, and art, for instance, Michael Polanyi advances the "conception of religious worship as a heuristic vision," to be aligned "with the great intellectual systems, such as mathematics, fiction and the fine arts, which are validated by becoming happy dwelling places of the human mind."[16] The following passage can be taken as a good summary of Polanyi's general position:

> In view of the high imaginative and emotional powers by which Christian beliefs control the whole person and relate him to the universe, the specification of these beliefs is much more colorful than are the axioms of arithmetic or the premises of natural science. But they belong to the same class of statements, performing kindred fiduciary functions. We owe our mental existence predominantly to works of art, morality, religious worship, scientific theory and other articulate systems which we accept as our dwelling place. . . . Objectivism has totally falsified our conception of truth. . . . In trying to restrict our mind to the few things that are demonstrable, and therefore explicitly dubitable, it has overlooked the acritical choices which determine the whole being of our minds and has rendered us incapable of acknowledging these vital choices.[17]

Polanyi's fiduciary epistemology does not deny the importance, indeed the indispensability, of external experience in the process of knowledge; but such experience serves only "*as a theme* for an intellectual activity which develops one aspect of it into a system that is established and accepted on the grounds of its internal evidence."[18] Such systems or frameworks develop into highly complex, articulate, and rigorous structures offering the minds that choose to inhabit them the opportunity to fully exert their "intellectual passions" (the heuristic passion, the persuasive passion, etc.). Validity, then, in any one of these systems is ultimately determined by internal and not external criteria. Obviously, there is no reason to consider the criteria of validity in any one of these systems as being more demanding or strict or exemplary, and therefore deserving to be introduced in all other systems. Furthermore, such criteria are not given once forever: in each one of the great heuristic frameworks, creation and subsequent refinement or reassessment of the whole "explanatory structure" are the rule, and stasis appears always as a temporary exception.

It is my view that Polanyi's general model of a plurality of coexisting heuristic systems, seen as many "happy dwelling places" of the mind, can be better understood if it is considered from an aesthetic vantage point rather than from the religious angle suggested by his insistence on the "fiduciary" basis of knowledge. And this is so, among other reasons, because aesthetic beliefs and judgments have always been more naturally dialogical and tolerant, that is to say, more spontaneously pluralistic. The self-conscious fictionality of the work of art, its traditional freedom from the constraints of literal truth, and its almost universally recognized ludic dimensions account for both the individualistic and the pluralistic vocations of artistic activities.

Polanyi himself is aware of the close connection between his postcritical view of religion and the experience of literature and the arts. "Artistic creation and enjoyment," he writes, "are contemplative experiences more akin than mathematics to religious communion. Art, like mysticism, breaks through the screen of objectivity and draws on our preconceptual capacities of contemplative vision."[19] The essential distinction between aesthetic and other beliefs is not so much that the former tend to be weaker than the latter; aesthetic beliefs can be quite strong, after all. What sets them apart is, I would maintain, the fact that they are rooted in a deeper sense of plurality.

V. AESTHETIC DUALISM AND PLURALISM

As I have suggested earlier, ontological dualism (and this is even more so in the case of religious dualism) has led, as a rule, to extremely strong versions of axiological monism. There is, however, one type of dualism that clearly represents a major step in the direction of true pluralism. This is the aesthetic dualism that prepared the emergence of romanticism and, more broadly, constituted perhaps one of the first working models of true philosophic pluralism. The "message" of aesthetic dualism can be summarized in the simple statement that there are two distinct types of beauty—the classic type and the romantic type—and that both of them are *equally legitimate artistically.*

Let us take the "classic/gothic" antinomy as it occurred in English criticism in the second half of the eighteenth century. The major implications of this opposition are illustrated, among many others, by Richard Hurd in his *Letters on Chivalry and Ro-*

mance (1772). Hurd speaks of *classic* and *gothic* as two perfectly autonomous worlds, neither of which can be considered superior to the other. Quite naturally, one who approaches the gothic with classical criteria will be unable to discover in it anything except irregularity and ugliness. But this, obviously, does not mean that the gothic has no rules or goals of its own by which its achievements should be judged. "When an architect examines a Gothic structure by Grecian rules," Hurd writes, "he finds nothing but deformity. But the Gothic architecture has its own rules, by which when it comes to be examined, it is seen to have its merit, as well as the Grecian." Hurd, who tries to defend the use of "gothic" fictions in poets like Spenser and Tasso against neoclassical rationalistic attacks, argues that a poem like *The Faerie Queene* must be read and criticized according to the idea of a gothic, not of a classical poem, in order to be adequately understood: "And on those principles, it would not be difficult to unfold its merit in another way than has been hitherto attempted." But even Hurd, as his argument unfolds, turns out to be less of a consistent aesthetic dualist than we might have expected. Going beyond the scope of a mere defense, Hurd's discussion of Tasso concludes with the typically early romantic pronouncement that gothic customs and fictions are superior to classical ones, after all, at least insofar as "poetic truth" is concerned. Hurd says: "The fancies of our modern bards are not only more gallant, but . . . more sublime, more terrible, more alarming, than those of the classic fablers. In a word, you will find that the manners they paint, and the *superstitions* they adopt, are more poetical for being Gothic."[20]

I have used the example of aesthetic dualism not so much for its intrinsic interest as for its didactic clarity. It offers the simplest model of what I understand by axiological pluralism. Whether we are faced with a duality or with a plurality, the obvious problem is always a problem of choice. Preference is unavoidable in the long run, particularly when the alternatives that are presented to us are alternatives of *doing* something (and even reading or pure aesthetic contemplation is a way of *doing* something in the Austinian sense in which we always do things with words, and in which even statements that appear as totally "constative" are actually "performative"). What aesthetic dualism or pluralism shows is simply that a choice does not necessarily imply a summary dismissal or ignorance of other available alternatives. On the contrary, when a choice is made in full awareness of the meaning and possibilities offered by other alternatives, the chances are that this choice will be more fruitful, more satisfying, and more insight-producing.

In this sense, any consistent pluralism implies a theory of freedom, and specifically of freedom of thought and discussion. The best formulation of such a theory to date is, I believe, John Stuart Mill's *On Liberty* (1859). According to Mill, "the collision of opinions" always works a "salutary effect." "Not violent conflict between parts of the truth," Mill writes, "but the quiet suppression of half of it is the formidable evil; there is always hope when people are forced to listen to both sides; it is when they attend only to one that errors harden into prejudices, and truth itself ceases to have the effect of truth, by being exaggerated into falsehood." Thus, freedom of thought and discussion is the main precondition of the "mental well-being of mankind."[21] As for truth, in the general sense in which Mill uses this concept, it is always scattered: to attain complete truth is an impossibility; to claim a monopoly on truth is a "formidable evil." We note in passing that, for clarity's sake, Mill also uses a "dualistic" working hypothesis: he divides the truth into two halves, one always more visible and more easily apprehended than the other. There is little doubt, though, that he is one of the first true radical pluralists. And his decisive influence on a typically postmodern philosopher of science like Paul Feyerabend (who applies quite faithfully the Millian theory of the liberty of discussion to the specific problems of the history and philosophy of science), may be interpreted as a sign that Mill's pluralism, a term that he himself never used, is perhaps more fertile today than ever.

VI. NEGATIVITY AND RELATIVITY: FROM "TRUTH" TO "RIGHTNESS"

Like romanticism, which both precedes it and renders it possible, aesthetic modernity has been defined in such a wide variety of fashions as to make its very concept almost ungraspable.

Some clarity, though, may be gained if we see these definitions as falling within two distinct categories: the first emphasizes the negative values of modernity, singling out such features as anti-traditionalism, polemicism, agonism, systematic subversion, nihilism, "dehumanization" (in Ortega's sense), deformation, unpopularity, etc.; the second category, without necessarily underestimating the role of negativity, stresses the positive diversity of styles, languages, and ultimately idiolects that not only coexist within modernity but give it a sort of fluid, changing, unpredictable, though never totally unrecognizable, identity. An example of the second way of approaching modernity, which is on the whole less frequent than the first, is found in the definition of Symbolism (for which read modernism) advanced by Edmund Wilson: "Symbolism may be defined as an attempt by carefully studied means—a complicated association of ideas represented by a medley of metaphors—to communicate unique personal feelings."[22] Modernism is seen here as an implicit pluralism rooted in the pursuit of individual expression under conditions of freedom from objectively imposed (positive or negative) constraints. But the problem raised by this and other similar definitions is: How free is the modernist artist to express himself through the complex "medley of metaphors" that Wilson speaks of? The fact is that, even when they recognize the tendency for stylistic pluralization, students of modernism are usually inclined to qualify and limit it by introducing the countertendency toward negativity, crisis, chaos, and even self-destruction.[23]

The will to freedom, uniqueness, visionary self-expression, and revelation of the new is always there in the art of the modernist, but its very condition of possibility seems to be a deep sense of negativity and, indeed, an urge for crisis, destruction, or chaos. That is why modernist (and even more so avant-gardist) experimentalism is primarily an experimentalism of negation. Being of one's time, or preferably in advance of one's time (the claim of the avant-garde), appears the same as adopting an unflinchingly adversary attitude toward both the past and its numerous deceptive survivals in the present.

Historical relativism, whose first far-reaching intimations date from the eighteenth century, received its most articulate and refined formulations in the romantic period. But even for the great romantics, historical consciousness—the sense of universal historical relativity or "chronotopicity," to use the term coined by Bakhtin—had only a partially liberating influence and, more often than not, became a principle of tension which, with the advent of modernity, was only increased. What does this principle of tension consist of? What kinds of polarities make it up? To find a convenient answer to such questions is to understand one of the cardinal features of the modern mind. To begin with, let us remark that historical relativism, with its implicit axiological pluralism and, at the same time, with its inability to make intercultural value judgments, poses a great challenge to our human-all-too-human need for order. The fact remains that the consciousness of historical relativity by itself cannot establish any kind of transhistorical validity of the order of "truth," unique "categorical imperatives," harmony with strict "universal laws," and so forth. For the modern mind, intent on demystification and intracultural criticism, this may be an advantage. But the dangers involved in this stance are also obvious. Unbounded historical relativism often ends up transforming history "with a capital 'H' and in the singular" into a new kind of unpredictable and incoherent God. Hence, among numerous other consequences, is the modernist's typically ambivalent attitude toward history, which he perceives as both a locus of hope and a "nightmare."

If we direct our discussion to aesthetic activity taken as a model for other related theoretical activities of the human mind, a more constructive solution of the dilemmas posed by historicism seems to emerge: if there is no general (aesthetic) "truth," if no universally recognized set of rules can be used to determine such "truth," why not resort to certain weaker, but in no way arbitrary, criteria such as "consistency" or "rightness"? Although judgments of consistency or rightness can be tested and retested against similar judgments until some kind of consensus is reached, the process—while being as rigorous and exacting as anything—is less exclusive and "coercive" (in Nozick's sense) than the process by which truth in the strict sense is established. Furthermore, even when we work with the most unambiguous definition of truth, we may be faced with situations in which conflicting truths about the same matter are obtained. As Nelson Goodman points out: "That truths conflict reminds us effectively that truth cannot be the only consideration in choosing among statements or versions. . . . Even where there is no conflict, truth is far from sufficient. Some truths are trivial, irrelevant, unintelligible, or redundant; too broad, too narrow, too boring, too bizarre, too complicated; or taken from some other version than the one in question, as when a guard, ordered to shoot any of his captives who moved, immediately shot them all and explained that they were moving rapidly around the earth's axis and around the sun."[24] We may therefore accept that "a statement is true, and a description or representation right, for a world it fits." As Goodman concludes: "Rather than attempting to subsume descriptive and representational rightness under truth, we shall do better . . . to subsume truth along with these under the general notion of rightness of fit."[25]

The concept of rightness of fit is clearly inspired, primarily if not exclusively, by fundamental aspects of aesthetic experience. Translated philosophically, aesthetic experience does not reject truth in the name of some historical-epistemological relativism or some random plurality of existing (artistic) worlds; what it does is simply to limit the relevancy of truth by spelling out certain larger requirements of appropriateness that apply both to truth and to what Goodman calls "fictional versions" (verbal or pictorial or in a broader sense aesthetic). This means that true versions as well as fictional versions are subject to similar criteria of selection by means of which those versions which are too loose, or too rigid, or too banal, or, in a word, too boring, will be eliminated. As we can easily see, within each world or collection of worlds posited by such a pluralistic-aesthetic conception, the notion of rightness of fit (closely connected with the activist notion of "efficacy of understanding") not only renders axiological chaos impossible, but introduces positive, if usually competing, standards for establishing articulate and forceful hierarchies of values. If such hierarchies or schemes are convincing, it is not because they imply (as well they may) some universal thesis or principle, but because, to quote Goodman again, they may have the quality of "calling attention to a way of setting our nets to capture what may be significant likenesses and differences" within one system or another or between systems (pictorial, verbal, etc.).[26] Similar views, although articulated from a "possibilistic" as opposed to "actualistic" perspective, are advanced by Robert Nozick in his *Philosophical Explanations,* a book that ends, significantly, with a statement on "Philosophy as an Art Form." Nozick underscores the notion of the "artistic reshaping" of the world by a philosopher who is committed to a vision of truth (and transcendence) that is clearly more closely related to that of artists than it is to the pursuit of those seekers of "knockout arguments" and "proofs" who, perhaps unwittingly, attempt to establish a sort of Cartesian-Orwellian "thought-police." As Nozick remarks: "The philosopher aimed at truth states a theory that presents a possible truth and so a way of understanding the actual world (including its value). . . . In his artistic reshaping, he also may lift the mind from being totally filled with the actual world. . . . We can envision a humanistic philosophy, a self-consciously artistic one, sculpting ideas, value, and meaning into new constellations."[27] Is our age witnessing, due in part to the revival of aesthetic consciousness, a rebirth of old-new philosophy from its analytic "ashes"?

From the vantage point of the foregoing remarks, modernism as a vast cultural movement may be seen as illustrating the difficulties and contradictions characterizing the middle point on the road between earlier, predominantly monistic or dualistic world views, and the consistent pluralism and dialogism that our postmodern age seems to be preparing. I have discussed elsewhere some of the outstanding *aporias* of modernist consciousness and their exacerbation in the experimentalism of the avant-garde.[28] Such *aporias* are usually brought about by the clash between the negative monism or monologism of a radically antitraditional attitude (an attitude which views tradition as *one* enemy) and the unsuspected but real pluralist implications of historical-aesthetic relativism. The category of *relation* itself is certainly not unambiguous, and its modernist interpretation in terms of "will to power" (power of the *cogito* or the self, or conversely, powerlessness and inauthenticity of the self before the Other, whether History, the Unconscious, the socioeconomic Base, etc.) is a possible interpretation, although a narrow one. For the mind of today, which tries to go beyond the restrictions of positive or negative monologism while acknowledging the centrality of the problem of language, dialogic pluralism is the key to a new interpretation of the category of relation. Freed from the inescapably linear unfolding of modernity's concept of time, as well as from the natural attempt to escape that ineluctable linearity (which took the form of various philosophical or scientific abstract schemes of *totally reversible* and ideally controllable concepts of time), historical relativity tends to appear as a vast network of reciprocal determinations in which the irreversibility of certain vital choices creates new patterns of reversibility; it tends to appear as an ongoing process of "creative evolution" without any "objectively" preestablished *telos* or *eskhaton.* Our consciousness exists in a multiplicity of (actual and possible) worlds in perpetual "chronotopical" change.

VII. CONCLUSION

Instead of a "normal" conclusion that would simply summarize the arguments of the foregoing essay, I would prefer to raise again the problem with which I began: Can we really speak of a pluralist renaissance in today's Western culture? In trying to answer this question I must begin by admitting that a pluralist renaissance in contemporary thought, as I see it, is as much a phenomenon-in-the-making as a *desideratum,* to both of which I feel committed, but without being able to entertain any kind of certainty with regard to their success. The pluralistic-dialogic frame of mind is essentially fragile. Its delicate balance can be tipped not only by resurgent fanticisms or intolerant monologic orthodoxies but also by the odd phenomenon of ideologies that work without anyone believing in them. Such ideologies can no longer be defined as forms of "false consciousness." Under totalitarian conditions (and no part of the present world is completely safe from the dangers or "temptations" of totalitarianism), ideology seems to function best when no one believes in it; more than that, belief, and even belief in the ideology's own principles and assumptions, appears as its greatest enemy. Utopia is not the triumph of (rational) belief but, on the contrary, the total interdiction of belief. Wittingly or unwittingly, the great modern philosophies of suspicion and derealization have brought their modest contributions in that direction (the influence of ideas on history being fortunately limited).

In this rather gloomy context, one must note with some cautious optimism that the very fragility of the pluralistic outlook can become an unsuspected source of strength. As we saw earlier, pluralist thought and its immediate consequences (a plurality of world views, a plurality of conflicting beliefs that articulate themselves ever more forcefully and vigorously to become "happy dwelling places of the mind") are possible only on the basis of the type of freedom of expression and discussion that John Stuart Mill defined in *On Liberty*. In spite of numerous limitations, constraints, and risks, such liberty has always existed to some degree, and often to a higher degree than the powers that be would have been prepared to tolerate. And this is so because liberty is not only an idea or ideal, but a fundamental need of human consciousness, and as such one of the factors that have played a direct role—sometimes larger, sometimes smaller, and very often quite invisible at first sight—in the shaping of history.

To come back to our main focus, what consequences could the new (postmodern) pluralism have in the circumscribed area of culture that I have been concerned with in this paper? I will state them very briefly. To begin with, if the trends that I have succinctly and perhaps disjointedly described continue, the chances are that both *inter*cultural and *intra*cultural dialogue will become increasingly active. This dialogue will certainly be more than a dialogue for the sake of dialogue: it will provide new insights into old matters and possible solutions to the new puzzles that the world we live in requires us to solve. The authors of a recent essay in the philosophy of contemporary science, Ilya Prigogine and Isabelle Stengers, suggest that this new kind of dialogism is rendered possible by a rediscovery of a value that did not rank high in the axiology of modernity, namely, the value of *respect*: respect for nature (restored to its ancient Greek status of "*physis*") in the physical sciences, and, above and beyond that, cultural respect, in contrast with the earlier cultural suspicion of the moderns. The authors write: "We must learn no longer to patronizingly judge the population of knowledges and know-hows ("*savoirs*"), of the practices, and of the cultures produced by human societies but, on the contrary, how to combine them and how to establish among them new forms of communication which would increase our ability to cope with the unprecedented demands of our age."[29]

The new (postmodern) pluralism also promises, after several centuries of modern scientific "disenchantment of the world," a "reenchantment of the world," another important idea of Prigogine and Stengers. We might add that this process of "reenchantment," which is at the same time a process of "rehumanization," applies not only to the sciences but to other theoretical disciplines and forms of activity as well, including philosophy, the arts, and history itself. In connection with the latter, there are signs that a new historicism is emerging, a historicism that sees the past neither as a normative paradigm (the old traditionalist view) nor as an opponent (the modernist view which conceives novelty exclusively in terms of rupture), nor as a collection of "facts" that should be carefully gathered because one day they may reveal general patterns and universal laws (the positivistic view), nor yet as pure intertextual circularity (the structuralist view, ultimately as sterile as the positivisitic approach that it opposes), but rather as a "storehouse" of alternatives and counteralternatives, of stories and counterstories, of smaller and larger narrative scenarios, involving not only individuals but also groups, societies, beliefs, ideas, emotions, myths, and ultimately worlds and "ways of worldmaking." Such a new approach to history, rigorously imaginative and imaginatively rigorous, constitutes, I would argue, one of the great joys and strengths of the pluralist mind.

NOTES

1 For a more comprehensive overview of pluralist thought at the turn of the century, Jean Wahl's *The Pluralist Philosophies of England and America* (London: The Open Court, 1925), is still very useful.
2 The quotation is from Ihab Hassan, *The Right Promethean Fire* (Urbana: University of Illinois Press, 1980), p. 17. The author refers to a specific work by François Châtelet, Gilles Lapouge, and Olivier Re-

vault d'Allones, *La Révolution sans modèle* (Paris: Mouton, 1975), but the comments and questions occasioned by the reading of this book have an obviously much wider application.

3 Yves Bonnefoy, *Hier régnant désert* (Paris: Mercure de France, 1964), p. 33.

4 See Michael Holquist, "The Politics of Representation," in *Allegory and Representation: Selected Papers from the English Institute, 1979-1980,* ed. Stephen J. Greenblatt (Baltimore: Johns Hopkins University Press, 1981), pp. 163-83.

5 Ibid. See also Holquist's introduction to M. M. Bakhtin, *The Dialogic Imagination: Four Essays,* trans. Caryl Emerson and Michael Holquist (Austin: University of Texas Press, 1981), pp. xix-xx. The problem of "heteroglossia" is discussed at length by Bakhtin in the fourth essay in the quoted book, "Discourse in the Novel," pp. 259-422. For Bakhtin's theory of dialogue and dialogic consciousness, see also Mikhail Bakhtin, *Problems of Dostoevsky's Poetics,* trans. R. W. Rotsel (Ann Arbor, Mich.: Ardis Pubs., 1973), especially pp. 87-113 of ch. 4.

6 From a different angle, the link between pluralism and Christianity is also suggested by Wayne Booth in his *Critical Understanding* (Chicago: University of Chicago Press, 1979). For the specifically theological treatment of the question of pluralism, Booth refers to such works as David Tracy's *Blessed Rage for Order: The New Pluralism in Theology* (New York: Seabury Press, 1975); or Hans Urs von Balthasar's *Die Warheit ist symphonisch: Aspekte des christlichen Pluralismus* (Einsiedeln: Johannes Verlag, 1972).

7 Bakhtin, *The Dialogic Imagination,* p. 271.

8 Ibid., p. 273.

9 Paul Ricoeur, *Freud and Philosophy: An Essay on Interpretation,* trans. Denis Savage (New Haven: Yale University Press, 1970), pp. 32-33.

10 Michael Polanyi, *Personal Knowledge: Towards a Post-Critical Philosophy* (Chicago: University of Chicago Press, 1958), p. 241.

11 André Glucksman, *Les Maîtres penseurs* (Paris: Éditions Bernard Grasset, 1977).

12 See Matei Calinescu, "L'Intellectuel et le dialogue," *Cadmos* 2, no. 7 (1979): 59-83, and "Persuasion, dialogue, autorité," *Cadmos* 3, no. 11 (1980): 16-36.

13 Nelson Goodman, *Ways of Worldmaking* (Indianapolis: Hackett Pub., 1978), p. 2.

14 Ibid., pp. 4-5.

15 We note that today's scientific discourse has largely overcome the prejudices of "scientism" and may even welcome certain forms of aesthetic self-consciousness. For the latter, see the enlightening collection *On Aesthetics in Science,* ed. Judith Wechsler (Cambridge, Mass.: M. I. T. Press, 1978).

16 Polanyi, *Personal Knowledge,* p. 280.
17 Ibid., p. 286.
18 Ibid., p. 279.
19 Ibid., p. 199.
20 Quoted after Matei Calinescu, *Faces of Modernity* (Bloomington: Indiana University Press, 1977), pp. 36-37.
21 John Stuart Mill, *On Liberty,* ed. David Spitz (New York: W. W. Norton, 1975), p. 50.
22 Edmund Wilson, *Axel's Castle* (1931; reprint ed., New York: Charles Scribner's Sons, 1969), pp. 21-22.
23 Cf. Malcolm Bradbury and James McFarlane, *Modernism (1890-1930)* (Baltimore: Penguin Books, 1978), pp. 26-27.
24 Goodman, *Ways of Worldmaking,* pp. 120-21.
25 Ibid., p. 132.
26 Ibid., p. 129.
27 Robert Nozick, *Philosophical Explanations* (Cambridge: Harvard University Press, Belknap Press, 1981), p. 647.
28 Calinescu, *Faces of Modernity,* pp. 95-150.
29 Ilya Prigogine and Isabelle Stengers, *La Nouvelle alliance: Métamorphose de la science* (Paris: Éditions Gallimard, 1979), pp. 294-95.

III / PERSPECTIVES ON

Postmodernism

14 /

Postmodern Psychoanalysis

Norman N. Holland

To say what I mean by Postmodern calls for a brief history of twentieth-century culture. That is, for me, Postmodernism is the third stage in a series of movements that almost all the arts in our century have gone through, perhaps the sciences too, and certainly, I think, psychoanalysis. I fear this will not sound terribly original, but I shall call these stages — and they are not purely chronological — Early Modern, High Modern, and (despite hesitations about the term) Postmodern. I would have preferred to set this up according to playwright Sam Shepard's formula: "A play should have a beginning, a middle, and an end, although not necessarily in that order." That would be a truly Postmodern program. But in this first paragraph we are, by definition, still Early.

The first of these movements corresponds to the end of what we term, in American literature, realism or naturalism. In fiction, late naturalism took the form of pointing literature toward two things: the doings of ordinary people, particularly people at the bottom of the social heap; and sexuality as a force in the doings of all people. Among American novelists, I think of Crane, Norris, or Garland; in England, Galsworthy or Bennett or Conrad; in France, Rolland or Malraux. In poetry, Imagism provides precisely a poetic that points to an ordinary world outside itself. The paradigm would be Pound's "In a Station of the Metro":

> The apparition of these faces in the crowd;
> Petals on a wet, black bough.

In painting, I think of the so-called "Ashcan School," the works of such realists as Remington, Bellows, or Hopper, although in a larger sense the movement is represented by the lush reworkings of reality we associated with Monet and Cézanne, or by the even more sexual languors of *Art Nouveau* or *Jugendstil*—precisely Pound's translation of faces in a subway to petals. In sculpture, I think of two aspects of Rodin's work: the erotic statues and the *Burghers of Calais.* In drama, I would point to the realistic Edwardians like Pinero, Jones, or the early Shaw, Chekhov, Gorky's *The Lower Depths,* or the seafaring plays of Eugene O'Neill. The film came into being during this Early Modern period, and it bears the marks thereof: it has always focused on sexuality and the doings of ordinary people.

The Early Modern concentration on sexuality and ordinariness represented a change in values, but it continued a characteristically nineteenth-century way of thinking about the arts. Since people thought of the arts primarily as representational, as statements about something other than the art work itself, the way to appreciate art was to read through the fiction or the painting to the other side, as it were, to the reality behind the canvas or the screen or the page. Critics treated drama or sculpture as a representation of something other than itself. Hence an Early Modern critic tended to talk about the space between the work of art and that hypothetical something it represented. You would compare the faces in the crowd to petals. How "true" is Pound's idea? How precisely does H. D. render the feeling of pine boughs or ocean waves?

As always, the criticism of Shakespeare provides a convenient example. Critics in the first quarter of this century talked about Shakespeare as representing the sufferings of ordinary English folk under Henry VI or Macbeth's sexualized ambition or Iago's homosexual longings toward Othello. The plays represented fictional or historical realities outside themselves.

In the second phase of modernism, the accent shifted from the work of art as a representation of something else to the work of art as an end in itself, as self-contained. We changed from poems about the Great War, like those of Owen or Brooke or Blunden, to poems about nothing at all, or, more properly, to poems as ends in themselves, like the works of Eliot, Pound, Stevens, Valéry, or Rilke. In these works, the poem becomes a structure of its own, not a representation of some other, realer world outside itself. The poem might draw on an attitude, a morality, a politics, a metaphysics from outside itself, but often not even that and only for its own purposes. In MacLeish's felicitous cliché, "A poem should not mean, but be."

This surely is what we think of as the aim of High Modernism. Proust, Joyce, Mann, or Faulkner: these giants of modern fiction are only a handful among hundreds of lesser writers of the High Modern period who created their own special worlds in their fiction and verse. Joyce worked out the paradigm as he moved from the naturalistic portrayal of Dublin in *Dubliners* to a mythically structured Dublin in *Ulysses,* to the almost wholly self-sufficient poetry of *Finnegans Wake.* We can read Picasso as paradigmatic in the same way. He moves from the early paintings, with their systematic distortions of reality through either color or analytical Cubism, to paintings, like *Guernica,* which are essentially complete in themselves: any external reference provides only an occasion, like the Dublin of *Finnegans Wake.*

In painting, this shift culminates in the Abstract Expressionism of the forties and early fifties. In sculpture, we changed from Brancusi's portraits to wholly abstract work like that of Jacques Lipschitz. In music, we moved from a folkloric base with Sibelius, Bartok, Vaughan Williams, or Charles Ives, toward the twelve tone experiments of Schönberg or the pointillism of Webern. Stravinsky, like Joyce, is paradigmatic, moving from the naturalistic core of *Le Sacre du printemps* toward experiments and a neoclassicism like that of Hindemith. Film evolved from Griffith's representations of ancient Rome or Huguenot France to the creation of worlds that belong to the film: the myths of the Western, of the gangster, of Dracula or Frankenstein or King Kong.

Again, marking the change as a Shakespearean, I would indicate the shift from perceiving Shakespeare as representing a world outside the plays to treating the plays as self-contained lyric poems in the manner of the New Criticism. That very New Criticism became the voice that spoke exactly for High Modernism, asking us to look at a poem or picture as an end in itself.

If Early Modern dominates the first quarter of the century and High Modern the second quarter, the third phase comes into being after World War II, around 1950. If the first movement treated the text as representing something outside itself and the second treated the text as an end in itself, the third treats the text as calling itself into question or, more exactly, calling into question the relationship between its audience and itself. This, it seems to me, is what people mean by Postmodernism.

For myself, I pinpoint the transition as that between Brecht and Ionesco. That is, Brecht insists on his plays as not representing anything outside themselves; we are not to empathize or identify. Nevertheless, the play makes it own self-contained statement, taking a strong ideological stand. It is High Modern. Ionesco is equally nonrepresentational, but his plays take no such position; rather, they shift and equivocate in a typically Postmodern way. They ask us to examine our relationships to the play. What is a play? What is it to be an audience? How is it possible to take phrases from conversation in a language textbook and call that a play, as in *The Bald Soprano*? In the same way, Beckett changes from the self-contained structure of his earliest works to the metafiction of the later novels, which call into question the very act of writing them. Ultimately, beyond the Theatre of the Absurd are the experiments of Peter Brook, plays in nonlanguage which ask us if we can create the feelings appropriate to a play out of minimal materials, a birdcall, a stomp, a rug on an African plain.

In the visual arts, we change from the powerful sculptures of a Jacques Lipschitz, a David Smith, or an Eduardo Chillida, to conceptual sculpture where, again, the question is: Is this a sculpture? Is a piece of paper describing how to make a chair a sculpture of a chair? In painting, Postmodernism moves from the canvas as an end in itself, Abstract Expressionism for example, toward paintings that ask us to consider what painting is: Op Art, Pop Art, or Neorealism. Postmodern architecture uses buildings to make whimsical comments on architecture itself, like the ill-starred lobbies of Hyatt hotels or that expensive joke, the new A. T. & T. skyscraper with its Chippendale roof.

In music, we changed from the special worlds of sound created by Schönberg or Hindemith to the music of John Cage or Pierre Boulez or Karlheinz Stockhausen, music that is made up from the coughs and foot-shufflings of the audience, or which the audience creates by voting, or which is decided by a throw of the dice—music, in short, which asks us to consider if what we are hearing is, in fact, music.

Films become films about films. For me the key moment comes in Godard's *Breathless* (1960), when the Belmondo character looks at a poster of Humphrey Bogart and rubs his thumb across his lips in Bogart's characteristic gesture. At that moment, this film becomes a movie about a man in a movie. Nowadays it has become routine for film critics to identify the *hommages* in a new movie, the visual echoes of earlier films and directors.

In tracing Postmodernism, I see the career of John Barth as paradigmatic. His early novels, *The Floating Opera* or *The End of the Road,* use philosophical ideas and myths for their structure, much in the tradition of *Ulysses.* By the time of *The Sot-Weed Factor* and *Giles Goat-Boy,* Barth has turned his attention more and more to the problematics of narrative. In his three most recent books, *Lost in the Funhouse, Chimera,* and *Letters,* he has increasingly made his own novels the subject of his novels, focusing entirely on the nature of narrative itself.

Finally, we return to that minor index, Shakespeare criticism. Today's Shakespeare critic looks to the decisions of the director and the reactions of the audience, and most recently to those points where Shakespeare calls attention to the play as play. Hamlet says,

> Remember thee?
> Ay, thou poor ghost, while memory holds a seat
> In this distracted globe.

We have learned to hear that "globe" with a capital G and read those lines as a reference to a seat in Shakespeare's theatre. We turn drama into metadrama.

In general, Postmodern criticism has turned decisively to the relation between reader and text. Think of Roland Barthes's explorations of the pleasure of the text or the paracriticism of Ihab

Hassan or the recent writings of Geoffrey Hartman, which make criticism into the poetry which used to be its subject matter. Shakespearean criticism is only one small sign of a general interest in the relation between reader and text that has made criticism more theoretical than it used to be when we called it formalist or "New." Transactive criticism in America asks the critic to build his essay from his own response rather than from a work of art imagined as having a being all its own. The German development of *Rezeptionsästhetik* focuses on the relation between the work of art and its audience through literary history. My own interest, reader response theory, uses psychoanalysis and cognitive psychology to explore that space between work and reader within which the experience of literature is created. Similarly, deconstructive criticism, derived from Derrida, is a way of calling the work into question if it will not call itself into question. It, too, points to a reader, although the deconstructivist likes to cover his tracks and deconstruct himself.

I see modernism, then, as incorporating three stages. First, there was Early Modern representing an opening from the nineteenth century into new subject matters, both sexual and socioeconomic. Early Modern arts remain representational, however, in the manner of the nineteenth century, although they greatly expand the range of permissible contents and styles. With High Modernism, the arts become self-contained structures, ends in themselves, nonreferential, nonrepresentational, expressionist, abstract. In Postmodernism, the arts take as their subject matter the relationship between the work of art and its artist or between the work of art and its audience. It is as though we changed the subject matter of our arts from something behind the canvas to the canvas itself and now to the space between the canvas and us.

Obviously nobody can mark off these three stages with neat little fences. They overlap. Some older artists like Beckett become Postmodern before some younger ones like John Updike. Some never become modern at all. Our bestsellers these days are mostly Victorian novels with lots of sex—Jacqueline Susann or Barbara Cartland are really Early Moderns. "We are all," writes Ihab Hassan, "a little Victorian, Modern, and Postmodern, at once." Nevertheless, I find these three stages or configurations convenient, and I think they do reflect some general trends in twentieth-century culture.

It seems to me that we can trace this same progression in the sciences. I see in constructivist mathematics a Postmodern development. I can think of an Early Modern physics which broke down the continuous world of nineteenth-century physics to new subject matters. Then followed a High Modern period represented, say, by the Bohr model of the atom. Now we find physicists concerned with the nature of the modelling process as much as with the models they are building. Similarly, in biology we can see a movement from the study of particular biological structures, like genes or cells, to the setting of these parts in systems that extend from the minute to geological and ecological events. The study of artificial intelligence, for example, or the "new look" in perceptual or cognitive psychology, focus precisely on the relationship between perceiver and perceived, much in the manner of a conceptual painter.

I am less sure about these speculations on science, but I do feel confident that I can find in psychoanalysis a similar development from Early Modern to High Modern to Postmodern. In the beginning, Freud broke the great Victorian silence about sexuality. He persuaded us to focus on the ordinary as opposed to the exceptional or the contrived. Just as the naturalistic painter or novelist brought common people and the events of everyday life into the foreground, so Freud focussed attention on the trivial and prosaic aspects of our experience: dreams, jokes, or slips of the tongue. As Freud said, "Psychoanalysis is accustomed to divine secret and concealed things from despised or unnoticed features, from the rubbish-heap, as it were, of our observations." Psychoanalysis as the Ashcan School. Nor do I need to emphasize that psychoanalysis brought sexual forces to the fore. In this sense, psychoanalysis began as an Early Modern movement.

Freud, however, very quickly took psychoanalysis into its High Modern period, that is, the phase when psychoanalysis itself or its various entities would be regarded as self-contained, ends in themselves, like an abstraction by Miro or a poem by Wallace Stevens. For example, Freud assigned as the most basic motivation for a person the pleasure principle. The individual sought to gratify drives based in his own biology or to avoid feelings of guilt or anxiety based in his own psyche. All these things were "in" the individual the way his liver or his lungs were. A later source of motivation was the reality principle, but this Freud placed as definitively in relation to the outer world as the pleasure principle had been tied to the inner world. Later, Freud would suggest as the deepest motivation of all the nirvana or constancy principle: the need to keep the tension between the satisfaction and dissatisfaction of one's drives at a constant level. This homeostatic process was also located wholly within the individual. As we know, Freud treated "the unconscious" as a thing in itself, almost like a bodily organ with certain functions and activities. Sometimes he almost spoke as though the unconscious were a place or location. (One still finds people speaking of "the unconscious" with its "content" as though the unconscious were a bucket to pour feelings or libido into or out of.)

In later writings, after 1922, at the height of High Modernism, Freud revised his theories. He no longer divided the mind into conscious, unconscious, and preconscious. Instead, he adopted the so-called structural hypothesis of id, ego, and superego. The unconscious had been a noun; now it became an adjective which could be applied to these structures. The id was wholly unconscious, but one could speak of unconscious ego, unconscious superego, and conscious ego. Id, ego, and superego now became the important self-contained entities, ends in themselves, like a Mondrian painting or a story by Faulkner.

In this context, psychoanalysis itself became such an entity. When I first became involved with psychoanalysis, around 1957, analysts told me that psychoanalysis was an automatic, self-correcting process. The differences between different analysts, between a male analyst and a female, say, made no difference. One knew a correct interpretation entirely by the feedback, that is, the change in the patient's associations. If the analyst made a wrong interpretation, the patient would simply reject it. The analyst could go on making interpretations until he got feedback that told him he had arrived at a correct reading. Similarly, if the patient simply associated long enough, he would eventually bring to light all the contents of his unconscious ego. Psychoanalysis was a closed system. The human being was made up of clear boundaries within which everything had a place and was in its place. One could find the truth about oneself like finding a lost glove.

The beginning of the Postmodern phase of psychoanalysis came with the dethroning of Oedipus. That is, for the early Freud, the most important event in human development was the period of rivalry beginning about the third year of life between the child and its parent of the same sex for the love of the parent of the opposite sex. The boy challenges his father to win his mother. The girl challenges her mother to win her father. It was these sexual, naturalistic (if you will), Oedipal triangles that emerged when Freud's neurotic patients free associated. He believed these triangles determined the shape of all later relationships in a human life, much as a Hardy or a Dreiser would read a life deterministically.

Nevertheless, as early as 1930, Freud called attention to the first months of life when the baby does not perceive its mother as separate from itself. Indeed, the child perceives no boundaries at all between itself and the world that surrounds it. This is an altogether different kind of relationship from the love and hate triangle that Freud found in the later Oedipus crisis. This is a global relationship rather than one directed toward a particular person. It gives a feeling like that of a mystic or poet being swept up into eternity. It is like being in love with love rather than being in love with a particular person. This early stage was to the classical Oedipal phase, Freud said, as Mycenaean-Minoan civilization was to classical Greece some thousand years later. It was the submerged basis for the Oedipal rivalry, but it was also a whole new discovery, a developmental stage with its own issues, tasks, and outcomes, and its own decisive impact on later life.

Freud himself pushed no further toward Postmodern psychoanalysis than these opening generalizations. It remained for later psychoanalysts like Melanie Klein or René Spitz or Margaret Mahler to unfold this earliest stage. They pointed out that one of the child's tasks during this first year is to achieve "self-object differentiation." The infant is born innocent of the boundaries between self and other, but about the eighth month of life, it loses that innocence. Because an infant depends so totally on an other (mother or "primary caretaker"), it must sometimes wait to be fed because that other is simply not there. Out of that waiting (or, to French analysts, *absence*), the child begins to realize there is an other which must be separate from its self, because that other does not coincide with the infant's inner needs and wishes, and cannot do so. The first other is frustration. By so painfully learning that its mother is not self, the infant learns there is a self and learns to differentiate the two. Later, in a great advance in sophistication, the child of two or three years becomes able to give up that boundary so painfully won, for the sake of play, art, and other yieldings of self ("regression in the service of the ego", Kris called it).

Because of the waiting and frustration that the separation of self necessarily demands, a second task for the first year of life is learning to live with ambivalence. The child must become able to tolerate massive feelings of love and hate simultaneously toward the same person — usually his mother on whom he is totally dependent for satisfaction but who has to, in the nature of things, frustrate him. In effect, the child must learn to love what he hates and to hate what he loves, to fear what he wishes and to wish for what he fears. The ambivalence of the first year of life is the emotional core of what many years later we would learn to call, in a philosophical sense, deconstruction. Each of our feelings has in it the seed of its opposite. As Marion Milner has eloquently demonstrated, the very idea of a separate self draws on a reservoir of aggression from those first, biologically dictated frustrations.

Freud had anchored his psychology in the biology and neurology of the human animal. He had, first in the Early, then in the High Modern, manner treated man as a sexual being who has a self-contained structure based on biological drives which defined pleasure. After Freud, indeed after World War II, this interest in early infancy, with its ambivalence and fluid boundaries between self and other, led toward a distinctly Postmodern mode of thought. Freud's *intra*psychic picture of the mind was giving way to an *inter*psychic model. The self (the mind, the ego) has a permeable interface with the world. One cannot separate a person from his or her *Umwelt* any more than from the air or the water from which our bodies make an interior ocean. One cannot separate the human infant (or adult) from the humans on whom a human depends. The psychoanalytic human being is social as well as biological.

The English object-relations theorists in the 1950s and 1960s, people like W. R. D. Fairbairn, Harry Guntrip, Marion Milner, or D. W. Winnicott, proposed relations with other significant humans as a better basis for understanding human motivation than biological drives. In this frame of reference, pleasure becomes a two-way street. One way, people satisfy our drives. The other way, the wish for pleasure is what enables us to relate to people. Drives define pleasure, but people define drives. Object-relations theory decenters man so that we are never alone, always in relation. We are born related to an object. We are, in short, Postmodern.

No one has put this relatedness more tellingly than Winnicott with his "transitional object" and "potential space." Originally the "transitional object" was the teddy bear or security cloth, a found, real object — an other — endowed with the symbolic value of the union of baby and mother: an object with which the child can ease, symbolize, and act out the separation of self from other. But as analysts have realized that that boundary is provisional, to be given up and reimposed in everyday life, it has become clear that for adults many "objects" can be transitional: a treasured possession, a lover, an ideology, a hobby, or a psychoanalyst.

Similarly, "potential space" began in Winnicott's work as the space between infant and mother, a space which is neither inner psychic reality nor wholly external reality, neither subjective nor objective, neither inside nor outside — always both. It is the space occupied by the mother when she is in transition between being merged with the infant and being perceived as a separate object. Winnicott concluded that this potential space continued in the child's experience of play (neither wholly "in here" nor wholly "out there") and, still more important, in the "cultural experience" of the adult: religion, art, and all creative living. Again, as analysts have come to agree that transition between self and other is the usual state of affairs, not something confined to infancy or religious ecstasy or romantic passion as Freud thought, they have also come to agree that the concept of potential space describes the normal and usual space between self and any other.

In a sense, we could reread Erik Erikson as part of the same trend. For Erikson, we are born into a community which gives us identity as we give the community identity. The individual human grows up through his relationship to a community which he in turn transforms. We are from beginning to end in relation.

One could look at Jacques Lacan from the same point of view. Where Erikson talks about the society that an anthropologist or a sociologist would talk about, Lacan renders it in linguistic terms. The child must enter a linguistic network of signifiers and signifieds, shaping that network to his own individual style with gaps, short circuits, and all kinds of sudden turns, leaps, and cavortings. Where the English theorists see human relations as motivation, Lacan substitutes chains of language.

In the United States, the late Heinz Kohut pioneered a "psychology of the self" in which the patient's relation to the analyst becomes crucial. To the extent the patient idealizes or makes grand the analyst or himself, he repeats an early state of his development. The child, who at first knew no boundary between itself and the world, tries to keep that first feeling of omnipotence despite the checks of reality. Hence the child transforms its own former omnipotence into grandiose or idealized images of its parents, from which, in turn, it builds its own psyche. Then the adult projects these feelings onto others in adult relationships. The exploration of the patient's relation to the analyst thus becomes crucial in this kind of analysis, alongside the uncovering of unconscious crises from Early Modern psychoanalysis or the strengthening of ego from High Modern.

For all these thinkers the self is both something to be called into question and the something that calls the self into question. This self or identity is an agency, the subject of verbs as in "I see," "I remember," or "I repress." It is a subject sometimes deliberately lost and found in deconstructivist or other Postmodern discourse as writers use abstractions ("visions," "memory," "repression") in which one then finds a "trace" or "suture" of that lost "I." But in psychoanalysis an I must always be present, for it is the agent initiating the systematic creation of I (or identity), including the creation and change of self on the couch.

Conversely, the I — identity, the self — is also always what is being created as the individual brings already-existing identity to new experiences: the "I" that is being created as "I see," "I remember," or "I repress." Hence identity in Erikson's sense or the self in object relations or *le sujet* of Lacan always has two correlative senses: it is an agent, and it is what the agent creates. Identity is a paradox.

Less mysteriously, identity is always involved in feedback. First fully understood and applied to human and animal adaptations in World War II, feedback has emerged as a central concept in brain physiology, artificial intelligence, and (in the work of Emanuel Peterfreund and Robert Rogers) psychoanalysis. We should now speak not just of self but of a self-system. What is in that potential space? A feedback from self to other and back again.

There remains, however, yet another step in Postmodern psychoanalysis. I have in mind Heinz Lichtenstein's conception of identity. Where Erikson, Lacan, and the English object-relations theorists treat identity as a sense of identity, an inner feeling of coherence and meaning, Lichtenstein suggests a more observable kind. Lichtenstein points to the mixture of sameness and difference which is human life. We are constantly doing something new, yet each new thing we stamp with our personal, characteristic style. Lichtenstein suggests that we can think of the sameness in a human life as a theme, not unlike the theme of a piece of music. We can then understand the newnesses and the changes as variations on that theme, each new and different, yet each retaining the personal style of this particular individual.

It seems to me, however, this concept of identity is itself High Modern, not Postmodern, because Lichtenstein centers identity at some essential core of an organically whole human being. Lichtenstein was a student of Heidegger in the 1930s, and he creates the human being as a self-contained entity in itself, like a play by W. H. Auden or a sculpture by Alexander Calder. But I am Postmodern, and it seems to me an essential corollary of Lichtenstein's theme-and-variations idea that identity only comes into being as someone perceives it. Identity is not found but made — ficted. It is I who create the fiction of someone's identity by looking at that person as a theme and variations. If you were looking at that person you would inevitably create another identity, because your interpretation would be a function of your identity.

We could of course compare our two readings for the number of details they bring into the theme-and-variations pattern and the directness of those connections. One or the other of our interpretations might be the "better" of the two, more comprehensive, more direct. Instead of awarding judgments, however, it would be more interesting to ask: What is the relation of your interpretation to you and of mine to me? One can use interpretations to enrich one another rather than cancel one another out. In other words, it seems to me that identity theory makes an interpretation the occasion not for a verdict but for a discussion. In the Postmodern manner, identity theory treats the interpretation of a person (or anything else) not as an end in itself but as a way of exploring the relation of oneself to that person (or anything else). And the same process view would apply to *any* interpretation of anything.

Further, when you interpret me as a theme and variations, you create a new variation on *your* theme — which is itself a theme someone else sees. Your identity is something I see as a function of my identity, and my identity is something somebody sees as a function of his or her identity, and that identity is a function of somebody else's identity, and so on.

If I look at myself to discover my own theme (as in a psychoanalysis, say), I thereby create a new variation which must be taken into account in the theme I am trying to discover. That is, when a person seeks to understand himself (as in a psychoanalysis), that self includes the act of trying to understand oneself. That act is, like all acts, a feedback.

In other words, this theme-and-variations concept of identity decenters the individual in a distinctly Postmodern, metafictional way. You are ficted, and I am ficted, like characters in a Postmodern novel. The most personal, central thing I have, my identity, is not in me but in your interaction with me or in a divided me. We are always in relation. We are among. Whereas psychoanalysis began as a science of human individuality within each human skin, Postmodern psychoanalysis is the study of human individuality as it exists *between* human skins.

Psychoanalytic therapy, from this point of view, is not a self-contained, self-correcting process. Neither is it the same for every analyst. Rather, psychoanalysis is a relationship between analyst and patient, and each such relationship is new and different. One analyst will interpret differently from another, and the analysis that a patient and an analyst build between themselves will be different from an analysis that the same patient might build with a different analyst.

André Green, who has written some of the most intelligent essays on Postmodern psychoanalytic therapy, goes even farther. The meaning of a dream or symptom does not exist prior to the analytic situation. Rather, the psychoanalytic process constitutes that meaning. Meaning is not discovered, it is created—just as the "reader-response critics" say of literary meaning. Green suggests thinking of psychoanalytic meaning as "absent" or "virtual." The analyst makes it potential by the game he sets up to play with the patient. Then they bring it into existence by their mutual discourse.

In this view of therapy, countertransference becomes an equal partner in the analysis with transference (although, as one can gather from Janet Malcolm's now famous account of the New York psychoanalytic scene, they have not yet heard of Postmodernism in the High Church of psychoanalysis, the New York Psychoanalytic Institute, which remains devoutly High Modern).

One could sum up this movement of psychoanalysis from Early Modern to Postmodern as a transition through three kinds of science. First, Freud thought he was creating a psychology which was equivalent to a biological, chemical, or physical science. It would respond to the mathematics and the experimentation of the neurology in which he had been trained and the Helmholtzian ideals of rigor to which he aspired. In the High Modern period of psychoanalysis, the period of Freud's own ego psychology and its evolution in America in particular, psychoanalysis became an observational science, like cultural anthropology or archaeology, to which Freud himself compared psychoanalysis. It is at this stage, for example, that Erikson enters the picture, with his essays studying Amerindians alongside cultural anthropologists. In still a third phase, however, we now recognize that psychoanalysis is a science of interpretation, as in the writings of Ricoeur or Lacan or Winnicott. Psychoanalysis is the science which helps us interpret what it is to be an individual and what it is to be an individual in relation to other individuals. Psychoanalysis allows us to explore the space between ourselves and the people and things around us, including other disciplines and sciences. In this larger sense, Postmodern psychoanalysis can claim to be the science that underlies all other sciences, the art of interpreting interpretation itself.

Accepting this growth and avoiding the temptation to freeze psychoanalysis into an orthodoxy pays tribute to Freud's extraordinary ability to grow and grow, even to the end of his long life. He was not only able to found such a science as psychoanalysis, launching the world into modern psychology, but, as early as 1930, he was able to take the first steps into Postmodern psychoanalysis and Postmodernism psychoanalysis and Postmodernism itself.

A POSTSCRIPT TO POSTMODERNISM: TOWARD AN IKONIC STYLE?

Already, by writing papers about it, by publishing books and special issues of journals, we announce we are through Postmodernism and out the other side. Once they can name it, artists can no longer "do" Postmodernism with the same half-knowing innocence as those who first called into question our relationship to the autonomous structures of the High Modern.

Through Postmodernism, but into what? At the risk of naming (and so ending) whatever that "what" is, I would like to report as an inveterate culture-watcher a trend: making a work of art the subject of a work of art. Obviously, like Modernism and Postmodernism, people have been doing that for a long time. As in every other movement, *Don Quixote* was there first. I sense something new, however, a self-consciousness that makes art out of its own self-consciousness. *Don Quixote* uses its Book I as the subject of Book II almost inadvertently. A post-Postmodern writer would proclaim that his use of Part I is the subject of Part II.

Consider the artful use of art in the *Superman* movie of 1978. Superman finds he can't change into cloak and tights in one of the new, bottomless phone booths. The new movie is joking on its own use of the old comic strips where the phone booths did offer the hero a necessary privacy. Similarly *Star Trek, The Movie* (1979) plays on the very fact it is a remake of a television series whose most memorable character was the pointy-eared Spock. The fact that the movie is a remake is a part of its "reality"; thus, for instance, the movie plot uses as part of its suspense, "How will they add Mr. Spock to the already established crew?" Such films do not simply render an old comic strip or television show in a new medium. Rather, the new work portrays its own portrayal of the older.

Consider also Philip Roth's novel *The Ghost Writer* (1980). The hero conjures himself into the image of a writer and then (in the first person) the Roth-writer portrays this act of becoming a writer. In his brilliantly surreal, Kafkaesque novel *The Silent Cry* (1968), Kenzaburo Oe portrays, in a startling mingling of realism with surrealism, a character living in such a way as to become a legend — which is the legend portrayed by the novel. Or to put it another way, the novel portrays the triumph of one character who believes in the legend the novel is creating over one who refuses to believe. One can read Gabriel García Márquez's *One Hundred Years of Solitude* (1967) or *The Autumn of the Patriarch* (1975) the same way, as novels that circle through time, portraying the creation of a legend which is itself the structure and subject of the novel that creates it.

I see something similar in the journalism of Tom Wolfe or the comedy of Robin Williams or Steve Martin. They make themselves into something — skeptical reporter, drug addict, jerk, portraying themselves in the roles with remarkable fidelity. That very fidelity then allows them to play against and joke about their own portrayals. The result? One cannot choose which is "real." The character portrayed? No, that's a fake. The act of portraying? No, because the portrayer steps out of character.

They give us the double refraction of Postmodernism, but in a new way.

Recently Janet Malcolm noted that today's photography and visual arts are trying to get away from the nineteenth-century preoccupation with vision. Whereas painters in the Middle Ages and the Renaissance put a whole conception of man on their canvasses, the Impressionists and post-Impressionists caught certain visual effects. The later painters tried to get us to think about seeing; the earlier tried to get us to see our thinking.

Now, think of the paintings of Alex Katz: a huge representation of what seems to be either a photograph or a smaller painting of the face. Or the Photo-Realists: a painting of a photograph. They are asking us to think, to ask ourselves: Which do you believe? The "original" photograph? The "actual" painting? None of the above?

What, then, can we name such a doubly refracted style? "Postmodern" was bad enough. "Post-Postmodern" would be too much. I suggest "Ikonic." The makers of ikons painted (usually), not a saint, but an earlier ikon of that saint, like these works of art out of the use of a work of art. The word also echoes the vacuum tube at the heart of television (the ikonoscope) which in turn seems at the heart of the Ikonic. For of all the media making roles out of roles, it is television that hour after hour, day after day, ikonizes our world. And then there is the theme of religion.

In the Ikonic, the dizzying double reflections we have come to expect from Postmoderns like Borges or Barth or Beckett are built in, but something more takes place. This style raises the question: What can you believe in? In a realistic portrayal of that which we know is not realistic, both are patently "so" and equally patently "just a story, just a picture."

The question arises sharply and painfully with our politicians. A man like Giscard d'Estaing or Ronald Reagan projects himself as an image and then tries to become that image *as an image,* as something to be seen on television. Compare Robert Altman's *Nashville* (1976). The actors who portray the country stars write the music that they sing. In effect, they "are" stars whom the movie then portrays as such. We have to believe in them, yet we cannot. Significantly, the film never shows the political figure whose image is a-building. He remains an offstage spirit, a deity about to be staged.

Is it because these works raise the question of belief that there hangs about them a vague aura of the mystic? Altman's *Popeye* (1980) carries his *Nashville* idea even further: human beings model themselves on comic strip characters whom the movie then photographs with meticulous realism. *Popeye* adds an element that recurs in this new mode: a vague set of religious overtones and symbols (death and rebirth, sacrifice, the miraculous child), a strange dimension for a comic strip. Richard Rush's underground success, *The Stunt Man* (1980), combines the same elements. The movie photographs the making of a movie. The characters are "themselves" but also the characters they "play" in the movie, and it is as the latter that the hero and heroine fall in love. What is "real" in a world presided over by the Dionysus-like director of the film within a film? The fictional film he is making? Or the undeniably real film we are watching—which is the film he (or somebody!) is making. And again, the presence of Dionysus and the odd death and rebirth open up the scintillations of a vague mysticism.

Most beautiful of all in this mode is the almost supernatural experiment of Peter Brook, *The Conference of the Birds.* The actors act themselves into very birds. The final mystical revelation makes the unreality of human birds into just that—final reality. As it always was. And wasn't. Or, simply, was Ikonic.

15 /

Modernisms/Postmodernisms

Malcolm Bradbury

I

My aim in this paper, which will be brief and very general, is to reflect on some of the problems we encounter in attempting to define the direction, the tendency, the episteme of the contemporary in the arts. I want to think about the various forms of periodization that go into the complex and collaborative critical process that is the writing of literary history, into the tactics of stylistic historicism. And I had better say straight away that I see these tactics, methods, and presumptions as partaking in some of the fictionality — sometimes the same *kind* of fictionality — that goes into the making of the creative arts themselves. For the making of the art involves, amongst the most serious practitioners, a deep historical realization; it is to the presence of such a historical realization that we allude when we talk of style, referring not simply to the personal signature of a work, but to the participative intervention into history and culture of those who self-consciously bring that work into existence. To write, to paint, to produce a piece of music is to enact and attempt to realize a form of historical consciousness; and part of the proper responsiveness of criticism is to share in and, further, to realize that consciousness. This is a familiar part of critical practice, but it is always to be found at its most dangerously sensitive when it deals with the arts that are contemporary, attempting to order, to classify, to clarify, and to correct their significance, their place, their mode of stylistic citizenship in the present world.

Now there are certain phases in the history of the arts when we sense, as critics and interpreters, the emergence of a general, a widespread, and a distinctive new phase of perception, structure, form, and style—a change that goes so deeply into the underlying formation of the arts that it is analogous to revolution or to radical reform in the social sphere. In such phases, the entire body of assumptions and the structure of social formation of the arts seem to shift so fundamentally that the artistic works produced no longer appear to witness to the same kind of consciousness, nor to refer to the same type of historical experience, nor to relate to the same processes of imagining, nominalizing, or alluding to exterior life as they did before. Theoretically such changes might arise from the logical development of aesthetic ideas and processes of generic evolution, and without any corresponding direct change in the social sphere; but they are undoubtedly deeply shaped by historical and social shifts and reconstitutions, and the form of artistic witness, the type of aesthetic justification the artist gives for change, regularly takes the form of a sociohistorical explanation. It is with these deep structural shifts, which call from us our largest critical and artistic generalizations, that I am concerned—those massive reconstitutions that we designate by our largest stylistic categories, like Romanticism and Modernism. Here we advance, usually *post facto* and for very large generalizing purposes, proposals that attempt to designate entire and long-lasting periods of artistic history and identify their distinctive qualities, the sum of the plural parts, the historical episteme. For our century, we have already settled on one such term, Modernism, and are in process of settling upon a second, Postmodernism. The terms propose a double fissure, one at or around the start of our century, the other toward the end of it; at the same time, the kinship between the two terms suggests that the second coming is not remote from the first. The aim of these comments is not to dissolve the terms but to inspect them and to indicate some of the kinds of skepticism and unease that we should bring into their employment.

II

It is somewhere in the last decades of the nineteenth century or in the first decade of our own that we have now agreed to find the crucial signs of that trembling of the veil, that new coming of things, that evidence of the great change that we have now agreed to call Modernism. That some sort of radical fracture, affecting all the arts and their underlying epistemology, generating a whole new set of mannerisms and forms that dislocated convention, did occur may no longer sensibly be denied. Its time, its place, its moment, its peak, its decline, its primary timetable, its essential characteristics may still be open to debate and dispute; but there can be little doubt that the early twentieth century saw a fundamental redirection of the nature, the character, and the meaning of a great many of our most significant artistic traditions. It took a long time to see the enormity of the change; but we now generally grant that enormity and perceive in the western arts a transformation as great as any other of those stylistic transpositions that shape our sense of the past—the emergence of Renaissance style, the coming of Romanticism—and possibly even greater, because of the scale of abandonment of previous art, the fullness of the break with tradition. Yet of all the great stylistic changes, Modernism still arouses some of the largest perplexities. This is not solely because of the complexity and difficulty of its products—a complexity and difficulty that, in the way of avant-garde gambles, time itself has helped dissolve. Rather it is because of the angled nature of Modernism's intervention, the complex relation it proposes between art's existence and the world's; for, from the start, Modernism secreted its own mystery in the oblique, divergent relation it proposed between the historical and the aesthetic, the world of modernization and the works of Modernism itself.

The mysteries and difficulties of Modernism are summed up in a term which was not novel with the tendency but which we need firmly in our minds to distill the peculiar way in which it specialized and abstracted artistic activity, broke its modes of mimetic allusion to the exterior world, and drew its practitioners away from the market place into specialist enclaves: the term *avant-garde.* A borrowed analogy, starting in military life, where it makes sense, it moved into political life, where again it is comprehensible as a form of radical action devoted to generating fundamental change derived from what its devotees saw as the necessary forward logic of history. But when it further moved, during the nineteenth century, across into the arts and literature, to speak to the artist's sense of his radical function and his attempt to intervene obliquely into the historical world, certain logical ambiguities arose. The analogy between the artist and the political radical, one who reaches beyond the present ideological order into the next state of affairs, has long been canvassed; it is a deep-seated proposal in Romanticism, in, for example, Shelley's *Defense of Poetry,* which itself compounds many of the paradoxes of the process of aesthetic and stylistic legislation. The term *avant-garde* implies that the arts develop through or in relation to some comprehensible and comprehended historical process; and yet much avant-garde art seems devoted more to its own aesthetic than to some specifically historical realization. It suggests the artist's role in cultural struggle; yet the avant-gardist's characteristic location is often one of cultural separatism. It seems to point toward artistic activism; yet after the disillusionments of 1848 it is most conspicuously implicated in a deep disenchantment with the historical world, and it characteristically expresses itself in formalism, narcissism, decadence, subjectivism, and nominalism.

Thus, for all the activist associations of the term, the avant-garde has created its prime achievement not through an aestheticized politics or a direct historical intervention, but rather through a concept of stylistic formation, a sense that the historically modern has its logical outcome precisely in style—in a new mode of perception, a new set of structures for consciousness, a new set of linguistic discourses or perceptual iconographies. Yet the avant-garde does not offer a style as such; it is rather a posture, a set of tactics, a mode of social organization of the arts, a sociological location for the generation, reception, testing and protection of styles. Indeed, the avant-garde is likely to generate stylistic pluralism, since it functions socially through movements and tendencies, themselves subject to schism, proliferation, pluralization, and dissent. Thus, to define Modernism, we need to impose upon the evolution of the avant-garde a model of stylistic coherence, a notion of an aesthetico-historical realization. To do this, we have conventionally come to look at the aesthetic mixtures of turn-of-the-century Europe, at a time when naturalism contended with symbolism and aestheticism, when the arts that offered themselves as experiments in the manner of science contended with those that offered themselves subjectively as an "impression"; and out of this complex and the disorders it generated, disorders consistent with those in the development of science, with its new theories of relativity and uncertainty, and its changing theories of consciousness and subjectivity, we can find a new set of tactics for the stylistic realization of that ever-evanescent entity, "the modern." We can read, through most of the Western countries, a deep sense of historical and epistemological transition. We can read analogies across from the disturbances in one Western culture — say the Russian — to those in another — say the Italian. We can see new arts of surprise, new forms of influence and association, new excitements; we can see "the modern" as an international chiliastic preoccupation.

Yet our characterization must necessarily be speculative and incomplete. One country's modern was not another's. For analogous forms and experiments in different nations, we do not have matching dates. Modernism becomes a comprehensible proposal because it refers to a polyglot, international, and temporally wide-ranging achievement that penetrated and disturbed the minds of a very large number of the major artists and performers of the age; but it is worth reminding ourselves that—except in Latin America, where there was a local "Modernist" movement— most of the writers, painters, musicians, philosophers, psychologists, architects, designers, and scientists whom we might regard as variously engaged in the enterprise did not summon up their historical function by calling themselves "Modernists." Some of them might have acknowledged membership in that generalized entity, the avant-garde, and been conscious of their separatism or bohemianism; some, indeed, took up specific movement identifications, calling themselves "symbolists," "decadents," "impressionists," "*fauvistes,*" "cubists," "post-Impressionists," "expressionists," "futurists," "constructivists," "*imagistes,*" "vorticists," "dadaists," "surrealists" and so on, though not necessarily for describing the sum of their work, for such movements were often visited and then abandoned. Certain recurrent aesthetic ideas and presumptions, styles and forms, circulated freely among the different movements, if often for quite contradictory justifications. And it is largely from these recurrences, which give us a sense of more fundamental processes at work of which the specific movements represent episodes, that we derive our conviction that we can register a general style or period that we call Modernism.

Yet our constitution of Modernism has been, essentially, a *post facto* enterprise, a validation of the avant-garde gamble as such; of course in validating it, we have generated the final paradox that the arts that meant to live on surprise and outrage no longer surprise us and have become conventional—in that process moving from being a present style to a past one. It is we who have generalized Modernism into a crucial and definitive creative enterprise of international significance, finding its effects radical if not cataclysmic, its forms and styles commanding and necessary, its primary supporters and expressers the central canon of early twentieth-century arts and ideas. We have, albeit selectively, validated the avant-garde claim to speak with the voice of the modern far beyond the measure of its own expectation, moving the fringe to the center, the eccentric to the middle, granting to these arts and ideas their claim to speak to the chaos, the crisis, and the need of modern history. What we call Modernism is, however, a variety of movements and individual performances, from a variety of countries, in a variety of arts, at a variety of times; the term thus gives coherence to a collage of different tendencies and movements, often epistemologically at odds with or in revolt against others, arising from a variety of different traditions and lineages, different political and cultural situations, different stages in modern historical evolution, different periods themselves segmented from each other by the cataclysm of a world war, and with deeply various views of what the modern situation is and so of the nature and species of the artistic expression it should duly call forth. And at the same time we have come to deny a whole contending history of twentieth-century forms deriving from those artists, writers, and thinkers who did *not* accept Modernist experimentalism and its characteristics as the dominant style of twentieth-century art. Indeed, throughout the century in most Western traditions we may see a pattern of systematic challenge of Modernism—from the continuing stock of nineteenth-century liberal realism and from those developments of Naturalism which pointed the way toward a new scientific realism, often a directly political realism.

In this matter, our latter-day judgment is in one clear sense correct. Modernism exists, and recognition may not be withheld, even in traditions of thought like Marxism which have sought to deny it. But what should be visible to us is the complexity of the exercise of identification and definition. What we have behind us are many Modernisms, and according to the location we stand in —Paris or London, Berlin or New York, Rome or Moscow—we will see its story and meaning as being very different. Expressionism, for example, is not a natural equivalent to imagism, though both roughly coincide in time; surrealism shares little with impressionism, though both emphasize the psychological constituent of artistic perception. Futurism and vorticism may have generated analogous forms but derive from different and contradictory premises. To perceive Modernism, we need to perceive Modernisms. No single nation invented the new styles, and no single precursory tradition explains it; Modernism was a pattern of international and polyglot transactions and, often, misapprehensions, deriving from the remarkable internationalism of the period and the emigré and expatriate movement of many of its participants. As it was polyglot, it was also polygeneric and eclectic, assimilating irreconcilables and incorporating these gradually within its own aesthetic self-definition. To comprehend Modernism we need in ourselves a parallel eclecticism; we need plural methods, a complex historiography, and a multinational and multilingual awareness, one which is likely to challenge many of the conventional definitions, often national in form, of what Modernism is and what its main motifs, preoccupations, and culture-readings amount to. We need likewise to recognize that the term does not conveniently cover many essential modern artistic forms and events; that as Modernism was constantly in quarrel with itself, with many of the later movements overtly hostile to the earlier ones, so there were many cultural programs and ideas in quarrel with its entire experimentalist and avant-gardist presumptions, its notions of crisis, its apocalyptics.

In sum, we need to recognize that Modernism is not a neutral descriptive term, but a form of acceptance of the formal and historical anxieties and expectations that ran variously through many minds and many arts over an extended and disturbed period of modern experience. And to comprehend Modernism in anything like its significance and power, we need to recall the anxieties that A. O. Lovejoy brought to our understanding of another primary concept of periodization, that of Romanticism. Lovejoy urged the discrimination of Romanticisms, pointing to the many different definitions, the many different threads and tendencies, the many contradictions and counteractions that we seek to incorporate into that stylistic term in order to historicize the period. We need a similar discrimination of Modernisms, a sense of the contention, variety, and plurality that we seek to contain within the term. Criticism has indeed grown more polyglot, more discriminating, more curious in its defintions; it has also, often, grown more assertive in its historicism, more certain that it knows what the heart of the matter is. The danger of *post facto* criticism is a process of historical reification. It then needs to be added that we can easily bring such reifications to the immediate works of our own time.

III

We might argue that the moment when Modernism became an entity was roughly the moment when we assumed that the entire tendency lay behind us, in the past. And in this sense Modernism may be distinguished from Postmodernism, a term that began to be necessary once we had displaced Modernism from the immediately contemporary scene. For this process an important episode is undoubtedly the period between 1939 and 1941, the period over which a European war and a rising threat of world fascism developed into the century's Second World War. Throughout the 1930s, the Modernist excitements of the previous three decades had been progressively amended and modified by a new political concern and by powerful new claims from naturalism and social and socialist realism to be the true art-movement of a politically horrifying century, a century of historical, cultural, and economic collapse in which nominalist speculation had to give way to the real enormities of history. The thirties saw many apostasies from Modernism and the coming of new languages of disturbed realism; the outbreak of war brought home the sense of the need to recover the values of democratic liberalism in the face of totalitarian threat. Many European writers fled before Hitler to America, carrying not only the lore of Modernism but the liberal secrets so often hidden within it. The season between 1939 and 1941 also saw a number of significant deaths among those who had exemplified various aspects of the modern experiment: W. B. Yeats, Virginia Woolf, and James Joyce; Sherwood Anderson, Scott Fitzgerald, Nathanael West. Careers were arrested; for many writers silence came. "Periods end when we are not looking . . . ," noted Cyril Connolly in *Horizon,* the British literary magazine he started as the war began and in which he reflected the changing style and taste of the entire decade of the 1940s. "An epidemic of dying has ended many movements. . . ."

This historicizing of Modernism is a visible theme in the cultural mood of the West in the 1940s and 1950s. Many of the new writers who emerged then or became dominant wrote in a context of perceived historical transition. Authors like Saul Bellow in the United States or Angus Wilson in Britain measured their modern anguish against the need for new humanist commitments, commitments called for in the era of holocaust, atomic anxiety, and continued totalitarian threat. In European countries which had suffered defeat and occupation on the continent, the sense of historical urgency was equally powerful; and in the fiction of Sartre and Camus, the drama of Brecht, the novels and plays of Günther Grass and Max Frisch, we can feel the steady tempering of the Modernist stock. Modernism, and particularly the historically urgent lineage of Modernism exemplified by writers like Dostoevsky, Kafka, or Mann, spoke in the direction of alienation and despair, though also of that bloodied, postliberal sense of

319

evil and pain which was part of the modern condition. Existentialism in particular came to seem the discourse of recovery, qualifying its identification of the absurd with a new act of faith and a hunger to assert man's social responsibilities and his need to find a kind of moral and social realism. The voice of that realism, mitigating absurdism and pointing toward a liberal redemption, runs through much of the writing of the 1940s and 1950s, and one of its consequences was an offered recovery of the liberal realist tradition of nineteenth- and even eighteenth-century art. Modernism remained an uneasy presence in much of this writing, but it was Modernism perceived as an emendable option.

It was now, indeed, that Modernism began to be canonical, to be perceived as a modern tradition open for selective reuse. Critics in the 1950s began to incorporate it into the essential tradition of literature, shifting writers like Proust, Joyce, Pound, Eliot, Williams, and Faulkner from marginal to central positions, and recognizing in the modernist abyss and its images of cultural disaster, its wasteland visions, its modes of mock-epic and antimyth, the fabulous discourse of the century. The recognition coincided with a weakening of innocent politics, especially the politics of the left, and a deepened sense of historical horror and unease; the great Modernists in turn became those who had seen the heart of darkness in history and the human soul, seen culture in chaos and myth and ritual displaced from significant reference. It also coincided with a questioning of innocent naturalism, and an art of uneasy social doubts and alienations which hungered for moral insight and mythical constitution.

It was this Modernism which helped to feed much of the writing of the 1950s; and that period's elaborate attempts to intersect modernist insights with an art of moral recovery and rediscovered realism might well be defined as a "Postmodern" episode. Indeed, this was precisely the proposal of Irving Howe in a fascinating essay of 1959 called "Mass Society and Post-Modern Fiction," where he inspected the American fiction of the period of cold war and recovered affluence, the fiction of a "relatively comfortable, half welfare and half garrison society in which the population grows passive, indifferent, and atomized," and saw in the half-alienated, anxious novel of the times a new set of "Post-Modern" forms.

Howe's usage is interesting because it precedes and differently defines the current intent of the term Postmodernism to discuss and characterize the significant arts of the later twentieth century, for it largely predates the main artistic events that the better-known explorers and users of the term Postmodernism have sought to characterize. During the 1950s in Europe there were, in the emergence of the Theatre of the Absurd and of the French *nouveau roman,* clear signs of revival of experimental and avant-garde activity, work offering itself as stylistically novel and contemporary. In the United States, where the assimilation of Modernism had been considerable, movements like "Beat," talked about from 1952, and striking new attempts at abstract and performance art and writing, were opening up a new mood. This mood began visibly to distill around 1960, in the Kennedy years, when the arts marvelously came together in multimedia events, performance theatre, happenings, street theatre, openform or aleatory art and writing, and a new behavioral avantgardism that linked youth culture and events in the pop scene to the world of the supposedly serious arts. Related to the youth culture, the experimental phenomenon was as loosely structured, as international, and as flexible as that culture itself; its underlying ideas, theoretics, and instincts were heterodox, and so were the styles of its products, which were often multigeneric, parodic, and collageist. Provisionality and elusive registration became paramount qualities; anarchism and revolutionary subjectivism replaced concepts of ordered form or mythic coherence. But while the American contribution was significant and in some sense a clearinghouse for experimental events elsewhere, other foci were of profound importance, including Latin America, Africa, India, and Japan. By the 1980s it had become possible to see that a major new generation of serious artists did evolve with new experimental ideals out of the texture of the youth culture and the new polyglottism of the 1960s and 1970s; and this was true on an extraordinarily international scale.

With this advent, it became relevant to ask whether the new

tendencies were best read as a continuation of Modernism, or whether they represented a radical variation away from its main tendencies and presumptions, the coming of a new episteme. All new movements are convinced of two things: their total novelty and their ultimate "realism"; and it was natural for those engaged in the many movements and tendencies that became active during the fluid art-scene of the 1960s to believe in the lore of a radical break from the past, a lore that indeed helped feed the revolutionary apocalyptics of 1968. It was clear in fact that many of the elements of the new experimental arts of the 1960s did owe much to Modernism; indeed, a good number of the most decisive mentors — Samuel Beckett, Jorge Luis Borges, Vladimir Nabokov, Charles Olson, for example — had begun their work in contexts of prewar Modernism. There was evidently a significant overlap from prewar Modernist tendencies like Dada and Surrealism, or the revolutionary subjectivism of Hermann Hesse, or the political and agitprop neo-Modernism of Brecht, or the "Revolution of the Word" of Joyce and Stein into the new experimentalism. On the other hand, the role and historical context of the avant-garde had clearly changed; now experiment, far from causing bourgeois outrage, became a bourgeois cause. There was also a new stylistic multiplicity, ranging from the *chosisme* and minimalism of French experiments to the excess and over-registration of a writer like Thomas Pynchon, from the magical realism of Latin American writers to the metafictionality of a Nabokov or a Barth, and from work in Europe and the United States to work in India and Japan. That new artistic energies were evident and that the new work offered fascinating new challenges to cultural forms already in existence was not in doubt; but there remained complex problems of characterization and definition.

Some of the best critics of the new tendencies were firm in recognizing a continuity onward from Modernism, perhaps most notably Frank Kermode, who distinguished two Modernisms — Palaeo-Modernism, the more formalist and concerned with symbolist transcendence, and Neo-Modernism, more chanceful, spontaneous, and aleatory, yet compelled to use and articulate form in order to subvert it. Others in an apocalyptic season urged the case for an epochal change: "My plan has been to argue that in the 1950s radically new conventions for the language of art were developed by writers, musicians and painters who wished to break away from modernism," observes another British critic, Christopher Butler, explaining the schema of *After the Wake* (1980), his interesting brief book on the contemporary avant-garde. Many American critics, particularly those sympathetic to the countercultural revolts of 1968, have likewise emphasized the epochal nature of the change, and have found in the counterculture and the new spontaneity a radical new posthumanist consciousness, the mode-of-being of what Leslie Fiedler has called "the new mutants." And similar apocalyptics have been apparent in a good deal of the French criticism that has emerged from structuralist and deconstructionist contexts, with their convictions of primary historical fracture and the hastening collapse of the sign. In some respects the debate is futile. In his spectacular essay "*post*modern*ism*," republished in *Paracriticisms* (1975). Ihab Hassan observed both continuities and discontinuities, rightly stressing that Postmodernism is continuous in its chiliasm and apocalypticism with Modernism, but that it presumes a different historical locus and a different causal historiography for its creations and events; Modernism provides a necessary prehistory for the existence of Postmodernism, but that existence redefines Modernism and offers a basis for its continuance.

What Modernism and Postmodernism share in common is a simple adversary, which is, to put it crudely, realism or naive mimesis; both are forms of post-Realism. They likewise share in common a practice based on avant-garde and movement tactics and a sense of modern culture as a field of anxious stylistic formation. Since there is no single Modernism, it is hard to find a point of closure or variation which permits us to characterize a successor movement, and indeed Postmodernism, when inspected broadly and eclectically, is no more single than Modernism. The definitions multiply according to the canon chosen; part of the theoretical disillusionment that one finds in some quarters with the concept arises from the elusiveness of its formulations and the preference found in many proponents of Postmodernism's existence for theoretical generalization rather than critical specificity. Is Postmodernism simply a recent American movement, a tendency among those American writers and performers who have incorporated the modernist avant-garde inheritance into their practice and who have in some fashion fulfilled Gertrude Stein's prophecy that Modernism may have started in Europe but would go to the United States to happen? Or do we set broader boundaries, incorporating movements like the French *nouveau roman* and Latin American magical realism? Is Postmodernism predominantly metafictional or metatheatrical, or do we include within its territory those forms of hyper-realism and photo-realism that bring the naturalist secrets back into the fold? Are we talking of the profitable association of a set of similar-seeming tendencies in different arts and different nations, or are we seeking a definition which is larger, and must therefore be more open? In short, are we not facing on a tighter time scale, and now with a vastly stronger critical intervention, the problems of Modernism as a concept over again?

IV

There are perhaps two kinds of view that might be taken of the extraordinary, vigorous, and international new arts that have come from writers, painters, actors, and musicians over the last twenty years, fascinating and preoccupying us, displaying their immediacy, their relevance, their sense that in some serious stylistic fashion they are "ours." One is to see this complex and international display of forms which in fact expresses an extraordinary stylistic promiscuity and a deep stylistic anxiety as a display of remarkable eclecticism, the art of what Al Alvarez has called an age of No Style. André Malraux once perceived our age as one of the "imaginary museum," a time when mechanical storage, culture overlap, and pluralism, and the global village assimilativeness of modern consciousness, made most styles of the past and the present, from whatever sources, simultaneously available and useable. Hence we no longer possessed a style but a vast compendium of styles, jostling each other in threatening and often parodic relation. In art and architecture this view of our times as being a period of outstanding eclecticism, generating an enormous jumble of contradictory styles and movements, has been commonplace. But there is an alternative view, vastly more strong-minded. This proposes that we do live in a distinct stylistic period, one with its own recognizable grammars and epistemologies. It sees the stylistic excess and variation as itself part of the stylistic equation, generating the self-skepticism and metaparodic manner of much contemporary art. Yet, across that art, in music and painting, writing and theatre, common characteristics can be read, a historical condition interpreted.

Now it is my assumption in these comments that terms like Modernism and Postmodernism are not simply neutral descriptions of artistic texts, events, and movements, each of which proclaim in every tissue and pore their stylistic nature. They are themselves creative theoretical constructs arising from the conduct of creative artists themselves and from the conduct of those who specialize in commenting and interpreting, if not legislating for, their activities, which is to say the critics. Aesthetic proposals and generalizations in criticism may arise pragmatically from, let us say, the problems of reading certain perplexing works (Pynchon's *Gravity's Rainbow* and Robbe-Grillet's *La Jalousie,* Calvino's *Castle of Crossed Destinies* and Márquez's *One Hundred Years of Solitude*); or they may arise from theories about language, form, and history applied to certain convenient and appropriate artistic instances and occasions. They may arise from scholarly-humanistic ways of perceiving artistic development, as a process of evolving traditions, transforming, merging, and waning; or they may arise from intellectual tendencies like Structuralism, post-Structuralism, and revisionist Marxist aesthetics, which seek to discover in artistic expression evidence of forms of historical and social crises which have to some degree been determined by and originated from other sources. In short, it may be that the contemporary arts are, in their innovation, their generic transformation, and variation, revealing a new and radical episteme which is disabling to traditional critical practice, requiring the critic to reach toward new understandings; or it may be that contemporary criticism is itself creating a new epistemology seeking to read the world and the book in ways which are consistent with its own radical theories, and is seeking a canon, both contemporary and traditional, for that purpose.

The growth and institutionalization of criticism, and the development of new critical theory of a generalizing and totalizing kind, is undoubtedly part of the equation of Postmodernism. Historically, it was largely the creators themselves who, in the stylistic deliverances of their own works, in aesthetic statements, in participation in movements, offered to utter the meaning of art at their given historical moment; it was the critics who, coming later, then sought to derive the broader episteme— Romanticism, Modernism. Today we see a notable acceleration of that process, as the critics, institutional and powerful, ever more confident in their deconstructive authority, surer than ever in their chiliastic historiography, seek to hasten the historical moment by their own interpretative intervention. In a time of changing forms we have a theoretics of a situation which is in many respects contradicted by the practice; "Postmodernism" has in some ways become a critic's term without ever quite being an artistic movement. This itself is a significant intervention and it can, at its best, itself have a generative influence upon the arts, constituting a context for their interest and importance. Its dangers lie in a process of over-determination or excessive legislation; artist and critic share in common the need to realize the style of the historical moment, but for different ends. For the artist it is a making and an achievement; for the critic it is a hypothesis turning toward a theory. And the state of the term "Postmodernism" is at the present somewhere between these two modes of usage.

We are indeed in a time of stylistic proliferation and generic transformation, creating a fascinating art-scene which will seem, I believe, as powerful and notable to the future as the Modernist one does to the present. Much of our theory of Postmodernism has arisen from a transformation in the critical forum, and has expressed itself in a spirit of theoretical nominalism, funded by a large philosophical reassessment of both idealist and empiricist practice. Its theory has arisen in part from a mode of synchronic and diachronic interpretation of literary history which has tended to generate over-constituted models both of Realism and Modernism, models which "Postmodernism" is then seen to deconstruct. There may, however, be other ways of proceeding toward an adequate account of the contemporary situation and character of our most serious, interesting, and pressing arts. I have said that in the end the study of Modernism can only be the study of Modernisms, and that the study must be international, comparative, eclectic, and various. The same, I propose, is true of the study of Postmodernisms. For an essential recognition is that while we do indeed live in an age of extraordinary change in the contemporary arts, that change is a remarkably various, contentious, and international affair. We live in a late twentieth-century phase in which the arts are, as they were at the century's turn, in international intersection, when many tendencies, some apparently parallel, some contradictory, some western and some not, some nominalist and some idealist, are appearing in different cultures and then intersecting radically. It is a time when the aesthetic-historical situation is not defined for us by the achievement of artists in a narrow canon, but by a wealth of experimental activities deserving plural and comparative analysis. The danger is to reach the point of critical closure too soon and too confidently, a danger always present in critical ambition. If our portrait of the arts of the twentieth century is to form under the stylistic heads of Modernism and Postmodernism, it must be a portrait of an age in which those critical methods are not solution but themselves phenomenon: part of the cooperative historical fiction out of which stylistic assertion is made.

16 /

Answering the Question: What is Postmodernism?

Jean-François Lyotard

A DEMAND

This is a period of slackening—I refer to the color of the times. From every direction we are being urged to put an end to experimentation, in the arts and elsewhere. I have read an art historian who extols realism and is militant for the advent of a new subjectivity. I have read an art critic who packages and sells *Transavantgardism* in the marketplace of painting. I have read that under the name of postmodernism, architects are getting rid of the Bauhaus project, throwing out the baby of experimentation with the bath water of functionalism. I have read that a new philosopher is discovering what he drolly calls Judaeo-Christianism, and intends by it to put an end to the impiety which we are supposed to have spread. I have read in a French weekly that some are displeased with *Mille Plateaux* because they expect, especially when reading a work of philosophy, to be gratified with a little sense. I have read from the pen of a reputable historian that writers and thinkers of the 1960 and 1970 avant-gardes spread a reign of terror in the use of language, and that the conditions for a fruitful exchange must be restored by imposing on the intellectuals a common way of speaking, that of the historians. I have been reading a young philosopher of language who complains that

Continental thinking, under the challenge of speaking machines, has surrendered to the machines the concern for reality, that it has substituted for the referential paradigm that of "adlinguisticity" (one speaks about speech, writes about writing, intertextuality), and who thinks that the time has now come to restore a solid anchorage of language in the referent. I have read a talented theatrologist for whom postmodernism, with its games and fantasies, carries very little weight in front of political authority, especially when a worried public opinion encourages authority to a politics of totalitarian surveillance in the face of nuclear warfare threats.

I have read a thinker of repute who defends modernity against those he calls the neoconservatives. Under the banner of postmodernism, the latter would like, he believes, to get rid of the uncompleted project of modernism, that of the Enlightenment. Even the last advocates of *Aufklärung,* such as Popper or Adorno, were only able, according to him, to defend the project in a few particular spheres of life — that of politics for the author of *The Open Society,* and that of art for the author of *Ästhetische Theorie.* Jürgen Habermas (everyone had recognized him) thinks that if modernity has failed, it is in allowing the totality of life to be splintered into independent specialties which are left to the narrow competence of experts, while the concrete individual experiences "desublimated meaning" and "destructured form," not as a liberation but in the mode of that immense *ennui* which Baudelaire described over a century ago.

Following a prescription of Albrecht Wellmer, Habermas considers that the remedy for this splintering of culture and its separation from life can only come from "changing the status of aesthetic experience when it is no longer primarily expressed in judgments of taste," but when it is "used to explore a living historical situation," that is, when "it is put in relation with problems of existence." For this experience then "becomes a part of a language game which is no longer that of aesthetic criticism"; it takes part "in cognitive processes and normative expectations"; "it alters the manner in which those different moments *refer* to one another." What Habermas requires from the arts and the experiences they provide is, in short, to bridge the gap between cognitive, ethical, and political discourses, thus opening the way to a unity of experience.

My question is to determine what sort of unity Habermas has in mind. Is the aim of the project of modernity the constitution of sociocultural unity within which all the elements of daily life and of thought would take their places as in an organic whole? Or does the passage that has to be charted between heterogeneous language games—those of cognition, of ethics, of politics—belong to a different order from that? And if so, would it be capable of effecting a real synthesis between them?

The first hypothesis, of a Hegelian inspiration, does not challenge the notion of a dialectically totalizing *experience;* the second is closer to the spirit of Kant's *Critique of Judgment,* but must be submitted, like the *Critique,* to that severe reexamination which postmodernity imposes on the thought of the Enlightenment, on the idea of a unitary end of history and of a subject. It is this critique which not only Wittgenstein and Adorno have initiated, but also a few other thinkers (French or other) who do not have the honor to be read by Professor Habermas—which at least saves them from getting a poor grade for their neoconservatism.

REALISM

The demands I began by citing are not all equivalent. They can even be contradictory. Some are made in the name of postmodernism, others in order to combat it. It is not necessarily the same thing to formulate a demand for some referent (and objective reality), for some sense (and credible transcendence), for an addressee (and audience), or an addressor (and subjective expressiveness) or for some communicational consensus (and a general code of exchanges, such as the genre of historical discourse). But in the diverse invitations to suspend artistic experimentation, there is an identical call for order, a desire for unity, for identity, for security, or popularity (in the sense of *Öffentlichkeit,* of "finding a public"). Artists and writers must be brought back into the bosom of the community, or at least, if the latter is considered to be ill, they must be assigned the task of healing it.

There is an irrefutable sign of this common disposition: it is that for all those writers nothing is more urgent than to liquidate the heritage of the avant-gardes. Such is the case, in particular, of the so-called Transavantgardism. The answers given by Achille Bonito Oliva to the questions asked by Bernard Lamarche-Vadel and Michel Enric leave no room for doubt about this. By putting the avant-gardes through a mixing process, the artist and critic feel more confident that they can suppress them than by launching a frontal attack. For they can pass off the most cynical eclecticism as a way of going beyond the fragmentary character of the preceding experiments; whereas if they openly turned their backs on them, they would run the risk of appearing ridiculously neo-academic. The *Salons* and the *Académies,* at the time when the bourgeoisie was establishing itself in history, were able to function as purgation and to grant awards for good plastic and literary conduct under the cover of realism. But capitalism inherently possesses the power to derealize familiar objects, social roles, and institutions to such a degree that the so-called "realistic" representations can no longer evoke reality except as nostalgia or mockery, as an occasion for suffering rather than for satisfaction. Classicism seems to be ruled out in a world in which reality is so destabilized that it offers no occasion for experience but one for ratings and experimentation.

This theme is familiar to all readers of Walter Benjamin. But it is necessary to assess its exact reach. Photography did not appear as a challenge to painting from the outside, any more than industrial cinema did to narrative literature. The former was only putting the final touch to the program of ordering the visible elaborated by the Quattrocento; while the latter was the last step in rounding off diachronies as organic wholes, which had been the ideal of the great novels of education since the eighteenth century. That the mechanical and the industrial should appear as substitutes for hand or craft was not in itself a disaster — except if one believes that art is in its essence the expression of an individuality of genius assisted by an elite craftsmanship.

The challenge lay essentially in that photographic and cinematographic processes can accomplish better, faster, and with a circulation a hundred thousand times larger than narrative or

332

pictorial realism, the task which academicism had assigned to realism: to preserve various consciousnesses from doubt. Industrial photography and cinema will be superior to painting and the novel whenever the objective is to stabilize the referent, to arrange it according to a point of view which endows it with a recognizable meaning, to reproduce the syntax and vocabulary which enable the addressee to decipher images and sequences quickly, and so to arrive easily at the consciousness of his own identity as well as the approval which he thereby receives from others—since such structures of images and sequences constitute a communication code among all of them. This is the way the effects of reality, or if one prefers, the fantasies of realism, multiply.

If they too do not wish to become supporters (of minor importance at that) of what exists, the painter and novelist must refuse to lend themselves to such therapeutic uses. They must question the rules of the art of painting or of narrative as they have learned and received them from their predecessors. Soon those rules must appear to them as a means to deceive, to seduce, and to reassure, which makes it impossible for them to be "true." Under the common name of painting and literature, an unprecedented split is taking place. Those who refuse to reexamine the rules of art pursue successful careers in mass conformism by communicating, by means of the "correct rules," the endemic desire for reality with objects and situations capable of gratifying it. Pornography is the use of photography and film to such an end. It is becoming a general model for the visual or narrative arts which have not met the challenge of the mass media.

As for the artists and writers who question the rules of plastic and narrative arts and possibly share their suspicions by circulating their work, they are destined to have little credibility in the eyes of those concerned with "reality" and "identity"; they have no guarantee of an audience. Thus it is possible to ascribe the dialectics of the avant-gardes to the challenge posed by the realisms of industry and mass communication to painting and the narrative arts. Duchamp's *ready made* does nothing but actively and parodistically signify this constant process of dispossession of the craft of painting or even of being an artist. As Thierry de Duve penetratingly observes, the modern aesthetic question is not "What is beautiful?" but "What can be said to be art (and literature)?"

Realism, whose only definition is that it intends to avoid the question of reality implicated in that of art, always stands somewhere between academicism and kitsch. When power assumes the name of a party, realism and its neoclassical complement triumph over the experimental avant-garde by slandering and banning it—that is, provided the "correct" images, the "correct" narratives, the "correct" forms which the party requests, selects, and propagates can find a public to desire them as the appropriate remedy for the anxiety and depression that public experiences. The demand for reality—that is, for unity, simplicity, communicability, etc.—did not have the same intensity nor the same continuity in German society between the two world wars and in Russian society after the Revolution: this provides a basis for a distinction between Nazi and Stalinist realism.

What is clear, however, is that when it is launched by the political apparatus, the attack on artistic experimentation is specifically reactionary: aesthetic judgment would only be required to decide whether such or such work is in conformity with the established rules of the beautiful. Instead of the work of art having to investigate what makes it an art object and whether it will be able to find an audience, political academicism possesses and imposes a priori criteria of the beautiful, which designate some works and a public at a stroke and forever. The use of categories in aesthetic judgment would thus be of the same nature as in cognitive judgment. To speak like Kant, both would be determining judgments: the expression is "well formed" first in the understanding, then the only cases retained in experience are those which can be subsumed under this expression.

When power is that of capital and not that of a party, the "transavantgardist" or "postmodern" (in Jencks's sense) solution proves to be better adapted than the antimodern solution. Eclecticism is the degree zero of contemporary general culture: one listens to reggae, watches a western, eats McDonald's food for lunch and local cuisine for dinner, wears Paris perfume in Tokyo and "retro" clothes in Hong Kong; knowledge is a matter for TV games. It is easy to find a public for eclectic works. By becoming kitsch, art panders to the confusion which reigns in the "taste" of the patrons. Artists, gallery owners, critics, and public wallow together in the "anything goes," and the epoch is one of slackening. But this realism of the "anything goes" is in fact that of money; in the absence of aesthetic criteria, it remains possible and useful to assess the value of works of art according to the profits they yield. Such realism accommodates all tendencies, just as capital accommodates all "needs," providing that the tendencies and needs have purchasing power. As for taste, there is no need to be delicate when one speculates or entertains oneself.

Artistic and literary research is doubly threatened, once by the "cultural policy" and once by the art and book market. What is advised, sometimes through one channel, sometimes through the other, is to offer works which, first, are relative to subjects which exist in the eyes of the public they address, and second, works so made ("well made") that the public will recognize what they are about, will understand what is signified, will be able to give or refuse its approval knowingly, and if possible, even to derive from such work a certain amount of comfort.

THE SUBLIME AND THE AVANT-GARDE

The interpretation which has just been given of the contact between the industrial and mechanical arts, and literature and the fine arts is correct in its outline, but it remains narrowly sociologizing and historicizing—in other words, one-sided. Stepping over Benjamin's and Adorno's reticences, it must be recalled that science and industry are no more free of the suspicion which concerns reality than are art and writing. To believe otherwise would be to entertain an excessively humanistic notion of the mephistophelian functionalism of sciences and technologies. There is no denying the dominant existence today of techno-science, that is, the massive subordination of cognitive statements to the finality of the best possible performance, which is the technological criterion. But the mechanical and the industrial, especially when they enter fields traditionally reserved for artists, are carrying with them much more than power effects. The objects and the thoughts which originate in scientific knowledge and the capitalist economy convey with them one of the rules which supports their possibility: the rule that there is no reality unless testified by a consensus between partners over a certain knowledge and certain commitments.

This rule is of no little consequence. It is the imprint left on the politics of the scientist and the trustee of capital by a kind of flight of reality out of the metaphysical, religious, and political certainties that the mind believed it held. This withdrawal is absolutely necessary to the emergence of science and capitalism. No industry is possible without a suspicion of the Aristotelian theory of motion, no industry without a refutation of corporatism, of mercantilism, and of physiocracy. Modernity, in whatever age it appears, cannot exist without a shattering of belief and without discovery of the "lack of reality" of reality, together with the invention of other realities.

What does this "lack of reality" signify if one tries to free it from a narrowly historicized interpretation? The phrase is of course akin to what Nietzsche calls nihilism. But I see a much earlier modulation of Nietzschean perspectivism in the Kantian theme of the sublime. I think in particular that it is in the aesthetic of the sublime that modern art (including literature) finds its impetus and the logic of avant-gardes finds its axioms.

The sublime sentiment, which is also the sentiment of the sublime, is, according to Kant, a strong and equivocal emotion: it carries with it both pleasure and pain. Better still, in it pleasure derives from pain. Within the tradition of the subject, which comes from Augustine and Descartes and which Kant does not radically challenge, this contradiction, which some would call neurosis or masochism, develops as a conflict between the faculties of a subject, the faculty to conceive of something and the faculty to "present" something. Knowledge exists if, first, the statement is intelligible, and second, if "cases" can be derived from the experience which "corresponds" to it. Beauty exists if a certain "case" (the work of art), given first by the sensibility without any conceptual determination, the sentiment of pleasure independent of any interest the work may elicit, appeals to the principle of a universal consensus (which may never be attained).

Taste, therefore, testifies that between the capacity to conceive and the capacity to present an object corresponding to the concept, an undetermined agreement, without rules, giving rise to a judgment which Kant calls reflective, may be experienced as pleasure. The sublime is a different sentiment. It takes place, on the contrary, when the imagination fails to present an object which might, if only in principle, come to match a concept. We have the Idea of the world (the totality of what is), but we do not have the capacity to show an example of it. We have the Idea of the simple (that which cannot be broken down, decomposed), but we cannot illustrate it with a sensible object which would be a "case" of it. We can conceive the infinitely great, the infinitely powerful, but every presentation of an object destined to "make visible" this absolute greatness or power appears to us painfully inadequate. Those are Ideas of which no presentation is possible. Therefore, they impart no knowledge about reality (experience); they also prevent the free union of the faculties which gives rise to the sentiment of the beautiful; and they prevent the formation and the stabilization of taste. They can be said to be unpresentable.

I shall call modern the art which devotes its "little technical expertise" (*son "petit technique"*), as Diderot used to say, to present the fact that the unpresentable exists. To make visible that there is something which can be conceived and which can neither be seen nor made visible: this is what is at stake in modern painting. But how to make visible that there is something which cannot be seen? Kant himself shows the way when he names *formlessness, the absence of form,* as a possible index to the unpresentable. He also says of the empty *abstraction* which the imagination experiences when in search for a presentation of the infinite (another unpresentable): this abstraction itself is like a presentation of the infinite, its *negative presentation.* He cites the commandment, "Thou shalt not make graven images" (*Exodus*), as the most sublime passage in the Bible in that it forbids all presentation of the Absolute. Little needs to be added to those observations to outline an aesthetic of sublime paintings. As painting, it will of course "present" something though negatively; it will therefore avoid figuration or representation. It will be "white" like one of Malevitch's squares; it will enable us to see only by making it impossible to see; it will please only by causing pain.

One recognizes in those instructions the axioms of avant-gardes in painting, inasmuch as they devote themselves to making an allusion to the unpresentable by means of visible presentations. The systems in the name of which, or with which, this task has been able to support or to justify itself deserve the greatest attention; but they can originate only in the vocation of the sublime in order to legitimize it, that is, to conceal it. They remain inexplicable without the incommensurability of reality to concept which is implied in the Kantian philosophy of the sublime.

It is not my intention to analyze here in detail the manner in which the various avant-gardes have, so to speak, humbled and disqualified reality by examining the pictorial techniques which are so many devices to make us believe in it. Local tone, drawing, the mixing of colors, linear perspective, the nature of the support and that of the instrument, the treatment, the display, the museum: the avant-gardes are perpetually flushing out artifices of presentation which make it possible to subordinate thought to the gaze and to turn it away from the unpresentable. If Habermas, like Marcuse, understands this task of derealization as an aspect of the (repressive) "desublimation" which characterizes the avant-garde, it is because he confuses the Kantian sublime with Freudian sublimation, and because aesthetics has remained for him that of the beautiful.

THE POSTMODERN

What, then, is the postmodern? What place does it or does it not occupy in the vertiginous work of the questions hurled at the rules of image and narration? It is undoubtedly a part of the modern. All that has been received, if only yesterday (*modo, modo*, Petronius used to say), must be suspected. What space does Cézanne challenge? The Impressionists'. What object do Picasso and Braque attack? Cézanne's. What presupposition does Duchamp break with in 1912? That which says one must make a painting, be it cubist. And Buren questions that other presupposition which he believes had survived untouched by the work of Duchamp: the place of presentation of the work. In an amazing acceleration, the generations precipitate themselves. A work can become modern only if it is first postmodern. Postmodernism thus understood is not modernism at its end but in the nascent state, and this state is constant.

Yet I would like not to remain with this slightly mechanistic meaning of the word. If it is true that modernity takes place in the withdrawal of the real and according to the sublime relation between the presentable and the conceivable, it is possible, within this relation, to distinguish two modes (to use the musician's language). The emphasis can be placed on the powerlessness of the faculty of presentation, on the nostalgia for presence felt by the human subject, on the obscure and futile will which inhabits him in spite of everything. The emphasis can be placed, rather, on the power of the faculty to conceive, on its "inhumanity" so to speak (it was the quality Apollinaire demanded of modern artists), since it is not the business of our understanding whether or not human sensibility or imagination can match what it conceives. The emphasis can also be placed on the increase of being and the jubilation which result from the invention of new rules of the game, be it pictorial, artistic, or any other. What I have in mind will become clear if we dispose very schematically a few names on the chessboard of the history of avant-gardes: on the side of *melancholia,* the German Expressionists, and on the side of *novatio,* Braque and Picasso, on the former Malévitch and on the latter Lissitsky, on the one Chirico and on the other Duchamp. The *nuance* which distinguishes these two modes may be infinitesimal; they often coexist in the same piece, are almost indistinguishable; and yet they testify to a difference (*un différend*) on which the fate of thought depends and will depend for a long time, between regret and assay.

The work of Proust and that of Joyce both allude to something which does not allow itself to be made present. Allusion, to which Paolo Fabbri recently called my attention, is perhaps a form of expression indispensable to the works which belong to an aesthetic of the sublime. In Proust, what is being eluded as the price to pay for this allusion is the identity of consciousness, a victim to the excess of time (*au trop de temps*). But in Joyce, it is the identity of writing which is the victim of an excess of the book (*au trop de livre*) or of literature.

Proust calls forth the unpresentable by means of a language unaltered in its syntax and vocabulary and of a writing which in many of its operators still belongs to the genre of novelistic narration. The literary institution, as Proust inherits it from Balzac and Flaubert, is admittedly subverted in that the hero is no longer a character but the inner consciousness of time, and in that the diegetic diachrony, already damaged by Flaubert, is here put in question because of the narrative voice. Nevertheless, the unity of the book, the odyssey of that consciousness, even if it is deferred from chapter to chapter, is not seriously challenged: the identity of the writing with itself throughout the labyrinth of the interminable narration is enough to connote such unity, which has been compared to that of *The Phenomenology of Mind.*

Joyce allows the unpresentable to become perceptible in his writing itself, in the signifier. The whole range of available narrative and even stylistic operators is put into play without concern for the unity of the whole, and new operators are tried. The grammar and vocabulary of literary language are no longer accepted as given; rather, they appear as academic forms, as rituals originating in piety (as Nietzsche said) which prevent the unpresentable from being put forward.

Here, then, lies the difference: modern aesthetics is an aesthetic of the sublime, though a nostalgic one. It allows the unpresentable to be put forward only as the missing contents; but the form, because of its recognizable consistency, continues to offer to the reader or viewer matter for solace and pleasure. Yet these sentiments do not constitute the real sublime sentiment, which is in an intrinsic combination of pleasure and pain: the pleasure that reason should exceed all presentation, the pain that imagination or sensibility should not be equal to the concept.

The postmodern would be that which, in the modern, puts forward the unpresentable in presentation itself; that which denies itself the solace of good forms, the consensus of a taste which would make it possible to share collectively the nostalgia for the unattainable; that which searches for new presentations, not in order to enjoy them but in order to impart a stronger sense of the unpresentable. A postmodern artist or writer is in the position of a philosopher: the text he writes, the work he produces are not in principle governed by preestablished rules, and they cannot be judged according to a determining judgment, by applying familiar categories to the text or to the work. Those rules and categories are what the work of art itself is looking for. The artist and the writer, then, are working without rules in order to formulate the rules of what *will have been done.* Hence the fact that work and text have the characters of an *event;* hence also, they always come too late for their author, or, what amounts to the same thing, their being put into work, their realization (*mise en oeuvre*) always begin too soon. *Post modern* would have to be understood according to the paradox of the future (*post*) anterior (*modo*).

It seems to me that the essay (Montaigne) is postmodern, while the fragment (*The Athaeneum*) is modern.

Finally, it must be clear that it is our business not to supply reality but to invent allusions to the conceivable which cannot be presented. And it is not to be expected that this task will effect the last reconciliation between language games (which, under the name of faculties, Kant knew to be separated by a chasm), and that only the transcendental illusion (that of Hegel) can hope to totalize them into a real unity. But Kant also knew that the price to pay for such an illusion is terror. The nineteenth and twentieth centuries have given us as much terror as we can take. We have paid a high enough price for the nostalgia of the whole and the one, for the reconciliation of the concept and the sensible, of the transparent and the communicable experience. Under the general demand for slackening and for appeasement, we can hear the mutterings of the desire for a return of terror, for the realization of the fantasy to seize reality. The answer is: Let us wage a war on totality; let us be witnesses to the unpresentable; let us activate the differences and save the honor of the name.

(Translated by Régis Durand)

CONTRIBUTORS

INDEX

CONTRIBUTORS

HERBERT BLAU is a founder of the San Francisco Actor's Workshop and former Director of the Repertory Theatre at Lincoln Center. He has recently published *Take Up the Bodies* (1982), a study of his work with the KRAKEN theatre group which he also founded. Blau is the author of *The Impossible Theatre: A Manifesto* (1964) and *Blooded Thought: Occasions of Theatre* (1982) and currently teaches English at the University of Wisconsin-Milwaukee.

WAYNE C. BOOTH is George M. Pullman Professor of English at the University of Chicago and 1982 President of the Modern Language Association. He has written *The Rhetoric of Fiction* (1961), *A Rhetoric of Irony* (1974), *Modern Dogma and the Rhetoric of Assent* (1974), *Now, Don't Try to Reason With Me* (1970), and *Critical Understanding: The Powers and Limits of Pluralism* (1979).

MALCOLM BRADBURY, novelist and critic, is Professor of English and American Studies at the University of East Anglia. Among his novels are *Eating People is Wrong* (1959), and *The History of Man* (1975), recently serialized on BBC television. He has also written short stories and parodies, *Who Do You Think You Are?* (1976), in addition to *All Dressed Up and Nowhere To Go: The Poor Man's Guide to the Affluent Society* (1962), and *Possibilities: Essays on the State of the Novel* (1973). He has co-edited *Modernism* (1976) and *Introduction to American Studies* (1981).

MATEI CALINESCU is Professor of Comparative Literature and West European Studies at Indiana University. His most recent book is *Faces of Modernity: Avant-Garde, Decadence, Kitsch* (1977). A study of postmodern culture and a book-length essay on Mircea Eliade are forthcoming. Calinescu has published poetry, novels, and criticism in Rumania.

RALPH COHEN is the editor of *New Literary History* and Kenan Professor of English at the University of Virginia. He is the author of *The Art of Discrimination* (1964) and *The Unfolding of the Seasons* (1970) and has edited *New Directions in Literary History* (1974).

DIDIER COSTE, novelist, poet, and critical theorist, teaches at the University of Pau. He has written, among other books, *La Lune avec les dents* (1963; English translation 1974), *Le Voyage organisé* (1968), and *Vita Australis* (new edition, 1981). He has contributed articles to many journals, including *Critique, Poétique, Digraphe,* and *Sub-Stance.*

RÉGIS DURAND teaches American literature at the University of Lille. He has published widely in French and English on the theatre and on contemporary literary theory. His recent publications include *Melville, Signes et métaphores* (1980), *La Relation théâtrale* (1981) which he edited, and a short story in *Minuit.*

LESLIE A. FIEDLER holds the Samuel Clemens Chair of American Literature at the State University of New York at Buffalo. He is the author of many seminal works of literary criticism, cultural history, and fiction, including *An End to Innocence* (1952), *Love and Death in the American Novel* (1960), *Waiting for the End* (1964), *Nude Croquet* (1969), *The Stranger in Shakespeare* (1973), and, most recently, *Freaks* (1978).

GEOFFREY H. HARTMAN is Karl Young Professor of English and Comparative Literature at Yale University and Director of the School of Criticism and Theory. He has written *The Unmediated Vision* (1954), *Wordsworth's Poetry* (1964), *Beyond Formalism* (1970), *The Fate of Reading* (1975), *Criticism in the Wilderness* (1980), and *Saving the Text* (1981).

IHAB HASSAN is Vilas Research Professor of English and Comparative Literature at the University of Wisconsin-Milwaukee. He is the author of *Radical Innocence* (1961), *The Literature of Silence* (1967), *The Dismemberment of Orpheus* (1971), *Contemporary American Literature, 1945-1972* (1973), *Paracriticisms* (1975), and *The Right Promethean Fire* (1980).

SALLY HASSAN is Research Associate in English and Comparative Literature at the University of Wisconsin-Milwaukee and a freelance writer. She also helped edit, together with Ihab Hassan, *Liberations: New Essays on the Humanities in Revolution* (1971).

NORMAN N. HOLLAND, James H. McNulty Professor of English, is founder and former Director of the Center for the Psychological Study of the Arts at the State University of New York at Buffalo. Among his many works on psychoanalysis and reader response theory are *Psychoanalysis and Shakespeare* (1966), *The Dynamics of Literary Response* (1968), and *5 Readers Reading* (1975).

DOMINICK LACAPRA, Professor of History at Cornell University, is the author of *Émile Durkheim: Sociologist and Philosopher* (1972), *A Preface to Sartre* (1978), and *Madame Bovary on Trial* (1982). He has written numerous essays on intellectual history and is an editor of the forthcoming *Modern European Intellectual History: Reappraisals and New Perspectives*.

JEAN-FRANÇOIS LYOTARD is Professor of Philosophy at the University of Paris VIII. His many books on art, philosophy, and politics include *Discours, figure* (1971), *Des Dispositifs pulsionnels* (1973), *Économie libidinale* (1974), *Instructions païennes* (1977), and *La Condition postmoderne* (1979).

PAUL NOACK is Professor of Political Science at the University of Munich and a frequent media commentator on political events. He is the author of *Deutsche Aussenpolitik seit 1954* (1972), *Internationale Politik* (1977), *Das Scheitern der Europäischen Verteidigungsgemeinschaft* (1977), *Was ist Politik? Eine Einführung in ihre Wissenschaft* (1978), and *Die manipulierte Revolution* (1979).

RICHARD SCHECHNER is founder and was director of The Performance Group (1967-1980), Professor of Performance Studies at

New York University, and a theorist of experimental theatre. He has written *Public Domain: Essays on the Theatre* (1969), *Environmental Theatre* (1973), *Essays on Performance Theory* 1970–1976 (1977), and *The End of Humanism* (1982).

CLAUS UHLIG holds the Chair of English and American Studies at the University of Marburg. Apart from many articles on Renaissance literature and literary theory, his publications include *Traditionelle Denkformen in Shakespeares tragischer Kunst* (1967), *Hofkritik im England des Mittelalters und der Renaissance* (1973), *Chaucer und die Armut* (1974), with Ludwig Borinski, *Literatur der Renaissance* (1975), and *Theorie der Literarhistorie: Prinzipien und Paradigmen* (1982).

INDEX

Abrams, M. H., 265
Abstract Expressionism, 293
Absurd, Theatre of the, 162, 294, 321
Absurdism, 320
Academicism, 333–34
Action: ranges of potential, 152–53;
freedom of, 155–56, 157n4
Actors, double bind of, 168
Adorno, Theodor, 101–2, 330–31
Aeschylus, 205
Aesthetic(s), 213–17, 221, 250, 274–79,
281–93, 324–41 passim
Africa, 321
After the Wake (Butler), 323
Against Method (Feyerabend), 22, 264
Agamemnon, 133
Alienation, 319–20, 321
Altamont Festival, 179
Altieri, Charles, 124
Altman, Robert, 308–9
Alvarez, A., 324
Ambilectic, 27
Ambivalence, 300
Americanization, 131
Ananke (Cixous), 249
Anarchism, science as, 22
Anderson, Sherwood, 319
Annales school, 43
Anti-ideologies, 271
Anti-intellectualism, 98, 169
Apocalypticism, 134, 166–67, 322–23
Apolitical tradition, dance's, 174

Apollinaire, Guillaume, 339
Appearance (in theatre). *See* Representation
Aquarius, Age of, 179
Architectonics of Answerability (Bakhtin), 269
Architecture, postmodern, 294
Arendt, Hannah, 102, 104
Aristotle, 41, 265f., 336
Armies of the Night (Mailer), 89
Arnold, Matthew, 93, 94–95
Art(s), 60–62, 145, 216–17; functions
of (ancient and modern), 101; theories of, 101; nonconformity, and
achievement in, 102; performance
theory and, 213–17, 252–53; coproductions of the, 219; conflict between
science and, 274–75; philosophy as
form of, 283; in twentieth-century
culture (brief history of), 291–97
Artaud, Antonin, 166–67, 183ff., 186,
215, 217, 218–22
Artist, fate of becoming an, 141–44
Art Nouveau, 292
Art Novels, 236ff., 240–41
Ashcan School, 292
Association of American Publishers,
239–40
Asynchrony, of simultaneity, 42
Audience, the: literalist art and, 214–
15; for novels, 228–33. *See also*
Spectatorship/spectacles

Aufklärung, 330
Augustine, 336
Austen, Jane, 92, 143, 154–55
Authentic history (Heidegger), 17
Authenticity. *See* Reality
Authority/authorities, questioning, 10, 269
Autumn of the Patriarch (García Márquez), 307
Avant-Garde, 24, 43, 244, 280, 332; breakdown of classification of, 151–52; in theater, 164, 176; language use and, 244, 329–30; Modernism, Postmodernism, and the, 314–17, 322ff.; the sublime and, 335–38
Axiologies, monistic or pluralistic, 267–71, 278

Bakhtin, Mikhail, 56–57, 101, 269–71, 281
Balinese cockfight, the, 203–4
Ballanche, Pierre-Simon, 91
Balzac, Honoré de, 232
Barba, Eugenio, 170
Barrault, Jean-Louis, 180–81
Barth, John, 228, 295, 322
Barthelme, Donald, 228, 240
Barthes, Roland, 10, 16, 28, 91, 101–2, 110n9, 180, 185–86, 211–12, 218–19, 295
Bateson, Gregory, 192, 195
Baudelaire, Charles, 24, 330
Baudrillard, Jean, 174, 251–52, 256, 260–61
Baum, L. Frank, 234
Bausch, Pina, 174
Bayreuth, 178
"Beat" movement, 321
Becker, Ernest, 16
Beckett, Samuel, 61, 162, 176, 238, 244, 258, 294, 322
Beliefs, stability of, 146–47. *See also* Religion
Bell, Daniel, 25–26, 27, 30
Belle de Jour, 193–97
Bellow, Saul, 35n47, 226–27, 241, 319

Benjamin, Walter, 102, 332
Benn, Gottfried, 83n13
Berliner Ensemble, The, 170
Best sellers, 237–38, 296. *See also* Mass Culture
Beuys, Joseph, 165
Binarism, 50, 58, 97, 183, 251
Bio-theatre, 217
Birth of Tragedy, The (Nietzsche), 127
Blanchot, Maurice, 91
Blau, Herbert, 8, 28, 161–88, 220, 345
Blindness and Insight (de Man), 116
Bloch, Ernst, 71, 249
Bloom, Harold, 91
Body: repression of, 16; language, 172–74; art, 184, 217; feminists on the female, 244–45, 249. *See also* Sex(uality)
Bonnefoy, Yves, 267
Book-burning moralists, 239
Book of Daniel, The (Doctorow), 88
Book of Laughter and Forgetting (Kundera), 88
Boorstin, Daniel, 18
Booth, Wayne C., 8, 131–59, 265–66, 268, 345
Borges, Jorge Luis, 228, 322
Bougé, 250, 258
Boulding, Kenneth, 25
Boulez, Pierre, 178
Bouvard and Pécuchet (Flaubert), 59, 61–62
Bracher, Karl Dietrich, 82n4
Bradbury, Malcolm, 9, 311–27, 345
Brando, Marlon, 168
Brecht, Bertold, 167, 170, 177, 212, 215, 223–24n11, 294, 319, 322
Brecht, George, 179
Breuer, Lee, 220
Bricolage, 169
Brook, Peter, 170, 294, 309
Brower, Reuben, 115
Bruce, Lenny, 165
Brzezinski, Zbigniew, 66–67
Buber, Martin, 269
Buck, Pearl, 228

Bucknell Review, 265
Burden, Chris, 184
Buren, Daniel, 180, 217, 338
Burgheart, Catherine, 197
Burke, Kenneth, 102, 109–10n9, 113, 265
Burroughs, Edgar Rice, 234
Butler, Christopher, 323

Cage, John, 174, 179, 186, 197, 216, 219
Caldwell, Taylor, 240
Calinescu, Matei, 9, 28, 41, 263–88, 345–46
Calvino, Italo, 161, 325
Campbell, Joseph, 17
Camus, Albert, 319
Canonical texts, 54–55
Capitalism, 26, 332, 335–36. *See also* Marx, Karl
Capote, Truman, 88
Carnivalesque, the, 56–58, 62
Castle, The (Kafka), 234
Castle of Crossed Destinies (Calvino), 325
Castration: feminism, and issues of, 247–48, 260–61
Catastrophe, learning through, 79–81
Catcher in the Rye (Salinger), 237
Causse, Michèle, 244–46, 251
Centres Dramatiques, 170
Cervantes, Miguel de, 306–7
Change: perspectives on, 3–12, 15–84; chronography of, 7, 39–46; models of, 17–24; temporal aspects of, 42–43; theatricality, performance theory, and, 213–17; feminist, 250–51
Chantage à la théorie, Le (Barthes), 186
Characterizations, postmodernist, 307–8
Chereau, Patrice, 178
Chicago Critics, 136
Chicago School, 266
Child development, theories of, 299–302

Chiliasm, 323
Christie, Agatha, 152
Chronography, 7, 39–46. *See also* Time
Chronotopicity, 281, 284
Cinema. *See* Film
Circus Maximus, 193
Cities, beginning of, 31, 37n67
Cixous, Hélène, 249, 257–58, 259–60
Classicism, 332
Classic world view, 278
Closure, possibility of, 98
Clubs of Rome, 132, 134
Cockfights, Balinese, 203–4
Cognitive dissonance, 75
Cohen, Ralph, 8, 111–30, 346
Collective behavior, concept of, 118–19
Colonna, Vittoria, 248
Comédie Française, 165
Commentary magazine, 227
Common-Sense School, 96–99
Complexity, reduction of, 79
Concepts, reality and, 65–67
Condition postmoderne, La (Lyotard), 26–27
Conflict: crisis and, 77–78; social dramas from, 205; aesthetics of (theatrical), 221
Conformism: non-, 102; mass, 333
Connolly, Cyril, 319
Consciousness: of modernism, 121, 283–84, 312–24; false, 271; aesthetic, 280–84; historical, 281; passim, 311–12
Conspiracy, evidence of, 163–64
Constancy principle, 298
Content. *See* Meaning, questions of
Context(s): texts and, 52, 54–58; play as matter of, 192–93
Continuity, theatre's, 161–62
Cooper, James Fenimore, 232
Coproductions (of the arts), 219
Correspondance (Flaubert), 60–61
Coste, Didier, 8–9, 243–62, 346

Counterculture, of the oppressed, 255–56
Countertransference, 305
Coup de dés, Un (Mallarmé), 249
Crane, Ronald, 265–66
Cratylus, 16
Creation/re-creation, heroic/mythic views of, 16, 18
Creative Criticism (Spingarn), 93
Creative process/creativity: change and, 24; of literary criticism, 93–94, 127; negativity and, 190
Crews, Frederick, 97
Crisis: of legitimacy, 26–27, 72; concept and reality of, 65–69; as perspective on change, 72–80, 103
Critical Understanding (Booth), 265, 268
Criticism. *See* Literary criticism
Criticism in the Wilderness (Hartman), 91–92
Critique of Judgment (Kant), 331
Croce, Benedetto, 93
Cruelty, Theater of, 221
Crystallization theory, 70–71, 83n13
Culler, Jonathan, 58–59
Cultural change. *See* Change
Cultural Contradictions of Capitalism, The (Bell), 26
Cultural crystallization, 83n13
Cultural Revolution, 236
Culture, perspectives on, 8–9, 225–88
Cunningham, Merce, 173–74, 219
Cybernetic machine, theatre as kind of, 211, 218

Dada, 322
Dance, theatrical performance and, 172–76 passim
Dardigna, A.-M., 244
Darwin, Charles, 20
Death, metaphoric uses of, 15–18, 56–57; feminist thought and, 255–60 passim
Debray, Régis, 84n18
Decadence, theatre's, 194–95, 196

Deconstruction, 50, 98, 101, 105, 116–17; the atomic self, 144, 149; of reasoning, 148; of world as a stage, 162–63; feminist textual practice as, 246–47; negative monism and, 272
Dedalus, Stephen, 140–45
de Duve, Thierry, 333–34
Defense of Poetry (Shelley), 127, 314
Deleuze, Gilles, 28, 256
de Man, Paul, 105, 107n5, 114–16, 124, 128
Democratic societies, 72, 74–75, 78, 103
Derrida, Jacques, 28, 50, 57, 91, 98, 121–22, 166, 168, 182–83, 249, 259, 272
Descartes, René, 146, 149, 156, 336
Desire, oppositional definition of, 250–51
Determinism: fear of, 134–35; Skinner and, 156–57n4
Détruire dit-elle (Duras), 249, 258
Dewey, John, 149
Dialogical (dialogue), 49–58 passim; reader-text relation as, 119; monism, pluralism and, 269–74 passim, 284, 285–86; intracultural, 275–77, 285
Dialogic equality, principle of, 269
Dickens, Charles, 232
Dickinson, Emily, 189, 208–9
Dictionary of Received Ideas (Flaubert), 38
Diderot, Denis, 337
Dilthey, Wilhelm, 107n5
Dionysus, 309
Disappearance, as subject of performance, 184
Disconfirmation, postmodernist condition of, 26–27
Discovery. *See* Invention
Displacement: historicity, tradition, the postmodern, and, 50–51; replacement as (in theatre), 218; signifiers, signifieds, and, 222
Dispositives, performances as, 217, 221

Doctorow, E. L., 88, 229
Documentation, for intellectual history, 52-55
Donne, John, 89
Don Quixote (Cervantes), 306-7
Dostoyevsky, F. M., 140, 232, 238, 319
Doubt. See Suspicion
Douglas, Lloyd, 239
Doxiadis, C. A., 37n67
Dracula (Stoker), 234
Drama. See Theatre
Drama Review, The, 196
Dreyfus, Hubert L., 37n63
Dualism, 267-68, 269, 277-79. See also Dialogical (dialogue); Pluralism
Dubliners (Joyce), 293
Duchamp, Marcel, 333, 338
Dune tetralogy (Herbert), 227
Dunn, John, 82n5
Dupréel, Eugène, 265
Durand, Régis, 8, 211-24, 341, 346
Duras, Marguerite, 249, 257, 258-59

Eagleton, Terry, 254, 261
Ecclesiastes, 16
Eclecticism, of contemporary arts, 324-27, 334-35
Economie libidinale (Lyotard), 245
Education, mass, 105, 107n4
Eighties, the (1980s), 179-80, 185-86
Einbildungskraft, 24
Einstein on the Beach (R. Wilson), 175
Eliot, T. S., 6, 91, 92-94, 320
Elites, popular culture and, 56
Emerson, Ralph Waldo, 231
Empedocles, 264
Empson, William, 98
Encontre, L' (Causse), 244-46
Energies, theater of, 219-20
English influences (literary criticism), 92-93, 94
Enlightenment, the, 330
Enric, Michel, 332
Épistémè, 40
Epistemology, 270, 275-77
Erikson, Erik, 302-3, 306

Erinnerung, 245
Eros and Civilization (Marcuse), 245
Eternal Return, 176
Evolution, 4-5, 20-21; neoteny in, 152, 158n12; feminist perspectives on, 245-46, 251
Existentialism, 320
Experimentalism, of negation (avant-garde's), 280
Experimentation, demands for ending, 329-32
Expressionism, 317; Abstract, 293
Expressivity, in theatrical (and dance) performance, 172, 174

Fabbri, Paolo, 339
Faerie Queene, The (Spenser), 278
Faith. See Beliefs
Falsity. See Truth
Fantasies, communal or private (in theatre), 171
Fascism, 104, 318-19
Faulkner, William, 320
Faust, 140
Federalist Papers, 154
Federman, Raymond, 28
Femininity, feminists on, 259-60
Feminism, in dance, film, 173-74
Feminist criticism, 109-110n9, 155, 159n14, 243-62
Feyerabend, Paul, 21, 22-23, 264
Fiction, 88-90, 97-98, 277, 291, 320-21; in 1960s, 236-38; truth and, 282-83. See also Novel, the
Fiedler, Leslie, 8, 28, 225-42, 323, 346
Film, 174, 292-93, 295, 308-9, 332-33
Finnegans Wake (Joyce), 293
Fish, Stanley, 123
Fit, rightness of, 282
Fitzgerald, Scott, 319
Flaubert, Gustave, 48, 56, 58-62, 238, 340
Fluxus group, 179
Folk theatre, Belle de Jour as authentic, 194

Foreman, Richard, 172
Forgetfulness, theoretical problem of, 185
Formlessness, 337-38
Foucault, Michel, 17, 28-29, 40, 121, 163, 168
Frankenstein (Living Theatre), 179
Frankfurt School, 110
Freedom: concept and possibility of, 8, 135-38, 147; rhetorical, 138; of choice (in Christianity), 139-40; artist's valuation of, 141-44, 145; existentialists on, 148; of interpretation, 150-56
Free indirect style, 157n5
French influences, 94, 243-62
French school (*Annales*), 43
Freud, Sigmund, 16, 271-72, 297-301, 305-6
Fried, Michael, 8, 213-17, 223-24n11
Frisch, Max, 319
Fritsch, Bruno, 79
Frye, Northrup, 90, 119, 136
Fulguratio, 5
Fuller, Buckminster, 29
Future/futurists, 5, 15, 71-73, 131-32, 238; feminist discourse, the possible, and, 246, 248-49
Futurism, 317

Gadamer, Hans-Georg, 110n10
García Márquez, Gabriel, 307, 325
Gardner, Erle Stanley, 237
Gass, William, 228
Geertz, Clifford, 113, 203-5
Gehlen, Arnold, 70, 83n13
Genesis, 236
Genet, Jean, 163, 167, 194
Geneology of Morals, The (Nietzsche), 100
German influences, 92
Germany: Nazi, 102, 334; theatrical performances in, 173-74, 176-78
Geschehen, 17
Ghost Writer, The (Roth), 307

Giles Goatboy (Barth), 228
Glas (Derrida), 91
Glucksman, André, 272
Godard, Jean-Luc, 295
Gödel's Proof of Incompleteness, 28
Goethe, J. W. von, 23, 93
Goffman, Erving, 191, 203, 206-7
Gone With The Wind (Mitchell), 229, 234
Goodman, Nelson, 274, 282-83
Gothic world view, 278
Graff, Gerald, 97, 120-21, 122, 138, 252-53
Graham, Martha, 173
Grass, Günter, 170, 319
Gravity's Rainbow (Pynchon), 325
Gray, Spaulding, 217
Green, André, 305
Gross, Bertram, 174
Grotowski, Jerzy, 165, 182-83
Guattari, Félix, 28, 256
Guérillères, Les (Wittig), 246-47
Guevara, Che, 181
Gurdjieff, G. I., 165

Habermas, Jürgen, 12n9, 26-27, 330-31, 338
Haggard, Rider, 234
Haley, Alex, 229
Hamlet (Shakespeare), 295
Handke, Peter, 168
Happy Days (Beckett), 162
Hardwick, Elizabeth, 234-35
Hartman, Geoffrey, 7-8, 87-110, 128, 296, 346
Hassan, Ihab, 7, 15-38, 91, 125, 127-28, 138, 264, 266-67, 296, 323, 346-47
Hassan, Sally, 347
Hazard, Paul, 67
Hegel, G. W. F., 19, 92, 97-98, 102
Heidegger, Martin, 17, 91, 98, 100, 107-8n6, 110n10
Heilbroner, Robert, 4
Heilbrun, Carolyn, 109n9
Heinlein, Robert, 236, 237-38

Heisenberg, Werner, 28, 38n68
Hellman, Lillian, 88
Hemingway, Ernest, 234
Heraclitus, 4, 16, 108n6
Herbert, Frank, 227
Hermeneutics, 21, 119, 122-23, 266,
    271-72
Heroes, 16, 18, 140
Hersey, John, 88, 89
Hesse, Hermann, 322
Heuristic vision, 275-77
Higgins, Dick, 179
Hiroshima (Hersey), 88-89
Hirsch, E. D., 110n10, 136
Historicity, 49-50, 52, 281, 286, 319-
    21
Historic materialism, 251
Historiography, 7, 39-46, 47-48, 49,
    54; Modernism's, 311-21
History, 7, 17, 18-20, 42-44, 99-104,
    121, 122-23; intellectual, 47-63;
    language of, 48-49, 54; fiction and,
    89-90; literature, criticism, and, 90-
    92, 97; feminist discourse on, 246,
    248-49; relativism of, 280-84 pas-
    sim. *See also* Propaganda
History and Class Consciousness (Lu-
    kács), 98
Hofstadter, Douglas, 29
Holderlin, Friedrich, 16, 177
Holiday, 182
Holland, Norman N., 9, 28, 291-309,
    347
Holocaust, 104
Holquist, Michael, 269
Hope, principle of, 71, 79
Horkheimer, Max, 102
Howe, Irving, 320-21
Hoy, David, 119
Humanism/humanities, 6, 95, 104-5,
    113-14, 136-37, 251-52
Human Potential Movement, 181
Hume, David, 146
Hurd, Richard, 277-78
Hutton, James, 20

Hypnerotomachia (Colonna), 248
Hyvrard, Jeanne, 249, 255-57, 259

Ibsen, Henrik, 206
Identity: quest of, 254; psychoanalytic
    conceptions of, 303-5
Ideologies, dualism, pluralism, and
    monologic, 271-72, 284-85
Idiot de la famille, L' (Sartre), 59
Ikonic style, 308-9
Imaginary, the female/feminist, 244,
    245-46
Imagism, 291-92, 317
Immanences, tendency of, 29-31
Impressionism, 317
In-betweenness, performance and, 190
Incompleteness, Gödel's Proof of, 28
In Defense of Reading (Brower, Poi-
    rier), 114-15
Independence, concept of learning,
    115-16
Indeterminacies, 7, 27-29, 44; in dance
    performance, 174; structural, 185-
    86
India, 321-22
Indication, representation and, 167-68
Individual, crisis-susceptibility of the,
    75-77
Individuality, documentation of, 163
Information: crises of, 75, 80; theatre's
    polyphony of, 211
Informatique, 29, 30
Innovation(s), perspectives on, 5-6, 7-
    9, 16, 18, 24, 85-287; crises as
    means for, 78-79. *See also* Change
Innovationism, temptations of, 131-
    36
Institutional theory, 124
Integrity, artist's pursuit of, 141-44
Intellectual history, 7, 47-63
Intensities, the (theatre, 1960s), 180-
    81, 182-83
Interactionism, change as, 22-23
Interdependency, worldwide, 11
Internationalism, 317, 327

Interpretation: language competency and, 124; literary theory and, 128; innovation, and tradition of, 136–38; truth, 'destructive' critique, and, 271; psychoanalysis as, 304–5, 306
Intracultural dialogue, 275–77
Invention, 5–6
Ionesco, Eugène, 294
Iran, U.S. hostages in, 185–86
Irigaray, Luce, 244–45, 260
Iser, Wolfgang, 117, 123
Isolation, artist's choice of, 142–43, 144

Jalousie, La (Robbe-Grillet), 325
James, Henry, 183, 233, 238
James, William, 40, 271, 274
Jameson, Fredric, 118
Jantsch, Erich, 34n38
Japan, 321–22
Jauss, Hans Robert, 123
Jesus Christ, 269
Jews, 91, 102, 104, 108–9n8, 241
Jonathan Livingston Seagull (Bach), 236
Journeys to Berlin/1971 (film), 173
Joyce, James, 140–44, 228, 233, 238, 293, 319–20, 322, 340
Judgments: of greatness, 55; ability to make, 75

Kafka, Franz, 233, 319
Kahn, Charles H., 108n6
Kant, Immanuel, 119, 331–40 passim
Kaprow, Allan, 179
Katz, Alex, 308
Kennedy, J. F., 321
Kermode, Frank, 322
Kerouac, Jack, 237
Kesey, Ken, 229
King Lear (Shakespeare), 176, 204
Kitsch, 334–35
Knowledge, 148–49, 334, 336
Kohut, Heinz, 302
KRAKEN group, 171
Krantz, Judith, 123

Kristeva, Julia, 28, 57–58, 171, 216
Kuhn, Thomas, 21–22, 114
Kundera, Milan, 88

LaBarbara, Joan, 217
Lacan, Jacques, 16, 302–3
LaCapra, Dominick, 7, 47–63, 347
Ladder System, The, 244, 246
Lamarche-Vadel, Bernard, 332
Landscape plays, 172
Language, 26–27, 48–49, 54, 82n4, 100–106, 124; feminist (French), 8–9, 243–62; meta-, 16; media's role in shaping, 29–30; other symbolic modes and, 52–53; of renewal, 149–50; withdrawal of the Sacred into, 171; meaning and, 176, 202–3; avant-garde and, 244, 329–30; child's development of, 302; Proust's, 339–40. *See also* Dialogical (dialogue); Literary criticism; Metaphor
Last Tango in Paris (film), 168
Laszlo, Erwin, 29
Latin America, 315, 321–22, 324
Leakey, Richard, 4
Learning process, 77–81 passim, 105, 115–16
Leavis, F. R., 94
LeCompte, Elizabeth, 217
Legitimation/legitimacy: crisis of, 26–27, 72; historical claims of, 100
Leonard, John, 88
Letters on Chivalry and Romance (Hurd), 277–78
Levin, Harry, 6, 263
Lévi-Strauss, Claude, 19
Lewis, Sinclair, 228
Liberal tradition, 319
Liberty, 279, 285
Lichtenstein, Heinz, 303
Life and Times of Joseph Stalin, The (R. Wilson), 181
Liminality: in theatre, 190, 196–97; TV news as paradigm of, 207–9
Literacy, language and, 103, 105

Literalist art, theatricality of, 213–17
Literary criticism, 24, 87–110, 295–96;
  periodization of, 9, 311–12; bounda-
  ries of, 90–91; two cultures of, 92–95;
  creativity of, 93–94, 127; practical,
  95–96; Common-Sense School of, 96–
  99; aesthetics of, 324–27. See also
  Fiction; Novel; Text(s)/textuality
Literary response, 124
Literary theory, 7–8, 24–25, 87–159;
  map of contemporary, 112–29
Literature, twentieth-century, 291–97.
  See also Fiction; Novel
Literature Against Itself (Graff), 120
Lives of Performers, 173
Living Theatre, The, 163, 165, 166,
  179
Lodge, David, 121
Logos, 108n6
Lolita (Nabokov), 229
Loneliness: self, society, freedom,
  and, 143–44
Lorenz, Konrad, 5
Love and Freindship (Austen), 143
Lovejoy, A. O., 318
Lovell, Sir Bernard, 20–21
Lowell, Robert, 88
Luhmann, Niklas, 79
Lukács, Georg, 97–98, 107n5
Lyell, Charles, 20
Lyotard, Jean-François, 9, 26–30 pas-
  sim, 138, 180, 212, 218ff., 245, 254–
  55, 256, 261, 329–41, 347

Macbeth (Shakespeare), 163
Macherey, Pierre, 253, 261
MacLeish, Archibald, 293
McLuhan, Marshall, 25, 178
Madame Bovary (Flaubert), 59, 61–62
Madness, femininity as, 255–56
Magic Mountain, The (Mann), 234
Mailer, Norman, 88–89
Malcolm, Janet, 305, 308
Mallarmé, Stéphane, 171, 249
Malraux, André, 88, 100ff., 181, 324
Malthus, Thomas R., 20

Mandel, Ernest, 251
Mann, Thomas, 228, 233, 319
Man's Hope (Malraux), 88
Marcuse, Herbert, 245, 338
Márquez, Gabriel. See García Már-
  quez
Marx, Karl, 19, 29, 172, 261, 271
Marxism, 19–20, 76–77, 99, 118–19,
  223–24n11, 255, 317
Mass Culture, novels of/for, 229–33.
  See also Best sellers
Mass media, 29–30, 75, 84n18, 90, 333
Mastery, 17–18, 79, 272
Matter-form-composition, 251
Maya, veil of, 162
Maya-lila, 208
Meaning, questions of, 176, 202–3
Measure for Measure (Shakespeare),
  163, 169
Medawar, Sir Peter, 35n46
Media. See Mass media
Medium and message, 25, 44
Mencken, H. L., 93
Mère la mort (Hyvrard), 240
Merleau-Ponty, Maurice, 172
Meta-: language, 16; narrative, 26–27;
  theories, 191; fiction, 324; theatre,
  324
Metanoia, 4
Metaphor, 8, 15–16, 65, 280
Metaphysics, 98, 221–22, 251
Methodology. See Theory
Middlebrow fiction, 238–39
Mill, John Stuart, 279, 285
Millenarian sects, 132–33
Mille Plateaux, 329
Miller, Hillis, 117
Milner, Marion, 300
Mimesis, 252–53, 323
Mind Is a Muscle, The (Nietzsche), 173
Minimal art, 213–17, 294
Mr. Sammler's Planet (Bellow), 227
Mitchell, Margaret, 234
Mitzman, Arthur, 59
Mnouchkine, Ariane, 178
Moby Dick (Melville), 233

Models: of change, 7, 17–24; questions about, 266–67; epistemological, 275–77. *See also* Theory(ies)

Modern, the (contemporary), 50, 333–34, 340–41

Modernism, 8, 24–25; consciousness of, 121, 283–84, 312–24; freedom in tradition of, 150–51; aesthetics of, 213–14, 250; feminist discourse and, 244; negative monism and, 272–75

Modernity: monism and, 263–64, 272; conflict between science and art and, 274–75; definitions of aesthetic, 279–80

Money, aesthetic criteria and, 335

Monism: relations between pluralism and, 256, 267–71; modernity and, 263–64; negative, 272–75

Monk, Meredith, 174

Monod, Jacques, 20

Monolingualism, democratic societies', 103

Monological, the, 57, 272

Monologism, negative, 271–75

Monopolistic systems, 274

Moral issues (of art, theatre, and innovation), 213–14

Mormons, 132–33

Mortality. *See* Death

Mother Kills Self and Kids (Saperstein), 88

Moynahan, Julian, 90

Multiplex signals, 220

Mumford, Lewis, 31, 37n67

Music, twentieth-century, 216, 293, 295

Mysticism, Jewish, 91

Mythopoesis, 19

Myths, 17–18, 22, 66

Nabokov, Vladimir, 91, 228–29, 322

Naipaul, V. S., 227

Narr, Wolf-Dieter, 68

Narrative: displacement of status of theatrical, 220–21. *See* Fiction; Novel

Nashville (film), 308–9

National Book Awards, 227, 239–40

Naturalism, 291, 317, 319–20, 324

Nazi Germany, 102, 334

Negation: in feminist discourse, 225; of avant garde, 280

Negative monologism, and pluralism alternative, 271–75

Negativity: the creative, 190; and relativity, 279–84

Nel, Christof, 178

Neoconservatism, 330–31

Neomarxists, 150

Neo-Modernism, 322

Neorealism, 294

Neoteny, 152, 158n12

Neumann, Erich, 17–18

New, the. *See* Change; Innovation(s)

New Criticism, the 93–94, 101, 136, 293–94

New Dance, rhetoric of the, 174–75

Newnovelism, 246–47

News, performance theory, and, 189–201, 207–9

Nietzsche, Friedrich, 23, 57, 98, 185, 271–72, 336, 340

Nihilism, 58ff., 218, 257, 336

Nin, Anaïs, 246

Nirvana principle, 298

Noack, Paul, 7, 65–84, 347

Nobel Prizes, 227–28

Normalcy, theory of, 68

Nouveau roman, 321, 324

Nouvelle rhétorique, La, 265

Novation. *See* Change; Innovation

Novel, the, 225–42, 270, 307; bestselling, 237–38, 296. *See also* Fiction

Nozick, Robert, 265, 268, 283

Oakeshott, Michael, 41

Objectification: of art, 213–14, 254; of women, 243–44, 261

Objectivism, 276–77

Object-relations theorists, 301

Object/subject polarity, 49

Oc, Kenzaburo, 307

Oedipal rivalry, Freud's theories about, 299
Offending the Audience (Handke), 168
Olbrechts-Tyteca, L., 265
Oliva, Achille Bonito, 332
Olson, Charles, 322
One, the. *See* Monism
One Flew Over the Cuckoo's Nest (Kesey), 229
One Hundred Years of Solitude (García Márquez), 307, 325
On Liberty (Mill), 279, 285
On the Road (Kerouac), 237
Ontological-Hysteric Theatre, 172
Op Art, 294
Open Society and Its Enemies (Popper), 269
Opoponax, The, 246, 248
Oppressed, counterculture of the, 255-56
Ordinariness, in twentieth-century arts, 291-92
Orghast (Brook), 170
Originality, questions about, 5-6
Origin of Species, The (Darwin), 20
Origins (Leakey), 4
Origins of Totalitarianism (Arendt), 104
Orpheus (Ballanche), 91
Orwell, George, 87, 99
Overcivilized society, 81
Overstanding, 155

Paik, Nam June, 179
Painting, twentieth-century, 292ff., 308, 338-39
Palaeo-Modernism, 322
Pale Fire (Nabokov), 91
Pantomime, theatre as, 219
Paracriticisms (Hassan), 264, 323
Paradigms, humanities', 21-23
Past, study of. *See* History
Paz, Octavio, 263
Peirce, C. S., 218
Pepper, Stephen, 148

Perception, 16, 23
Perelman, Chaim, 149, 265-66
Perfection: search for, 133; as image of the void, 267
Performance: issues of innovation or renovation in, 161-88; apocalyptic radicalization of, 166-67; abuse of, 168; reconstrual of, 168-71; nature of, 171-72; everyday life and, 185, 206-7; innovation as, 185-86; training for, 189-90; postmodern, 215-17
Performance in Postmodern Culture (Feyerabend), 264
Performance theory, 8, 161-224; news, sex, and, 189-201; transformations of the theatrical and, 211-24; Barthes on theatre, theatricality, and, 212-13; art and, 213-17, 252-53
Personal Knowledge (Polanyi), 272
Phallocentrism, feminist perspectives on, 174, 244, 248, 255, 260-61
Phenomenology of Mind, The, 340
Philosophical Explanations (Nozick), 265, 283
Philosophies blanches, 28
Philosophy, as art form, 283
Photography, 332-33
Photo-Realists, 308
Physicalism, 275
Picasso, Pablo, 293, 338
Pirandello, Luigi, 167
Planchon, Roger, 169-70
Plato, 6, 98, 108n6, 184, 268-69
Play: the remission of, 161-88; hegemony of, 180-81; relationship between theatre and, 192-93, 195
Pleasure of the Text, The (Barthes), 101, 180
Pleasure principle, Freud's, 297-98, 301
Plumb, J. H., 39
Pluralism, 263-88; innovation and, 264-65; hermeneutical, 266; axiologies of monism or, 267-71, 278; negative monologism and alterna-

Pluralism (*continued*)
tive of, 271-75; aesthetic dualism and, 277-79; contemporary renaissance of, 284-86
Pluralistic Universe, A (W. James), 274
Polanyi, Michael, 21, 149, 272, 275-77
Political aspects: of language, 82n4, 100-102, 103-4, 109-10n9; of theatre, 176-77, 180-81, 183, 185-86; of the novel, 227
Political change. *See* Revolution; Sociopolitical change
Political situation, the arts and, 134, 319-20, 334
Political system, crisis of, 82n7
Politicians, images of, 308-9
Popaioannou, J. G., 37n67
Pop Art, 178, 294
Popeye (film), 309
Pop Novels, 230, 235-37, 239
Popper, Karl, 21, 269, 271, 330
Popular culture, elites and, 56. *See also* Mass Culture
Population, explosion of human, 30
Pornography, 240, 333. *See also* Sex(uality)
Portrait of the Artist as a Young Man (Joyce), 140-44, 145
Postmodernism: as perspective on change, 6-7, 9, 25-27; chronology, and concept of, 40, 294; aesthetics of, 215-17; epistemological models within, 275-77; psychoanalysis and, 291, 297-309; historical consciousness (and defining) of, 318-27; answering the question: what is, 329-41
Postmodern society, 8, 47-63
Poststructural theory, 97-99
Potential space, between self and other, 301-2
Pound, Ezra, 6, 178, 291-92
Power: in the theatre, 166-67, 169, 218ff.; truth viewed in terms of, 171-72; sex differences in structure

of, 247; denials of, 252; will to (of the self), 283-84
Practical criticism, 95-96, 106n3
Pragmatists, 149
Prague Formalists, the, 213
Presentness, concept of, 214-15, 216
Present time, intellectual history, and defining, 47-63
Pride and Prejudice (Austen), 154-55
Prigogine, Ilya, 285-86
Production/reproduction, in French feminist discourse, 243-62
Progress, social change, and concept of, 66
Propaganda, language and, 82n4, 100-102, 103-4, 109-10n9
Proust, Marcel, 228, 233, 320, 339-40
Psychoanalysis: postmodern, 9, 291-309; language/jargon of, 108n7; feminist approaches to, 244-45; rehearsal and, 260-61
Psychology of Art (Malraux), 102
Psychophysical exercises, 166
Pynchon, Thomas, 88, 123, 228, 322, 325

Ragtime (Doctorow), 229
Rainer, Yvonne, 173-74
Rajneesh, Bhagwan Shree, 133
Rauschenberg, Roy A., 216, 219
Reader-text transaction, 116-19
Reading: documentary, 52-55; finding freedom, and, 154-55; literary language, and act of, 116-19
Realism, 292, 317-27 passim, 331-35
Reality, 65-67, 191, 252-53, 336; television, mass media, and, 75, 84n18, 90, 193, 207-9; theatre and, 162, 190-95 passim, 203, 219, 222; feminist discourse, and, 258; pluralism on, 267-71
Reality principle, 298
Reason, science and, 22
Rebirth: transformation images of, 17-18; revolution and myth of, 66
Reception, aesthetics of, 123

Reconstruction, rhetoric of, 150–56
Redemption, 132–33, 139–41
Reduction: of complexity, 79; monism, pluralism, and, 274
Redundancy: requirement of, 168; rehearsal repetitiousness, and, 175–76
Reenchantment, process of, 286
Regeneration, cell, 175–76
Rehearsal: -behavior, 9; redundancy and, 175; as alternative to production/reproduction, 243–62; feminist time structure as, 257–58; psychoanalysis and, 260–61
Relatedness (interpersonal), theories of, 301–6
Relation, category of, 283–84
Relativism: in literary theory, 119–20; negativity and, 279–84; historical, 280–84 passim
Religion, 17–18, 83n13, 104, 132–33, 236, 275–77. See also Beliefs; Myths
Remembrance of Things Past (Proust), 234
Renewal: renewal of, 131–59; language of, 149–50
Renovation. See Innovation
Repetition: in theatre, 175, 183f.; in TV news, 207; theory of, 257–58
Representation: theatre, and issues of, 167–68, 169ff., 181–82; the arts as, 292, 294
Repression, literary, 103
Reproduction. See Production/reproduction
Respect, value of, 285–86
Reversibility, of choices, 284
Revolution: concept and reality of, 65–68, 70–71; decay of, 69–71; crises instead of, 72–73; individual's crises susceptibility and, 76; in writing, 137–138
Rezeptionsästhetik, 296
Rhetoric: renewal of, 148–50, 265; of reconstruction, 150–56
Ricoeur, Paul, 28, 91–92, 146, 271
Rightness, from "truth" to, 279–84

Right Promethean Fire, The (I. Hassan), 264
Rilke, Rainer Maria, 11, 190
Rings trilogy (Tolkien), 227, 236
Rituals, of passage, 17–18
Robbe-Grillet, Alain, 175, 325
Robe, The (Douglas), 239
Romanticism, 312, 314, 318
Roots (Haley), 229
Roth, Philip, 307
Rousseau, Jean Jacques, 152
Roustang, François, 260
Rumold, Inca, 81
Rush, Richard, 309

Sacred, the, theatre and, 171
Sacre du printemps, Le (Stravinsky), 293
Sado-masochistic theatre, 193–97
Sahlins, Marshall, 158
Sainte-Beuve, Charles Augustin, 91
Salammbô (Flaubert), 59
Salinger, J. D., 237
Salvation, 132–33, 139–40
Samizdat, 165
Saperstein, Al, 88
Sartre, Jean-Paul, 58–59, 61, 91, 319
Saving the Text (Hartman), 91–92
Scarpetta, Guy, 219
Schechner, Richard, 8, 189–201, 220, 347–48
Schmidt, Siegfried J., 125–26
Schneider, Monique, 260
Scholarship, propagandists' dictatorship of, 102
Scholem, Gershom, 91
Schwartz, Delmore, 25
Schwartzkohler, Rudolf, 24
Science fiction, 237–38
Science(s)/scientific worlds, 6, 21–23, 95, 99, 274–75, 297, 306, 336–37. See also Evolution
Scientisms, 137–38, 275
Scott, Sir Walter, 232
Sculpture, twentieth-century, 292, 294

Self, the, psychoanalytic theories about, 299–306
Self-mastery, 17–18, 79, 272
Self-purgation, 100
Self-referential activity, 53–54
Self-transcendence, 34n38, 100
Self-transformation, 23
Semiotics, 8; theatre's, 211–12, 218–23
Sense and Sensibility (Austen), 143
Sense perception, extending limits of, 180
Sentimental Education (Flaubert), 59, 62
Serial Threshold Theory, 175–76
Sermons (Donne), 89
Seven Against Thebes (Aeschylus), 205
Sex(uality): performance and, 193–97; feminists on female, 245; in twentieth-century arts, 291f., 296; Freud, psychoanalysis, and, 297–301. *See also* Body
Shakespeare, William, 163, 169, 176, 193, 292–93, 295
She (Haggard), 234
Shelley, Percy Bysshe, 314
Shepard, Sam, 291
Signs/signifiers, of theatricality, 211–12, 218–23
Silent Cry, The (Oe), 307
Simplicity, societal, 81
Simultaneity, asynchrony of, 42
Singer, Isaac Bashevis, 241
Singularities, science encounters with, 20–21
Sirens of Titan (Vonnegut), 236
Six Characters in Search of an Author (Pirandello), 167
Sixties, the (1960s), 177–85 passim, 216, 236–38, 321–22
Skinner, B. F., 156–57n4
Slaughterhouse Five (Vonnegut), 229, 239
Slippages, 175
Social drama, 205
Sociopolitical change, 66–72 passim, 79–81. *See also* Revolution

Socrates, 108n6
Soleri, Paolo, 29
Sonfist, Alan, 184
Sophocles, 177
Soviet Union, 72–73, 102
Space (between self and other), concept of "potential," 301–2
Space (theatrical): experiments with, 181–82; in performance theory, 189–90; Squat's spheres of, 201–2; literalist art, time, and, 214
Spectatorship/spectacles, 191–92, 195–96, 221. *See also* Audience
Spenser, Edmund, 278
Spingarn, J. E., 93
Squat, 163–64, 177, 197–203; *Pig, Child, Fire!*, 198–201; *Mr. Dead and Mrs. Free*, 200–202
Stabilities, 83n13; undermining of, 146–47
Stage, all-the-world a, 191
Staging (of plays), primacy of, 165–66
Stalinist Russia, 102
Stanislawski, C., 165–66
Star Trek, The Movie, 307
State, the, 73–75, 79. *See also* Political aspects
Stein, Gertrude, 172, 261, 322, 324
Steinbeck, John, 228
Steiner, George, 11
Stengers, Isabelle, 285–86
Stevens, Wallace, 222
Stevenson, Robert Louis, 232–33
Stoker, Bram, 234
Stowe, Harriet Beecher, 231–32
Stranger in a Strange Land (Heinlein), 236
Stravinsky, Igor, 293
Structuralism, 97, 98–99, 100, 168, 325
Stunt Man, The (film), 309
Style, eclecticism of contemporary, 324–27, 334–35
Subject/object polarity, 49
Sublime, avant-garde and, the, 335–38
Subtext, 117–19

Superman (film), 307

Surrealism, 317, 322

Surrender, freedom through, 154–55

Suspicion, philosophies of, 146, 271–72, 285

Symbolism, 280. *See also* Modernism

Symposium (Plato), 127

S/Z (Barthes), 91

Tableau entier, 30

Tarzan of the Apes (Burroughs), 234

Tasso, Torquato, 278

Taste. *See* Aesthetic(s)

TAT, 177

Technology: social effects of, 73–75, 103, 336–37; theatre and, 178–79

Teilhard de Chardin, Pierre, 20, 29

Television: ikonization by, 308–9; news on, 196, 207–9; reality created by, 75, 84n18, 90, 193

Temptation of the West, The (Malraux), 100

Temptations of Saint Anthony, The (Flaubert), 59, 61–62

Tension: crises and, 68; principle of, 281; Freud's constancy principle and, 298

Text(s)/textuality, 49, 52–55, 117–18; context and, 52, 54–58; reader transaction with, 116–19; use of, instead of "work," 121–22; theory, history, and, 122–23; nature of a, 127–28; as resources for freedom, 151–52; in theatrical performance, 165–67, 169, 171, 178, 180, 185; eroticizing of, 180; decadence of practice of, 252

Theatre, 8, 161–62, 168, 171, 215–16, 292

Théâtre du Soleil, 164, 178

Théâtre Libre, 167

Theatre on Chekov Street, the, 170–71

Theatricality, change, performance theory, and, 213–17

Theory(ies): of change, 7, 17–24; history and, 7, 42–44, 99–104, 121, 122–24; science and, 95; formulating/writing, 111–33; vocabulary, and practice, of, 123–24; quest of a, 254–55. *See also* Literary theory; Models; Performance theory

Theory of the Novel (Lukács), 97–98

Therapy, theatre and, 182–83

Thomas, D. M., 91

Thought, performance as species of, 172

Thought-control, totalitarianism, the media, and, 108–9n8

Threshold, liminality as, 190

Time: change, and sense and scale of, 23; acceleration of, 43; literalist art's preoccupation with, 214; feminist perspectives on, 245, 257–59; concepts of, 284. *See also* Change; Evolution

Time Machine, The (Wells), 234

Timerman, Jacobo, 108–9n8

Tolkien, J. R. R., 227, 237

Tolstoy, Leo, 232, 238

Tompkins, Jane, 157n5

Totalitarianism: literature and, 98–99; rise of, 104, 319, 330; thought-control, ·the media, and, 108–9n8; fight for freedom from, 135; tyranny of wholes as potentially, 266–67, 269

Totalization, 107n5, 266–67, 269

Total Theatre, 162

Toynbee, Arnold, 29

Tradition(al), the, 50, 55, 94–95, 136–38; breakdown of classification of, 151–52; and theatre in society, 168, 177; dance's apolitical, 174

Traité de l'argumentation (Perelman, Olbrechts-Tyteca), 265

Transavantgardism, 329, 332

Transcendence: of irony, 59; self-, 34n38, 100; language usage in defining the present, and, 49ff.

Transformation(s), 4, 17–18, 21–22,

Transformation(s) (*continued*)
27–28; self-, 23; socio-political factors in, 80–81; of the theatrical, and performance theory, 211–24
Transgression, feminist program of, 257
Transitional object, 301
Tree of People, The, 182
Trinity, Western humanism's holy conceptual, 151–52
Trucage, 90. See also Reality
Truth: individual's choice versus received, 140–41; approached as lying, 271–75; pluralism of, 279; to "rightness" from, 279–84; aesthetic, 281–82
Turner, Victor, 204–5
Twain, Mark, 232

Uhlig, Claus, 7, 39–46, 348
Ulysses (Joyce), 293
Uncertainty Principle, Heisenberg's, 28
Uncle Tom's Cabin (Stowe), 231
Unconscious (Freud's), 298
Understanding: of "pure" art, 60–62; change to overstanding from, 155; efficacy of, 282
Unheimlichkeit, 28
Uniformitarianism theory (of change), 20
United States: and Europe (theatrical influences), 92, 94, 161–66 passim; future orientation of, 131–32; hostages in Iran, 185–86
UnschärfeRelation, 67
Ussher, James, 20
Utopias: historians' language usage and, 49, 52; weaknesses of, 71–72, 271; feminist, 246, 249–50, 257, 259–60; belief and, 284–85

Validity, criteria for, 276
Value(s): literary, 114–15; of students and teachers, 124; of self versus society, 143–44; lack of positive, 144–47; of art, 145; monism versus pluralism, 268–69; of respect, 285–86; of sexuality and ordinariness, 292. See also Freedom
Value-free judgments, 120
Verfremdungseffekt, 162
Vico, Giambattista, 18, 148
Vilar, Jean, 165
Village Voice, 196–97
Visual arts, twentieth-century, 29ff., 308
Vonnegut, Kurt, 229, 236, 238–39
Vorticism, 317

Wagner, Richard, 178
Waiting for Godot (Beckett), 181
Wallace, Alfred Russel, 20
Ways of Worldmaking (Goodman), 274
Weber, Max, 77
Weizsäcker, C. F. von, 80–81
Wellmer, Albrecht, 330
Wells, H. G., 232, 234
Werfel, Franz, 81
West, Nathanael, 88, 234, 319
White, Hayden, 51–52
White Hotel, The (Thomas), 91
Whitman, Walt, 235
Williams, William Carlos, 320
Wilson, Angus, 319
Wilson, Edmund, 280
Wilson, Peter J., 158n12
Wilson, Robert, 175, 181–82
Winnicott, D. W., 301
Wittgenstein, Ludwig J. J., 149, 331
Wittig, Monique, 246–49, 257, 259–60
Wizard of Oz (Baum), 232, 234
Woman's Romance, the, 240, 296
Women, 8–9, 255–57. See also Femininity
Woodstock, Love-In at, 179
Woolf, Virginia, 319
Words. See Language; Reading; Texts
Wordsworth, William, 114–15

World community, theatre as means of achieving, 170–71
World-Play, 162–63, 171, 179
World Wars (I and II), 104, 318–19

Yeats, William Butler, 93, 319
Youth Revolution, 237–38

Zamyatin, Yevgeny, 3

DESIGNED BY GUY FLEMING
COMPOSED BY METRICOMP, GRUNDY CENTER, IOWA
MANUFACTURED BY THOMSON-SHORE, INC., DEXTER, MICHIGAN
TEXT IS SET IN TIMES ROMAN, DISPLAY LINES IN BULMER

Library of Congress Cataloging in Publication Data
Main entry under title:
Innovation/renovation.
(Theories of contemporary culture)
Includes index.
1. Civilization—Modern—20th century—Addresses,
essays, lectures. 2. Arts—History—20th century—
Addresses, essays, lectures. 3. Intellectual life—
History—20th century—Addresses, essays, lectures.
4. Literature—Philosophy—Addresses, essays, lectures.
5. Postmodernism—Addresses, essays, lectures.
6. Creation (Literary, artistic, etc.)—Addresses,
essays, lectures. 7. Originality—Addresses, essays,
lectures. I. Hassan, Ihab Habib, 1925-
II. Hassan, Sally. III. Series.
CB425.I53 1983   306   82-23888
ISBN 0-299-09390-5